Modern China's Network Revolution

Modern China's Network Revolution

CHAMBERS OF COMMERCE AND SOCIOPOLITICAL
CHANGE IN THE EARLY TWENTIETH CENTURY

Zhongping Chen

Stanford University Press
Stanford, California

Stanford University Press
Stanford, California

Printed in the United States of America on acid-free, archival-quality paper

Library of Congress Cataloging-in-Publication Data
Chen, Zhongping, Ph. D., author.
  Modern China's network revolution : chambers of commerce and
sociopolitical change in the early twentieth century / Zhongping Chen.
    pages   cm
  Includes bibliographical references and index.
  ISBN 978-0-8047-7409-3 (cloth : alk. paper)
  1. Boards of trade—China—History—20th century.   2. Social
networks—China—History—20th century.   3. Social change—
China—History—20th century.   4. China—Politics and government—
1644–1912.   I. Title.

HF331.C6C44   2011
381.06'0951—dc22   2011000529

Typeset by Westchester Book Composition in Bembo, 10.5/13.5

To the memory of my parents

Contents

Illustrations

Preface

In Search of a Broader and More Dynamic Network Approach to Chinese Studies

When I first began the study of the more than 200 chambers of commerce that popped up from 1902 to 1912 in the Lower Yangzi region around Shanghai, I approached it as an organizational analysis. I concerned myself primarily with the chambers' reformist, revolutionary, nationalistic, and business activities in this key economic region of modern China. However, over the course of the last decade, the analytical focus of my work broadened: the research now spans a longer historical period of late Qing and early Republican China and covers the expansion of the chamber networks and their sociopolitical influence beyond the Lower Yangzi region. From this broader perspective, the development of the Chinese chambers from this region marked not only the emergence, for the first time in China's millennial history, of the legally sanctioned associations (*faren shetuan*).[1] Their network development from the local to the national level also represented revolutionary change in the sociopolitical relations of the most populous country of the world.

The inspiration for such a network analysis came initially from my reflections following an academic conference and from a personal experience during subsequent air travel in China. In July 2000 I traveled from Montreal to Hong Kong to present at the Third International Conference on Chinese Business History. The theme of the meeting was relations between chambers of commerce and business networks (*wangluo*) in modern China, and this naturally prompted me to consider revising my work on chambers of commerce from a similar angle. However, the network approach still seemed inapplicable to my research because of its focus on interpersonal ties in Chinese studies.

Indeed, around 2000, the major subject of such network analysis was Chinese *guanxi* (literally "connections"). This Chinese colloquialism has a negative connotation and refers primarily to the interpersonal ties "based on ascribed or primordial traits such as kinship, native place, and ethnicity," as well as shared personal experiences in the same schools, working units, business deals, unusual events, and so on. Previous studies of *guanxi* assumed that such interpersonal ties would thrive in the absence of institutional structures like formal organizations and rational laws but decline after the establishment of the latter.[2] In other words, they treated formal organizations and other institutional relationships only as context rather than a component of social networks.

In rare cases, some early studies of Chinese chambers of commerce and a few papers at the Hong Kong conference also made use of the Chinese term *wangluo*, or network. However, such research was still limited to the scope of organizational analysis because it stressed only interorganizational links among the chambers and other organizations but skipped their interpersonal ties, the primary focus of conventional network analysis.[3] Thus, during the three days of meetings, I began to think about the possibility of combining the network and organizational analyses in the study of Chinese chambers of commerce.

After my airplane took off from Hong Kong and flew northward, I put my methodological questions aside and started worrying about my travel arrangements at the destination, Lukou, the newly built international airport far away from Nanjing. Although I had lived in Nanjing a decade earlier, I did not have any knowledge of how to get from the new airport to the city, nor did I have a hotel booked for the night. However, a casual chat with another traveler made my worries disappear and led me to see the network issue in a new way.

It turned out that I and the passenger were fellow alumni; he was a vice president of the university where I had worked before. The university arranged to send a car to pick him up from the airport, and he offered me a ride to the city. Moreover, he promised to help me find a room in the campus hotel. In our conversation, the university officer further discovered that we were from the same county, and he became more excited and immediately invited me to dinner at his home. Due to his familiarity with the airport officers in Lukou, I received the most courteous treatment from the customs officers in my travel across any national borders. With his help, I also arrived at the university in Nanjing and settled at the hotel without any difficulty.

My fortuitous encounter with this university officer threw me into deep thought, and his generous help moved me profoundly. This episode reminded

me of the importance of friendship among people from the same native place
and same working unit as well as other interpersonal relations in Chinese society, an importance that network analysis in Chinese studies has always stressed.
But it also raised doubts about the overemphasis of the analytical model on
interpersonal ties and on their negative implications.

In this case, the home county that the university officer and I came from
was not only our "ascribed or primordial" birthplace but also an administrative institution (it was later turned into a suburban district). Even though we
enjoyed learning that we came from the same county, our relationship likely
would have ended soon after this trip if we had not also worked for the same
university. It was mainly through this university and similar institutions in
China and Canada that I had maintained personal contacts with my former
Chinese colleagues for our academic exchange and collaboration at the institutional level. Undoubtedly, institutional links could merge with interpersonal
ties and make the latter become stronger, broader, and more socially significant. Network analysis, I then realized, might incorporate both types of relations into its analytical framework rather than separate them artificially.

A new twist from my encounter with the university officer in Nanjing
alerted me to another side of Chinese social networks. Nearly one year after
our unexpected meeting, one of my high school classmates in my hometown
heard about it and made an international call to me in Montreal. His nephew
had just taken the college entrance examinations, but the resultant grades barely
reached the minimum requirements of the university in Nanjing. This former
classmate hoped to take advantage of my acquaintance with the university
officer and further use our local ties with the latter to secure his nephew's
admission into this university. After politely rejecting his request, I became
both amazed by the globalization of Chinese personal relations and alarmed
at its potential implications. If personal cliques and interpersonal ties could
uninhibitedly control and corrupt institutions and institutional ties, the con-
sequence would be more harmful to society than previous studies of personal
networks suggested.

This episode reminded me of numerous encounters with Chinese social
networks in different circumstances, and such practical experience led me to
turn from organizational to network analysis in my book project. The network paradigm initially attracted me as a new way of examining hundreds
of Lower Yangzi chambers of commerce and their numerous participants
within interconnected frameworks. Even the initially abstruse jargon of network analysis—"density," "connectivity," "centrality"—fascinated me as new
techniques for accurately processing relational data in historical documents.[4]

My critical reading of the existing literature in network analysis, however, also confirmed my worries about its methodological deficiencies. Although this approach promises to examine social relations from the whole to the part and from structure to individual, "social network analysts often study personal networks rather than whole networks."[5] The scholarly tendency to stress interpersonal ties at the expense of their institutional structures finds typical expression in a "classic" definition of personal relationships:[6]

> A relationship involves a series of interactions between two individuals known to each other. Relationships involve behavioural, cognitive and affective (or emotional) aspects. Formal relationships are distinctive from personal relationships.

By contrast, institutional analysis, especially historical institutionalism, indicates that "institutions" include "both formal organizations and informal rules and procedures that structure conduct."[7] That is, institutional structures comprise not merely formal organizations, organizational principles, and inter-organizational relations. They also include socially established "rules" at the personal level, ranging from formal marriage to informal customs in inter-personal relationships, which further involve the interpersonally behavioral, cognitive, and affective interactions beyond institutionalized "rules." Thus, historical institutionalism confirmed my previous perception that institutional structures would not necessarily wipe out interpersonal relations like Chinese *guanxi*. Their formal frameworks could also incorporate, extend, and transform the latter, but such a process of relational institutionalization has not received attention from network analysis of Chinese *guanxi* or organizational analysis of chambers of commerce.

An examination of my documental record for this book project in its early stage also made me realize that the conventional network approach has analytical strength in describing social relations but paradigmatic weakness in explaining relational changes. As an advocate of this paradigm in Asian studies admits, "social network analysis does not handle change well unless one can do repeated iterations of the net over time."[8] Even if historical data allow such research, it is still hard to reveal dynamics for network changes. Thus, it became evident that I could not simply apply the network theory and its jargon to my research. Rather, I had to refine the preexisting theory and develop new concepts through my own network analysis of data.

Consequently, the painstaking process of research for this book project also became an exciting journey in search of a broader and more dynamic network approach. As a result, this book is fundamentally different from the preexisting organizational analyses of Chinese chambers of commerce. It also distinguishes itself from conventional network analysis by its new analytical approach. This approach not only expands network analysis to include both interpersonal and institutional relations but also emphasizes relational transformation and its dynamics in the chamber networks.

A central concept in this book is that of "associational networks." I use it to distinguish my new approach from conventional network analysis and to differentiate the chamber networks of the Lower Yangzi region from the preexisting social relations in Chinese history. This key concept aligns the historical narrative in this book along a central argument: the associational networks of these Lower Yangzi chambers demonstrated strength and significance because they expanded through both personal and institutional relations, increasingly brought different individuals and organizations into interactions, and thereby provided dynamics for varied sociopolitical changes, including the general trend of social integration and long-term transformation of society-state relationship. In particular, such chamber networks exerted deep influence on reformist, revolutionary, and nationalist politics, as well as economic revitalization and modernization in late Qing and early Republican China.

To summarize the theme of the book in a single sentence, the associational networks of the Lower Yangzi chambers of commerce embodied a *network revolution* because they achieved unprecedented level of relational institutionalization, expansion, diversification, and interaction in the sociopolitical landscape of modern China. In terms of both its expression and influence, such a radical and structural change in Chinese sociopolitical relations was comparable to and even more comprehensive than what Eiko Ikegami calls "the Tokugawa network revolution," the sudden expansion of communicative networks at a critical moment of Japanese cultural history.[9]

It is in this sense that this book suggests that the Lower Yangzi chambers of commerce were not merely pioneers and models of the chambers in the whole country and similar kinds of state-legitimized social associations in other professions but were also the vanguards and representatives in the network revolution and attendant sociopolitical change up to the national level. Certainly, the analytical focus of my book is still on the chambers of commerce within the Lower Yangzi region. In fact, it goes beyond previous studies on individual chambers in large cities or at the national level mainly through network analysis of hundreds of chambers in small cities and market towns of the region.

In such a local historical context, the Lower Yangzi chambers of commerce displayed their chief characteristics because their network development among a large number of small cities and market towns had few parallels in other regions of China during the early twentieth century.[10] In view of the specific character of the Lower Yangzi chambers, this book explores and employs a wealth of local historical sources, such as archives, statistics, gazetteers, newspapers, and magazines, as well as personal diaries, memoirs, biographies, and anthologies that include previously untapped information about lower-level chamber networks. It also makes full use of quantitative analysis to process such historical data.

The combination of local historical analysis with a broad and dynamic network approach enables this book to focus on the regional characteristics of the Lower Yangzi chambers of commerce but also to shed light on their nationwide connections, influence, and significance. However, due to the primary mission of this historical research, I have tried to follow basic principles of network analysis while avoiding its technical jargon. Moreover, my network approach also abstracts new concepts from empirical research and adopts useful notions from organizational, institutional, and class analyses, as well as other research methods in disciplines such as anthropology, sociology, business studies, and political science.

It is my hope that this full and dynamic understanding of Chinese social networks may offer a key intervention into scholarly discussions about class and elites in Chinese historiography and about Chinese *guanxi*, informal politics, civil society, and the public sphere across the social sciences. Such historical understanding also has practical significance for China today because it points to a new way of building the public sphere, civil society, and society-state relations on the solid basis of institutionalized networks, which certainly could include institutional checks on unhealthy *guanxi* in Chinese society and politics. Therefore, this book is not only about China's past but also about its present and future.

Acknowledgments

Due to the decade-long nature of my work, I have benefited from the help of too many individuals and institutions to acknowledge them all here. I would first like to thank Mark Granovetter, a pioneer in the field of social network theory. He recommended my manuscript to Stanford University Press and further encouraged me "to move network analysis away from a purely interpersonal framework, into one where history, culture and institutions interact with networks in a mutually causal way" (e-mail message to author, August 31, 2009). Two anonymous reviewers for the press also offered encouraging and insightful comments. Their advice helped shape the final version of the manuscript and sharpen its central theme. Two editors of the press, Stacy Robin Wagner and Jessica Walsh, showed equal enthusiasm about the book project and guided me during the final revision through their professional, efficient, and patient work.

Sincere thanks are also due to the following colleagues and friends who had read all or parts of the manuscript in its different versions: Gregory Blue, Arif Dirlik, Linda Grove, Xiaorong Han, Liam Kelley, Richard King, Elizabeth J. Perry, John Price, Mary Backus Rankin, Edward R. Slack Jr., and Robin Yates. Their advice, concern, and encouragement constantly boosted my spirit and bolstered my confidence. Dr. Rankin merits special thanks for her repeated readings of different versions of the manuscript and thought-provoking criticism. Dr. Perry's early suggestion for conceptual clarification and Dr. Guoguang Wu's remarks on institutional analysis also influenced the evolution of my network approach. Moreover, I appreciate Ole Heggen's help with the map, and I am grateful for the editorial assistance of Donald Bar-onowski and the late Neil Burton.

Among my colleagues in China, Zhang Kaiyuan, Ma Min, and Zhu Ying of Wuhan, Yu Heping and Liu Dong of Beijing, Xu Dingxin, Tang Lixing, and Ma Xueqiang of Shanghai, Lü Zuoxie, Zhang Xianwen, and Fan Jinmin of Nanjing, Chen Xuewen of Hangzhou, and Zhang Shouguang of Chong-qing deserve my deep gratitude. They had either shared with me their research on Chinese guilds and chambers of commerce or provided assistance in data collection. Two of my former students, Tao Tao of Beijing and Zhao Ji of Shanghai, were very helpful in collecting sources.

Support for my documentary work also came from the staff at the archives and libraries in Shanghai, Nanjing, Suzhou, Hangzhou, and Nantong, as well as the libraries at the University of Hawaii, McGill University, the University of British Columbia, and the University of Victoria. Special assistance with data collection was provided by Mi Chu at the Library of Congress. Financial support for the book project at its different stages came from the East–West Center, the *China Times* Cultural Foundation, the Center for Chinese Studies at the University of Hawaii, the Social Sciences and Humanities Research Council of Canada, and the Center for Asia-Pacific Initiatives of the Univer-sity of Victoria.

I would like to extend sincere thanks to my longtime mentors, Harry J. Lamley, Kwang-ching Liu, Jerry H. Bentley, Sharon Minichiello, Sen-dou Chang, and Tien-yi Tao. Their sage advice and careful guidance helped me build a solid foundation for this book. My deepest gratitude goes to Professor Lamley and the late Professor Liu, who pushed me to expand my research interest from economic into sociopolitical history of China. Professor Bent-ley opened my eyes to different theories in the vast field of world history and inspired me to apply my newly developed network approach to the study of the global Chinese diaspora and the ecological networks across China and the Indian Ocean world.

Finally, I wish to thank my wife, Limin Huang, for her support and sac-rifice for my academic pursuits during our two dozen years of common life. Our son, Victor Houwei Chen, was born right after I joined the University of Victoria in 2002, and his birth earned me half a year of parental leave, during which I began to write this book intensively. He made a special con-tribution to this book because his first cry after birth, frequent smiles in in-fancy, and boyish laugh in our house always brought me joy during what was otherwise a lonely journey. Victor also pushed me to work harder and faster after he claimed to have already produced a few Picasso-style "books" at the age of five. My own book is dedicated to my father, Chen Zhaojiang, and mother, Cui Wenying. My parents raised me during the hard times of the great famine and the Cultural Revolution in China, and they had to endure my wandering in the remote past and distant places thereafter. Neither of them survived to see the completion of the project, but both bequeathed me the spiritual force to do my best in any circumstances.

Parts of Chapters 1, 2, and 6 have appeared in two of my articles, "The Origins of Chinese Chambers of Commerce in the Lower Yangzi Region," *Modern China* 27, no. 2 (2001): 155–201, and "The Quest for Elite Dominance, Associational Autonomy and Public Representation: The Lower Yangzi Chambers of Commerce in the 1911 Revolution," *Twentieth-Century China* 27, no. 2 (2002): 41–77. Both articles have been further revised and reorganized for incorporation into this book and its new theoretical framework. I thank the two journals and their publishers, Sage Publications and the University of Michigan Press, for allowing me to reuse the two previous publications.

Abbreviations

ACC	affiliated chamber of commerce
BCC	branch chamber of commerce
CCA	commercial consultative association
GCC	general chamber of commerce
GCCC	general chamber of cotton commerce
HSLB	*Huashang lianhebao* (Journal of united Chinese merchants)
MQSG	Suzhou lishi bowuguan and Jiangsu shifan xueyuan lishixi, *Ming-Qing Suzhou gongshangye beikeji* (Collection of stone inscriptions concerning handicraft industry and commerce in Ming-Qing Suzhou)
NGST: I	*Nonggongshang bu tongjibiao: Diyici* (Statistical tables prepared by the Ministry of Agriculture, Industry, and Commerce: First collection)
NGST: II	*Nonggongshang bu tongjibiao: Di'erci* (Statistical tables prepared by the Ministry of Agriculture, Industry, and Commerce: Second collection)
SBZX	Shanghai bowuguan tushu ziliaoshi, *Shanghai beike ziliao xuanji* (Selected materials from Shanghai stone inscriptions)
SSDC	Zhang, Liu, and Ye, *Suzhou shanghui dang'an congbian, 1905–1911* (Collection of archival materials of the Suzhou General Chamber of Commerce, 1905–1911)

SSZT: 1906   *Shanghai shangwu zonghui tongrenlu: Bingwuinian* (Register of the Shanghai General Chamber of Commerce, 1906)

SSZT: 1908   *Shanghai shangwu zonghui tongrenlu: Dingweinian* (Register of the Shanghai General Chamber of Commerce, 1907) [This register actually lists members and leaders of the general chamber in 1908]

SSZT: 1909   *Shanghai shangwu zonghui tongrenlu: Jiyounian* (Register of the Shanghai General Chamber of Commerce, 1909)

SSZT: 1910   *Shanghai shangwu zonghui tongrenlu: Gengxunian* (Register of the Shanghai General Chamber of Commerce, 1910)

SSZT: 1911   *Shanghai shangwu zonghui tongrenlu: Xinhainian* (Register of the Shanghai General Chamber of Commerce, 1911)

SWGB   *Shangwu guanbao* (Gazette of Commercial Administration)

SWGS   *Shanghai wanguo guanshang shishen zhiye zhuzhilu* (Occupations and addresses of Chinese and foreign officials, merchants, and gentry in Shanghai)

SZZZ   Shanghai shi gongshangye lianhehui and Fudan daxue lishixi, *Shanghai zongshanghui zuzhishi ziliao huibian* (A collection of materials concerning the organization of the Shanghai General Chamber of Commerce)

TSDH   Tianjin shi dang'anguan, Tianjin shehui kexueyuan lishi yanjiusuo and Tianjin shi gongshangye lianhehui, *Tianjin shanghui dang'an huibian, 1903–1911* (Collection of archival materials of the Tianjin General Chamber of Commerce, 1903–1911)

WGCC   [Western] general chamber of commerce

ZGHS   Peng, *Zhongguo gongshang hanghui shiliaoji* (Collection of historical materials concerning the artisan and merchant guilds of China)

Introduction

Chambers of commerce developed in early twentieth-century China as a key part of its sociopolitical changes. In 1902, one year after the Qing court launched the New Policy Reform (*xinzheng*), the first Chinese chamber of commerce appeared as the Shanghai Commercial Consultative Association (Shanghai CCA, Shanghai shangye huiyi gongsuo) and soon received official approval. In 1904, such chambers of commerce became the earliest nongovernmental organizations legitimatized by state law in Chinese history. When the Qing dynasty and two millennia of imperial rule ended with the 1911 Revolution, over 1,000 general chambers (GCCs, *shangwu zonghui*), affiliated chambers (ACCs, *shangwu fenhui*), and branch chambers (BCCs, *shangwu fensuo*) had been established throughout China. They achieved increasing integration, and their collective actions deeply influenced nationalistic, reformist, and revolutionary movements as well as economic modernization.[1]

These chambers of commerce could bring about broad sociopolitical changes beyond their business world, not only because they achieved a significant degree of organizational integration and expansion but also because their participants included varied merchants with widespread influence and relations in both business and politics. According to the commercial law drafted by the late Qing chambers of commerce and enacted by the Republican government in 1914, "merchants" included those in various businesses, industries, service trades, financial activities, brokerage, and the like.[2] Actually, the late Qing chambers of commerce were composed of more diverse merchants, such as gentry-merchants (*shenshang*) who owned commercial wealth and official titles, leaders of urban guilds, merchant managers of semiofficial enterprises, and so on.[3] Based on the newly developed chamber networks, these elite merchants formed interconnections and greatly expanded their influences from local business into the larger society and state politics. Thus, these chambers of commerce spearheaded relational changes among social elites and in the society as a whole. Their networks also helped transform business-government and society-state relationships permanently in early twentieth-century China. Such profound relational change constituted an initial and also an important part of the general network revolution in modern China.

The historical significance of these chambers of commerce has manifested itself in the increasing number of monographs on their organizational development and activities at the national level or in large cities like Shanghai and Suzhou. However, the overwhelming majority of the chambers in small cities and market towns as well as their networks from the local to the national level have not received much attention.[4] This book fills this scholarly gap by examining more than 200 chambers of commerce within the Lower Yangzi region, the socioeconomic heartland of modern China, and it focuses especially on their network development and extensive influence on sociopolitical changes in the early twentieth century.

The Lower Yangzi region included Shanghai and two prosperous provinces of modern China, Jiangsu and Zhejiang, especially the highly commercialized and urbanized Yangzi delta. However, the socioeconomic conditions of the regional core in the Yangzi delta were still very different from those of the peripheral areas, and large cities like Shanghai and Suzhou also differed from smaller cities and market towns.[5] Therefore, this study covers the chambers of commerce in the entire region not for their environmental or organizational homogeneity but for their interconnections and network expansion. Furthermore, chambers of commerce also prompted sociopolitical change from the local to the national level because their networks had already expanded beyond the region itself and influenced the larger society and state politics in the early twentieth century.

Lower Yangzi Ecology and Elite Initiative in Chambers of Commerce

The Lower Yangzi chambers of commerce and their networks developed on the basis of long-established urban and administrative systems in this region. Lying at the mouth of the Yangzi River, Shanghai had become the national center of commerce and industry from the mid-nineteenth century. Its In-

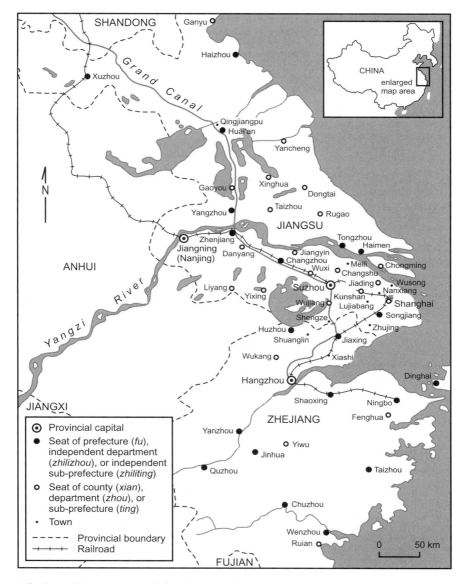

The Lower Yangzi region in the late Qing period.

ternational Settlement and French Concession attracted radical reformers and revolutionaries because of Western cultural influence and the political protection under foreign administration there. Guarding the upper reaches of the Yangzi River within this region, Jiangning (Nanjing) was the seat of the Liangjiang governor-general. This ranking official administered Jiangsu, Anhui, and Jiangxi provinces in eastern and central China, and he also held the position of imperial commissioner for treaty ports in southern China (*Nanyang dachen*). Linking the imperial capital of Beijing and northern China with the Lower Yangzi region, the Grand Canal cut across the Yangzi River and passed through Suzhou, a commercial center and the seat of the governor of Jiangsu Province. Standing at the southern end of the canal, Hangzhou was another commercial center and the seat of the governor of Zhejiang Province.[6]

While general chambers of commerce usually appeared in Shanghai and other metropolises, their affiliated and branch chambers further developed in smaller cities and market towns in the Lower Yangzi region. Such urban centers and marketplaces comprised dozens of prefecture-level cities, more than 100 county-level cities, and thousands of market towns.[7] By the 1910s, the population was about 1 million in Shanghai and between 170,000 and 270,000 in Jiangning, Suzhou, or Hangzhou. Within and near the Yangzi Delta, populations varied between 10,000 and 100,000 in most prefecture-level cities and between 1,000 and 10,000 in the county-level cities and large towns.[8]

The Lower Yangzi region had also been successful in producing the politically active gentry (*shenshi*) and wealthy merchants. The gentry included former officials and other titleholders who had earned academic degrees through civil service examinations, and all of them acted as elite leaders in local society. They became hybrid gentry-merchants because of their involvement in business, as did many rich merchants after their purchase of academic degrees and official titles from the government. This hybrid social group also developed through the division of gentry and merchant functions among the male members of a family or clan, through intermarriage between gentry and merchant families, and through their concurrent leadership in guilds and charitable institutions.[9] These wealthy and prestigious elite merchants had long dominated commercial and community organizations before they formed the chambers of commerce in Lower Yangzi cities and towns at the beginning of the twentieth century.

By the late Qing period, a majority of such elite merchants still combined their pursuit of community leadership and even Confucian scholarship with the management of old-style businesses in the Lower Yangzi region, especially in inland cities and towns. However, in modern cities like Shanghai, it was common for them to expand their economic activities into new-style industries and businesses, enter semibureaucratic services for governmental enterprises, and serve as compradors for foreign firms. Because of their direct competition or contacts with foreign business organizations, these elite merchants made the earliest efforts to initiate Western-style chambers of commerce in China.[10]

One leading elite merchant promoter of chambers of commerce in the late Qing period was the well-known gentry reformer and industrialist Zhang Jian, a native of Tongzhou independent department in Jiangsu Province. Zhang spent more than twenty years to prepare for and pass the three-level civil service examinations, but he realized his dream to become the top scholar in the palace examination only in 1894 when Qing China suffered disastrous defeat in its war with Japan. In view of both the national crisis and new business opportunities in his home place, Zhang ended his official career in the Qing court and turned to the textile industry in Tongzhou. He succeeded in the industrial adventure because of his gentry connections with both officials and merchants.[11] Thus, Zhang decided to pursue his social and political ambitions by "facilitating the government-business linkage" (*tong guanshang zhiyou*). From the mid-1890s, he began to promote chambers of commerce as a device to unite merchants and officials for the vitalization of Chinese business.[12]

In contrast with Zhang, the major founder of the Shanghai CCA, Yan Xinhou, exemplified most elite merchants from the business world. Yan came from a poor family in Ningbo Prefecture of Zhejiang Province, but his native-place connections helped him become a Shanghai shop clerk at a young age. Through the recommendation of a Zhejiang native, he further entered the retinue of Governor-General Li Hongzhang, a major leader of military modernization and early industrialization in late Qing China. With Li's help, Yan received the title of expectant *daotai* (circuit intendant) and made a fortune by managing the Changlu Salt Administration (*Changlu yanyunsi*) in Zhili Province after 1885. However, he soon left officialdom for Shanghai, involving himself with both old-style businesses and new industries. Yan gained high social prestige as a leader of merchant guilds, charitable institutions, and semi-official enterprises.[13] From 1899 he joined Zhang Jian, other elite merchants, and Qing officials in establishing the Shanghai Bureau of Commerce (*Shanghai shangwuju*), an unsuccessful copy of Western chambers of commerce. Eventually, in 1902, Yan received governmental encouragement to found the Shanghai CCA, and his plan for the first chamber of commerce of Qing China expressed the aspiration to end the estrangement between Chinese officials and merchants in the face of foreign economic intrusion.[14]

Zhang and Yan's backgrounds illustrate the social diversity of the late Qing elite merchants in the Lower Yangzi region, but the two of them made common efforts to initiate chambers of commerce for the purpose of strengthening government-business cooperation against foreign intrusion. This fact raises questions about the class and organizational analyses of the late Qing chambers of commerce in previous studies, especially those in mainland China. This line of scholarship has usually stressed the common class interest or homogeneous identity of the merchant participants in these chambers of commerce and has focused on their hostile relationship with the state.[15] In order to go beyond such rigid class and organizational analyses, the present book adopts a new network approach in its examination of the Lower Yangzi chambers of commerce and their sociopolitical influence in early twentieth-century China.

Network Dynamics and the Rise of Chinese Chambers of Commerce

The network approach has become an established paradigm in Western academia.

> It conceives of social structure as the patterned organization of network members and their relationships. Analysis starts with a set of *network members* (sometimes called nodes) and a set of *ties* that connect some or all of these nodes. Ties consist of one or more specific *relationships*, such as kinship, frequent contact, information flows, conflict, or emotional support.[16]

This approach has the potential to analyze interrelations between both individuals and organizations, and it could supplement the standard social scientific research that focuses on individual attributes and behaviors or organizational structures and functions.[17] In particular, an emphasis on interactive relations between both individuals and organizations can help reveal the full dynamics for the rise of the Lower Yangzi chambers of commerce, the starting point of the network revolution in modern China.

 Chinese scholars such as Liang Shuming and Fei Xiaotong noticed the predominance of *guanxi* or interpersonal relationships in Chinese society long ago. Recently, the Western network approach has been used to analyze such relationships.[18] This line of network analysis naturally shows a tendency to emphasize interpersonal ties at the expense of institutional links, and it has led scholars to focus on kinship and local fellowship in their studies of Chinese businesses, including *guanxi* capitalism.[19] Historical studies of labor unions and native-place associations in modern Shanghai have also shed light on the continuity and dominance of such primordial relations.[20] However, the relational changes inside the new institutional contexts and especially dynamics for such changes still need to be examined beyond the limitation of conventional network analysis.

Previous analysis of personal networks in Chinese studies has also tended to stress their cliquish and corruptive orientations. Anthropological studies of Chinese interpersonal relationships have mainly treated them as the source of rampant corruption, although there have been discoveries of personal affection and social autonomy based on such relationships.[21] Historians and political scientists in Chinese studies have especially blamed personal relationships for factionalism and have affirmed their detrimental impact on political development.[22] By contrast, recent works on personal networks in modern China have paid more attention to their intersection with social organizations and business corporations.[23] This scholarly trend has led to the discovery of "the new style of networking" based on newly formed institutions in modern Chinese history,[24] although the trendy research still "focuses on personal networks."[25]

As a study of Chinese chambers of commerce in the late Qing and early Republican periods, this book expands network analysis from its focus on interpersonal ties to include the dimension of institutional links. In particular, it adopts the concept of "associational network" to denote particular groups of persons and their intertwined interpersonal and institutional relations, as well as their interactions with other socioeconomic and political forces. This expanded concept affirms the continuity of kinship, friendship, local fellowship, and other interpersonal relationships in chambers of commerce and similar associations. However, it also indicates that the new institutional norms, organizational principles, and hierarchical structures could incorporate, transform, and transcend interpersonal relationships.

Historically, preexisting organizations such as lineages, guilds, and charitable halls (shantang) had already achieved different degrees of relational institutionalization and expansion in China, but their organizational development was mainly based on the personal ties among the finite groups of kinsmen, fellow townsmen or provincials, people in the same trades or occupations, and other acquaintances in individual cities, towns, or rural townships. Their interrelations above the local level of urban and rural societies were usually sporadic, informal, and unstable.[26] In contrast, the chambers of commerce first developed formal membership, leadership, hierarchy, and other institutional relationships that retained the strength of interpersonal ties but also wove the latter into their organizational frameworks and widespread networks ranging from the local to the national level, as is detailed below.[27] Thus, research on the associational networks of these chambers can combine network and organizational analyses but also go beyond their respective foci on either interpersonal ties or formal organizations.

Such a network approach can also assimilate valuable perspectives from the class analysis of the late Qing chambers of commerce but avoid overemphasis on common class interests of their merchant members and on their class struggles with the Qing government. Network analysis affirms that people with intimate kinship and shared economic relations could form personal cliques and social classes in pursuit of cliquish and class interests. But it also suggests that "as [relational] systems increase in size and complexity, organizational imperatives [could] surpass family and class interests."[28] Thus, as the Lower Yangzi chambers of commerce expanded their associational networks beyond the limits of interpersonal ties, they could rally merchants, especially elite merchants, from different social backgrounds. Through the extensive chamber networks, these elite merchants could elevate their private interests into public concerns and effectively change their relations with the state through multiform interactions with officials, not merely class struggles.

A network analysis of such relational changes offers new insights into the origins of Chinese chambers of commerce in the Lower Yangzi region. Negishi Tadashi, Shirley S. Garrett, and other pioneer scholars had long stressed the organizational evolution from late Qing guilds to chambers of commerce under Western influence, and they even regarded these chambers as superguilds or as guild federations in "Western garb."[29] However, Wellington K. K. Chan's research on late Qing chambers of commerce basically regards them as the result of official efforts to expand governmental control from state-initiated enterprises and bureaus of commerce into the larger business community. By contrast, Mary Backus Rankin attributes the development of these chambers and other new associations mainly to social elite mobilization from the mid-nineteenth century.[30] All of these previous studies are instructive for further research on the issue. However, it is still hard to explain why centuries of guild evolution in the Lower Yangzi region and decades of reformist elite mobilization in the late nineteenth century did not produce any citywide merchant organization until 1902, but thereafter chambers of commerce and their networks suddenly spread to the whole region, especially the market towns beyond direct official control, in a few years.

From a network perspective, Chapters 1 and 2 present a comprehensive explanation for the origins of the Lower Yangzi chambers of commerce through a broad analysis of long-term relational changes among both their institutional predecessors and their elite and official initiators. Both the old and new organizations within the business world provided an institutional foundation for elite merchants to expand their formal leadership and interrelations, to intensify interactions with other social elites and officials for business and public affairs, and to share a common concern about foreign economic intrusion, including that from Western chambers of commerce. The institutional development and expansion of guilds, semiofficial enterprises, and bureaus of commerce, especially the interactions of their merchant leaders with other reformist elites and officials, provided the fundamental dynamics for the rise of chambers of commerce and their networks among Lower Yangzi cities and towns during the era of the New Policy Reform.

These newly formed chambers of commerce in the Lower Yangzi region usually came under the leadership of their elite merchant initiators and relied heavily on the latter as linkage men in their continuous interactions with governments and other sociopolitical organizations. However, elite merchants not only dominated these chambers but also helped expand their relations with other organizations. Such network expansion influenced a broad range of social change within and beyond the business world. Thus, the emergence and development of these chambers reflected and further reinforced relational change in the society as a whole.

Chambers of Commerce, Elite Merchant Webs, and Social Integration

The late Qing chambers of commerce have aroused widespread interest in previous scholarship largely because they included so many wealthy, prestigious, and powerful merchants. While the aforementioned class and organizational analyses of these elite merchants have tried to define them as homogeneous members of a bourgeois class and even as identical participants in the organizations of this social class, another scholarly tendency is to depict them as diverse elites with different socioeconomic resources.[31] A network analysis of relational changes around the Lower Yangzi chambers of commerce can reconcile and refine the two different lines of scholarship.

Actually, these chambers expanded their networks to integrate bourgeois entrepreneurs and more heterogeneous merchants through their relational diversification, especially through their incorporation of merchant leaders from different guilds and other business groups. The chamber networks also expanded beyond the business world through their links with diverse sociopolitical organizations. Thus, the network expansion and diversification of the Lower Yangzi chambers of commerce constituted two interrelated aspects of their relational revolution, but such highly diversified chamber networks could integrate their merchant participants rather than disintegrate into personal factions mainly because of their increasing institutionalization.

As Chapters 3 and 4 demonstrate, all the chambers of commerce in Lower Yangzi cities and towns developed roughly similar structures to incorporate elite and nonelite merchant participants into different levels of membership, elections, meetings, and so on. Annual elections and other institutional devices for mandatory personnel change also enabled these chambers to recruit influential leaders from increasingly diverse guilds, other merchant groups, and commercialized gentry strata. Similarly, their links with different community and professional organizations gradually expanded from the personal to the institutional level. As a result, the chamber networks not only integrated diverse elite merchants beyond the cliquish limits of kin, local, and occupational groups but also promoted general social integration in their merchant community and the larger society.

Indeed, the Lower Yangzi chambers of commerce incorporated not only wealthy and prestigious elite merchants but also their relations with numerous guilds and other merchant groups. Although these chambers have long been regarded as superguilds by Japanese and Western scholars, their relationship with merchant guilds has remained a major controversy among Chinese historians. Ma Min and Zhu Ying's collaborative study of chambers of commerce around late Qing Suzhou argues that they differed fundamentally from the closed and inert guilds because the chambers admitted all businessmen of the same encouraged commercial competition and innovation, and granted t democratic rights. On the contrary, guilds restricted themselves ific regional or occupational groups, prohibited merchant compe- d enforced feudal control over their participants.[32]

st Chinese historians, however, hold that the preexisting guilds were orporated into chambers of commerce, either because the former had modernized themselves as the latter or because both of them were traditional organizations to some extent. Therefore, all of these historians emphasize the distinction between traditional and modern organizations and agree that these chambers could admit only homogeneous members from the guilds of their own kind.[33] What they fail to notice is that these chambers were associational networks that could encompass diverse members from both "traditional" guilds and "modern" business institutions.

Another issue is whether these chambers admitted only the elite leaders or all participants of guilds into their membership. Ma and Zhu's aforementioned study has noticed the inclusion of guild leaders into full membership (*huiyuan*) of the chambers of commerce around late Qing Suzhou. However, they argue that these chambers admitted common participants of guilds and other small merchants only as associate members (*huiyou*) or peripheral members (*waiwei chengyuan*) who did not have the actual right to take part in chamber activities. Ma's subsequent research still treats all such chamber members as gentry merchants, but Zhu's new study instead argues that the associate members of these chambers were "actual" participants.[34] Clearly such strict organizational analysis has difficulty lumping the varied merchants into homogeneous membership in these chambers.

The network approach to the Lower Yangzi chambers of commerce challenges such organizational analysis, especially the conventional class analysis that identifies them with a small and impotent bourgeois class. In mainland China, historians used to regard the late Qing chambers as the instruments of the bureaucratic comprador bourgeoisie that controlled state-sponsored enterprises and served foreign imperialists. More recently, these scholars have instead emphasized the chambers' relations with a national bourgeoisie composed of anti-imperialist industrialists and commercial entrepreneurs, in particular, and of pro-revolution intellectuals and other social forces, in general. However, both the earlier and recent studies tend to stress the weakness of the Chinese bourgeois class and its chambers of commerce because of the small number of bourgeois entrepreneurs and the unsteadiness of their revolutionary spirit around the 1911 Revolution.[35]

By contrast, Marie-Claire Bergère defines the late Qing chambers as the organizations of a more inclusive bourgeoisie, the "urban elite connected with modern business," such as those in the manufacturing and transport industries and in Western-style commercial and financial activities. However, she still believes that this bourgeois class and its chambers of commerce were too immature and impotent to lead the 1911 Revolution, except in a few modern cities like Shanghai.[36] My study also finds that the late Qing bourgeois class was weak in the Lower Yangzi region because its members constituted only a minority in a small number of chambers even when Bergère's broad definition of an inclusive bourgeois class is used in statistical analysis. However, these chambers on the whole were not weak bourgeois organizations but powerful networks of more diverse elite merchants, including the wealthiest and most influential ones.

The emphasis on the diversity of the chamber leaders and members brings this research close to previous scholarship on the local elites at the county and lower levels of Chinese society. In North America, the gentry society paradigm had deeply influenced Chinese studies from the 1950s, and it also led Edward J. M. Rhoads to depict the late Qing chambers around Canton as organizations of gentry-merchants, including commercial and industrial entrepreneurs with gentry titles. His point found an echo in Wellington K. K. Chan's more general discussion about chambers of commerce of late Qing China. The notion of gentry-merchants has recently been elaborated by scholars in mainland China to broaden their understanding of these chambers and the related bourgeois class.[37]

Meanwhile, Joseph W. Esherick, Mary Backus Rankin, and other scholars have redefined gentry-merchants, bourgeois entrepreneurs, guild leaders, and other social notables as local elites in terms of their dominance in the social arena at and below the county level. According to these scholars, these elites controlled varied material and social and symbolic resources and cannot be categorized simply as undifferentiated holders of state-granted gentry titles or members of a specific bourgeois class. Thus, the inclusive concept of local elites reveals their more diverse and changeable attributes than previous scholarship suggested.[38] local elites → inclusive concept

This book elaborates on the diversification and transformation of the elite merchant participants in the Lower Yangzi chambers, but its network analysis lays more stress on their interconnections. These elite merchants were more diverse than the local elites defined by Esherick and Rankin. They ranged from the local merchant notables in market towns to the gentry-merchants of provincial capitals and the bourgeois entrepreneurs in national metropolises like Shanghai. They could be classified as "local elites" only in the sense that their business dominance was concentrated on the "local" arena of their cities and towns. In fact, many merchants kept relations with their remote birthplaces and with long-distance trade, not to mention their new chamber networks.

Certainly, the hierarchical distinction among general, affiliated, and branch chambers in the Lower Yangzi region still affirms Philip Kuhn's hypothesis about social cleavages between elites at the national, provincial, and local levels. Their different degrees of network development between the regional core and its peripheral areas also reflected the social rupture between core and peripheral elites, as Rankin stresses.[39] Nevertheless, the primary impact of the chamber networks on these social elites was the intensification of their interconnections. The network expansion of such chambers allowed many of their elite merchant participants to act as local elites in their respective cities or towns and to pursue influence at the provincial and national levels at the same time. It also brought the elite merchants in core and peripheral areas into closer contact than ever before.

network expansion of c-c → allowed elite merchants
to act as local elites
connected core and perip. elite merchants

Furthermore, through personnel and, in particular, institutional interconnections, the Lower Yangzi chambers of commerce and other new associations linked up elite merchants and more diverse elites in other social circles. As a result, these elites achieved unprecedented integration in spite of their geographical dispersion, social diversification, and professional specialization. In particular, the engagement of the chambers and their leaders in varied public activities, such as nationalist mobilization, municipal reform, and management of township charities, facilitated social integration of both elites and the populace. Such social transformation certainly influenced political change in society-state relations.

Chamber Networks, Elite Associational Activism, and Society-State Relations

The associational networks of the Lower Yangzi chambers of commerce increasingly integrated their elite merchants and brought them into organized activities, including collective actions taken by themselves and joint actions undertaken with other sociopolitical forces. Such associational activism led the chamber leaders and members into more intensive and complicated interactions with both the populace and officials. It marked the climax of the relational revolution around these chambers of commerce in the early twentieth century because the tripartite interactions among their elite merchants, the general public, and the governments produced strong dynamics for sociopolitical change in this region and the whole country, including longterm transformation of the society-state relationship in modern China.

Because the Lower Yangzi chamber networks incorporated the kinship, local fellowship, and other personal relationships of their elite merchant leaders and members, their activities naturally reflected the familial, parochial, and other private interests of these elites. However, it is more important to note that the chamber networks also expanded the social relations of these elite merchants above the personal level, and the relational expansion naturally linked their private interests with their public concerns for the larger society. As a result, the chamber leaders and members engaged not only in collective actions by themselves but also in joint actions with the populace in some circumstances. Such relational change around the chamber networks has not received enough attention in previous studies of Chinese local elites or the bourgeois class.

Previous scholarship on the local elites in late Qing China has often shown a tendency to stress their pursuit of social dominance and their clashes with the populace. As early as the 1960s, Chūzō Ichiko presented a well-known hypothesis that the late Qing gentry, especially those at the local level, supported official reforms and developed reformist organizations for the purpose of self-preservation. They increased their prestige, power, and profit at the expense of both governmental control and popular welfare. Edward J. M. Rhoads's research on the late Qing chambers of commerce around Canton reveals their more positive impact on industrial development and political change, but his work still stresses that their activities were mainly aimed at strengthening the dominance of the local elites.[40] To some extent, the motivation for local elite dominance can indeed explain many activities of these chambers, including their clashes with the populace in local markets. However, it fails to account for their collective actions over larger areas and especially their joint actions with the populace in social protests against governmental or foreign encroachments on their shared public interests.

Among scholars in mainland China, class analysis of the late Qing chambers of commerce has offered a more influential explanation for their activities. In particular, it uses the class interest of the new yet impotent bourgeoisie to interpret their limited participation in the 1911 Revolution and their eventual withdrawal from the revolutionary camp.[41] However, as noted before, bourgeois members never formed a majority among the late Qing chambers in the Lower Yangzi region. Thus, their class interest could hardly motivate a majority of chamber leaders and members into collective actions. Contrary to this assumption, the bourgeois members of the metropolitan chambers and most chamber participants in old-style businesses of small cities and towns did not share a common class interest. Nonetheless, they often took concerted action because the chamber networks coordinated their different interests and brought them together through public rhetoric that had wide appeal.

Evidently, the associational networks of these late Qing chambers transformed the pursuits of elite merchants by bringing them into collective actions beyond the scope of their personal, local, and even class interests. Thus, Mary Backus Rankin reinterprets such chambers and similar elite associations as a portion of the "public sphere" in which social elites managed public affairs distinct from their private pursuits and official administration. According to Rankin, the public activities of these elites and their associations increasingly involved conflicts with the Qing state and brought them into an irreversible process leading toward the 1911 Revolution.[42] Moreover, William T. Rowe, David Strand, and other scholars have further introduced into Chinese studies Jürgen Habermas's concept of the public sphere, a realm where rational and critical discourse develops and defends society and the public good against state intrusion.[43]

Rowe and a few other scholars, however, still insist on the distinction of the Chinese public sphere from the Western idea of "a civil society autonomous and counterpoised to the state."[44] In contrast, Zhu Ying has directly interpreted the late Qing chambers of commerce as the main component of a Chinese civil society (*shimin shehui*), or the social associations embodying democratic principles, self-regulating authority, and organizational autonomy from the state. He argues that these chambers represented broad social interests in their increasing conflicts with the Qing court and especially in their eventual involvement in the 1911 Revolution.[45] His new interpretation downplays the bourgeois class nature of these chambers and echoes Edward Shils's notion of civil society. In Shils's opinion, such civil society differs from the family, the locality, and the state and rests on the civic virtue of its citizen members in giving precedence to the public good over individual interests and in following the law to regulate their own behavior and limit state power.[46] Thus, based on the public sphere or civil society model, recent works on Chinese chambers of commerce have highlighted the public and social motivations of their elite merchant participants as the new dynamic that drove their actions.

From the network point of view, however, the public motivations of these elite merchants developed in connection with, rather than separately from, their private interests. As Habermas's concept of the bourgeois public sphere in early modern Europe suggests, it was the realm of private persons of the bourgeois class who engaged in public discourse versus state authority.[47] By contrast, the chambers of commerce in late Qing and early Republican China were composed of diverse elite merchants with more differing personal, group, and class interests. Thus, they could bring their elite and even nonelite merchant participants into collective actions because their associational networks effectively linked up the different interests of such diverse merchants and further bound them together with public issues of wide concern in the larger society.

More important, the Lower Yangzi chambers of commerce derived dynamics for their associational actions not only from the intertwined private and public interests of their elite merchant participants but also from their multiform interactions with the governments. In regard to this issue, previous studies under the influence of public sphere and civil society discourses have offered valuable insights into the vigorous struggles of the chambers and other

social organizations for public authority and associational autonomy from
the state. However, their overemphasis on such society-state contention has
also drawn criticism from other scholars. As one of their critics, Philip C. C.
Huang instead treats the late Qing chambers as an example of the "third realm"
in which state and society overlapped and cooperated.[48] Even though Kohama
Masako uses the concept of the "public sphere" to depict varied social associations in modern Shanghai, her work stresses the collaboration of these
urban organizations with officials and their failure to change society-state
relations.[49] Xiaoqun Xu's study of professional associations in Republican
China also deplores their "lack of complete autonomy" from the state and pro-
poses the concept "symbiotic dynamics" to highlight their interdependent
relations with the state.[50]

 By contrast, my concept of associational networks stresses interactive
dynamics and changeable relations between society and state. Specifically
speaking, it focuses on dynamic forces generated by multiform interactions
between social organizations and the governments and on subsequent relational changes beyond mutual cooperation or confrontation. Most important,
my network analysis suggests that the chambers of commerce in early twentieth-
century China did not simply seek "complete autonomy" from the state. In
fact, what these chambers pursued in their relations with the state was "structural autonomy," by which network analysis denotes the ability of network
members to acquire necessary resources while reducing control by other members through their interactive relations.[51]

Indeed, it was through different forms of interaction with the late Qing
government that the Lower Yangzi chambers of commerce acquired legal
sanction and further developed their widespread networks beyond direct
official control. The network institutionalization, expansion, and diversification in turn enabled these chambers to rally and represent their merchant
community and even the larger society in their multiform interactions with
the governments from the local to the national level. Thus, the chambers increased their structural autonomy and sociopolitical influence because their
interactive relations with both the state and the general public progressively
expanded in scale and complexity.

Chapters 5 and 6 respectively scrutinize the associational activities of the
Lower Yangzi chambers and their influence in late Qing business and politics. These chambers expanded their activities from local markets to provincial railroads, a national fair, and Sino-American joint ventures because they
actively pursued both the private and public interests of their elite merchants
through cooperation, confrontation, or other forms of interaction with the

Qing officials and foreign capital. The chambers of commerce, especially those in the Yangzi Delta, also accelerated constitutional reform and facilitated the success of the 1911 Revolution through their multiform interactions with the Qing officials, varied reformist organizations, and the anti-Qing revolutionary parties. Their associational activities promoted economic modernization and political transformation and also enhanced their public image and authority, even though there was still class tension between their elite merchants and the populace at the local level.

Although the focus of Chapters 1–6 is on the associational networks of the late Qing chambers of commerce in the Lower Yangzi region, my documentary and theoretical analyses refer frequently to the influence of their network revolution beyond this region. In particular, Chapter 7 documents the nationwide network development of these chambers and their interactions with the various Republican regimes. In the Conclusion, a theoretical summary of such network revolution and its historical legacy in the late twentieth century further highlights how the Lower Yangzi chambers of commerce influenced long-term social integration and society-state interaction in modern China.

Certainly, the associational networks of the Lower Yangzi chambers of commerce in the early twentieth century reflected only the beginning and a primary aspect of the relational revolution in modern China. Such network revolution did not happen in a historical vacuum but was based on centuries of relational evolution in Chinese society. In fact, even the Lower Yangzi chambers themselves were a product of long-term relational changes among urban guilds, elite merchants, and officials in late imperial China.

1

Guilds and Elites in the Face of Domestic
and Foreign Challenges

For Western visitors to late nineteenth-century China, one striking discovery was that ["the people crystallize into associations; in the town and in the country, in buying and selling, in studies, in fights, and in politics."[1] Foreign intrusion from the mid-nineteenth century reinforced the Chinese tendency to act as social groups for self-defense, while the influence of social Darwinism also galvanized late Qing elites to organize themselves for national survival and revival.[2] Thus, in addition to the traditional clans, guilds, charitable institutions, secret societies, and so on, anti–Qing revolutionary organizations began to appear from 1894, and reformist associations such as study societies also experienced ephemeral development before the failure of the 1898 Reform.[3] Among these organizations, merchant guilds were the direct predecessors of Chinese chambers of commerce, which also displayed strong foreign influence.

However, the Lower Yangzi chambers of commerce were neither the natural results of guild evolution nor simple imitations of their Western counterparts. Like the late Qing reformist and revolutionary organizations, these chambers represented the collective responses of social elites, especially guild leaders and other elite merchants, to domestic and foreign challenges. Therefore, the rise of such elite merchant leadership in the guilds preconditioned the development of chambers of commerce. It also reflected relational changes more important than organizational evolution from guilds into chambers.

Chinese guilds have usually been divided by previous studies into regional guilds of merchants from the same native places and occupational guilds

C.C. → responses of social elites
to foreign and domestic
challenges

of people within specific trades. Actually, the guilds in late Qing China developed along both regional and occupational principles, as is shown by Goodman's research on native-place associations and other merchant organizations
in Shanghai. Nevertheless, these merchant guilds are still treated roughly as
native-place or common-trade associations in my study simply because they
emphasized one or the other of the two organizational principles in their titles,
memberships, functions, and so on.[4] Such merchant guilds could develop because of informal patronage rather than legal guarantee from local governments, and their elite leaders were crucial in helping them acquire such patronage from local officials.[5]

In order to develop, defend, and dominate such merchant groups under
business competition, governmental intervention, social unrest, and foreign
economic intrusion, guild leaders in the Lower Yangzi region made constant efforts to expand and intensify their regional, occupational, and official
connections. As a result, they promoted guild development and also turned
their personal and familial dominance into formal elite leadership. In the face
of domestic and foreign challenges from the mid-nineteenth century onward,
these guild leaders expanded their associational activities from business into
community affairs such as charities, because of their concern not only for
market and social crises but also personal wealth and power. Such elite merchants also joined radical reformers in response to the challenge from Western chambers of commerce in treaty ports, and they planned similar Chinese
organizations with the double purpose of strengthening their socioeconomic
dominance and saving Chinese business and the nation. However, their plans
also included designs for widespread chamber networks, a matrix of the future
relational revolution.

The Growth of Guilds and Elite Merchant Leadership:
The Shanghai Case

The guilds in late imperial China included urban organizations with various titles, such as *huiguan* (meeting hall) and *gongsuo* (public office). The
Lower Yangzi region nurtured some of the earliest merchant guilds in late
imperial China, and it was also one of the few regions with large numbers
of guilds by the late Qing period.[6] Although this study argues against the
assumption that these guilds directly federated themselves into chambers
of commerce, their organizational development still provided an institutional foundation for the latter. In particular, the institutionalization and expansion of their elite merchant leadership and their interrelations directly

prepared for the advent of the Shanghai CCA and successive Lower Yangzi chambers.

After *huiguan* began to appear as native-place clubhouses for officials in the imperial capital of Beijing from the 1420s, sojourning merchants and officials from the same native places also founded similarly titled organizations in Suzhou around the beginning of the seventeenth century.[7] In this Lower Yangzi city, a *gongsuo* for silk weavers had probably existed as early as 1295, although merchants did not make wide use of this term for their associations until the mid-seventeenth century.[8] The unique features of these Chinese guilds, especially their regional and official connections, contrasted sharply with those of their European counterparts. Thus, some scholars have tried to distinguish the common-trade *gongsuo* from native-place *huiguan* and deny the guild nature of the latter.[9] Actually, these merchant organizations used the titles *huiguan* and *gongsuo* interchangeably and developed similar guild functions for self-protection, mutual assistance, and promotion of common interests.[10] These guilds could perform such important functions because they used regional, occupational, and other socioeconomic ties to bond merchants together, and their leaders formed close relations with other social elites and officials.

In 1886, D. J. MacGowan, a missionary from the United States, had already noticed the close relations between guilds and officials in late Qing China: "Chief among edifices in mercantile emporiums are buildings erected by guilds for headquarters—places of meeting, theatrical representations, and as lodging-houses for high officials when traveling, and for scholars en route to metropolitan examinations." He further divided the Chinese *huiguan* and *gongsuo* into merchant and craftsman guilds and likened them to chambers of commerce and trade unions in the West.[11]

MacGowan's early work initiated the trend for Negishi Tadashi, Shirley S. Garrett, and other scholars to define late Qing chambers of commerce as guild federations under a Western signboard. Soda Saburo and Kurahashi Masanao also argue that these chambers resulted from the confederation of Chinese guilds against foreign aggression and from their need for business administration and social control.[12] Yu Heping's more recent work further emphasizes the tendency of the late Qing guilds to federate into chambers of commerce because they had gradually reduced regional and occupational exclusiveness under the influence of modern economic development.[13]

These previous studies have correctly indicated that merchant guilds laid an institutional foundation for chambers of commerce, but their analyses have oversimplified the relational changes among merchant organizations.

Because social relations tended to become denser, stronger, and more intimate among merchants from a smaller area or a specific trade, regional and occupational guilds would naturally multiply and even subdivide into more localized and specialized organizations once they accumulated sufficient members and resources. In William T. Rowe's study of late Qing Hankou, he indicates that regional and occupational guilds in this city gradually formed alliances because of the prolonged residence of nonnative merchants in this city and their need to cooperate with locals in trade and in the face of official and foreign interference. By contrast, late Qing guilds in the Lower Yangzi region rarely confederated along regional or occupational lines, and that was true even for Shanghai, the largest treaty port under direct imperialist dominance.[14]

Actually, the Lower Yangzi guilds in the late Qing period experienced continual multiplication and subdivision because their merchant participants increasingly formed regional and occupational ties at a more intimate level. However, they also developed interconnections through both interpersonal and institutional links in the face of domestic and foreign challenges. Moreover, elite merchants often held concurrent posts in various guilds because of their diverse business involvements and widespread social relations. They further formalized such guild leadership through their intermediary role between guilds and governments. It was through such relational changes that the Lower Yangzi guilds paved the way for the future chambers of commerce.

As Table 1 shows, the Lower Yangzi guilds began to appear around the beginning of the seventeenth century. They developed not only in Suzhou and Shanghai, the two successive centers of commerce in the region, but also in other provincial, prefectural, and county cities, as well as in market towns. Their number gradually increased from the year 1600 on because of long-term commercialization and urbanization in the Lower Yangzi region, but their numerical increase greatly accelerated after 1800. Because most guilds in this region were rebuilt or created after the Taiping Rebellion (1851–1864) was suppressed, their development reflected mainly the associational activism of merchants, especially elite merchants, in the face of mounting social and national crises from then on.

These elite merchants used regional and occupational relations to create a large number of new guilds and also subdivided the existing guilds into more numerous organizations for more localized groups of merchants or more specialized trades. By creating and subdividing such organizations, they expanded their interrelated leadership in varied guilds and also intensified

TABLE 1

The development of guilds in Lower Yangzi cities and towns, 1601–1912

City and town	Founding year[a]								Total
	1601–1650	1651–1700	1701–1750	1751–1800	1801–1850	1851–1900	1901–1912	Unknown	
Suzhou	4	7	14	17	32	35	13	66	188
Shanghai			1	9	13	55	25	47	150
Jiangning (Nanjing)			1	1	3		1	44	50
Hangzhou					1			38	39
Four prefectural cities[b]	1			1	3		3	29	37
Seven county cities[c]				1	5	11	6	2	25
Twenty-four towns[d]		2	8	4	19	14	8	25	80
Total	5	9	24	33	76	115	56	251	569

Source: Data from Fan, Ming-Qing Jiangnan shangye de fazhan, 283, 286–309. Fan's data include some associations for officials and artisans only.

[a] Because Chinese sources date the emergence of many huiguan and gongsuo to the reigns of emperors, their founding years are reckoned as the last years of the reigns during which they appeared.

[b] The four prefectural cities were Changzhou, Huzhou, Jiaxing, and Zhenjiang.

[c] The seven county cities were Deqing, Fuyang, Jiading, Jiangyin, Kunshan, Wucheng, and Wuxi.

[d] The twenty-four towns were Hushu, Jiwang, Linghu, Luxu, Nanxiang, Nanxun, Pingwang, Puyuan, Qingyang, Shengze, Shuanglin, Si'an, Tongli, Wangdian, Wangjiangjing, Wuqing, Xiashi, Xinchang, Xinshi, Yushan, Zhapu, Zhenze, and Zhoupu.

their communications with local governments concerning guild affairs. The relational changes among these Lower Yangzi guilds and their influence on future chambers of commerce can be clearly seen when one examines a case study of the dozens of merchant organizations that provided elite leaders for the Shanghai CCA and its successor, the Shanghai GCC.

The major founder of the Shanghai CCA, Yan Xinhou, came from the Ningbo Guild (Siming gongsuo), which became a large and complex native-place association mainly through its organizational subdivision and relational expansion under interrelated elite merchant leadership. Around 1797, the Ningbo Guild appeared in Shanghai as a regional association at the prefectural level; it developed further through a fundraising campaign led by two of the Fang brothers. One of their nephews, Fang Chun, succeeded to the leadership and successfully petitioned Lan Weiwen, the Ningbo-born Shanghai magistrate, to exempt their guild properties from taxes. From the 1870s, new generations of upstarts from Ningbo, such as Yan Xinhou, got rich through quasi-official services and the management of family businesses and modern industries. They soon joined the Fangs and other established elite families in the leadership of this regional guild.[15]

By 1911, the Ningbo Guild had spawned one native-place association for merchants from Dinghai subprefecture, and forty-two occupational guilds or groups. These formal guilds and informal groups had more than 300 "major and minor directors" in 1901, and they all maintained personal and institutional links with the prefectural-level guild. Meanwhile, the Fangs and other wealthy Ningbo lineages in Shanghai gradually established their empires in businesses ranging from the sugar and silk trades to native banking and coastal shipping, and formalized their familial dominance in the Ningbo Guild. By 1836, these elite merchants had already developed a stable guild leadership composed of four directors (dongshi), including two of the Fangs; they also established the position of assistant director.[16]

At the beginning of the twentieth century, the Ningbo Guild was still under the leadership of four "annual directors" (sinian dongshi), including Yan and one of the Fangs. Under them, about a dozen monthly directors (siyue dongshi) were selected from the affiliated occupational groups for supervising business affairs, while two salaried managers (sishi) were appointed by these directors to handle general and accounting affairs.[17] Although this guild experienced continuous subdivision after its emergence and did not even affiliate with the Shanghai CCA in 1902, such elite merchant leaders as Yan Xinhou still used their concurrent positions in occupational guilds, semiofficial enterprises, and so on to found and dominate the first Chinese chamber of commerce.[18] Thus, the link between the Ningbo Guild and the Shanghai CCA reflects how the Lower Yangzi guilds led relational changes toward chambers of commerce through the development of formalized and inter-locked elite merchant leadership rather than through the progressive confed-eration of their organizations.

In late Qing Shanghai, Cantonese people were rivals of those from Ningbo, but elite merchants in both groups had significantly formalized their leader-ship, and so joined together in the Shanghai CCA despite the rivalry. After Lan Weiwen, the aforementioned Ningbo-born official, suppressed the Small Sword Uprising (1853–1855) that involved many Cantonese in Shanghai, the early guilds of the latter were forcibly moved out of the walled city and soon became extinct. However, in 1872, the new Shanghai magistrate was a Canton-ese. With his encouragement, the Guang-Zhao Guild (Guang-Zhao gongsuo) was formed by elite merchants from Guangzhou and Zhaoqing, two prefectures around Canton.[19]

The founders of this guild included several wealthy merchants who had purchased gentry titles and had even held comprador positions in foreign firms, such as Xu Rongcun and his nephew, Xu Run. These elite merchants amassed a large sum donated by merchants and officials from these two prefectures. Their guild leadership was then expanded to include gentry-directors (shen-dong) in charge of people from each county of the two prefectures, monthly directors who served as accountants in rotation, and a small group of perma-nent directors at the top. Within this prefectural-level guild, the merchant members from Nanhai and Shunde counties later split off to form their own native-place associations, but the three merchant organizations undoubtedly maintained ties through their elite merchant leaders. As mentioned above, the same phenomenon characterized Ningbo guilds at that time. Thus, the sub-division of the Guang-Zhao Guild did not prevent its leaders from joining the Shanghai CCA on behalf of the entire Cantonese group. As one major leader of this prefectural guild, Xu Run later entered the Shanghai GCC in 1904, but he became its first vice president mainly because of his association with semiofficial enterprises.[20]

Another major group of Guangdong merchants in Shanghai came from Chaozhou Prefecture east of Canton, but its merchants were close to those from southern Fujian Province in terms of their speech and trade interests. Both Chaozhou and Fujian merchant guilds underwent internal subdivision, but they affiliated themselves with the Shanghai CCA through shared elite merchant leadership. After the Chaozhou Guild (Chaozhou huiguan) ap-peared in Shanghai in 1759, merchants from Jieyang, Puning, and Fengshun

guilds – diverse, elite members

counties in addition to those from Chaoyang and Huilai counties successively broke away and formed two separate guilds around 1822 and 1839. Although Fujian merchants had a provincial-level guild in Shanghai before the Small Sword Uprising in the mid-1850s, they did not rebuild it after the uprising failed. On the contrary, one of their native-place associations at the prefectural level, the Fuzhou Guild (Sanshan gongsuo), was founded around 1863 but later split into two guilds: one in the Chinese district of Shanghai and another in the International Settlement.[21]

In spite of such organizational subdivision, the regional guilds of Chaozhou and Fujian incorporated diverse elite merchants into a similar type of formal leadership. Around 1804, the Chaozhou Guild successively hired two provincial graduates (*juren*), who were paternal cousins, as its directors. Among Fujian people in Shanghai, the guild for merchants from Jianning and Tingzhou prefectures was created mainly by Zeng Guqing in the late 1790s. Zeng, his two sons, and one of his grandsons successively managed this guild until the late 1880s. Zeng Chutai was a director, from the 1860s, of another native-place association for merchants from Fujian's Quanzhou and Zhangzhou prefectures, before his son, Zeng Zhu, succeeded to the position. In 1902, the junior Zeng represented the regional groups of both Fujian and Chaozhou merchants in the Shanghai CCA soon after helping its major official patron and a leading bureaucratic industrialist, Sheng Xuanhuai, found a branch of the Red Cross in China.[22]

The two remaining native-place guilds with direct affiliation to the Shanghai CCA were for merchants from Jiangxi and Sichuan provinces. These two guilds developed at the provincial level because each of them could gather sufficient members only from a province, not because they confederated prefectural and county-level merchant organizations. Available documents about the Jiangxi Guild (Jiangxi huiguan) indicate that it also developed elite merchant leadership, just as the aforementioned regional guilds did. In 1841, six Jiangxi merchants with gentry titles advanced money to purchase a building as their guildhall, and their effort was soon endorsed by the Shanghai magistrate at the time, one of their fellow provincials. The six elite merchants thus became the earliest directors. In 1894, both the Shanghai *daotai* and the magistrate happened to be Jiangxi natives. Thus, merchant leaders from Jiangxi Province, especially Chen Runfu, launched a new fundraising campaign with support from the two local officials and other Jiangxi natives in the government and successfully expanded their guild. Moreover, Chen later became a founder of the Shanghai CCA because of his leadership in the guild for southern remittance shops.[23]

Actually, most regional guilds in the treaty port were not formally affiliated with the Shanghai CCA, but their leaders joined the latter as representatives of more than twenty occupational guilds. Although these common-trade guilds also tended to subdivide, they had long developed close relations among themselves and with native-place guilds through the gradually institutionalized and interlocking leadership of elite merchants. In particular, these occupational guilds actively recruited prestigious gentry figures of local origin into their elite merchant leadership for their dealings with local governments. Thus, their development, especially the expansion of their elite merchant leadership through official contacts, had a direct effect on the rise of the Shanghai CCA.

The Merchant Shipping Guild (Shangchuan huiguan) appeared in 1715 as the earliest occupational guild in Shanghai, and large merchant owners of seagoing vessels originally served in rotation as its monthly managers. However, this guild began to establish the permanent position of director in the mid-nineteenth century, when it participated in the seaborne transportation of tribute rice for the Qing government. Between 1844 and 1891, this guild successively hired fifteen directors to work with its monthly managers of merchant origin and serve as its links with local officials. These directors included prestigious gentry from official families and even former officials.[24] In 1819, rich Ningbo merchant families in the coastal shipping business, such as the Dongs, Fangs, and Lis, founded a separate Zhejiang-Ningbo Guild (Zhe-Ning huiguan). However, Lishenji and Zhenkang, the family business establishments of the Lis and another Ningbo lineage, had held leaderships in both the Merchant Shipping Guild and the Zhejiang-Ningbo Guild by the 1890s. Thus, one leading merchant from the Li lineage, Li Yongshang, later became a representative of all coastal shipping merchants in the Shanghai CCA.[25]

Coastal shipping merchants in Shanghai had long transported soybeans, soybean cake, and soybean oil from northern to southern China. Thus, guilds in these trades developed close relations with each other and maintained contacts with local governments through their similar and often shared leaderships, although all of their organizations experienced subdivision. After the Soybean Guild (Douye gongsuo-Cuixiutang) appeared around 1813, merchants from Qingkou town of northern Jiangsu Province and those from southern Anhui Province founded another guild in this trade around 1822. Nevertheless, the Soybean Guild retained its control over the trades of soybeans, soybean cake, and soybean oil because it received official sanction to maintain a major building inside the Yu Garden (Yuyuan) of the City God Temple (Chenghuangmiao) and to collect "contributions to the temple" (*miao-*

guilds in coastal shipping developed close
relations w/e. other + local govts.

jun) from all merchants in these trades. This guild also led twenty occupational groups, including fifteen occupational guilds and the groups for actors, beggars, and the like in maintaining all buildings in the Yu Garden. At least five of these occupational guilds later sent elite merchant leaders as their representatives into the Shanghai CCA.[26]

As a typical example of these common-trade organizations, the Soybean Guild originally had an unstable leadership composed of a few monthly managers from the 1840s to the 1880s. In 1890, its eight monthly managers were selected by the manager of a shipping business establishment alone. In other related trades, grain brokers and rice retailers originally formed a joint guild in 1867, but they quickly split to found the Guild of Grain Brokers (Mimai zaliang gongsuo-Rengutang) in 1869 and the Guild of Rice Retailers (Miye gongsuo-Jiagutang) the next year. In 1898, merchant leaders of the Guild of Rice Retailers selected a provincial graduate as its director and received recognition of the new leader from local governments. In the following year, monthly managers in the Soybean Guild and the Guild of Grain Brokers also began to select local gentry figures as their joint directors and representatives to the local governments. One of their directors, Zhang Lejun (Jianian), later represented both the soybean and rice trades in the Shanghai CCA.[27]

Through extending financial services for coastal shipping, soybean, rice, and other trades, the Shanghai native banking business gradually came to dominate the local market. The first guild in this business appeared in the Inner Garden (Neiyuan) of the City God Temple around 1776, and its twelve early directors managed to obtain official protection of their guildhall because of their promise to help the local government maintain the garden. Native bankers then split into one guild in the Shanghai county city in 1883 and another in the International Settlement in 1889. After this organizational subdivision, leaders of the two new guilds continued to maintain joint management of the Inner Garden, which they turned into the office of the General Guild of Native Banks (Qianye zonggongsuo), where they held their annual or special meetings. Both guilds established directors for external contacts, and their memberships gradually included native bankers from Zhejiang, Jiangsu, Anhui, and Guangdong provinces, as well as merchants from dyestuff, foreign goods, and other major trades. Meanwhile, such Ningbo merchant lineages as those of the Lis and Fangs expanded their dominance from the aforesaid coastal shipping and soybean trades into the native banking business. The managers of their family banking establishments, Tu Yunfeng and

Xie Lunhui, were long-term guild leaders in this business and its representatives in the Shanghai CCA in 1902.[28]

Like the early guilds in the interrelated coastal shipping, soybean, grain,
and native banking businesses, new occupational guilds in the Shanghai
treaty port also formed stable and even shared leaderships in spite of their
organizational subdivision and rapid multiplication. Elite merchants in these
guilds usually developed formal leadership and acquired official recognition
of their power by performing tax-collecting duties for local governments.
They would later use a similar pattern of interactions with the Qing government to establish the Shanghai CCA. guilds further interacting w/govt

In the export trade of modern Shanghai, silk and tea merchants founded
a joint guild in 1855, but they soon split into two groups. In 1860, the governor of Zhejiang Province requested Shanghai merchants to fund his anti-
Taiping campaign with a silk surcharge (*sijuan*). Eight merchant titleholders
in Shanghai's silk trade arranged the surcharge but also petitioned the governor for a *huiguan* to run charities for silk dealers. In response, the governor
contributed a thousand taels to the *huiguan* and permitted it to keep a portion
of the silk surcharge as its own funds. The eight founders of the Silk Guild (Siye
huiguan) claimed that it would nourish friendship among silk merchants
from different places, although most were elite merchants from Zhejiang and
Guangdong provinces. These elite merchants established themselves as perma-
nent directors, each serving in turn as active director for one year. Moreover,
they hired two gentry figures as manager and assistant manager in charge of
the guild's general affairs.[29] close govt. relations w/guilds

A separate Tea Guild (Chaye huiguan) also appeared in 1870, after its elite
merchant leaders had donated the joint silk-tea guildhall to local officials as
a charitable institution. These tea merchants hired a provincial graduate as a
director to manage their guild affairs and make representations to the government, and they employed another gentryman as an accountant to handle
financial matters and the collection of *lijin* (transit tax) for the government.
Moreover, this *huiguan* selected twelve elite merchants in the tea trade to serve
as monthly managers in rotation and to assist the two gentrymen in handling
general and financial affairs. One major founder and a long-term manager of
this guild was the aforementioned Xu Run, the leader of the Cantonese merchants' and silk traders' guilds and the first vice president of the Shanghai
GCC.[30]

Similarly, the guilds in both native and foreign cotton cloth trades brought
gentry figures into their elite merchant leaderships and developed formal
directorships because the former had once supplied native cotton cloth to

the Qing government and the latter had helped local officials collect the *lijin* tax on the foreign cotton cloth trade in the International Settlement. Such guild leaderships also appeared in cotton, coal, fruit, timber, pawnshop, and other trades by the end of the nineteenth century. Available data indicate that the guild leaders in the coal and foreign cotton cloth trades, among whom were Chen Leting and Xu Chunrong, were involved in the native-banking guilds, although it is hard to detail the interrelations among all these guild leaders.[31] Therefore, the institutionalized and interlocked guild leaderships had significantly integrated diverse elite merchants in this treaty port and brought them into closer contact with officials before these elites gathered to form the Shanghai CCA through further interactions with the Qing government.

Links of Guilds and Elite Merchants beyond Commercial and Community Bounds   guild leaders→ public activities

From Shanghai to other Lower Yangzi cities and towns, the late Qing guilds under elite merchant leadership demonstrated a similar trend toward organizational multiplication and subdivision as well as relational institutionalization and expansion. Many guilds not only formalized their elite merchant leadership but also developed linkages across different cities and towns. Their leaders further joined other social elites in public activities such as management of local charities, and these elites even helped officials with famine relief for remote provinces. As a result, these guild leaders expanded their social relations beyond the limits of their own commercial and communal affairs. This kind of relational change among guilds and their elite merchant leaders directly led the future chambers of commerce to develop associational networks across and beyond the Lower Yangzi region.

In late Qing Shanghai, large guilds gradually formed institutional relations with their counterparts in other cities and towns within or outside the Lower Yangzi region. The Ningbo Guild of Shanghai founded a branch office in the city of Ningbo as early as 1882, and the two units worked closely in the service of their members, especially in transporting the coffins of dead members to their home places. This guild later expanded such institutional relations with other Ningbo guilds in the Lower Yangzi region and even with those in other regions. Since the early 1870s, the Tea Guild in Shanghai had also begun collaborating closely with its counterpart in Hankou, another treaty port in the Middle Yangzi River valley, in regulating their trade. It is noteworthy that the leaders of the Ningbo and the tea guilds included Yan

Xinhou and Xu Run, the first president and vice president of the future Shanghai GCC.[32]

Merchant guilds in Shanghai also undertook public activities within and beyond their urban community, and such activities further brought elite merchants into citywide institutions before the rise of chambers of commerce. These guilds began to supply regular funds for charitable halls in Shanghai and in the prefectural capital of Songjiang as early as 1789. Based mainly on such guild support, the Hall of Impartial Altruism and Support for the Fundamental (Tongren fuyuantang) in 1855 merged two preexisting charitable halls in Shanghai county city and then founded two branches in the International Settlement and the French Concession, respectively. It also took over control of three charitable halls for foundlings, widows, and ferry passengers. Under the leadership of dozens of gentry, guild leaders, and other elite merchants, this umbrella charity expanded its activities into municipal services, such as the organization of militias, erection of road lamps, maintenance of street sanitation, and the construction of roads, bridges, and temples.[33] *public activities of merchant guilds in Shanghai*

Leaders of merchant guilds and charitable halls in Shanghai and other Lower Yangzi cities even organized famine relief effort for Zhili, Henan, Shanxi, and Shaanxi provinces around 1878, a large-scale institutional collaboration that foreshadowed the development of the future chamber networks. Jing Yuanshan, a merchant philanthropist of Zhejiang origin, and Zheng Guanying, a former Cantonese comprador and future advocate of chambers of commerce, played leading roles in this campaign. In 1879, they gathered more than twenty gentry and elite merchants from Jiangsu, Zhejiang, and other provinces to found the Shanghai Office for Relief Cooperation (Shanghai xiezhen gongsuo), which was located first in Jing's native bank and then in Zheng's house. This office had about ten branches within and outside the Lower Yangzi region, which cooperated closely with many guilds, charitable halls, and merchant shops to collect and distribute funds for famine victims in northern China.[34] *merchant guilds → famine relief*

Mary Rankin's research on the management of charitable activities and this famine relief by Zhejiang elites has stressed how they expanded the public sphere with interests distinct from their private pursuits and governmental administration.[35] However, Jing Yuanshan led the famine relief also because he hoped that his philanthropic deeds would help him have male offspring at the age of forty. The birth of his oldest son in 1880 further inspired his enthusiasm for charitable activities. Right after the famine relief, both Jing and Zheng Guanyin received appointments from Zhili Governor-

General Li Hongzhang to manage semiofficial enterprises in Shanghai.[36] Clearly, the charitable institutions and activities channeled the personal interests of elite merchants into their public activities and facilitated their pursuit of personal influence and prestige as well as official connections. Thus, in addition to commercial guilds, these charitable halls in Shanghai and other Lower Yangzi cities also provided an institutional precedent and prepared elite merchant leadership for the rise of chambers of commerce later on.

One typical example of such elite merchants was Xu Run, a leading figure in the Cantonese merchant group and the guilds for tea and silk trades in addition to being a director of three charitable halls in Shanghai. In Xu's autobiography, he indicated that charitable activities from 1868 had enabled him to make friends with such officials as Sheng Xuanhuai, the sponsor of the future Shanghai CCA, and with several Jiangsu and Zhejiang gentrymen. The leadership in charitable halls further institutionalized such interpersonal relations among elite merchants. For instance, the Shanghai Hall for Benevolent Assistance (Shanghai renjitang) recruited Xu and other Cantonese elite merchants as its directors and brought such Zhejiang elite merchants as Yan Xinhou and Zhu Baosan into its leadership. Yan, Zhu, and Xu later would become major leaders of the future Shanghai CCA and the succeeding Shanghai GCC.[37]

Both merchant guilds and charitable halls appeared in Suzhou earlier than in Shanghai, and their development there reflected a longer period of relational changes that resulted in the rise of chambers of commerce. Elite merchants in late Qing Suzhou, like their peers in other long-running commercial and political centers, had stronger gentry backgrounds and closer official connections than their counterparts in Shanghai. They also made earlier efforts to establish their permanent directorships within guilds and to expand their charitable activities beyond the merchant community and their city, although the Suzhou GCC did not appear until 1905, three years later than the Shanghai CCA.[38]

By 1620, Cantonese merchants and officials had already founded the Guangzhou Guild (Lingnan huiguan) in Suzhou as a native-place association at the prefectural level. Thereafter, merchants from Guangdong Province formed at least one provincial-level guild, two prefectural-level guilds, and two county-level guilds. They even worked with incumbent officials from both Guangdong and Guangxi provinces to establish a dual-province guild in 1878. Nevertheless, neither the provincial-level guild nor the dual-province guild incorporated the existing guilds of Guangdong merchants because all of them still appeared as separate organizations in local gazetteers of the late Qing period.[39]

These regional guilds developed elite merchant leaderships similar to those of their counterparts in Shanghai, and these guild leaders also formed interrelations across different Lower Yangzi cities and towns before the appearance of chamber networks in this region. As one native-place association for the Guangdong merchants in the Lower Yangzi region, the Chaozhou Guild first appeared in Jiangning and then moved to Suzhou around the mid-seventeenth century. This guild preceded its Shanghai counterpart in establishing the post of director with a tenure of three years. Between 1781 and 1784, its director was a Chaozhou native and official candidate who had earned the degree of metropolitan graduate (*jinshi*) but was waiting for governmental appointment. The dual-province guild of Guangdong and Guangxi even linked merchants and incumbent officials who came from the two provinces and acted in Suzhou and nearby cities. Around 1878, it built a guildhall with donations from such officials and "gentry-merchants" in Suzhou, Shanghai, and other cities. One of these elite merchants was the aforementioned Xu Run, the future vice president of the Shanghai GCC.[40]

Other sojourning groups in Suzhou formed about ten native-place associations at the provincial level, twenty at the prefectural level, four at the county level, and one at the township level by 1912. Available data indicate that at least five of the ten provincial-level *huiguan* were founded by merchants together with their fellow provincials in governments, or by officials alone, and at least eight prefectural-level *huiguan* and *gongsuo* were jointly founded by merchants and officials.[41] None of these regional guilds had direct affiliation with the Suzhou GCC later on, but many of their elite merchants joined the latter as leaders of occupational guilds because the two types of guilds had long formed interrelations through their interlocking leaderships.[42]

Among the occupational guilds in Suzhou, those in the silk fabric trade provided the general chamber of commerce in this city with the largest number of elite merchant leaders in 1905, and they also offered the most dramatic examples of guild multiplication, subdivision, and relational expansion in the Lower Yangzi region. As early as 1295, the Suzhou Silk-Weaving Gongsuo (Sujun jiye gongsuo) had already appeared as a precursor of craftsman guilds in this region, as mentioned before. By the mid-nineteenth century, there were four different guilds for silk weavers in the city, and at least one of their guildhalls was built by local gentry.[43]

Merchants in this trade also tended to form more localized and specialized guilds before the advent of the Suzhou GCC. Local brokers in the silk fabric business formed a quasi-guild before 1723. Then, the silk fabric merchants from Hangzhou Prefecture of Zhejiang Province founded an occupational guild of their own in 1758, while those from Huzhou Prefecture of Zhejiang and from Wu'an county of Henan Province established their guilds in 1789 and 1886, respectively. The merchants who engaged in silk fabric production also formed the Brocade Guild (Yunjin gongsuo) in 1822.[44]

In addition to the nine artisan and merchant guilds, Hu Shoukang, an imperial college student (*jiansheng*), organized the Silk Fabric Guild (Qixiang gongsuo) in 1843 as a charity for wholesalers and retailers in this trade. Hu and another elite merchant each loaned 500 taels to purchase a garden compound to use for the guildhall. They petitioned the Suzhou prefect and provincial officials and received permission to collect 0.5 percent of sales by all silk fabric shops as the charitable fund in this trade. The Suzhou prefect even contacted his subordinate magistrates in Wu, Wujiang, and Zhenze counties, as well as the prefects of Jiaxing and Huzhou prefectures in Zhejiang Province, ordering all silk fabric merchants in these places to donate to Hu's charity.[45] The magistrates in Wu, Wujiang, and Zhenze counties of Suzhou Prefecture and in Wucheng County of Huzhou Prefecture issued similar notices to their local merchants.[46]

With such official sponsorship, this guild expanded its influence into silk fabric markets within the three prefectures, and it also developed formal elite merchant leadership. Its major founder, Hu Shoukang, was confirmed by the Suzhou prefect as a director. Hu in turn invited one of his elite associates to serve as an accountant. These elite merchant leaders operated this *gongsuo* both as a charitable institution to support aged and disabled merchants in this trade and as an occupational guild to regulate the price and quality of silk fabrics. By 1859, the leadership of this *gongsuo* was expanded to include two imperial college students and five other elite merchants, one of them being Hu Shouzang, a brother or paternal cousin of Hu Shoukang.[47]

Although the Silk Fabric Guild did not confederate the extant guilds in this trade, its elite merchant leaders dominated the silk fabric market with official support, and they also engaged in public activities beyond their business interest. In 1890, You Xianjia, a gentryman from one such silk fabric merchant family, even became a manager of famine relief for southern Jiangsu and other provinces. He was also a director of two charitable halls thereafter and a major leader of local militias during the Boxer Uprising around 1900. Thus, You became a major founder and first president of the Suzhou GCC in 1905. He and other elite merchants also established this general chamber in the building of the Silk Fabric Guild.[48]

_ guild leaders + elite merchants formed guanxi
_ through charitable work
34   GUILDS AND ELITES

According to a local record of Suzhou around 1843, the Silk Fabric Guild,
Foreign Goods Guild (Yongqin gongsuo), and other occupational guilds all
built their guildhalls after petitioning the local officials (chengguan gongjian).[49]
The contacts with officials over such guild affairs obviously allowed elite
merchants to develop their formal leadership in these common-trade organizations as in the Silk Fabric Guild. These guild leaders and other elite merchants also formed their interrelations through their involvement in charitable
institutions. For instance, You Xianjia, the major founder of the Suzhou GCC,
had a relationship with the major guild leader in the pawnshop trade through
marriage, and the two shared a common interest in local charities.[50]

The case of the Sauce Guild (Jiangye gongsuo) in Suzhou further reflects
how elite merchants expanded their relationships and leadership from their
regional groups and occupational guilds into public activities before they
jointly founded the general chamber of commerce in this city. This guild was
formed in 1873 by eighty-six merchants from the cities of Suzhou and Jiangning as well as Anhui and Zhejiang provinces, but three of its four earliest
directors were Pan clansmen from Suzhou and Hangzhou. The Pan lineage
had long moved from Anhui to Suzhou, and it also engaged in salt trade in
Hangzhou. In the Qing period, its Suzhou branch alone produced eleven
metropolitan graduates, thirty-one provincial graduates, and twenty imperial
students (gongsheng). Among the Pans in the Qing court, one was a grand secretary (daxueshi) and another a grand councilor (junji dachen). The petition from
such influential elite merchants to create a gongsuo for managing charity and
regulating business in the sauce trade easily received official approval.[51]

The Pans dominated the Sauce Guild's leadership thereafter, and one elite
merchant from this powerful lineage, Pan Zuqian, was also active in local
public activities. After China suffered defeat in the Sino-Japanese War and
Suzhou became a treaty port under the terms of the Treaty of Shimonoseki
of 1895, Pan, the aforesaid You Xianjia, and Zhang Lüqian (Yuejie), a leading
native banker and merchant titleholder, were even officially entrusted with
powers to delimit the Japanese concession in the suburbs of this city. In 1902,
Pan and two other gentrymen, Wu Zihe and Peng Fusun, obtained support
from both officials and leaders of three charitable halls, including Xu Jun-
yuan, Ni Sijiu, and Pang Bingquan, for the construction of a bridge in Lumu
town outside Suzhou. They completed this project the next year, two years
before all of them joined You Xianjia, Zhang Lüqian, and other elites in
founding the Suzhou GCC.[52]

Like the Silk Fabric Guild in Suzhou, guilds in Hangzhou, Jiangning,
and other Lower Yangzi cities as well as the towns of Wusong and Luodian

also provided their premises for the future chambers of commerce.[53] However, guild leaders and other elite merchants helped organize these chambers through more important relational resources, including their formal leadership and interpersonal ties in business and public activities, as well as their connections with local officials.

In Hangzhou, the capital of Zhejiang Province, wealthy merchants and prestigious gentrymen had long been joint leaders in charitable activities, which enabled them to make a concerted effort to form a general chamber of commerce later on. In this city and its nearby towns, many guilds provided funds for a "charitable federation" composed of a dozen philanthropic organizations, and its "general directors of charities" (*shanju zongdong*) came from either a gentry or merchant background.[54] Thus, Fan Gongxu, a charity director of gentry origin, later led merchant guilds to found the Hangzhou GCC in 1906 and became its first president.[55]

From the aforesaid large cities to the smaller ones in the Lower Yangzi region, the guilds in the late nineteenth century universally established relatively formal leaderships composed of gentry titleholders and wealthy merchants, both of whom would become the founders and leaders of chambers of commerce later on. As MacGowan witnessed in Shanghai and two small treaty ports within the prefectural capitals of Ningbo and Wenzhou around 1886:[56]

> The [guild] officers consist of a general manager; a committee who are elected annually, but eligible for re-election. . . . The most important functionary is the permanent secretary, a salaried scholar of literary rank, who, in virtue of his literary position, has the right of personally interviewing the mandarinate, and, as guild delegate, has a recognized official standing. He is a medium of all correspondence, and at the Yamens appears as the guild's legal representative, pleading for its interests, demanding redress for its injured members, defending and protecting his constituents as occasion requires. He is useful to local authorities in soliciting from his guild subscriptions for public works, charities, and extraordinary exigencies.

It is noteworthy that the mixed elite merchant leaders in these guilds used not only institutional norms such as annual elections but also official connections to formalize their power. Through contacts with local officials, they further expanded their associational activities into public affairs. Indeed, in Ningbo, merchants in native banking, herbal medicine, pawnshops, and other businesses usually recruited gentrymen as their major leaders and dubbed them the "secretaries of public-minded guilds" (*gonghang xiansheng*).[57] In Wenzhou, merchant guilds either held periodic selections of their leaders from large business establishments or hired gentry titleholders as their secretaries and managers.[58] Thus, in both cities, gentry and merchant leaders of local guilds jointly founded chambers of commerce later on, as is shown in Chapter 2.

Compared with the guilds in these cities, those in Lower Yangzi towns had more difficulty in gathering enough members and resources and in finding protection from prestigious gentry-merchant leaders or fellow provincials in local governments. Thus, the regional and occupational guilds at the township level would often expand their regional and occupational ties to recruit merchants from nearby towns and related trades into their memberships. Although many of these guild leaders lacked prestigious status, they still secured official and gentry patronage through their flexible use of regional relations, sponsorship of charitable activities, or services in tax-collecting activities. Thus, the township guilds and their less prestigious leaders also developed widespread relations as the network basis for their future chambers of commerce.

In Shengze, a silk fabric town south of Suzhou, local guilds provided a rare example of organizational merger, but their relational expansion was more crucial for the formation of an affiliated chamber of commerce there. In this town, two guilds for merchants from Huizhou and Ningguo prefectures of Anhui Province jointly built a guildhall in 1809, although both guilds still kept their respective premises. This joint project received financial support from their prefectural fellows in several towns and marketplaces in southern Jiangsu and northern Zhejiang provinces, but it did not lead to further mergers of other guilds in the town.[59] guild merger

By the late nineteenth century, nearly twenty regional and occupational guilds existed in Shengze town, and those in the silk fabric trade formed especially extensive networks. In addition to their guilds in the town itself, silk fabric merchants from Shengze founded an informal group in Suzhou and a formal guild in Shanghai, and the latter was one of the sponsors of the aforesaid Shanghai Hall for Benevolent Assistance and its charitable activities. Naturally, a merchant titleholder in the silk fabric trade became the major founder and first president of the affiliated chamber of commerce in this town in 1906, and the affiliated chamber was located in a charitable hall. Like the aforementioned guilds in this town, this affiliated chamber opened its membership to merchants in nearby towns. It also pledged to collaborate with the general chambers in Suzhou and Shanghai with regard to silk fabric matters.[60]

In another case, merchant guilds in Shuanglin, a major silk and silk fabric town in western Zhejiang, skillfully used their tax-collecting services for the government to build their elite merchant leadership in this trade itself and in local charities. Merchants in this town founded about six regional and occupational guilds from the early eighteenth century, but their early guild-halls were mostly destroyed during the Taiping rebellion. When local offi-cials began to levy *lijin* in 1865, silk merchants selected a gentryman as their guild director to collect both the tax for the government and the funds for three charitable halls in the town. In 1870, they further selected a few man-agers, who took monthly turns handling accounting affairs for the halls.[61]

Meanwhile, in the Huzhou prefecture in which Shuanglin was located, silk merchants universally selected gentry titleholders as their guild directors for the tax-collecting activities. In the town itself, silk fabric merchants also chose a gentry titleholder, Shen Shantong, as their director, and they made an attempt to rebuild a guildhall in 1902. Because Shen could not accumu-late sufficient financial resources for the project among silk fabric merchants, he solicited donations from the silk merchants. These silk and silk fabric mer-chants then founded a joint guildhall under the leadership of Shen. Similarly, the guilds in the rice, pawnshop, and other trades successively selected their directors. However, these elite merchant leaders did not amalgamate their guilds as did those in the silk and silk fabric trades. It was not until 1907 that these guild leaders formed a branch chamber of commerce under the en-couragement of an official of local origin. They vowed that their new orga-nization would not only unite local merchants but also "champion public wellbeing" (*weichi gongyi*).[62] ~formal elite merchant leadership in towns~

The Shuanglin case shows that guilds in the Lower Yangzi region had ~as~ formalized their elite merchant leadership not only in large cities but also in ~well~ market towns by the beginning of the twentieth century. These guild leaders, especially those in large cities, had also extended their relations and interests into public affairs beyond their business world and local communities. As a result, leading elite merchants in this region were ready to join reformist li-terati to cope with new foreign challenges, including those from Western chambers of commerce. Having built widespread relationships through guilds and charitable halls, these elites naturally planned chambers of commerce as their associational networks beyond individual cities and towns.

Reactions of Literati and Elite Merchants to Western Chambers of Commerce

Western chambers of commerce entered China alongside foreign commercial, military, and political expansion during the 1830s, the decade before the Opium War (1839–1842). These China-based Western chambers of commerce, unlike their counterparts in Europe and North America, operated not only as national and international organizations for foreign merchants but also as political partners of foreign governments for their common ventures in China. Thus, the earliest response to these Western chambers by literati reformers in the Lower Yangzi region was to design similar Chinese organizations for the purpose of uniting Chinese merchants beyond the regional and occupational limits of guilds and promoting government-business cooperation against foreign incursion. Subsequently, leading elite merchants presented more creative plans to develop widespread chamber networks from provincial capitals to county cities and to demand governmental sponsorship rather than bureaucratic control of these new merchant associations.

The first Western chamber of commerce appeared in China in 1834, when the chief superintendent of British trade in Canton, William John Napier, was trying to expand British interests through direct communications with Qing officials instead of with the *Cohong* merchants, the government-licensed brokers who monopolized foreign trade in Canton. When Napier's attempt met with resistance from Chinese officials and merchants, a British chamber of commerce was formed at his suggestion and appeared in the foreign factories of Canton on August 25, 1834.[63] Its major purpose was to "insure unity of action at the time when Lord Napier was trying to force open the door of China."[64] In 1836, a general chamber of commerce further incorporated British and other foreign merchants in Canton and Macao; the chamber played various commercial and even political roles until its dissolution at the beginning of the Opium War.[65] Western chamber of com.

After this war opened the door of Qing China, more Western chambers of commerce developed in the new treaty ports, including Shanghai, Xiamen, Fuzhou, Hankou, and Tianjin, as well as in the British colony of Hong Kong. In Shanghai a British chamber of commerce quickly came into being in 1847. In 1863, it incorporated other foreign merchants in the treaty port and renamed itself the Shanghai [Western] General Chamber of Commerce (Shanghai WGCC).[66] The Shanghai WGCC provided both a model and leadership for other foreign chambers in the treaty ports of China. It also had direct contacts with Chinese guilds and governments in the Lower Yangzi region and thereby exerted a conspicuous influence on the Chinese elite merchants in their effort to organize similar organizations.

The Shanghai WGCC consisted primarily of British firms, along with American, German, and French firms, until the 1880s. By that time, it was annually electing an executive committee composed of "four English, two Americans and two members of continental nationality," namely, French and German businessmen in the city.[67] From 1891 onward, this Western chamber began to accept Japanese and other foreign firms into its membership, as Table 2 shows. By 1901, the Shanghai WGCC had turned into much more of an international merchant association, with ninety-two members from eleven nations. Nevertheless, it remained a predominantly Western organization because its members were all European and American firms, excepting three Japanese companies.

In the late nineteenth century, the Shanghai WGCC consistently restricted its membership to large foreign companies by rejecting individual merchant members and charging high membership fees.[68] However, the general chamber actively recruited individual members from foreign diplomatic bodies and military forces. According to its rules, the Shanghai WGCC would accept prominent visiting officials from foreign governments as guest members without charging fees. It would also invite diplomatic and naval officials of foreign powers as honorary members; the former did not pay any admission fees, while the latter paid at a reduced rate.[69] This set of rules later influenced the Shanghai GCC, which claimed to have "objects and regulations similar to those" of the Shanghai WGCC.[70]

TABLE 2

*Nationalities of members of the Shanghai WGCC,
1880, 1890, and 1900*

Nationalities of members	Number of members		
	1881	*1891*	*1901*
British	33	29	47
German	6	6	21
American	3	4	7
French	4	2	6
Japanese		1	3
Swiss			3
Belgian			1
Danish			1
Dutch			1
Italian			1
Russian			1
Total	46	42	92

Sources: Data from Shanghai [Western] General Chamber of Commerce, *Annual Report for 1880*, 4; *Annual Report for 1890*, 5; *Annual Report for 1900*, 5. Each of these annual reports actually listed members for the next year.

The Shanghai WGCC impressed Chinese elites not only with its regulations but also with its actions, including its effort to establish direct relationships with foreign governments. At its general meeting of 1869, F. B. Johnson,
the representative of Jardine, Matheson and Company, proposed that "the
chamber should make its voice heard by addressing the foreign offices of treaty
powers, and by placing itself in communication with the leading commercial bodies in Europe and America."[71] In response to this proposal, F. Porter,
the committee chairman, expressed the worry that such efforts would make
the Shanghai WGCC a political rather than a commercial body and overex-
tend its financial capacity. However, in December 1869, the meeting of the
general chamber adopted Johnson's suggestion and raised membership dues
to finance this plan.[72]

 As Porter had predicted, the Shanghai WGCC broadened its concerns
from business to politics and operated more like a political organization than
a commercial one. An American account of the Shanghai WGCC concurs:[73]

> The General Chamber of Commerce . . . differed from the general idea of a chamber
> of commerce in the United States in that it was not a "trade promotion" body. . . .
> It came to exercise broad powers and was looked upon by the foreign consular
> authorities and the Chinese as having almost semiofficial status. In brief, if the general
> chamber recommended certain action in reference to trade matters it usually was
> adopted as a matter of course, the foreign consuls recommending the action to their
> own nationals as well as to the Chinese government.

Indeed, the Shanghai WGCC had cooperated closely with foreign powers
to gain economic and political concessions from the Qing government. During the Anglo-Chinese negotiations for the revision of the Treaty of Tianjin
in 1868, the British consul, Rutherford Alcock, invited the Shanghai WGCC
to express an opinion and also asked it to supply information for the opening
of additional treaty ports in China. Subsequently, the Shanghai WGCC
called a general meeting to advocate the opening of new ports and even "the
whole country to foreign capital and skill." Meanwhile, the general meeting
selected three members to work with the executive committee in gathering
information about the proposed new treaty ports. The responses from the
Shanghai WGCC reached all the foreign ministers in Beijing, the British
and Dutch foreign secretaries, members of the British Parliament, and chambers of commerce in Britain and France.[74]

There was also close cooperation between the Shanghai WGCC and the
Municipal Council of the International Settlement in Shanghai. In 1897, the
Municipal Council sought the general chamber's support in an effort to ex-
tend the boundaries of the International Settlement into the Chinese districts.

The Shanghai WGCC rendered enthusiastic assistance by informing the diplomatic corps in Beijing of the "unanimity, strength, and reasonableness of public opinion on this subject in the Shanghai foreign community."[75]

As an active and powerful organization of foreign firms in China, the Shanghai WGCC had long engaged in commercial competition and even confrontation with Chinese merchant guilds. In 1873, for example, a foreign firm refused to cash the promissory notes that its comprador had embezzled to pay his personal debt to a Chinese native bank. The Native Banks' Guild of Northern Shanghai (Shanghai beishi qianye huiguan) took up the issue and urged the Shanghai WGCC to conform to the native banking practice of cashing promissory notes regardless of their holder. When this request was rejected by the Shanghai WGCC, the guild forced the latter to recognize the native banking practice through a successful boycott against all foreign firms early in 1874.[76]

Although Chinese merchant guilds had direct contact and even clashed with the Shanghai WGCC, they did not automatically imitate this Western chamber of commerce or federate into a similar organization beyond regional and occupational limits. However, a few literati reformers in late Qing China, together with leading elite merchants in the Lower Yangzi region, had long expressed interest in the Shanghai WGCC, and they began to draft different plans to establish similar Chinese organizations from the early 1880s.

Zhong Tianwei, a leading Shanghai scholar of Western learning and a pioneer reformer in late Qing China, presented the earliest proposal to establish Western-style chambers of commerce, or shanghui, in China.[77] In 1884, his petition to Liangguang Governor-General Zhang Zhidong, a new leader in the early industrialization of late Qing China, included the following suggestion:[78]

> A matter of prime importance is to form chambers of commerce. . . . [Chinese officials should] follow the ways of foreign consuls [in treaty ports], allow merchants in all trades to select gentry-managers, and grant them status and authority. In any business matter, the officials should allow the gentry-managers to contact the government. For business beneficial to China, the officials should authorize them to protect their interests rather than obstruct them with routine regulations.

Zhong evidently perceived the Western chambers of commerce mainly as a linkage device for government-business cooperation. Thus, he proposed the formation of similar Chinese merchant organizations through official support and for the purpose of strengthening the relations between merchants and the governments. Zhong's proposal did not receive a positive response from Governor-General Zhang at that time, but his literati and elite merchant followers in the Lower Yangzi region would again bring this issue to official attention a decade later and would further push the Qing government to promote nationwide chambers of commerce two decades later.

In 1888, two other reformist scholars in Shanghai planned new mercantile associations on the basis of native guilds or after the model of Western joint-stock companies, and their plans would also influence the discussions about Chinese chambers of commerce later on. Zhang Jie, a scholar in the Academy of Western Learning (Gezhi shuyuan), suggested that guild leaders in treaty ports should form business-promoting associations (*tongshang gonghui*), which could hold discussions on business affairs and protect merchants from official extortion and foreign oppression through direct communications with the central government. The principal of this academy and the more famous reformist scholar, Wang Tao, also called on the Qing government to follow the example of the British East India Company and establish general bureaus of commerce (*shangwu zongju*) as links between Chinese officials and merchants.[79]

Like Zhong's proposal for Chinese chambers of commerce, Zhang and Wang's plans did not receive immediate responses from the Qing government. However, their ideas inspired leading elite merchants to plan Western-style chambers of commerce around the mid-1890s, when China's defeat in the Sino-Japanese War shocked the nation as a whole. As a result of the war, the Treaty of Shimonoseki directly affected the Lower Yangzi region by opening Suzhou and Hangzhou, the provincial capitals of Jiangsu and Zhejiang provinces, to foreign trade and manufacturing activities.[80] In the face of new foreign economic intrusion, elite merchants in this region began to join literati reformers in the discussions and designing of Western-style chambers of commerce in China.

By the mid-1890s, Zheng Guanying had become a merchant manager of semiofficial enterprises in Shanghai after leading the aforementioned famine relief effort around 1878. He made an extensive examination of Western chambers of commerce and presented a systematic plan for similar Chinese organizations. Zheng's plan was included in his widely circulated book, *Shengshi Weiyan* (Warning to a Seemingly Prosperous Age), which influenced reformist scholars, officials, and even the young Guangxu emperor.[81] Zheng quoted Zhong Tianwei's proposal in his own writings, and he also used the Chinese term *shanghui* to refer to Western chambers of commerce. But he planned Chinese chambers of commerce with the title "bureau of commerce" or *shangwu ju*, the term used by Wang Tao before him. Because Zheng realized that "bureau" (*ju*) was a term for official institutions in the West, he evidently thought of bureaus of commerce as Western-style chambers of commerce with closer relations to the government.[82]

However, it was not only the Western model but also Zheng's involvement in guilds and charitable organizations that led him to plan the bureaus of commerce as new associational networks for merchants at different levels of urban centers. According to Zheng, all provinces should establish general bureaus of commerce, or *shangwu zongju*, in their capitals, and provincial officials should select prestigious gentry-merchants as these bureaus' directors. These directors would keep officials informed of merchant opinions and submit suggestions about business affairs to the provincial and even the central governments for endorsement. Officials at the prefectural and county levels should also instruct merchants and artisans to organize branch bureaus of commerce (*shangwu fenju*) and elect their directors. These directors would hold regular business discussions and submit their suggestions to the government through the provincial bureaus of commerce. Zheng believed that such organizations would bring merchants and officials together and eventually enable Chinese businesses to keep pace with Western ones.[83]

From the mid-1890s, the most radical reformer in late Qing China, Kang Youwei, also joined the Lower Yangzi literati and elite merchants in the call for Chinese chambers of commerce, and his call brought the issue to nationwide attention. Kang began to promote Western-style chambers of commerce in Qing China in May 1895, when he gathered more than 1,300 provincial graduates for a petition against the signing of the Treaty of Shimonoseki. In his draft of the famous "provincial graduate petition" (*gongche shangshu*), Kang lumped Western chambers of commerce together with joint-stock companies, such as the British East India Company and the Dutch East India Company. He claimed that the British occupation of India, the Dutch colonization in Southeast Asia, and Western aggression in China had all benefited from such "chambers of commerce." Thus, Kang requested that the Qing court resist the foreign intrusion with the establishment of similar institutions.[84] KYW advocates for C.C.S

Meanwhile, Kang's reformist associates, including Tan Sitong and Xu Qin, also expressed strong interest in chambers of commerce.[85] In February 1898, one of their reformist journals in Hunan Province published the first set of draft regulations for Chinese chambers of commerce. The editorial office of this journal proclaimed itself the headquarters of nationwide chambers of commerce, which would include a general chamber of commerce (*shangye zonghui huiguan*) in Beijing, affiliated chambers of commerce (*shangye zonghui xieguan*) in treaty ports and provincial capitals, and branch chambers of commerce (*zhihui*) in various trades. These chambers were to promote Chinese business by exploring new knowledge and to unite merchants by nourishing their mutual trust and friendship. The chamber leaders had to be selected through elections, and official sponsors could become members only if they accepted the chamber regulations. This set of regulations reflected the ambition of these literati reformers to build chambers of commerce as a part of their associational networks.[86]

The Lower Yangzi region remained the center in the nationwide discussions on chambers of commerce and in the early associational activities of the reformist elites. With support from Zhang Zhidong, the acting Liangjiang governor-general, Kang Youwei successfully founded the first reformist organization, the Study Society for National Strength (Qiangxuehui), in Shanghai in late 1895. It involved dozens of reformist elites and officials, as well as such leading elite merchants as Jing Yuanshan and Zheng Guanying.[87] Kang would eventually bring his proposal for chambers of commerce to the Qing court and push for the establishment of such organizations during the 1898 Reform, as is discussed in Chapter 2. By contrast, Lower Yangzi elite reformers developed more concrete plans for the development of chamber networks from the provincial to the local level. They also made stronger demands to the Qing government for legal protection and official support rather than bureaucratic control of chamber activities.

A major promoter of the chambers of commerce in the Lower Yangzi region was Zhang Jian, who had joined Kang's Study Society for National Strength in 1895 and then transformed himself from a metropolitan official into a gentry industrialist. When he helped Governor-General Zhang Zhidong draft a petition to the throne for resisting new foreign intrusions in 1895, Zhang Jian's proposal incorporated Zheng Guanying's ideas about bureaus of commerce. But Zhang Jian's writings of 1895, 1896, and 1897 regarded the bureaus of commerce, or *shangwuju*, and chambers of commerce, or *shanghui*, as similar organizations. He also emphasized their similar functions in binding merchants and linking the merchant community with the government for the purpose of promoting Chinese business against foreign aggression. His proposal not only planned general chambers of commerce at the provincial level and affiliated chambers at the prefectural level but also emphasized that these chambers should operate at the initiative of merchant leaders rather than officials.[88]

According to Zhang, different businesses should select and send their own "directors" into the chambers of commerce at the prefectural and provincial levels. At the prefectural level, the leaders of the affiliated chambers of commerce would investigate local conditions, discuss commercial issues, and submit their plans for business development to the merchant leaders in general chambers of commerce at the provincial level. Subsequently, chamber leaders at the provincial level would make decisions by themselves rather than wait for official approval. They simply needed to inform the governor-generals and governors of their decisions and obtain official support and protection. Most important, Zhang requested that the Qing court enact a "concise statute" (*jianyifa*), ensuring governmental support of such chambers and prohibiting official interference into their affairs.[89]

Another literati participant in the Study Society for National Strength, Wang Kangnian, published a series of articles from 1896 to 1898 in which he urged merchants to establish chambers of commerce by themselves. In his opinion, such chambers not only could enable merchants to protect themselves from foreign economic intrusion but also could raise their status in relation to officials and increase their influence on state policy on business issues.[90] A paternal cousin of Wang Kangnian, Wang Dajun, initiated a business study society in a Shanghai rice shop and began to publish a commercial journal in September 1898. He also used the journal to promote chambers of commerce for saving Chinese business under foreign aggression.[91]

This journal soon published a set of regulations for a general chamber of commerce in Shanghai. The preface to the regulations indicated that Western chambers of commerce were recognized but not organized by governments. Thus, this set of regulations stressed the general chamber in Shanghai mainly as a link between merchants and officials and requested that the Qing court appoint a supervisor to liaise between the general chamber and local officials. However, the general chamber itself would consist of leaders from merchant guilds in different trades, who would discuss business issues and make decisions by themselves, although their decisions would need governmental support. The journal also presented the planned general chamber of commerce in Shanghai as a model for similar organizations in the entire country.[92]

This set of regulations for chambers of commerce again expressed the common aspiration of reformist literati and elite merchants in the Lower Yangzi region in the era of the 1898 Reform. These diverse elites, ranging from commercialized gentry to wealthy merchants, had already fused through their leaderships in guild and charitable activities as well as their common pursuit of personal fame, family fortune, and public welfare. Through joint responses to Western chambers of commerce, reformist literati and elite merchants also made a common effort to promote Western-style commercial organizations

reformist literati & elite merchants
advocated for est. of c.c.s

why they wanted
C.C.
↓

in China for the revival of Chinese business, survival of the nation, and reform of late Qing politics. However, these elites designed Chinese chambers
of commerce not merely as the institutional device to unite merchants beyond
guild limits and promote government-business cooperation against foreign
aggression. They also tried to build these new organizations as part of the associational networks under their dominance.

Indeed, the reformist literati and elite merchants advocated chambers of
commerce together with other kinds of new associations to pursue their political power and ambitions. One elite merchant participant in Kang Youwei's
Study Society for National Strength, Zheng Guanying, even accepted a suggestion by Japanese diplomats and initiated the Shanghai Branch of the Asiatic
Study Society (Shanghai Yaxiya xiehui fenhui) in March 1898. This Shanghai-
based study society vowed to "revitalize Asia by enlightening people and developing resources," and it planned to establish branches throughout Asian
countries, their provinces, and counties. Its leaders and members included
Zheng himself, Zhang Jian, Wang Kangnian, and Yan Xinhou, all of whom
were literati and merchant advocates of chambers of commerce, as described
above.[93] Although the radical literati later failed to carry the 1898 Reform to
a successful conclusion, and their study societies were outlawed by the Qing
court, Yan and other elite merchants in the Lower Yangzi region continued
their interactions with reformist officials and finally established the earliest
Chinese chambers of commerce in this region.

– merchant guilds + gentry leadership
   began to impact gov. policy

– guilds have diverse wealth and
   leadership

   guilds began interacting more w/ gov
– participating in public activities/ public
   works

   developed links across cities + towns,
   networks w/ other social elites

   Shanghai WGCC – first chamber
   of commerce → western
   merchant shipping

   Reformist calls for Chinese c.cs
   including Kang Youwei

Elite and Official Interactive Movements
toward Chambers of Commerce

Qing influenced by li' reformists and elite merchants on c.c. issue

Because reformist literati and elite merchants from the Lower Yangzi region to the country as a whole expressed enthusiasm for chambers of commerce around the mid-1890s, the Qing government placed the issue on its agenda. However, only a few officials had acquired limited knowledge of such Western organizations by that time, and one of their pioneers was the first Chinese minister to Great Britain, Guo Songtao. In 1877, Guo arrived in London with a mission to obtain British ratification of the Zhifu (Yantai) Convention that imposed a tariff on opium imported to China. Guo's mission met protests from the Shanghai WGCC and the chambers of commerce in Bradford and Halifax. However, he also received support from the chambers in Liverpool, Manchester, Glasgow, and Kendal, which were more interested in the export of industrial products to China.[1] Although Guo had direct contacts with these Western chambers of commerce, he did not realize their difference from joint-stock companies. In his diaries, he coined the Chinese term *shanghui* (merchant society) to refer to both foreign companies and chambers, and simply regarded them as a similar device for grouping merchants together.[2] *C.C. as "merchant society"*

Meanwhile, Ma Jianzhong, a diplomatic attaché in Paris, also used the phrase *shanghui* to denote both Western companies and chambers of commerce, and urged official promotion of such organizations for merchant support. He reported to Zhili Governor-General Li Hongzhang in 1877:[3]

> I originally assumed that the European nations had been rich and strong because of
> their superior manufacturing skills and strict military discipline. After an examination

of their laws and administration, I realized that they pursued wealth by protecting *shanghui*, and became strong by winning popular support.

Because Li and other reformist officials had already launched joint-stock companies under "official supervision and merchant management" (*guandu shangban*) from the early 1870s, they naturally tried to found chambers of commerce under the same formula around the mid-1890s, when new national crises compelled the Qing government to seek merchant support. Meanwhile, these officials also adopted proposals from the Lower Yangzi elite merchants to organize bureaus of commerce for the revival of Chinese business and the nation, but such official versions of chambers of commerce still attempted to expand bureaucratic control over the merchant community.

In contrast, elite merchants in the Lower Yangzi region had long used different forms of interaction with officials to build and expand their formal leadership in guilds and charitable halls. They further intensified their interactions with the Qing government within the new business institutions for their pursuit of power and profit as well as an institutional solution to the mounting national crises. Such interactive movements directly caused the institutional transition from semiofficial companies and bureaus of commerce to chambers of commerce.

The formative process of general, affiliated, and branch chambers of commerce in the Lower Yangzi region represented the beginning of a relational revolution because it greatly institutionalized and expanded social networks in the merchant community, especially among elite merchants from large cities to market towns. The three-tier chamber networks also caused unprecedented change in government-business relations from the local to the national level.

Official Attempts at Joint-Stock Companies and Bureaus of Commerce

In the face of foreign economic aggression during the late nineteenth century, reformist officials eagerly enlisted elite merchant support by establishing semi-official enterprises at first and bureaus of commerce later on. Although they depended on merchant capital, managerial skills, and social connections in such efforts, the Qing court and provincial officials still strove and even competed for control over these business institutions. In contrast, elite merchant investors and managers regarded official control as a threat to their profits and power, and responded with vocal protests and passive resistance, including the withdrawal of capital and support. As the court's political and financial crises intensified, competing officials had to permit elite merchants more control over these enterprises and bureaus of commerce. The official and elite interaction and subsequent relational change led eventually to the earliest emergence of Chinese chambers of commerce in the Lower Yangzi region. A detailed examination of this complicated historical process is significant because previous studies have often deplored bureaucratic control in all of these business institutions or downplayed institutional transition from bureaus of commerce to chambers of commerce.[4] *officials had to 'give merchants control b/c of coua crisis*

Among the late Qing officials, Sheng Xuanhuai could become the major patron of the Shanghai CCA in 1902 because he had helped Governors-General Li Hongzhang and Zhang Zhidong to supervise a series of semiofficial enterprises starting from the early 1870s. He also brought many elite merchant investors and managers into these new business institutions. Most of these enterprises, such as the China Merchants' Steam Navigation Company (Lunchuan zhaoshangju), the Imperial Telegraph Administration (Dianbao zongju), and the Imperial Bank of China (Zhongguo tongshang yinhang), centered on Shanghai, and they later became affiliated with the Shanghai CCA, as did many merchant guilds.[5] Compared with the guilds, however, these enterprises brought reformist officials and elite merchants into more direct and intensive interactions, and they even enabled Sheng to plan a chamber of commerce before the appearance of the Shanghai CCA. *S.e. → closer official-merchant cooperation*

The semiofficial enterprises of late Qing China started with the establishment of the China Merchants' Steam Navigation Company in 1872 under Governor-General Li's sponsorship and Sheng's supervision. This company at first attracted elite merchants because Li promised to "strengthen the empire and reassure merchants" against foreign competition and because large merchant shareholders such as Xu Run received managerial powers and high rates of return from their investment. Thus, this enterprise expanded quickly during its first decade as a result of its efficient management by elite merchants and strong official support. Its initial success also inspired the joint efforts of these reformist officials and elite merchants to launch similar enterprises in telegraph, textile, and other industries around Shanghai and in the whole country.[6] *emergence of semi-official enterprises*

However, the increasing bureaucratization and gradual stagnation of these enterprises quickly caused disenchantment among elite merchant investors and managers, including Zheng Guanying, an early advocate of bureaus of commerce and chambers of commerce. In response, Sheng and other reformist officials had to entice merchant investors by turning the enterprises under official supervision and merchant management into ones under the joint-management of officials and merchants (*guanshang heban*) and even into ones under merchant management (*shangban*).[7]

The institutional modification of these new enterprises was a part of the official policy changes that would eventually allow elite merchants to establish chambers of commerce by themselves and under their leadership. Sheng and other officials, however, did so not simply in response to elite merchant criticism but as a scheme to ensure their personal dominance over these enterprises at the expense of the court's central control. Sheng's ambition to build and expand his economic empire brought him into conflict with the Qing court especially in his attempt to establish the Imperial Bank of China and a chamber of commerce as the bank's symbiotic institution.

Sheng made this attempt under the encouragement of his mentor, Li Hongzhang, who lost the position of Zhili governor-general and became a sinecure official in the court because of his responsibility for Chinese losses in the Sino-Japanese War. In October 1896 Sheng petitioned the throne to organize the first modern Chinese bank, and he argued strongly for merchant management rather than governmental control of this bank. However, he still stressed the need for the supervision of the bank by a high official, presumably himself. Sheng soon received Li Hongzhang's instruction to call the bank a *shanghui*, the term that had been used by some official and literati reformers to denote both joint-stock companies and chambers of commerce.[8]

Sheng readily acknowledged that *shanghui* was a "very new" term and named the planned bank *Zhonghua shanghui yinhang* (Chinese *Shanghui* Bank) in the first draft of the bank regulations.[9] In January 1897, Sheng changed the name to *Zhongguo tongshang yinhang*, or the Imperial Bank of China, and expanded Li's idea into a plan to establish a chamber of commerce as an adjunct to the modern banking system. In the draft bank regulations that Sheng submitted to the Zongli yamen (Office of Foreign Affairs) in February 1897, he made it clear that the head office of the bank would be in Shanghai, his own power base. Moreover, the bank would be managed by merchant directors, and its profits would go to the shareholders, although it would contribute 20 percent of its profits to the court. Most important, Sheng envisaged a chamber of commerce that would assemble merchant managers from all semiofficial enterprises and operate symbiotically with the bank to head all railroad, steamship, telegraph, and mining companies.[10]

Sheng's plan soon met with criticism from the Zongli yamen, which wanted the bank's head office in the imperial capital of Beijing, not in Shanghai. The yamen also demanded a 50 percent share of its profits and strict control over its silver reserves and capital transactions.[11] At the same time, Sheng's plan for a chamber of commerce also aroused the suspicion of a censor, Guan Ting-xian. In a memorial to the court, Guan warned that the planned chamber of commerce might interfere in the operation of government-sponsored enter-prises. In particular, Guan asked the court to restrict the chamber's functions to the general discussion of business affairs.[12]

[handwritten margin note: opposition to Sheng's bank plan + cc]

Two of Sheng's patrons, Governors-General Zhang Zhidong and Wang Wenshao, came to his defense because they were expecting to build the Beijing-Hankou railroad with capital from the bank. In a joint petition to the throne that was actually drafted by Sheng himself, Zhang and Wang rendered their support for Sheng's bank regulations and his plan for a chamber of commerce. This petition argued that such a chamber was necessary so that merchant man-agers of all companies could discuss business affairs and maintain close con-tacts among themselves. It also indicated that Chinese merchants had always suffered losses because they were not united. In contrast, Western merchants had organized chambers of commerce in Shanghai even though their num-bers were not large.[13] *[handwritten: support for plan from governors-general]*

This episode vividly demonstrates how intragovernmental competition for the control of new business ventures evolved into strife over a plan for a cham-ber of commerce. Although Sheng in the end failed to organize such a chamber, he was able to establish the Imperial Bank of China in Shanghai in early 1897. Among the first nine directors of the bank, Yan Xinhou, Yan Ying, Shi Zejing, Yang Tinggao, and Zhu Baosan, as well as the two bank managers, Chen Gan (Shengjiao) and Xie Lunhui, all participated in the Shanghai CCA later on.[14] Thus, under the Imperial Bank of China, Sheng had gathered the major leaders of the future chamber of commerce in Shanghai. *[handwritten: no CC, bank est. 1897]*

In the national emergency following the Sino-Japanese War of 1894–1895, the acting Liangjiang governor-general, Zhang Zhidong, also promoted bureaus of commerce in the Lower Yangzi region as the official version of chambers of commerce. However, his attempt to control these new business institutions soon brought him into conflict with elite merchants and the Qing court, and the failure of his attempt would teach him a hard lesson and turn him into an advocate of elite merchant leadership in chambers of commerce. In 1895, Zhang received an imperial edict to combat new foreign intrusions under the Treaty of Shimonoseki. In response, he included the aforesaid proposal of Zhang Jian for bureaus of commerce in his own report to the court, but he used his own subordinate officials rather than elite merchants to establish three bureaus of commerce in Jiangning, Suzhou, and Shanghai.[15]

[handwritten: Zhang's plan to form CCs led by his lower officials in Jiangning, Suzhou, Shanghai]

Through these bureaus Governor-General Zhang planned to raise 124 million taels in loans from foreign banks, the Qing government, and Chinese merchants to set up five reeling mills and five cotton mills. He envisioned that these ten Chinese textile enterprises would consume all the raw cotton and silk produced in Jiangsu province, so that Japanese and other foreigners could neither buy these raw materials nor sell textile products there. However, a shortfall in foreign and government loans soon forced Zhang to reduce his grandiose plan and seek Chinese merchant investment for only one textile mill in Tongzhou and two in Suzhou. To attract gentry and merchant capital, he turned from incumbent officials to local gentry for the organization of bureaus of commerce. In Tongzhou and Suzhou, respectively, he entrusted Zhang Jian and Lu Runxiang, two top metropolitan graduates (zhuangyuan), to found bureaus of commerce and textile mills.[16]

In late 1895, Governor-General Zhang personally instructed Lu to establish two textile mills under a bureau of commerce in Suzhou. However, the only financial sources he mustered were the merchant loans that the provincial government had previously arranged and was supposed to repay to the merchant lenders at the end of 1895. With permission from the court, Zhang shifted about 600,000 taels of merchant loans to the bureau of commerce as capital for a commercial company, one reeling mill and one cotton mill. At first, Zhang was elated at his scheme to transform merchant loaners into stockholders, but he soon discovered that his compulsory action was unpopular among the merchants.[17]

In the Qing court, Censor Wang Pengyun in early 1896 echoed Zhang's previous report with a proposal to establish bureaus of commerce in provincial capitals along the coast and to put them under the direct control of governors and governors-general. In Wang's plan, these provincial officials would appoint the bureau chiefs, who would order local guilds to select merchant leaders, deliberate business affairs with them, and then submit proposals to their respective provincial governments for approval. Only important issues would be transmitted from these bureaus through provincial officials to the Qing court. In response, the Zongli yamen approved the formation of bureaus of commerce in provincial capitals and county seats. However, it took careful measures to prevent the expansion of provincial power, ordering provincial officials to let merchants manage these bureaus rather than appoint bureau heads directly.[18] Thus, the power struggle of the Qing court with its provincial officials actually helped the future chambers of commerce to emerge under elite merchant leadership rather than bureaucratic control.

In the Lower Yangzi region, provincial officials were directly under pressure from elite merchants to relinquish bureaucratic control over bureaus of commerce. When Zhang Zhidong and Liu Kunyi resumed their respective positions as Huguang and Liangjiang governors-general in early 1896, Liu found that Suzhou merchants, especially those in native-banking and pawn-shop businesses, still resented Zhang's coercive measures concerning merchant loans. Moreover, these elite merchants were unhappy with Lu Run-xiang, who headed the bureau of commerce in Suzhou but had no experience in commercial affairs. Therefore, Liu had to instruct Lu to recruit merchant managers into the bureau.[19]

The reformist tide in 1898 brought Kang Youwei and other literati reformers into the Qing court, and they began to promote the merchant-managed bureaus of commerce as the precursors of chambers of commerce. After Kang helped the young Guangxu emperor launch political reform on June 11, he submitted a special proposal regarding commercial issues on July 19 and pushed for the establishment of bureaus of commerce in all provinces. In particular, Kang proposed that merchant leaders should be selected from the directors of charitable halls in Shanghai and Canton and allowed to run such bureaus of commerce in the two cities as an experiment. On July 25, the emperor ordered Governors-General Liu Kunyi and Zhang Zhidong to make arrangements for founding bureaus of commerce under such elite merchant leadership. The imperial edict further instructed them to make preparations for setting up commercial schools and newspapers as well as chambers of commerce.[20]

On August 2, Kang submitted another proposal regarding commercial affairs. He again suggested that the bureaus of commerce in all provinces should establish merchant leaderships by following the examples of guilds and charitable halls in Shanghai and Canton. They should also take responsibility for promoting chambers of commerce. Consequently, the emperor on the same day ordered provincial officials to implement his previous edict immediately. On August 29, a junior official and one of Kang's reformist fellows in the court, Wang Xifan, followed up with a new proposal. He argued that the bureaus of commerce were only an imitation of foreign business administration, but Western chambers of commerce were formed by merchants themselves. Their leaders came forward through merchant elections and received only recognition, not salaries, from the government. Thus, Wang proposed the establishment of chambers of commerce in addition to bureaus of commerce in all provinces, and he specifically suggested a general chamber in Shanghai. In response, the emperor issued a new edict to

Governors-General Liu Kunyi and Zhang Zhidong, ordering them to promote both bureaus of commerce and chambers of commerce in the Lower and Middle Yangzi regions.[21] b.C. + C.C. ordered by emperor

Kang and his followers were unable to establish the proposed chambers of commerce before Empress Dowager Cixi ended the reformist movement with a coup on September 21 and then put the emperor under house arrest. Nevertheless, the 1898 Reform helped bureaus of commerce develop from the Lower Yangzi region to the entire nation. In the Middle Yangzi region, Huguang Governor-General Zhang Zhidong appointed two officials to organize a bureau of commerce in Hankou in 1898 and to promote chambers of commerce there, but only silver shops and native banks in this city formed a joint guild in the name of a chamber of commerce (shanghui gongsuo) in 1900.[22] 1898 Reform helped b.C.s develop in LY and MY

In the Lower Yangzi region, Liangjiang Governor-General Liu Kunyi merged the Jiangning and Shanghai bureaus of commerce into the Jiangnan General Bureau of Commerce (Jiangnan shangwu zongju) in Shanghai by early September of 1898. This provincial bureau began with the gentry industrialist Zhang Jian as its head and gathered a group of such elite merchants as Yan Xinhou as its managers. After the failure of the 1898 Reform, this general bureau in May 1899 still received an imperial decree to expand its protection over merchants and thus founded a branch bureau of commerce in the Yangzi port of Zhenjiang. The two bureaus in Shanghai and Zhenjiang ceased operations for a short time in late 1899 because Gangyi, a conservative Manchu minister, stopped the governmental subsidy for them after his fiscal investigation of the Lower Yangzi region. However, the general bureau's merchant managers insisted on staying in office, petitioned to continue its operation, and even promised to contribute half of the bureau's funds.[23] Han vs Manchu conflict – political – reflected in b.C.

Gangyi's attempt to restrict provincial outlays for bureaus of commerce reflected the antagonism of conservative officials toward reformist institutions, and it led to a political conflict that crossed ethnic lines between Han and Manchu officials. In a petition to the throne in October 1899, Qingkuan, a Manchu official, claimed that Gangyi's order to terminate the bureaus of commerce had become a running joke among foreigners. In Qingkuan's opinion, the bureaus in Shanghai and Hankou had begun an effort that would enrich the state and regain Chinese economic rights from foreigners. Subsequently, the imperial court restated its support of provincial bureaus of commerce and again gave instructions to place these bureaus under gentry-merchant management.[24]

[Handwritten margin note top: "Shanghai bc- stable group of 4 merchants also directors of Imperial bank + later S.CCA leaders"]

With renewed support from the court, Governor-General Liu reopened the Jiangnan General Bureau of Commerce in Shanghai in October 1899. Later his subordinates renamed it the Shanghai Branch Bureau of Commerce (Shanghai shangwu fenju) and moved the general bureau to Jiangning in December 1900. Although its titles and heads kept changing, the Shanghai bureau retained a stable group of elite merchant managers, such as Yan Xinhou, Shi Zejing, Xie Lunhui, and Chen Gan. These four elite merchants were also directors or managers of the Imperial Bank of China and would all become the leaders of the Shanghai CCA in 1902.[25]

In December 1899, the general bureau of commerce in Jiangning also restored its branch bureau in Zhenjiang after receiving a petition from more than ten merchant titleholders in that city. In northern Jiangsu Province, similar merchant titleholders in the prefectural city of Huai'an and a town on the Grand Canal, Qingjiangpu, founded general and branch bureaus of commerce, respectively, after 1900. The leading merchant director in the Zhenjiang bureau would become a major founder of an affiliated chamber of commerce there, and the two bureaus in Huai'an and Qingjiangpu directly turned themselves into affiliated chambers later on.[26] In Zhejiang Province, provincial officials founded a general bureau of commerce in Hangzhou in 1902, and so did the local gentry and elite merchants in Jiaxing Prefecture in the same year. The former would help found the first general chamber of commerce in the province, and the latter simply renamed itself a chamber of commerce later on.[27]

[Handwritten margin note: "bc → direct precludes to CCs"]

Thus, these bureaus of commerce developed as direct preludes to chambers of commerce. When the Jiangnan General Bureau of Commerce reopened in Shanghai in late 1899, its regulations already included a plan for an embryonic chamber of commerce. According to this set of regulations, this general bureau would establish a general association (zong gongsuo) composed of six merchant managers from the general bureau itself and representatives from various merchant associations.[28] Although the plan for this general association never came to fruition, it was actually an official blueprint for future chambers of commerce that would be formed and led by elite merchants.

When the Qing court appointed Li Hongzhang as imperial commissioner for commerce (shangwu dachen) in December 1899, the veteran reformer and initiator of semiofficial enterprises realized that the preexisting bureaus of commerce had received endorsement merely from the Qing court rather than from merchants. Thus, Li called for the establishment of chambers of commerce starting with the Shanghai silk and tea trades. Although he still

[Handwritten note bottom: "bCs endorsed by Qing, not merchants"]

Sheng → bcs failed to unite Qing + merchants
b/c they only employed officials as managers

planned to establish a bureau of commerce in this treaty port, his choice of
the bureau head was not an official but Pang Yuanji, a Zhejiang silk merchant and a general director of charities in Hangzhou.[29] Li's former assistant
in semiofficial enterprises, Sheng Xuanhuai, was the newly appointed associate imperial commissioner of commerce (*huiban shangwu dachen*), and he made
a similar criticism of bureaus of commerce. In his opinion, these bureaus failed
to unite the merchants with Qing officials because they employed only officials rather than gentry-merchant managers. Thus, their activities were contrary to the idea of chambers of commerce in the West.[30]

Another sponsor of semiofficial enterprises in late Qing China and the
official initiator of bureaus of commerce in the Lower Yangzi region, Governor-
General Zhang Zhidong, came to the same conclusion. He also recognized
the importance of using elite merchants for the organization of chambers of
commerce. His new attitude was clear in a letter to the Qing court: "[Gov-
ernment] can encourage merchants to organize chambers of commerce by
themselves. It should neither provide funds nor order merchants to pay for
chambers of commerce organized by officials. Merchants are most resentful
of such official behavior."[31] *CCs should be merchant-led : Zhang*

As official promoters of joint-stock companies or bureaus of commerce
in late Qing China, Li Hong Zhang, Sheng Xuanhuai, and Zhang Zhidong
eventually recognized the difficulty of extending bureaucratic control over
these new business institutions because of their decades of interactions with
elite merchants. Thus, they all embraced the idea of chambers of commerce
under elite merchant leadership. The new official attitudes toward chambers
of commerce caused important changes in the state's commercial policies.
Such policy reforms and the subsequent elite responses led directly to the
rise of the general chambers of commerce in Lower Yangzi cities.

Elite and Official Interactions and the Birth of General Chambers of Commerce

After the Boxer fiasco of 1900, the unprecedented national crisis compelled
the Qing court to launch the New Policy Reform in haste. Nevertheless, the
Qing court did not formulate its policy toward chambers of commerce until
the Lower Yangzi elite merchants had already initiated such organizations
together with reformist officials. Thereafter, provincial and local officials
implemented the new policy of the Qing court both as a part of their administrative duties and as a way to extend their power into the new business organizations. However, elite merchants did not simply follow the state policy

and collaborate with officials to organize their chambers of commerce. They also launched subtle or public challenges to bureaucratic intervention. Such elite and official interactions led to successful organization of six general chambers of commerce in the Lower Yangzi region, as is listed in Appendix 1.

The debut of the Shanghai CCA was an epoch-making event in the history of Chinese chambers of commerce and other nongovernmental organizations. On February 22, 1902, on the occasion of the Lantern Festival beginning the new lunar year, the popular *Shenbao* (Shanghai Daily) reported that Sheng Xuanhuai, the associate imperial commissioner of commerce, had approved the petition of Yan Xinhou, the leading Ningbo merchant in the treaty port, to form the Shanghai CCA for the purpose of uniting merchants and communicating with officials.[32] Another Shanghai newspaper edited by the veteran reformer Wang Kangnian published an editorial praising Sheng's action as a breakthrough in the traditional barrier between the Qing government and its subjects. It even regarded the Shanghai CCA as the embryo of a future Chinese parliament and encouraged its merchant participants to deliberate business issues seriously and set an example for popular participation in domestic reforms and foreign affairs.[33]

The two newspapers, however, failed to catch the inside story. In fact, Sheng had proposed the formation of this merchant organization after the model of Western chambers of commerce by himself, and he conveyed this idea to Yan through the Shanghai *daotai* on October 19, 1901. Sheng came to the idea during his negotiations with foreign governments over new trade treaties mandated by the Boxer Protocol of 1901. In the early stage of the negotiations, he had noticed the close collaboration between foreign diplomats and Western chambers of commerce and thus requested Shanghai guild leaders to organize a *zonghui* (general association) as his consultative body.[34]

In response to Sheng's call, Yan blamed the estrangement between Chinese officials and merchants as the main reason for the foreign domination of business in Shanghai. His suggestion to Sheng was to form the new organization not only as the latter's advisory body for treaty negotiations but also as a key link between the government and merchant community. Yan further indicated that the organizational title suggested by Sheng, *zonghui*, had been indiscriminately used by merchant guilds for their recreational places. Thus, he proposed to adopt the term *huiyi gongsuo*, or consultative association, from the Japanese title for chambers of commerce, in naming the new organization. Yan also nominated one of his Ningbo fellows and a merchant holder of the expectant magistrate title, Zhou Jinbiao, as the general manager (*tidiao*) of this association.[35]

Sheng's reply to Yan's petition blamed both the government-business estrangement and the disunity of merchants themselves for the failure of Chinese business. He approved the formation of the Shanghai CCA and specifically ordered Yan to incorporate leaders of major Shanghai guilds into the new organization. With such official sponsorship, Yan raised funds, rented an office, and drafted a set of regulations for the Shanghai CCA by consulting the rules of the Western general chamber of commerce in the city and those of bureaus of commerce of the Qing government. On March 30, 1902, he gathered guild leaders and other elite merchants in Shanghai for a discussion about the regulations, and they formally inaugurated the Shanghai CCA.[36]

Sheng further instructed all guilds in the Shanghai county city and foreign concessions to select two directors each for the Shanghai CCA and let them elect one president (*zongli*) and two vice presidents (*fuzongli*). According to a Japanese source, a total of seventy-five elite merchants from regional and occupational guilds as well as semiofficial enterprises, merchant-owned business establishments, and the like joined this organization. They included the president and two vice presidents as well as thirteen deliberative members (*yiyuan*).[37] Many of them were Yan's associates in various guilds, charitable halls, the Imperial Bank of China, and the Shanghai Bureau of Commerce, as mentioned before, but the Shanghai CCA bound them with new institutional ties.

Yan and other elite merchants established the major leadership of the Shanghai CCA through both electoral formality and governmental approval. He originally selected only five leading figures from Ningbo, Guangdong, and Jiangxi merchant groups, including himself, as the general directors (*zongdong*) of the Shanghai CCA. On Sheng's instruction, the Shanghai CCA then held its election, with Yan and Zhou becoming its president and vice president, respectively. The nominee for second vice president, Mao Zumo, was a provincial graduate but not necessarily an official, as a previous study has assumed. In any case, his name was not submitted for official approval later on.[38] Thus, the Shanghai CCA was totally under elite merchant leadership.

These elite merchants voiced their political ambitions through the Shanghai CCA's regulations drafted by Yan Xinhou. He inserted into the regulations ambitious plans to promote joint-stock companies, to formulate business laws, and especially to unite merchants and strengthen their relations with the governments through the Shanghai CCA. These regulations demanded not only the advisory role stipulated by Sheng Xuanhuai for his treaty negotiations but also the right to communicate with the government on all commercial affairs, to regulate business practices in markets, and to mediate disputes among Chinese merchants.[39]

By October 22, 1902, the Shanghai CCA had successively received endorsement from the acting Liangjiang governor-general, Zhang Zhidong, and formal recognition by the Qing throne.[40] Thus, it became the first state-legitimatized association in Chinese history. Under its influence, commercial consultative associations also appeared in other Chinese cities in 1902 and 1903.[41] When the Ministry of Commerce (Shangbu) appeared in late 1903 and then drafted its policy on chambers of commerce,[42] it undoubtedly took into account these extant organizations. *SH CCA officially recognized in 1902*

Indeed, on January 11, 1904, the ministry submitted to the throne a proposal advocating chambers of commerce in the whole country, but that proposal directly echoed the Shanghai CCA's regulations. It envisioned chambers of commerce not only as a leading force in a commercial war with foreign powers but also as a useful antidote to the disunity among merchants and to their estrangement from the government. With the approval of the throne, the ministry issued its first set of rules for chambers of commerce and simply ordered the preexisting commercial consultative associations to rename themselves according to its new rules. It planned both general and affiliated chambers of commerce and granted them extensive rights to contact the government on behalf of merchants, to make decisions on local business through various meetings and discussions, and to handle merchant disputes before and even after official verdicts.[43] *expansion of C.Cs*

Ironically, such a policy reflected not only the court's responses to elite merchant demands but also the ministry's attempt to circumvent provincial and local officials in favor of central control over the new chambers and the merchant community. Under the ministry's rules, elite merchants received the right to form chambers of commerce and elect their leaders, but their regulations and leaderships had to obtain the ministry's direct approval. These chambers were also required to submit reports about local business to the ministry, help it register business establishments, and even enforce the use of standard accounting books issued by the ministry.[44]

In order to control these chambers, the ministry first targeted the Shanghai CCA. In February 1904, the Ministry of Commerce accepted Zhili Governor-General Yuan Shikai's proposal to assign its junior councilor (*youcanyi*), Yang Shiqi, the task of promoting chambers of commerce in Shanghai. Actually, as a cunning upstart in the late Qing military and politics, Yuan had already used Yang as a trusted aide to take control of the semiofficial enterprises in Shanghai from Sheng Xuanhuai. It was evident that both the ministry and the governor-general used Yang again to rid Sheng's influence and his elite merchant associates from the Shanghai GCC.[45]

Yang did make the Shanghai CCA change its title to the Shanghai GCC, as the ministry had required. He also ensured that Xu Run, Sheng's former rival in semiofficial enterprises and Yuan's merchant associate, replaced Zhou Jinbiao as the vice president of the Shanghai GCC. However, Yan Xinhou and most previous leaders retained their positions after the reorganization. They further institutionalized their dominant power by elaborating the aforementioned regulations of the Shanghai CCA into a new set of seventy-three articles for the Shanghai GCC.[46] The successively formed general chambers in the Lower Yangzi region basically adopted similar regulations and organizational structures. However, they grew out of different forms of elite and official interaction. CCA transition to GCC

Provincial officials in Jiangning, the seat of the Liangjiang governor-general, made the most aggressive attempt to organize local merchants into a general chamber of commerce, but they later had to give up such high-handed policy because of a cold response from merchants. In early 1904, the official director of the Jiangnan General Bureau of Commerce, Liu Shihang, personally founded the Jiangnan General Association for Commercial Affairs (Jiangnan shangwu gonghui) and simply turned all local guilds into its branches. Liu advanced funds, drafted regulations, and situated this new organization in the pawnshops' guildhall. He assumed the position of president himself and enlisted guild leaders in the city as members and deliberative members of this association. In late 1904, Liu changed the title of this organization into the Jiangning GCC as the Ministry of Commerce had required, and he further incorporated elite merchants from the new business establishments in foreign trades, insurance, and so on.[47]

In spite of such official effort, the Jiangning GCC enlisted elite merchants who rarely met its requirements for full membership and did not enjoy a high reputation among local merchants. By March 1905, this general chamber was able to pass and implement a single resolution to post daily lists of quotations for the money market, and such quotations were followed only by large money shops and not by the smaller ones. The chamber's members were so notorious that even President Liu launched a secret investigation of their behaviors and threatened to expel them from GCC membership. After a newspaper reported that one of the chamber members had committed suicide over embezzling, gambling, and whoring scandals, Liu left his official position and returned to his home province of Anhui as a gentryman.

not all GCCs influential/successful
↳ in this case b/c not led by
elite merchants

Thereafter, the general chamber gradually came under elite merchant leadership and established its reputation among merchants.[48]

Suzhou was another political center of Jiangsu province, and it was also a major manufacturing and marketing center of silk fabric and other commodities. However, a general chamber of commerce came to this city later than in Shanghai and Jiangning because local elite merchants could not see eye to eye with officials. From 1904 to early 1905, the Ministry of Commerce, the Liangjiang governor-general, and the Jiangsu governor successively urged the formation of a chamber of commerce in Suzhou. But these official appeals did not receive an active response from local elite merchants because the central and provincial governments were still reluctant to grant Suzhou a general chamber similar to the one in Shanghai.[49]

For their part, Suzhou elites expressed their aspiration for a general chamber of commerce through two successive petitions to the Ministry of Commerce on June 20 and 30, 1905, only ten days apart. The petitioners included leading gentry and elite merchants in local businesses and public activities, such as the aforementioned You Xianjia, Zhang Lüqian, Pan Zuqian, and Peng Fusun. A metropolitan graduate and former provincial official, Wang Tongyu, led the second petition. As they argued in the two petitions, Suzhou was a center of silk fabric production, the cocoon, silk, and cotton cloth trades, as well as the native banking business. The city had also become a treaty port like Shanghai, and the local market had suffered from a similar invasion of foreign goods. Moreover, Suzhou deserved a general chamber because it was also the political center of southern Jiangsu, and such an organization in this city could unite merchants and officials through its collaboration with the Shanghai GCC. In the second petition, the petitioners informed the Ministry of Commerce that they had prepared to build an office for the general chamber and would soon submit its regulations, register of members, and list of elected leaders.[50]

At a public meeting on July 1, 1905, Suzhou elite merchants, including many leaders of regional and occupational guilds, also called for the organization of a chamber of commerce in the city, and Wang again promised to support their plan through his official connections. As a result, the Ministry of Commerce approved the formation of a general chamber of commerce in Suzhou on July 17 and instructed it to maintain liaison with the Shanghai GCC. Thereafter, Wang and other initiators of the Suzhou GCC drafted its regulations by consulting those of the Shanghai GCC. On October 6, 1905, they gathered sixty-four guild leaders to hold an inaugural meeting and elected You Xianjia as the first president.[51]

Like the Suzhou GCC, another general chamber of commerce appeared in Jiangsu Province because of pressure from elite merchants rather than because of governmental planning. According to the ministry's rules of 1904, the capital of Tongzhou independent department was not qualified to have a general chamber of commerce because it was neither a provincial capital nor a prosperous metropolis. However, Zhang Jian, the prominent elite reformer of Tongzhou origin, had been a successful founder of the local textile industry and an advocate of chambers of commerce from the mid-1890s. Therefore, in 1904, the Ministry of Commerce specially entrusted him with the task of promoting chambers of commerce in the Lower Yangzi region. In response, Zhang warned the ministry against the hasty organization of citywide chambers of commerce and instead called for the establishment of such organizations for specific trades.[52] ☆ idea of C.C. for specific traders in smaller cities

In line with Zhang's idea, his elite merchant associates in late 1904 petitioned the Ministry of Commerce to form a general chamber of commerce for the local cotton trade, although they actually planned to include all trades in this new organization. Their ingenious ploy avoided the difficulty of obtaining official approval for a general chamber for all trades, such as their peers in Suzhou were facing at the same time. After their petition received approval from the Ministry of Commerce, Zhang Cha, Zhang Jian's older brother, business partner, and a former magistrate, became the president of the newly formed Tong-Chong-Hai General Chamber of Cotton Commerce (GCCC) (Tong-Chong-Hai huaye zonghui).[53] This general chamber seemed to limit its influence to the cotton market in Tongzhou independent department, Haimen subprefecture and Chongming County. In reality, it adopted regulations similar to those of the Shanghai GCC, and its membership was open to guild leaders and elite merchants in other trades.[54]

Because Jiangsu included Shanghai in the late Qing period, its elite merchants actually established four general chambers of commerce in a single province. They successfully organized the four general chambers beyond governmental limitation by using different forms of interactions with officials, including their subtle challenge and passive resistance to the Ministry of Commerce's rules. In contrast, elite merchants in Zhejiang Province established two general chambers through stronger confrontation or closer collaboration with officials, but their effort to organize a third general chamber failed to obtain governmental approval.

As the provincial capital of Zhejiang, Hangzhou was very similar to Suzhou in terms of its political importance and central position in regional commerce and industry, especially in silk fabric production and trade. But

(margin note: Tongzhou GCC - for cotton on paper but operated under same practice as SH GCC)

the formation of a general chamber of commerce in Hangzhou involved a more dramatic contest of Zhejiang gentry and elite merchants with provincial officials and their elite associates. In early 1904, the provincial bureau of commerce in Hangzhou founded a commercial consultative association after the model of the Shanghai CCA, locating it in the guildhall of the Jiangning merchant group in the city. This association quickly renamed itself the Zhejiang GCC, but it did not formulate any regulations until August 1905. Because very few merchant guilds joined this general chamber, it relied more on officials for financial support and even moved its office into the building of the provincial bureau of commerce later on.[55] *1905- Zhejiang GCC (Hangchau)*

Moreover, the two earliest presidents of the Zhejiang GCC were a gentryman and a former prefect, respectively. The second president, Shen Shoulian, assumed the position in July 1905 but immediately faced newspaper criticism for his attempt to build a railroad around Hangzhou together with a German company in the previous year. In August 1905, both Shen and the managing director (*zuoban*) of the Zhejiang GCC, Gao Ziheng, came under attack from provincial gentry for their sale of mining resources in Zhejiang to British and Italian companies. Meanwhile, Gao and Shen were under pressure from the provincial government to endorse its plan to grant an American company permission to build a railroad in the province, but their collaboration with officials in this matter also met strong protest from Zhejiang gentry and elite merchants.[56] *Zhejiang GCC pres. and directs forced out after railway protest*

Seven general directors of charitable halls in Hangzhou led the protest against this railroad project. Their major leader was Fan Gongxu, a metropolitan graduate, former provincial director of schools (*xuezheng*) in Shaanxi, and an advocate of new schools in Hangzhou.[57] The protest received support from the Ningbo merchant leaders of the Shanghai GCC, especially its president, Yan Xinhou. Although the Zhejiang GCC later rejected the American proposal for the railroad, President Shen and Managing Director Gao had become notorious. The provincial governor nevertheless still tried to save their faces by arranging for their resignations. Because neither Shen nor Gao would give up their positions voluntarily, the governor had to dismiss Gao in September 1905 and forced Shen to resign thereafter.[58]

Meanwhile, leaders of guilds in the silk fabric, native banking, and other trades selected Fan Gongxu as the new president of the general chamber and requested the provincial governor's approval. However, Fan refused to accept an official notice of approval until a new provincial governor replaced his unpopular predecessor in March 1906. Under Fan's leadership, the Zhejiang GCC changed its title to the Hangzhou GCC, adopted a new set of

1906- ZJ GCC - official approval
moved to charitable hall → less govt interference
64   ELITE AND OFFICIAL INTERACTIVE MOVEMENTS

regulations similar to those of the Shanghai and Suzhou GCCs, and eventually received approval from the Ministry of Commerce in October 1906. This general chamber then moved out of the building of the provincial bureau of commerce and later settled in a charitable hall because Fan considered it "an inconvenience" for merchants to stay together with officials.[59] Thus, it became less subject to governmental interferences, although President Fan was closer to the Qing government than his two predecessors.

In contrast with the Hangzhou GCC, a general chamber appeared uneventfully in the treaty port and prefectural capital of Ningbo because of close collaboration among local elite merchants, gentry, and officials. In September 1905, two wealthy merchants in the city initiated the formation of the Ningbo GCC, and the local prefect personally drafted its regulations in accordance with the rules of the Ministry of Commerce. Leaders of many guilds in the city joined this general chamber and selected a former prefect of Ningbo origin, Wu Chuanji, as its first president.[60] Ningbo G CC

In another prefectural city of Zhejiang Province, Jiaxing, local elite merchants also organized a general chamber of commerce, but their effort eventually failed due to both official disapproval and their internal dissension. As mentioned before, elite merchants in Jiaxing had already founded a general bureau of commerce by themselves in 1902, and they had selected a local gentryman, Sheng Pingzhi, as its general director (zongban). In January 1905, the general bureau received permission from the provincial government to turn itself into a general chamber. However, it was not until January 1906 that the Jiaxing GCC formally elected Sheng and Zhang Guang'en (Youqi), a young elite merchant, as its president and vice president, respectively.[61]

At the time, the Qing government had already required all general chambers of commerce to get approval from the Ministry of Commerce, but the Jiaxing GCC still petitioned the Zhejiang provincial government for recognition of its recent election. Unfortunately, the general chamber did not obtain governmental recognition of its new leadership but instead received an official order to turn itself into an affiliated chamber of commerce. President Sheng submitted another petition to the Zhejiang governor, arguing that Jiaxing was a city with prosperous trade and deserved a general chamber. After his request met with rejection from the governor, Sheng resigned from his position, and the young and energetic Zhang Guang'en became the new president through another election. However, Zhang was unable to continue the fight for the status of this general chamber because his qualification for the leadership soon came under attack from some founding members, and his position was then taken over by a senor elite merchant in December

1906. Due to the internal struggle, these local elites had to accept an affiliated chamber in Jiaxing Prefecture instead.[62] *accept affiliate c.c*

Therefore, the development of the general chambers of commerce in the Lower Yangzi cities was influenced by both interactions between elites and officials and the interrelations among the elite merchants themselves. These elite merchants established six general chambers of commerce in Jiangsu and Zhejiang provinces through different forms of interaction with officials, but their success always depended on their own solidarity. On the contrary, the internal strife of local elite merchants in Jiaxing prefecture impeded their effort to fight with officials for a general chamber. This pattern of elite and official interactions also characterized the formative process of affiliated and branch chambers in the region. However, the expansion of associational networks ranging from general to affiliated and branch chambers would bring greater unity to elite merchants, reduce their internal dissension, and change their relations with the Qing government.

Three-Tier Chamber Networks and New Government-Business Relations

After the Ministry of Commerce called for the formation of both general and affiliated chambers of commerce in 1904, it initially relied mainly on provincial and local officials to promote such merchant organizations, and these officials merely patronized a limited number of affiliated chambers in their administrative centers. This governmental approach did not change until the general chambers in Shanghai and other cities took the initiative to help organize their affiliated chambers beyond the official limitation. Moreover, Lower Yangzi elite merchants also created branch chambers of commerce beyond the original plan of the Qing government and thus formed three levels of chamber networks in this region, especially in the core area of the Yangzi Delta. Such chamber networks linked diverse elite merchants from large cities to market towns and effectively raised their status and influence in their interactions with officials.

The birth of the Tong-Chong-Hai GCCC in late 1904 immediately spurred the formation of the three earliest affiliated chambers in the Lower Yangzi region, and indeed the whole country. However, among the first group of affiliated chambers in the region, the majority had to get approval from the Ministry of Commerce through provincial officials, and their development was largely limited to prefectural capitals and county seats. Thus, by April 1906, more than two years after the ministry issued its rules for

GCC's organized affiliated chambers led to 3 levels of chamber networks

chambers of commerce, affiliated chambers numbered only thirteen in Ji-angsu and five in Zhejiang. Among the eighteen affiliated chambers, six were in provincial and prefectural capitals, nine in county seats, and only three in market towns.[63] *Slow development of accs, lack of merchant support*

At this stage, affiliated chambers of commerce experienced slow development mainly because their official promoters implemented the policy of the Ministry of Commerce without merchant support. In the prefectural capital and treaty port of Zhenjiang, Jiangsu Province, the prefect repeatedly received from the Ministry of Commerce instructions to organize a chamber of commerce in early 1904. Thus, he gathered local merchants in five major trades to discuss the issue in April of that year and chose a close friend, the local branch manager of the Imperial Bank of China, as chamber president. But the latter soon died, leaving a huge debt to the prefectural treasury. Under double pressure to make up the enormous deficit and to meet urgent demands from the ministry, the desperate prefect selected the manager of a native bank as new chamber president. Nevertheless, this local official was unable to establish the affiliated chamber before his dismissal in early 1906. It was not until May 1906 that Wu Zhaoen (Zemin), a gentry titleholder in local business and the major director of the local bureau of commerce, eventually founded the Zhenjiang ACC with support from local guilds, the new prefect, and the Jiangning GCC.[64]

In another prefecture of Jiangsu Province, Changzhou, the official promoters of an affiliated chamber met similar difficulty. The local prefect and other officials indeed pushed guild leaders to form an affiliated chamber of commerce as early as June 1905, but it still lacked genuine support from merchants. Because the official effort received help mainly from five influential gentrymen, including former officials of local origin, the Changzhou ACC did not select a president but instead accepted the five gentrymen as its directors. Although this affiliated chamber incorporated local guild leaders, it was mainly under gentry domination and relied heavily on official support because all of its funds came from these gentrymen and officials.[65]

Meanwhile, elite merchant initiators of affiliated chambers also faced difficulty in getting governmental approval through bureaucratic formalities. In Songjiang, the prefectural city near Shanghai, a merchant titleholder mobilized merchants in the pawnshop, clothing, native banking, and other trades to form an affiliated chamber by themselves in late 1905. Then they directly petitioned the Ministry of Commerce for recognition, but the ministry was suspicious of the petition without local official endorsement. It first consulted metropolitan officials from Songjiang for information about this merchant

accs led by officials struggled to get merchant support

accs run by merchants struggled to get govt approval

titleholder and then ordered an investigation of him by the prefect, magistrate, and local gentry in Songjiang. After these officials submitted a positive report to Beijing, the Songjiang ACC still had to submit a new petition to the ministry through the Jiangsu governor. It finally received governmental recognition in late 1906, nearly a year after its appearance.[66]

In Zhejiang Province, the Gongchenqiao ACC also met difficulty in getting official approval. Because it was initiated by elite merchants in the northern suburb of Hangzhou in mid-1905, its petition to the Ministry of Commerce for approval caused the ministry to order a similar investigation by the Zhejiang governor. During the investigation, the governor revoked the official stamp that the affiliated chamber had previously received from the provincial government, and he also forced it to revise its regulations. Eventually, it was through the sponsorship of this provincial governor that the Gongchenqiao ACC received the ministry's approval in April 1906.[67]

Because official endorsement was so crucial for these early affiliated chambers in getting governmental approval, they had to recruit prestigious gentry, especially former officials, into their leadership. In the prefectural capital and treaty port of Wenzhou, merchant leaders of six large occupational guilds planned an affiliated chamber and soon brought in other merchant groups. Although these leaders were gentry titleholders hired by guilds or wealthy merchants with purchased titles, they still selected a metropolitan graduate and former magistrate as their president. They also treated the latter as an official instead of a chamber president, rising to welcome him to each of their meetings. Under the leadership of this former official, the Wenzhou GCC quickly received approval from the Ministry of Commerce through the Zhejiang governor in April 1906.[68]

The ministry's policy of using officials to promote affiliated chambers failed to win over merchant support and also obstructed the organizational efforts of elite merchants, especially those in market towns. In Huzhou Prefecture, the prefect in early 1905 had already received the Zhejiang provincial government's order to establish an affiliated chamber of commerce, but merchants within the prefectural capital did not make any positive response until late 1906. On the contrary, in early 1906 silk merchants in the nearby town of Linghu founded an affiliated chamber by themselves. However, as late as November 1906, they had not received any endorsement from the Huzhou prefect and the Zhejiang bureau of commerce because the prefect was still trying to establish an affiliated chamber in the prefectural capital first. Meanwhile, the provincial bureau would allow the formation of only a single affiliated chamber in this city or a nearby county seat, rather than a market town.[69]

The Shanghai GCC first challenged this governmental policy toward affiliated chambers of commerce, especially those at the township level. In its petition to the Ministry of Commerce in early 1906, this general chamber reported that merchants in many prosperous towns and even rural market-places had expressed their enthusiasm for affiliated chambers. Because the ministry had not yet paid much attention to these township chambers, the Shanghai GCC requested that it issue a new set of rules for their development. In response, the ministry in April 1906 instructed all general chambers to take over the responsibility of promoting affiliated chambers in each province, and it kept provincial and local officials in charge of such organizational development only in places where general chambers had not appeared. In general, the ministry allowed each county or department to form only a single affiliated chamber in the most prosperous commercial center, not necessarily in the administrative center. It also permitted the formation of two affiliated chambers in a county that had more commercial centers.[70]

 Under the new set of rules, general chambers in the Lower Yangzi region largely replaced provincial and local governments in the promotion of affiliated chambers and facilitated their communications with the Ministry of Commerce and the succeeding Ministry of Agriculture, Industry, and Commerce (Nonggongshang bu).[71] As a result, affiliated chambers of commerce spread to most prefectural cities in the Lower Yangzi region and especially mushroomed in county cities and market towns. As Appendix 2 shows, at least 145 affiliated chambers had come into being in the Lower Yangzi region by 1911. gccs promoted accs - finally developed quickly

The general chambers of commerce in the Lower Yangzi region offered especially crucial help for the development of affiliated chambers in market towns. After the Suzhou GCC appeared in late 1905, the news quickly inspired elite merchants in Meili town of the adjacent Changshu County to form an affiliated chamber in early 1906. These merchants first contacted the general chamber in Suzhou for a copy of its regulations and for its help in getting governmental approval. Then, the Meili ACC used the Suzhou GCC as a model to develop its own regulations, which included a pledge to maintain close contacts with the general chamber and to unite merchants in the surrounding eighteen towns for the vitalization of local business. In May 1906, this affiliated chamber made an unsuccessful attempt to get approval from the Ministry of Commerce because its regulations encountered official criticism. After minor revision of the regulations, the Meili ACC finally received the ministry's recognition through the help of the Suzhou GCC.

gcc support dev of accs in market
towns g. Meili ACC

Later on, its regulations were basically adopted by the affiliated chambers in Shengze and other market towns as well as in county cities around Suzhou.[72]

Similarly, the Hangzhou GCC also provided help for the formation of an affiliated chamber in the Shangbai town of Wukang, a mountainous county of Western Zhejiang. In late 1908, an affiliated chamber was to appear in the county seat of Wukang, but elite merchants in Shangbai argued that their town was a more prosperous marketplace than the administrative center and a better location for the only affiliated chamber that the Ministry of Commerce's 1906 rules would allow to appear in such an underdeveloped county. Through the Hangzhou GCC, they appealed their case directly to the Ministry of Commerce and finally compelled it to agree on the formation of two affiliated chambers, one in Shangbai town and the other in the county city of Wukang.[73]

Because the Ministry of Commerce still limited the number of affiliated chambers to one or two in each county unit from 1906, elite merchants in the Lower Yangzi region further initiated branch chambers of commerce as a way to break through the numerical limitation. Such elite merchant initiative caused another significant change in government policies toward chambers of commerce. The policy reform would allow elite merchants to organize branch chambers of commerce without any limitation in number. As a result of such elite and official interaction, three levels of chamber networks expanded from large cities to market towns in the Lower Yangzi region, especially in the Yangzi Delta.

Elite merchants in the Shanghai county seat, the southern part of the urban complex, first petitioned for the formation of a branch of the Shanghai GCC in September 1906. In response, the Ministry of Commerce approved the establishment of the South Shanghai BCC (Hunan shangwu fensuo). Thereafter, elite merchants in both the town of Fenglichang in Rugao County and the town of Dongtangshi in Changshu County failed to obtain the Ministry of Commerce's permission to establish affiliated chambers of commerce because there had already been one or two such organizations in each county. Nevertheless, these township elite merchants still received the ministry's approval to form branches of the affiliated chambers in their counties.[74]

In November 1906, Zhou Tingbi, a director of the Shanghai GCC and the president of the Wuxi-Jinkui ACC, capitalized on these precedents and requested that the ministry promote branch chambers of commerce throughout the entire country. Zhou argued that chambers of commerce could achieve their primary goal of uniting all merchants only when they could solidify the business community in each town and then expand such merchant unity from the township level to the county level and upward. Hence he suggested that branch chambers of commerce be formed throughout market towns below the affiliated chambers of commerce in the county seats. In his opinion, branch chambers could be attached to an affiliated chamber as fingers and arms to a human body and provide both links for merchants and local information for the government. The Ministry of Commerce quickly adopted Zhou's proposal and called for the organization of branch chambers of commerce after the model of general and affiliated chambers of commerce.[75]

Therefore, the Qing government successively formulated and reformed its policies toward general, affiliated, and branch chambers of commerce through its constant interactions with the Lower Yangzi elite merchants. However, the development of the three-tier networks in the Lower Yangzi region not only reflected but also reinforced such elite and official interplay. In particular, the new associational networks brought the elite merchants at the township level into close contact with their counterparts in large cities and enabled them to engage in direct interactions with higher levels of government. As a result, these township elites increased their influence in struggles with officials for the development of more numerous chambers with heightened status.

In one of the aforementioned cases, Dongtangshi, in Changshu County, received governmental permission to found only a branch chamber of commerce in 1906 because the twin counties of Changshu and Zhaowen had already formed one affiliated chamber in their joint county seat and another one in the town of Meili on their shared border by November 1906. Nevertheless, the branch chamber in Dongtangshi continued its struggle to raise its status, and its effort received help from the affiliated chamber in Meili town. The Meili ACC claimed that its own location was inside Zhaowen rather than Changshu County, in which Dongtangshi still deserved to have an affiliated chamber. This forced argument received support from the Suzhou GCC, and it finally compelled the Ministry of Agriculture, Industry, and Commerce to grant an affiliated chamber to Dongtangshi.[76] With help from the Shanghai GCC, the South Shanghai BCC in 1909 also obtained the ministry's permission to turn itself into an affiliated chamber, and so did the branch chamber in the capital of Taicang independent department.[77]

Elite merchants in Taizhou, a county in the northern part of the Yangzi Delta, made the most adroit use of their relations with three different general chambers in their efforts to establish three affiliated chambers there. These local elites first formed an affiliated chamber in the county seat in

1906 and then a second one in the town of Haian in 1907. The two affiliated
chambers obtained governmental approval through the Jiangning and Shanghai GCCs, respectively. Thereafter, a rich merchant in another town of the
same county, Jiangyan, repeatedly petitioned the Ministry of Agriculture,
Industry, and Commerce for the formation of an affiliated chamber but received official sanction only for a branch chamber in the town. In 1908, this
branch chamber obtained the support of the Tong-Chong-Hai GCCC for a
new petition to the ministry and finally received the latter's permission to
raise itself to the status of an affiliated chamber. Thus, Taizhou became the
first county that had three affiliated chambers in the Lower Yangzi region
and the entire country.[78]

Even in Yancheng, the relatively underdeveloped county of northern
Jiangsu, chamber networks helped elite merchants in the small town of
Nanyang'an to found a branch chamber that had previously failed to get official approval. After an affiliated chamber had already appeared in a larger
town of the county, Shanggang, two merchant titleholders of Nanyang'an in
1910 led a petition to the Jiangnan General Bureau of Commerce in Jiangning for a branch chamber. But they met with a flat rejection from the provincial bureau because their petition did not include any detailed regulations and their chamber leaders were not chosen through merchant election.
The Nanyang'an elite merchants then contacted the affiliated chamber in
Shanggang for help, and the latter dispatched two directors to investigate
whether the official accusation was true. In fact, the two chamber directors
from Shanggang also helped draft a new set of regulations for the Nanyang'an
branch chamber and presided over its inaugural meeting and leadership election. Thereafter, the affiliated chamber in Shanggang submitted a petition
to the provincial bureau of commerce on behalf of the branch chamber in
Nanyang'an and helped it win official approval at last.[79]

While elite merchants usually used the new chamber networks to
strengthen their interconnections and compel officials to accede to their demands, their internal competition and local power struggles could also turn
their organizations into victims of official interference. In Yiwu, a peripheral county of southern Zhejiang, an affiliated chamber had already appeared
in the county seat in early 1909, but elite merchants in the town of Fotang
refused to subject themselves to its leadership. Instead, they petitioned provincial officials for another chamber with the same status on the ground that
their town was the center of local trade. Although this petition received governmental approval, the new chamber leaders in Fotang engaged in further

power struggles with other township elites, and thus their inaugural ceremony in March 1910 was stormed by the mob instigated by the latter.
Thereafter, the Fotang ACC continued to compete with the affiliated chamber in the county seat for control over merchants in nearby towns, but this
led to an official order that it rename itself a branch chamber.[80]

The Fotang ACC, like the aforementioned Jiaxing GCC, suffered a reduction in its status mainly because of internal strife among local elites, but
such cases were rare in the formative process of Lower Yangzi chambers of
commerce. Generally speaking, the development of the chamber networks,
including branch chambers at the township level, strengthened their interrelations and intensified their multiform interactions with officials, including their collaboration with the latter. In the town of Shuanlin in western
Zhejiang, Cai Song, a provincial graduate and an incumbent official, took
temporary leave from his office in 1907 and used the opportunity to plan a
branch chamber in his hometown. Cai gathered guild leaders in the rice,
silk, silk fabric, pawnshop, and other trades to hold five successive meetings
in a guildhall, and they elected leaders for the branch chamber. Cai received
the most votes but declined the chamber leadership because he was still an
official. Thus, the leader of the rice guild became the chief director of this
branch chamber, while Cai helped it gain governmental approval and find
office space in a local temple.[81]

The inaugural ceremonies of the branch chambers in Lower Yangzi towns
also provided opportunities for township elite merchants to engage in personal
contact with their urban counterparts and county officials. When the branch
chamber in the town of Sunduan in eastern Zhejiang held its inaugural meeting on May 30, 1909, it assembled more than fifty merchant members together
with students from two local schools, and its distinguished guests included
the magistrate of Kuaiji County and the president of the affiliated chamber
from the county seat. All those in attendance first sang the branch chamber
song, and students then played martial music. After the fanfare, the magistrate, the president of the affiliated chamber, and the chief director of the
branch chamber gave speeches in succession. Similar rituals were repeated
on a larger scale at the inaugural meetings of the branch chamber in Chonggu
town in 1909 and of that in Fengjing town in 1910, both towns adjacent to
Shanghai.[82] They all involved direct contacts between local elite merchants
and officials.

It was mainly through such elite and official interactions that the Lower
Yangzi region produced approximately 210 chambers of commerce by 1911,
including 6 general chambers, 145 affiliated chambers, and 59 branch cham-

bers, as shown in Table 3. The branch chambers numbered fewer than the affiliated chambers because they often appeared only in places where elite merchants could not establish more affiliated chambers than officials allowed. According to more detailed information on the 210 chambers presented in Appendixes 1–3, only 6 (3%) of them appeared in provincial capitals and major treaty ports, and 20 (9.5%) in prefectural capitals, but 80 (38%) of them were located in county cities, and 104 (49.5%) in market towns. The location of 87.5% of the chambers of commerce at the county and township levels demonstrated both the width and depth of their network development.

To be sure, the chamber networks experienced uneven development in the core and peripheral areas of the Lower Yangzi region. According to the data in Appendix 1, all six of the general chambers of commerce in the Lower Yangzi region were located in the Yangzi Delta and its southern coastal flank. As for the affiliated chambers listed in Appendix 2, their average number was nearly two for every county unit within Songjiang Prefecture around Shanghai, but it was as low as one for every two county units in Chuzhou, Taizhou, and Yanzhou, the three peripheral prefectures in southern Zhejiang Province. Because the Qing government usually allowed only one or two affiliated chambers to appear in each county unit, their average numbers within these administrative units still did not show significant difference between the core and peripheral areas.

By contrast, the branch chambers listed in Appendix 3 were developed by elite merchants beyond the state-imposed numerical limitation, and most of them appeared in the Yangzi Delta and its coastal flanks. Located in the center of the Yangzi Delta, the twin counties of Wujiang and Zhenze had fourteen branch chambers by 1908. By 1911 Shanghai County and the nearby

TABLE 3

The formation of chambers of commerce in the Lower Yangzi region, 1904–1911

Chamber	Year								Unknown	Total
	1904	1905	1906	1907	1908	1909	1910	1911		
GCC	3	1	2							6
ACC	3	7	32	32	30	27	8	6		145
BCC			3	9	20	12	12	1	2	59
Total	6	8	37	41	50	39	20	7	2	210

Sources: Data from Appendixes 1–3.

Note: This table does not include the early chambers of commerce that appeared in 1902–1903 and used the name of commercial consultative association or other titles. They usually renamed themselves as general chambers of commerce from 1904.

Fengxian County had three and four branch chambers, respectively.[83] Ji-angdu and Gaoyou counties in the northern delta as well as Fenghua County in coastal Zhejiang also had three to four branch chambers each.[84] Actually, an analysis of Appendix 3 shows that most of the fifty-nine branch chambers of commerce appeared in the core area. Only the Fotang, Haimen, and Nanyang'an BCCs were located in Chuzhou, Taizhou, and Huai'an, the three peripheral prefectures of the Lower Yangzi region.

ch.
thesis

Thus, the general, affiliated, and branch chambers of commerce mainly formed their three-tier hierarchy in the core area of the Lower Yangzi region, but their networks also expanded into the regional peripheries through the development of many affiliated chambers there. Because the chamber net-works linked up elite merchants from metropolises to small cities and market towns, they not only increased the elites' influence on official policies dur-ing the formative process of chambers of commerce but also transformed the government-business relations thereafter. Ironically, such relational changes resulted partly from competition among central, provincial, and local gov-ernments for the control of chambers of commerce.

leaders of gcc, on par w/ lower officials below govrank

In 1904, the Ministry of Commerce had already specified chambers of commerce as the major channel for communications between officials and merchants. In 1908, the Ministry of Agriculture, Industry, and Commerce issued a new ordinance to regulate communications of the chambers of com-merce with provincial and local governments. According to this ordinance, leaders of general chambers could send documents to provincial officials below the rank of governor in the form of "communication" (*yi*), implying their equal relationship with these officials. Only in their correspondences with governors and governors-general were the documents required to be in the form of "petition" (*cheng*), indicating their inferior position to these ranking officials. Although the ministry stipulated that affiliated chamber leaders should use "reports" (*diecheng*) in their correspondence with prefectural and county officials, it indicated that they were not subordinate to the latter.[85] This set of rules reflected the ministry's attempt to turn the new chamber networks into its own power base beyond the interference of provincial and local officials, but it actually raised the positions of the chamber leaders in their communications with provincial and local governments.

Evidently, the formation of the general, affiliated, and branch chambers as well as their hierarchical networks in the Lower Yangzi region brought their elite merchant participants into more intensive and institutionalized interactions with each other and with local, provincial, and central govern-ments. In their interactions with officials, the newly formed chambers of commerce quickly increased their influence because their associational networks enabled the diverse elite merchants in different cities and towns to draw help and strength from one another. In this sense, the development of the three-tier chamber networks caused revolutionary change not only in social relations within the merchant community but also in its political relations with the Qing government.

Because most chambers of commerce in the Lower Yangzi region, especially those in small cities and market towns, appeared after 1906, when the Qing court began to prepare constitutional reform and to grant legal recognition to new associations in education and other professions,[86] their network development also reflected the relational revolution in the whole of society. In particular, the change in their internal components and interrelations epitomized such relational revolution down to the personal level.

3 levels - general
affiliate
branch

- linked elite merchants in city to small towns + markets
- increased elite influence on official policy
- changed gov't-business relations
- GCC leaders become similar(ish) to low officials
- bccs did not develop rapidly until they were promoted by gccs
-

- bank dev before cc (1898), helped pave way
- bc as precursor to cc ('gov't led vs. merchant led (?))
- 1902 - SH CCA

3

Changes in Organizational Composition
and Interrelations

- dev. of LY ccs→beyond Qing expectations

- ACCs reported directly to ministry

The development of the Lower Yangzi chambers of commerce, especially their three-tier networks, went beyond the Qing court's expectation from the beginning. Although the Ministry of Commerce in its 1904 rules put affiliated chambers under the jurisdiction (*lishu*) of general chambers, it carefully restricted their vertical communications to the routine submission of regular business reports from the former to the latter and finally to itself. This set of governmental rules specifically required affiliated chambers to submit reports about important issues directly to the ministry.[1] Thus, the formation of the chamber networks in the Lower Yangzi region quickly got on official nerves and compelled them to take more stringent measures.

In March 1906, the Ministry of Commerce redefined the relationship between general and affiliated chambers as one of mutual "communication" (*lianluo*) and denied the jurisdiction of the former over the latter, allowing them to contact each other only in special circumstances. The ministry further divided the chambers of commerce in Jiangsu Province into four separate groups: the affiliated chambers in southern Jiangsu were to link themselves to the Suzhou or Shanghai GCC, those in southwestern and northern Jiangsu to the Jiangning GCC, and those in the cotton trade around Tongzhou independent department to the Tong-Chong-Hai GCCC. In 1909, provincial officials in Zhejiang also ordered the affiliated chambers in the coastal area and the rest of the province to maintain communications with the Ningbo and Hangzhou GCCs, respectively.[2]

- GCC did not have jurisdiction over ACC
- could contact e·other in special circumstances
→ official rules (unsuccessful)

LY chambers developed hierarchical structures for elite + non-elite merchants

The official attempt to divide and rule these chambers of commerce and their merchant constituencies was not successful. On the contrary, these Lower Yang chambers strengthened their interrelations and merchant solidarity by developing similar structures and expanding their institutional contacts and personnel overlap. Through manipulation of the governmental rules, these chambers universally developed hierarchical structures to encompass elite and nonelite merchants in accordance with their different socioeconomic statuses. In defiance of the official restriction, they built both horizontal and vertical relations from large cities down to market towns.

Because these Lower Yangzi chambers of commerce brought elite and nonelite merchants into different niches in their organizational structures and interrelations, their networks roughly reflected the class differentiation between these merchant participants. Nevertheless, this does not mean that the elite merchant participants had formed a distinctive bourgeois class, as the previously cited studies have assumed. Actually, most elite merchants joined chambers of commerce as representatives of regional and occupational guilds that were mainly composed of common merchants. Due to the inflow of elite merchants from more numerous and diverse guilds, these chambers experienced constant changes in their composition and gradually expanded their networks and representation in merchant communities.

Such compositional changes usually increased the diversity of elite merchant members and leaders in these Lower Yangzi chambers, as local elite studies in the aforementioned literature have suggested. However, what deserves more attention is that the chamber networks enabled elite merchants to expand their social relations beyond the limits of their kinship and regional groups as well as their local society. Thus, these chambers promoted the network revolution through both relational diversification and expansion, and their institutional development especially characterized such relational change.

chambers – diverse – elite & common merchants

Development of Internal Structures and Interconnections

After the birth of the Shanghai CCA in 1902, the Lower Yangzi chambers of commerce gradually developed multilayered memberships and leaderships as well as different levels of meetings and elections to accommodate their varied merchant participants. They also established interrelations through overlapping membership, interlocking leaderships, joint meetings, and other forms of contact. Such network development brought elite and nonelite merchants into institutionalized hierarchy and, in particular, bonded elite merchants within and across different cities and towns. However, this tendency ran counter to official policies.

In its rules of 1904, the Ministry of Commerce originally required all business establishments in a given city or town, except small peddlers, to register with their local chamber of commerce. This set of rules specified twenty to fifty directors, including a president and a vice president, in a general chamber, and ten to thirty directors, including one president, in an affiliated chamber.[3] However, the Shanghai GCC deliberately applied the ministry's rule for the directors of a general chamber to its own members, or *huiyuan*, and limited the membership to fifty persons. Moreover, it established eighteen deliberative directors (*yidong*), including a president and a vice president.[4] Between 1904 and 1909, the Shanghai GCC further developed seven categories of membership, including three types of full members and four kinds of associate members:[5] SH GCC - more members that govt stipulated

1. Regular members were guild representatives. They had to pay annual dues of 300 taels each, and their number was limited to three per guild.

2. Special members (*tebie huiyuan*) were representatives of large enterprises. They also paid 300 taels in annual dues and were limited to three persons for every enterprise.

3. Honorary members (*mingwang huiyuan*) were large donors with high social reputation, but the Shanghai GCC did not have any such members by 1912.

4. Leading associate members (*lingxiu huiyou*) were guild representatives who paid annual dues of less than 300 taels each.

5. Individual associate members (*geren huiyou*) were merchant participants, each of whom paid an annual fee of twelve taels. The annual dues were raised to thirty taels each in 1907.

6. Special associate members (*tebie geren huiyou*) were "honorable merchants" and "superior graduates" from the training programs of the Chinese militia in the International Settlement. They provided the general chamber with security but did not need to pay any dues.

7. Group associate members (*banghang huiyou*) were merchants in affiliated guilds, but the Shanghai GCC never clarified whether they included all or merely a part of guild participants.

Thus, the Shanghai GCC incorporated mainly wealthy and prestigious elite merchants into its three types of full memberships and the first three kinds of associate memberships, and it simply lumped common merchants of affiliated guilds into the symbolic category of group associate membership. This general chamber also granted the diverse merchant participants in the seven categories different rights in its multilayered elections and meetings, the major difference in their rights being between common merchants of group associate membership and elite merchants in other categories of membership. *common + elite merch. had diff. rights in elections + meetings*

Although the Shanghai GCC adopted the "method of secret ballot" (*jimi toutongfa*) for elections from 1904, its group associate members had only the limited right in the primary elections to choose the established guild leaders as their representatives, that is, as regular members of the general chamber. In the subsequent election for directors, the Shanghai GCC in 1907 stipulated that each full member, either a regular or special member, could cast three votes, and a leading associate member who paid annual dues of 100 or 200 taels could cast one or two votes, respectively. In 1909, the GCC further granted one vote to each of its special individual associate members in the election of directors. As the Ministry of Commerce required, all directors had to be respectable merchants who were more than thirty years old and in local business over five years, and they should also have been the founders of successful business ventures and owners or managers of large business establishments. But the Shanghai GCC further required its directors to have knowledge of official document formats and thus limited their candidates to the elite merchants with official connections and gentry training. Only these directors had the right to become voters and candidates in the highest level of election for president and vice president.[6] *GCC voting system + changed over the years*

The Shanghai GCC also stipulated three different kinds of meetings for its elite and nonelite merchant participants, although it required all meetings to reach decisions by a majority of the participants, who would throw white or black chess pieces into a box as affirmative or negative votes, respectively. All of its full members could attend annual meetings (*nianhui*) to check accounts, discuss budgets, and review business issues of the previous year. Ten or more full and associate members could also call for special meetings (*tehui*) to deal with emergency issues, but the group associate members from affiliated guilds probably never enjoyed such a right. By contrast, only directors, including the president and vice president, could attend the regular meetings (*changhui*) and make decisions for the general chamber.[7]

Through the different levels of membership, leadership, elections, and meetings, the Shanghai GCC brought mainly diverse elite merchants into its hierarchical but interconnected networks. In 1906, the Shanghai GCC included twenty-one directors in its highest power circle, of whom twenty had purchased the fourth or fifth rank of official titles such as the prestigious *daotai*. By contrast, five out of the remaining thirty-seven full members had no gentry title, and twelve had official titles lower than the fifth rank.[8] However, commercial wealth, social prestige, and political power were more important than these titles in determining their qualifications for full membership and leadership in the Shanghai GCC, as the case of Xu Run shows. wealth, social power more imp. than gentry titles

As a leading Cantonese merchant in Shanghai, Xu became the first vice president of the Shanghai GCC in 1904 right after he helped Zhili Governor-General Yuan Shikai seize the China Merchants' Steam Navigation Company from Sheng Xuanhuai. Although Xu lost the position of vice president in the annual election of the general chamber in late 1905, he remained a director because he was still a representative for this semiofficial enterprise and the Cantonese merchant group until1907. Unfortunately, his ambiguous action in the new round of power struggles between Yuan and Sheng made Xu lose his position in the China Merchants' Steam Navigation Company in mid-1907, and he was subsequently ousted from the Shanghai GCC. Xu was still able to establish a successful family enterprise in 1908, and he reentered the Shanghai GCC in 1910, but only as an individual associate member representing his own business venture.[9]

Table 4 provides available data about both directors and full members in nearly ten general, affiliated, and branch chambers of commerce between 1904 and 1911. Among them, the Shanghai GCC increased the number of its directors from eighteen to twenty-one during these eight years, while the number of its full members, including regular and special members, fluctuated between fifty and seventy. Apart from these full members, the number of its leading, individual and special associate members reached fifty-two in 1908 and seventy-four in 1911.[10] Thus, by 1911, this general chamber counted only 124 direct participants in a city with about one million residents.

However, many of these elite participants represented affiliated guilds that included numerous common merchants. These guilds usually conducted their relations with the Shanghai GCC through their elite merchant leaders, but some of them went further, following the organizational model of this general chamber and establishing more formal relationships with it. In 1905, the guilds in the grocery, seafood, and three other trades invited a director of the Shanghai GCC to preside over their joint meeting and reorganized themselves into a chamber of commerce under his leadership. Although local of-

TABLE 4

Members and directors in general, affiliated, and branch chambers of commerce, 1905–1911

Chamber of commerce	Year							
	1904	1905	1906	1907	1908	1909	1910	1911
Shanghai GCC[a]	50 (18)		58 (21)		70 (21)	66 (21)	69 (21)	50 (21)
Suzhou GCC		76 (16)	82 (18)		65 (18)	85 (21)	89 (22)	(25)
Huai'an ACC				(10)		46 (22)		
Kunshan-Xinyang ACC			25 (9)		(13)			
Wujiang-Zhenze ACC			44 (11)	45 (13)		(12)	(13)	
Meili ACC			30 (16)			31 (11)		
Shengze ACC			25 (9)	31 (11)	31 (11)	31 (11)	(11)	
South Shanghai BCC[b] / South Shanghai ACC					69 (17)			103 (17)
Zhenze BCC					15 (3)			

Sources: Data from NGST: I, 4:36b; SZZZ, 1:70–71; SSZT: 1906, 1a–7b; 1908, 1a–7a; 1909, 1a–7a; 1910, 1a–6a; 1911, 1a–7a; SSDC, 46–58, 76–84, 100–106, 121–33, 143–58; SWGS, section 2, 4–6; HSLB, 21 (1910): haineiwai shanghui tongrenlu 5–9; *Hunan shangwu fenhui baogao timingce*, sections 4–5.

Note: The figures for members refer to full members only and include those for directors (in parentheses). This rule also applies to Tables 5–8 in this chapter.

[a] SZZZ (1:94–122) includes lists of directors and full members of the Shanghai GCC between 1904 and 1911, but most of these lists are from indirect sources. They are inconsistent with the annual registers issued by the general chamber, and thus their data are not included in this table. A Japanese record of 171 "members" of the Shanghai GCC in 1904 is also included in SZZZ and has been widely cited by Xu Dingxin, Yu Heping, and others scholars. Actually, this list does not accord with either the Shanghai GCC's regulations or its yearly registers between 1904 and 1911. It was presented by the Shanghai GCC to foreign authorities for the protection of its full members and other "respectable and wealthy merchants" in affiliated guilds. See SZZZ, 1:67–68, 70, 94–122; Tōa dōbunkai, *Shina keizai zensho*, 4:69–76; Xu and Qian, *Shanghai zongshanghui shi,1902–1929*, 61; Yu, *Shanghui yu zhongguo zaoqi xiandaihua*, 150.

[b] The South Shanghai BCC became an affiliated chamber in 1909.

foreign good guilds→ common trade associations
fre, tobacco, sugar guilds → C.C.S

ficials in Shanghai forbade the formation of chambers of commerce in specific trades from 1906, the Guild of Rice Retailers renamed itself a chamber of commerce in 1908 and established a formal membership and leadership as well as rules for elections and regular meetings. It even decided to let the Shanghai GCC handle its important issues.[11] Under the Shanghai GCC, merchants in the tobacco and sugar trades also renamed their guilds chambers of commerce. Moreover, the guild leaders in the foreign goods, fur, cotton, insurance, and other trades formed common trade associations (*gonghui*), which would become the unitary title for all affiliated guilds of chambers of commerce later on.[12] Such organizational changes in various guilds strengthened their relations

with the Shanghai GCC and helped bring their numerous merchant participants into its networks.

The general chambers of commerce in other Lower Yangzi cities largely
modeled themselves after the Shanghai GCC, although their organizational
structures also reflected different social relations among their own elite and
nonelite merchant participants. Some of these general chambers further formed
institutional and interpersonal relations with the Shanghai GCC. In turn,
they became organizational models for their affiliated and branch chambers
in small cities and market towns and expanded their vertical connections with
these lower-level chambers through interlocking leaderships or more formal
contacts, such as annual conferences.

The available data show that the Suzhou GCC and the Tong-Chong-
Hai GCCC established similar categories of regular, honorary, and special
membership for their elite merchants, as well as group associate membership for common merchants in their affiliated guilds. At the outset, each of
the two general chambers also had fourteen or eighteen directors, including a president and a vice president. They even brought their elite and nonelite merchant participants into elections and meetings in the same way as
the Shanghai GCC did. When the Hangzhou GCC appeared in 1906, it
formulated its regulations on the basis of those of the Shanghai and Suzhou
GCCs.[13] Thus, these general chambers showed a high level of institutional
uniformity.

Nevertheless, in such long-established commercial and political centers as
Suzhou and Hangzhou, general chambers formed stronger ties with guilds and
gentry than had the Shanghai GCC. In 1905, at least sixty-four full members
of the Suzhou GCC, or 84 percent of its full membership, were leaders from
more than forty guilds, which accounted for nearly half the local merchant
groups. By 1908, these guild leaders brought 1,099 merchant shops into group
associate membership of the general chamber and contributed 8,184 silver dollars in membership fees, which accounted for 85 percent of its total income.[14]
Meanwhile, all of the full members in the Suzhou GCC had gentry titles,
and it also named two or three prestigious gentrymen and former officials as
honorary members. One of its honorary members was Wang Tongyu, a former provincial official in charge of schools. Because Wang took leave from
his official duties from 1903, he was able to help found the Suzhou GCC in
1905 and take on the honorary membership. Although Wang resumed his
official career in 1909, the general chamber continued his honorary membership and further promoted him to the position of an honorary director in
1911.[15] Similarly, in the Hangzhou GCC, twenty of its twenty-one directors

in 1909 were guild leaders with gentry titles, and the general chamber also included as many as eighteen honorary deliberative members (*mingyu yiyuan*), most of them former officials.[16]

The Jiangning and Ningbo GCCs developed simpler structures than the aforementioned four general chambers in the Lower Yangzi region. They listed only thirty-two and thirty-eight "directors," respectively, in 1909, and neither reported any regular members. Nevertheless, most of their directors were guild leaders, and all had gentry status. The Ningbo GCC even included prestigious gentrymen like former officials of the central, provincial, and county governments as well as a few provincial graduates among its directors.[17] JN and NB → also closer links to guilds + gentry

Similarly, affiliated and branch chambers used either multilayered systems of memberships, leaderships, elections, and meetings or slightly simpler structures to incorporate their elite and nonelite merchants. The data in Table 4 indicate that the systems of both directorship and full membership existed in the five affiliated chambers located in the prefectural city of Huai'an, the twin-county cities of Kunshan-Xinyang and Wujiang-Zhenze, and the towns of Meili and Shengze. Whereas the South Shanghai BCC evolved directly into the South Shanghai ACC, the Zhenze BCC developed a structure similar to that of the aforesaid affiliated chambers, which had copied general chambers.

Like the Shanghai GCC, the Meili ACC in 1906 translated the official rule concerning a maximum of thirty directors in each affiliated chamber into its own rule regarding the number of regular members and instead established a board of fifteen directors, in addition to one president. It even developed three similar categories of full membership for elite merchant participants: regular membership for affiliated guild leaders, honorary membership for prestigious gentry with commercial knowledge, and special membership for large donors. Ordinary merchant participants in the affiliated guilds could become only associate members, pay yearly dues, and receive protection from the affiliated chamber. However, they did not have the right to attend regular meetings or participate in leadership elections as did full members.[18]

Other affiliated chambers that are listed in Table 4, such as the Shengze, Kunshan-Xinyang, and Wujiang-Zhenze ACCs, basically modeled themselves after the Meili ACC. For example, the Shengze ACC in 1907 gathered its full and associate members for elections in three steps: first, all associate members in the affiliated guilds selected its thirty full members; these full members then elected ten directors; finally, the ten directors chose a president among themselves. In the election of 1910, its former and incumbent

Meili ACC - directors, 3 categories of full members, assoc. members

presidents received five votes each from the ten directors. An official supervisor in the election then drew lots for the two candidates and declared the
incumbent president the winner.[19]

Although Table 4 includes only available data from six affiliated chambers
in the Lower Yangzi region, they are sufficient to demonstrate that most
chambers had kept relatively small directorships and full memberships by
1911. Except for the Shanghai ACC, which had an exceptionally large number of full members in 1911, each of the five affiliated chambers in Huai'an,
Kunshan-Xinyang, Wujiang-Zhenze, Meili, and Shengze had only twenty-
five to forty-six full members and nine to twenty-two directors. A further
check of the status of the 178 full members in these five affiliated chambers
in 1907 or 1909 indicates that all of them had gentry titles, and most were
guild leaders. In the same two years, a total of 253 directors in fifteen other
affiliated chambers included only four persons who did not have such titles,
and many of these directors were also guild representatives.[20] Through such
prestigious elite participants, these affiliated chambers gained financial resources
from affiliated guilds and controlled larger numbers of common merchants
in their respective cities or towns.

Branch chambers in Lower Yangzi market towns usually had a smaller
number of participants or slightly simpler structures than affiliated chambers,
and the Ministry of Commerce initially did not even allow them to title their
major leaders "presidents." It was not until September 1911 that the Ministry
of Agriculture, Industry, and Commerce began to grant the title of chief director, or *zongdong*, to these leaders. Nevertheless, the branch chambers still
brought both elite and nonelite merchants into different categories of membership and organizational activities such as elections and meetings. As Table
4 shows, the Zhenze BCC had only three directors and eight full members, but the merchant shops under its control numbered 106. Even in the
northern periphery of Jiangsu Province, the branch chamber in the small
town of Nanyang'an also formed hierarchical structures and held multilayered elections. It started with more than sixty merchant participants, and
its inaugural meeting in 1910 assembled forty-three of them for elections.
These merchant participants first elected ten directors, who subsequently
selected two Chen cousins as the chief director and honorary chief director,
respectively.[21]

Through their multilayered compositions and activities, these chambers
were able to encompass diverse elite merchants and more numerous and heterogeneous common merchants in their cities and towns. By 1912, 148 chambers of commerce in Jiangsu (including Shanghai) and Zhejiang provinces

contained 4,962 "deliberative members," or an average of thirty-four full members in each chamber, but they rallied about 39,157 merchants or about 264 group associate members each.[22] More important, these diverse merchant participants were linked up not only by individual chambers but also by their networks across different cities and towns. large # of associate members by 1912

The Lower Yangzi chambers of commerce could establish their interrelations largely because of their institutional uniformity and contacts as well as personnel overlap. As a result of official disapproval of their interconnections, these chambers relied heavily on the personal relations of their elite merchant leaders and members for their network expansion. Nevertheless, they gradually developed more formal and regular relations among general, affiliated, and branch chambers in the Lower Yangzi cities and towns. relationships btw GCC's

The Shanghai GCC formed close relations with many chambers of commerce in the Lower Yangzi region, especially with the South Shanghai BCC and the succeeding South Shanghai ACC. In 1911, its directorship included President Wang Zhen and three directors of the South Shanghai ACC, Shen Manyun, Lin Liansun, and Su Benyan. More elite merchants held double membership in the two Shanghai chambers.[23] This general chamber also established relations with chambers of commerce outside of Shanghai through their shared leaders.

One long-term director in the Shanghai GCC, Zhou Tingbi, came from a small landlord family in Wuxi County but made a fortune as a comprador in Shanghai. Thus, he was able to purchase the prestigious title of *daotai* and became a major founder of the Wuxi-Jinkui native place association in Shanghai in 1888. After Zhou successively joined the Shanghai CCA in 1902 and the Shanghai GCC in 1904, he further established the Wuxi-Jinkui ACC in his home place in 1905 and served as its president until early 1907. Among his numerous business ventures, Xincheng Bank (Xincheng yinhang) had branches in several cities and received protection from chambers of commerce there. This bank was also managed by Shen Manyun, a director of both the Shanghai GCC and the South Shanghai ACC in 1911.[24]

Another long-term director in the Shanghai GCC, Zhu Dachun, succeeded Zhou as the president of the Wuxi-Jinkui ACC in 1907 and served continuously as a link between the two chambers. Zhu came from Jinkui, the twin county of Wuxi. Like Zhou, he was also a comprador, a holder of the *daotai* title, a founder of their native-place association in Shanghai, and an investor in many industrial ventures. In addition to his links with the Shanghai GCC and the Wuxi-Jinkui ACC, Zhu also joined the Suzhou GCC in 1909. In the same year, the first vice president of the Suzhou GCC,

Ni Sijiu, entered the Shanghai GCC as a special member and then became its director in 1910.[25]

The Suzhou GCC developed more formal relations with its affiliated and branch chambers through institutional arrangements. For instance, it received two-thirds of the membership fees from the affiliated chamber in the town of Pingwang in the adjacent Wujiang County. In turn, the Wujiang-Zhenze ACC received from its fourteen branch chambers one-third of their annual membership dues and thus included their major leaders as full members or directors.[26] *GCC relations w/ ACC + BCC in SZ – more formal*

Similarly, the Tong-Chong-Hai GCCC used both institutional and interpersonal ties to expand its networks. When this general chamber came into being in 1904, it turned a cotton cloth guild in Shanghai into its branch chamber and put it under the management of Shi Zejing, a director of the Shanghai GCC, around 1906. Moreover, its leadership included the president of the Tongzhou ACC from the beginning. After this general chamber helped elite merchants in the town of Jiangyan in the adjacent Taizhou County found a third affiliated chamber in 1908, it brought all three affiliated chambers in that county under its control. Thus, in March 1911 its title was changed from the Tong-Chong-Hai GCCC into the Tong-Chong-Hai-Tai GCC.[27]

Because the Shanghai GCC was originally dominated by Ningbo elite merchants, such as Yan Xinhou, it naturally kept close relations with the Ningbo GCC. In fact, two directors of the Ningbo GCC in 1909 had been partners of the Yan family in the first modern cotton mill in that city from 1894. The interpersonal relations between the two general chambers became formalized to some extent by 1909 because the chief secretary of the Shanghai GCC, Jiang Yixiu, held a concurrent position as the Shanghai-residing investigator (*zhu-Hu diaochayuan*) in the Ningbo GCC. Starting from 1907, the Ningbo GCC also formalized its relations with its affiliated and branch chambers by gathering them for annual meetings.[28] For the same purpose, the Hangzhou GCC in 1909 built a spacious meeting hall and began to assemble leaders of its affiliated chambers for two regular conferences each year. In 1910, the Jiangning GCC also established a special office to host delegates from affiliated chambers in northern Jiangsu and began to gather their leaders for general conferences from then on.[29] *Shanghai – Ningbo GCC ties*

Therefore, both the internal composition of the Lower Yangzi chambers of commerce and their interrelations underwent continuous institutionalization. As a result, these chambers bonded their merchant leaders and members through substantial relations, although their hierarchical structures reflected the social diversity and even class differentiation between their elite and

use of institutionalized + interpersonal ties in TCH GCC

nonelite participants. It was this institutional development that enabled the chamber networks to assimilate increasingly diverse participants and expand in size and complexity, rather than fall apart.

Transformation of Elite Merchant Members and Directors

Although all of the chambers of commerce in the Lower Yangzi region limited their leadership positions and the privileges of full membership to their elite merchant participants, this elite group experienced constant change because most were representatives of different guilds and subject to annual elections and other forms of personnel changes. The personnel reshuffling among these elite merchant members and directors usually increased their socioeconomic diversity rather than the tendency for them to form a homogeneous bourgeois class. In particular, the compositional diversification in these chambers gradually allowed them to develop beyond the oligarchic control of specific kin, local and business groups, or other elite cliques. As a result, they became more representative of the different merchant guilds and other organizations in their constituencies.

Based on available year-by-year registers of the two general chambers in Shanghai and Suzhou as well as the affiliated chamber in the town of Shengze between 1905 and 1911, Table 5 shows a similar pattern of personnel reshuffle in their directorships and full memberships. With some exceptions, the newcomers who entered the three chambers through annual elections and other institutional arrangements constituted between 24 and 33 percent of their directors (the exceptionally low and high rates were 18 and 48 percent, respectively), and between 26 and 38 percent of their full members (the unusually high rate was 49–52 percent). Other Lower Yangzi chambers of commerce did not leave such annual data, but their extant records support the above discoveries and even suggest larger margins of personnel change. In the Wujiang-Zhenze ACC of 1907, newcomers amounted to twenty-one of its forty-five full members, accounting for 47 percent of the full membership. Meanwhile, there were three newcomers among the chamber's thirteen directors, representing 23 percent of its directorships. In 1910, the number of new directors in this chamber rose to six, or 50 percent of its twelve directors. In the Kunshan-Xinyang ACC, a power struggle in 1908 brought in twelve new directors, or 92 percent of its thirteen directors.[30]

Another indication of the compositional changes in these chambers was the continuous decrease in the average ages of their directors and full members, although many elite merchant leaders and members still survived personnel

TABLE 5

New members and directors (in parentheses) of the Shanghai, Suzhou, and Shengze chambers of commerce, 1905–1911

Year	Shanghai GCC			Suzhou GCC[a]			Shengze ACC		
	Total	New	%	Total	New	%	Total	New	%
1905				76					
				(16)					
1906				82	40	49	25		
				(18)	(5)	(28)	(9)		
1907							31	16	52
							(11)	(3)	(27)
1908	70			65	18	28	31	8	26
	(21)			(18)	(5)	(28)	(11)	(3)	(27)
1909	66	18	27	85	32	38	31	8	26
	(21)	(10)	(48)	(21)	(5)	(24)	(11)	(2)	(18)
1910	69	21	30	89	24	27			
	(21)	(7)	(33)	(22)	(4)	(18)	(11)	(3)	(27)
1911	50	14	28						
	(21)	(7)	(33)	(25)	(6)	(24)			

Sources: SSZT: 1908; 1909; 1910; 1911; SSDC, 46–58, 121–33.

[a] The Suzhou GCC held its second annual election in late 1906 and its third in early 1908. Thus, its membership did not experience personnel changes from late 1906 to early 1908.

recruitment of younger merchants
reshuffles and their ages increased year by year. In the Shanghai GCC, the average age of its directors dropped from 52.9 in 1906 to 50.1 in 1911, and that of its full members also decreased from 49.3 to 46.9 during the five years.[31] In the Shengze ACC, the average age of its full members was 43.5 in 1907, but it declined to 40.5 in 1909. More dramatically, the average age of directors in the Kunshan-Xinyang ACC was 53.3 in 1907 but slumped to 42.6 in 1908. In 1909, the lists of the Jiangning and Hangzhou GCCs, as well as eighteen affiliated chambers in other Lower Yangzi cities and towns, also indicated that the average ages of their directors were between 37 and 52.[32] Clearly all of these Lower Yangzi chambers of commerce included elite merchants from different age groups, but most of these elite participants were in the prime of their life. The continuous recruitment of the younger and more energetic elite merchants ensured that these chambers were dynamic institutions in both business and political activities.

More important, through such compositional changes, these chambers of commerce broadened their constituencies by recruiting elite leaders from increasingly diverse regional groups of merchants in many cities and towns; this was especially evident in the immigrant city of Shanghai. Previous studies have indicated that the Ningbo native-place group had long dominated the Shanghai GCC from the late Qing period.[33] In Table 6, quantitative analysis of the birthplaces of directors and full members in this general chamber confirms the previous discovery. But it also indicates that Ningbo dominance in the Shanghai GCC showed significant decline between 1906 and 1911 because annual elections and other institutional arrangements inside this general chamber brought in more elite merchants from other regional groups.

As Table 6 shows, in the Shanghai GCC of 1906, Ningbo natives numbered fourteen among its fifty-eight full members, and eleven among its twenty-one directors, accounting for 24 percent of the former and 52 percent of the latter. Thus, they obviously dominated this general chamber at the outset, and their dominance was especially prominent in its directorship. However, these Ningbo elites faced increasing competition from the leaders of other regional groups, although they also complained about their sacrifice of time and energy for public service in this general chamber. Thus, the Shanghai GCC in 1909 adopted a new rule to limit the tenure of its directors, including its president and vice president. This rule compelled one-third of its incumbent directors to withdraw from the annual elections by drawing lots, although the retired directors could reenter elections after the lapse of one year.[34] Consequently, the Ningbo dominance in the Shanghai GCC declined dramatically. By 1911, Ningbo natives retained only nine positions in its full membership and three in its directorship, accounting for only 18 percent of the former and 14 percent of the latter.

Table 6 also shows that elite merchants from other parts of Zhejiang Province and from Jiangsu Province (including Shanghai) increased their respective proportions in the directorship from 10 to 29 percent and from 24 to 43 percent between 1906 and 1911. However, their percentages in the full membership did not show such a steady increase. In the same period, the proportion of elite merchants from provinces other than Jiangsu and Zhejiang remained at 14 percent in the directorship, but it increased steadily from 22 to 32 percent in the full membership. As a result, elite merchants from Jiangsu Province (including Shanghai) and those from the whole province of Zhejiang (including Ningbo) accounted for an equal 43 percent of directors in each of the three years from 1909 to 1911, although their respective ratios in the full membership fluctuated in favor of either Jiangsu or Zhejiang natives during the same three years. In 1911, the Shanghai GCC's list of the leading, individual, and special associate members also showed that Jiangsu

TABLE 6

Birthplaces of members and directors (in parentheses) of the Shanghai GCC, 1906–1911

Year	Jiangsu Province (including Shanghai)		Zhejiang Province (excluding Ningbo)		Ningbo Prefecture[a]		Others		Total	
	No.	%	No.	%	No.	%	No.	%	No.	%
1906	18	31	13	23	14	24	13	22	58	100
	(5)	(24)	(2)	(10)	(11)	(52)	(3)	(14)	(21)	(100)
1908	23	33	12	17	19	27	16	23	70	100
	(7)	(33)	(1)	(5)	(10)	(48)	(3)	(14)	(21)	(100)
1909	25	38	11	17	12	18	18	27	66	100
	(9)	(43)	(3)	(14)	(6)	(29)	(3)	(14)	(21)	(100)
1910	22	32	15	22	14	20	18	26	69	100
	(9)	(43)	(5)	(24)	(4)	(19)	(3)	(14)	(21)	(100)
1911	13	26	12	24	9	18	16	32	50	100
	(9)	(43)	(6)	(29)	(3)	(14)	(3)	(14)	(21)	(100)

Sources: SSZT: 1906; SSZT: 1908; SSZT: 1909; SSZT: 1910; SSZT: 1911.

[a] Ningbo natives were from the six counties of Ningbo Prefecture and Dinghai Independent Subprefecture, which became separated from the prefecture in 1841.

and Zhejiang natives numbered thirty and thirty-four, respectively.[35] Thus, by the end of the late Qing period, the Shanghai GCC was less the preserve of Ningbo natives and more a union of elite merchant representatives from Jiangsu, Zhejiang, and other provincial groups.

In addition to this general chamber, the South Shanghai BCC and the succeeding South Shanghai ACC had always been such a coalition of different regional groups, especially Jiangsu and Zhejiang merchants. Among the seventeen directors in the two successive chambers, Jiangsu and Zhejiang natives numbered eight each in 1908, and nine and seven, respectively, in 1911. Among the full members, their respective numbers were thirty-six and thirty in 1908, and forty-six and forty-three in 1911. Ningbo natives, as distinguished from other Zhejiang natives, numbered only four, or 24 percent of the directorship, in both 1908 and 1911. Although their number in the full membership category increased from eighteen in 1908 to twenty-five in 1911, their proportion actually dropped from 26 to 24 percent during the three years because the total number of full members in the two successive chambers increased from 69 to 103.[36]

Unlike the two chambers of commerce in the immigrant city of Shanghai, their counterparts in other Lower Yangzi cities and towns were mostly dominated by native rather than sojourning elite merchants at the outset. However, annual elections and compositional changes in these chambers led to a gradual increase of nonnatives in their full memberships and director-ships and thus expanded their constituencies to include more sojourning merchant leaders and different regional guilds. The available data assembled in Table 7 for the Shengze ACC indicate that the proportion of its nonnative participants steadily increased from 40 to 58 percent of its full members, and from 44 to 64 percent of its directors between 1906 and 1909. By contrast, native elite merchants dominated this affiliated chamber in 1906 but ac-counted for less than half of its full members and directors in 1909.

Between 1907 and 1910, the single-year registers of the four general cham-bers in Suzhou, Jiangning, Hangzhou, and Ningbo, as well as twenty-three affiliated chambers, indicate that they usually included both native and non-native elite merchants in their full memberships and directorships. Native merchants totally monopolized the directorships of the Shanyin-Kuaiji and Wuxi-Jinkui ACCs in 1909. Conversely, nonnative merchants constituted more than 50 percent of full members and directors in the Kunshan-Xinyang ACC in 1907, and their proportions were also higher than 50 percent in the directorships of the Baoying and Shipu ACCs in 1909. Because many nonnative elite merchants had already mingled with natives as long-term residents in these Lower Yangzi cities and towns, the chambers under their domination still could claim representation for the local merchant community.[37]

Another important strategy for these chambers to expand their represen-tation was to recruit elite merchant leaders from more numerous and diverse occupational groups and business institutions. In previous studies, an analyti-cal focus on the relations of these chambers with the urban elites in "modern

TABLE 7

Birthplaces of members and directors (in parentheses) of the Shengze ACC, 1906–1909

Year	Natives[a]		Nonnatives		Total	
	No.	%	No.	%	No.	%
1906	15	60	10	40	25	100
	(5)	(56)	(4)	(44)	(9)	(100)
1907	15	48	16	52	31	100
	(5)	(45)	(6)	(55)	(11)	(100)
1908	15	48	16	52	31	100
	(5)	(45)	(6)	(55)	(11)	(100)
1909	13	42	18	58	31	100
	(4)	(36)	(7)	(64)	(11)	(100)

Source: SSDC, 121–33.

[a] Natives include people from Wujiang and Zhenze counties around the town of Shengze.

8

business" has usually led to the discovery of a small bourgeoisie among these chambers and a consequent lamentation on the bourgeois impotence.[38] In fact, these chambers included more diverse and influential elite participants and developed more extensive and powerful networks than the so-called bourgeois organizations stressed in previous scholarship. That was true even in the most modernized cities like Shanghai.

On the basis of a Japanese record of membership in the Shanghai GCC in 1904, Xu Dingxin argues that this general chamber mainly represented the bourgeois class and capitalist economy from its beginning. Among its 171 members, only eighteen (10.5 percent) represented merchant guilds, and the remaining 153 (89.5 percent) were bourgeois entrepreneurs from industrial and commercial enterprises, which included one Western-style bank, one steamship company, five mechanized factories, twenty-five foreign firms, and 121 individual shops. Actually, Xu's data about the chamber membership include not merely the full members of the Shanghai GCC but also other "respectable and wealthy merchants" under its protection. More important, the "individual shops" on his list were mostly old-style business establishments in the silverware, silk fabric, sugar, sauce, and other trades, not necessarily "modern" business ventures.[39] not just bourgeois entrepreneurs

Table 8 is based on the yearly registers issued by the Shanghai GCC between 1906 and 1911. It reveals the different types of business institutions represented by the full members, including directors, of this general chamber in the late Qing period. Although the number of guild representatives fluctuated and even slightly decreased among the full members and directors, they usually accounted for more than 50 percent in either category. Only in 1910 did the proportion of guild representatives decrease to 49 percent of the full members and to 48 percent of the directors. Because the directors and full members from individual shops were mostly in old-style businesses, the representatives of the "modern business" ventures, such as Western-style banks, mechanized factories, and joint-stock companies, never formed a majority. According to a list of the seventy-four leading, individual, and special associate members in the Shanghai GCC of 1911, those from such "modern business" institutions numbered only twenty-five, accounting for 34 percent of the three categories of associate membership.[40] Thus, if the standard for the Chinese bourgeoisie in previous scholarship is to be followed, it is problematic to define the Shanghai GCC simply as a bourgeois organization, not to mention other chambers in small cities and market towns where far fewer bourgeois entrepreneurs would exist.

directors + members mainly in "old-style" class
businesses - not ny bourgeois capitalist class

TABLE 8

Business backgrounds of members and directors (in parentheses)
of the Shanghai GCC, 1906–1911

Business institution	1906		1908		1909		1910		1911	
	No.	%	No.	%	No.	%	No.	%	No.	%
Merchant guild	37	64	36	51	35	53	34	49	28	56
	(13)	(62)	(11)	(52)	(13)	(62)	(10)	(48)	(11)	(52)
Individual shop	7	12	11	16	5	7	6	8	1	2
	(3)	(14)	(5)	(24)	(2)	(10)				
Foreign firm (comprador)	2	3	2	3	1	2	1	2	1	2
	(2)	(10)			(1)	(4)	(1)	(4)	(1)	(5)
Western-style bank			3	4	7	10	8	12	7	14
					(2)	(10)	(4)	(19)	(4)	(19)
Mechanized factory	12	21	14	20	15	23	15	22	9	18
	(3)	(14)	(3)	(14)	(3)	(14)	(4)	(19)	(4)	(19)
Joint-stock company			4	6	3	5	5	7	4	8
			(2)	(10)			(2)	(10)	(1)	(5)
Total	58	100	70	100	66	100	69	100	50	100
	(21)	(100)	(21)	(100)	(21)	(100)	(21)	(100)	(21)	(100)

Sources: SSZT: 1906; SSZT: 1908; SSZT: 1909; SSZT: 1910; SSZT: 1911.

Note: In order to calculate all percentages in round numbers, the ratio of 1/21, or 4.76 percent, appears either as 4 or 5 percent in this table.

Actually, this general chamber was a more powerful organization of elite merchant representatives from commercial guilds, family businesses, and new-style enterprises. Quite a few of its directors and full members acted simultaneously as guild leaders, new entrepreneurs, and even compradors for foreign firms. Yu Qiaqing, a director of the Shanghai GCC in 1908, served as a representative of both the Foreign Goods Guild and a Dutch bank in this general chamber, and he also launched a modern bank together with his Ningbo fellows at that time. Although Chinese Marxist historians are still debating whether Yu represented the comprador or national bourgeois class, he and similar merchant leaders undoubtedly helped the Shanghai GCC expand its connections and influence into their guilds and other business institutions.[41]

It was precisely because the Shanghai GCC assembled the elite merchant leaders of the different business institutions ranging from guilds to industrial enterprises that it could claim representation for the merchant community beyond the small bourgeoisie in this city. In fact, it constantly expanded its constituency through such compositional diversification. At first, this general chamber was predominated by elite merchants from the few major business institutions, especially the Guild of Southern Remittance Shops (Nanbang huiye gongsuo) and two semiofficial enterprises, the China Merchants' Steam Navigation Company and the Imperial Telegraph Administration. In 1904, the two enterprises provided the Shanghai GCC with 12,000 taels, about half of its initial funds, and they sent a total of six representatives as full members between 1906 and 1909. But that number dropped to three in 1910 and to only one in 1911.[42] Similarly, the Guild of Southern Remittance Shops sent five representatives as full members of the general chamber until 1906, but that number dropped to two in 1908 and to one in 1911.[43] This guild and the China Merchants' Steam Navigation Company also produced the first president and vice president of the Shanghai GCC, Yan Xinhou and Xu Run, as well as three of its directors by 1906. By 1911, only one representative of this company was still on the directorship of the general chamber.[44] Naturally, representatives of more numerous guilds and private enterprises entered the full membership and directorship of the Shanghai GCC and brought their business institutions into its networks.

In the available registers of the Suzhou, Jiangning, Hangzhou, and Ningbo GCCs for 1909, their directors and full members generally reported connections with guilds or old-style businesses in the native banking, pawnshop, silk fabric, cotton cloth, jewelry, medicine, grain, grocery, and other trades. Among the 107 directors in these four general chambers in that year, only one in the Hangzhou GCC and five in the Ningbo GCC reported relations with new business and industrial ventures, such as mechanized factories and joint-stock companies. The register of the Suzhou GCC for 1909 included sixty-four full members, but none of them identified themselves as representatives of such "modern" businesses.[45] In reality, quite a few elite merchant leaders in these general chambers had engaged in new business ventures by that time, as is discussed in the next section. However, their tendency to identify themselves with guilds and old-style business establishments indicated that new business ventures were still not so important in the socioeconomic activities of these elite merchants. Thus, compositional changes in the four general chambers usually helped them recruit leaders from more diverse merchant groups but not necessarily bourgeois entrepreneurs from new business ventures.

When the Suzhou GCC came into being in 1905, guild leaders from the native banking, pawnshop, satin, gauze, and silk fabric trades constituted 63 percent of its full members, which included representatives from more than forty trades. The first four businesses also produced fourteen of the sixteen directors, or 88 percent of the directorship, in the general chamber. Elite merchants from these five businesses could initially dominate the Suzhou GCC partly because the general chamber allowed affiliated guilds to select more than three representatives each as its full members if any of their representatives had become its directors. Moreover, some small guilds like those for the pig brokerage and cured meat trades originally selected shared representatives as full members of the general chamber.[46]

In 1908, the Suzhou GCC began to prohibit affiliated guilds from sharing their representatives in order to expand its direct communications with more merchant groups. Such institutional arrangements, and especially annual elections, led to significant changes among the elite merchant components in this general chamber. Among its full members, the proportion of representatives from the aforementioned five major trades first dropped from 63 to 43 percent between 1905 and 1908, and then to 34 percent in 1909, although their guild leaders still amounted to nineteen, or 86 percent, of the twenty-two directors in 1911.[47] These compositional changes at least allowed the Suzhou GCC to recruit elite leaders from more numerous and different merchant groups into its full membership.

In smaller cities and market towns, elite participants in affiliated and branch chambers also came from different trades, especially from old-style businesses related to the traditional agricultural economy. Table 9 provides a survey of the business backgrounds of 368 directors, including presidents, in twenty-two affiliated chambers as of 1909. The trades of grain, native banking, delicacies from southern China, pawnshop, cotton cloth, silk, medicine, clothing, soy sauce, silk fabric, and cooking oil were in order the most important businesses represented by these chamber directors. Each of the eleven trades sent ten to thirty-three elite merchant directors to the twenty-two chambers. However, directors of these chambers also included representatives from more than forty trades that produced fewer than ten directors each. By contrast, only three (0.8 percent) of the 368 directors in the twenty-two affiliated chambers registered their relations with one mechanized factory and two joint-stock companies.

Actually, fragmentary records show that new business ventures attracted more leaders from these affiliated chambers. In particular, many of these leaders engaged in the railroad movements of Jiangsu and Zhejiang provinces from 1905, as is discussed in Chapter 5. However, their investment in the railroad projects resulted mainly from the nationalistic mobilization of their chamber networks and not necessarily from their capitalist entrepreneurship. In these affiliated chambers, some leaders also used their power to found new business ventures and then forced local merchants to invest in them, but

TABLE 9
Business backgrounds of directors in twenty-two ACCs, 1909

Trades	No.	%
Grain	33	9.0
Native banking	32	8.7
Delicacies from southern China	20	5.4
Pawnshop	18	4.9
Cotton cloth	18	4.9
Silk	16	4.3
Medicine	15	4.0
Clothing	13	3.5
Soy sauce	13	3.5
Silk fabric	12	3.3
Cooking oil	10	2.7
Tea	9	2.5
Lumber	9	2.5
Delicacies from northern China	9	2.5
Wine	8	2.2
Tobacco	8	2.2
Grocery	7	1.9
Paper	6	1.6
Candles	6	1.6
Fish	6	1.6
Dyehouse	6	1.6
Cotton	5	1.4
Satin	5	1.4
Pickled meat	5	1.4
Thirty other trades	52	14.1
Joint-stock company	2	0.5
Mechanized factory	1	0.3
Unknown	24	6.5
Total	368	100

Sources: SSDC, 94–95, 112–15, 131–32; HSLB (the section "haineiwai shanghui tongrenlu" in each issue), 7 (1909): 3–4; 11 (1909): 6; 12 (1909): 3–6; 16 (1909): 4–10; 18 (1909): 3–4; 21 (1909): 5–7, 9–11, 13–15; 22 (1910): 11–14.

Note: The twenty-two ACCs were located in the prefectural capitals of Huai'an, Huzhou, and Jiaxing, the county seats of Baoying, Fenghua, Huating-Lou, Ruian, Shanyin-Kuaiji, Wujiang-Zhenze, Wuxi-Jinkui, and Xiao, and the towns of Dongba, Haian, Linghu, Luodian, Pingwang, Shengze, Shipu, Xinshi, Zhoupu, Zhujing, and Zhuanghang. The thirty other trades produced fewer than five directors each.

such coercive measures actually reinforced their dominance in local business rather than conversion to a bourgeois class.

The first president of the Changzhou ACC, Yun Zuqi, provides a typical example. Yun came from a prominent lineage in Changzhou Prefecture and became a prefect in Fujian Province around 1894. His clash with Japanese there cost him the official position but made him into a patriotic hero. In his home place, he also acquired high standing as a gentry manager of public projects. Thus, Yun became a founder and major leader of the Changzhou GCC in 1905. After his creation of a new-style bank in 1907, he first pushed pawnbrokers and native bankers under the affiliated chamber to subscribe half of the bank's capital and then compelled other affiliated merchant groups to purchase the remaining half of the shares. Probably through similar means, Yun founded a processing factory for vegetable oil and tried to get official permission to monopolize vegetable oil production in Changzhou Prefecture. In addition to unsuccessful attempts to establish printing, paper-making, and canned food factories in Changzhou, he launched a land reclamation company in the adjacent Zhenjiang Prefecture. In 1910, his mismanagement of this company prompted complaints by its merchant shareholders and an investigation by the Qing government, but Yun kept his position in the Changzhou ACC and even defied the official investigation with the help of the Shanghai GCC.[48] Clearly, Yun received support from the elite merchant leaders of the Shanghai GCC because of their links based around the new chamber networks, not because of their common bourgeois commitment to capitalist entrepreneurship. links of chamber networks > bourgeois entrepreneurship

Therefore, the Lower Yangzi chambers of commerce encompassed and linked up diverse elite merchants ranging from metropolitan entrepreneurs and guild leaders to local gentry-merchants, such as Yun. These elite merchants brought in social prestige and connections with guilds and other socioeconomic institutions and promoted the expansion of chamber networks in their merchant communities. They also used the new associational networks to strengthen their own dominance in the business world. However, these elite merchants themselves and their social dominance in the new chamber networks still underwent significant transformation, as is shown by changes among major chamber leaders.

Personnel and Relational Changes among Major Leaders

Major leaders in the Lower Yangzi chambers of commerce included presidents and vice presidents in general chambers, presidents in affiliated chambers, and chief directors in branch chambers. Personnel and relational changes among them not only ensured the continuous inflow of leaders from different regional groups of merchants and the most important businesses but also shifted power from chamber leaders of gentry and even official origin to elite merchants with more extensive relations in the business world. In practice, chamber leaders from both gentry and merchant backgrounds worked hard to seek and maintain their dominant positions by expanding their interpersonal and institutional relations, such as partnerships in business ventures and collaboration in power struggles. A detailed examination of the diverse chamber leaders and their scrambles for profit and power can reveal how they helped expand the chamber networks by building their collective dominance and interrelations beyond specific kin groups, local factions, and other personal cliques as well as individual cities and towns.

In order to prevent the monopolization of power by individual leaders, the Suzhou GCC in 1905 not only stipulated annual election of its leaders but also limited the tenures of its president and vice president to a maximum of three consecutive years. The Ministry of Agriculture, Industry, and Commerce later enforced this rule in all chambers in its approvals of their annual elections for major leaders. Actually, the Lower Yangzi chambers underwent different degrees of personnel changes in their top leadership because they either followed the official rule to ensure the continuous recruitment of influential elite merchants or used various excuses to retain their incumbent leaders beyond the three-year limitation.[49] Nevertheless, these chamber leaders universally experienced significant changes in their social relations.

Appendix 1 includes the available names of presidents and vice presidents in the six general chambers of the Lower Yangzi region in the late Qing period. In many aspects, the Shanghai GCC typified the personnel and relational changes among these major leaders. From 1902 to 1905, Yan Xinhou had been president of the Shanghai CCA and the succeeding Shanghai GCC because of his official connections and the dominance of his family business and the Ningbo merchant group in the urban market, as mentioned earlier. In his new positions, Yan greatly strengthened his kin and local relationships through the chamber networks. When Yan initiated the creation of the Shanghai CCA in 1902, he made Zhou Jinbiao the first vice president because they were both Ningbo fellows and business partners in a cotton mill. After Yan died in late 1906, his son, Yan Yibin, became a director of the general chamber in 1908 and its vice president in 1909. Moreover, a manager of the Yans'

Yuanfengrun Remittance Shop (Yuanfengrun yinhao), Chen Ziqin, was a director of the Shanghai CCA and GCC from 1902 to 1909.[50]

However, the senior and junior Yans also used their leadership positions to find new business partners within and outside the Ningbo elite merchant group, and they even expanded their personal circles to include chamber leaders in different cities. In 1905, Yan Xinhou launched the Huaxing Fire and Flood Insurance Company (Huaxing shuihuo baoxian gongsi), and his eight partners were all directors, full members, and even major leaders of the Shanghai GCC. They included its first vice president of Cantonese origin, Xu Run; its second president of Fujian origin, Zeng Zhu; and its second vice president of Ningbo origin, Zhu Baosan. Moreover, Yan Xinhou's partners in other business ventures included chamber leaders outside of Shanghai, such as Shen Yunpei and Xu Dinglin, the first and second presidents of the Haizhou-Ganyu ACC in northern Jiangsu, not to mention his business partners inside the Ningbo GCC.[51]

In the annual election of the Shanghai GCC in late 1905, Ningbo elite leaders lost the office of president to Zeng Zhu, who came from the Fujian merchant group but had just become a national hero in the anti-American boycott of that year. Because Zeng had grown up in Shanghai, he had developed close relations with elite merchants from both Jiangsu and Zhejiang provinces. Thus, his tenure lasted for only one year not because of pressure from Ningbo leaders, as Xu Dingxin and Qian Xiaoming's work has assumed, but because of his ascent to the leadership of the citywide self-government institution. After Zeng's voluntary withdrawal from reelection in this general chamber, he partnered with Yan Yibin and other Ningbo leaders of the Shanghai GCC in the Jiangxi Porcelain Company (Jiangxi ciqi gongsi) in 1907. They even planned to establish more than a dozen branches of the company in China, Europe, and North America.[52]

Consequently, Li Houyou, an elite merchant member of the wealthy Li lineage from Ningbo, won the election for president in 1907, but the vice president was Sun Duosen, a merchant titleholder from a more powerful official family of Anhui origin. In addition to their different regional ties, both Li and Sun brought their familial relations into the general chambers. From 1905, Sun Duosen and his brother, Sun Duoxin, joined the Shanghai GCC together as representatives of their flour mill, and the former had been a director before he became vice president. The Suns' flour mill had founded more than seventeen branches in large cities including Beijing and Hankou as well as Lower Yangzi towns such as Jiangyan. In 1910, this mill led four other flour mills to form a specific association for managing the wheat trade (*banmai gonghui*) in Shanghai and the counties of Wuxi and Gaoyou as well as the town of Jiang-yan. Their petition received governmental approval because of strong support from the Shanghai GCC.[53]

Li Houyou also used the Shanghai GCC to expand his familial connections and businesses, but the expansion of such personal relations in return broadened the chamber networks. Although Li lost the position of president in 1908, he remained vice president of the general chamber that year. Between 1908 and 1911, his two brothers, Li Weizhuang and Li Zhengwu, successively joined the general chambers as individual associate members. His two other brothers, Li Hongxiang and Li Xieqing, at one point were full members.[54] Li Houyou's long engagement in the Shanghai GCC brought him into partner-ship with chamber leaders in many business ventures and in different cities. In 1908, he partnered with the former vice president of the Suzhou GCC, Ni Sijiu, and the major leader of the South Shanghai BCC, Wang Zhen, to form an insurance company. They also established branches of their com-pany in seven different cities and ensured that these branches would receive protection from chambers of commerce there. In 1909, Li Houyou even tried to establish the Chinese Merchant Bank (Zhongguo huashang yinhang) with capital from all Chinese chambers of commerce at home and abroad. His brother, Li Zhengwu, made a special trip to Southeast Asia to collect investment funds from Chinese merchants there. Their plan for this bank received positive responses from chamber leaders both inside and outside of China, although it ultimately proved too ambitious to realize.[55]

Li Houyou was succeeded as president by a more senior elite merchant of Ningbo origin, Zhou Jinbiao, a former magistrate, the vice president of the Shanghai CCA, and a veteran director of the Shanghai GCC from 1904. Because Zhou was the general manager of the Imperial Telegraph Adminis-tration, both his official connections and his Ningbo native-place ties helped him retain the position of president in the Shanghai GCC for three consecu-tive years from 1908 to 1910. The Ningbo dominance in the major leadership of the general chamber also experienced a heyday in 1908–1909, as the two successive vice presidents, Li Houyou and Yan Yibin, were Zhou's prefectural fellows.[56]

Nevertheless, the major leadership of the Shanghai GCC finally shifted away from the hands of these Ningbo elite merchants with close official connections. When the aforementioned lot-drawing method was first used to enforce partial retirement of incumbent directors at the beginning of 1910, both Yan Yibin and his family business representative, Chen Ziqin,

SH GCC use of chamber networks continued

lost their positions, as did Li Houyou. The final blow to Ningbo dominance in the Shanghai GCC came in late 1910, when the Qing court blamed mismanagement by Zhou Jinbiao for a stock market crisis and dismissed him from the office of president.[57]

In early 1911, Chen Runfu, a native banker of Jiangxi origin, won the election as president, not unexpectedly as previous studies have usually assumed. In fact, Chen was one of the very few directors who had survived personnel reshuffles in the Shanghai CCA and the Shanghai GCC between 1902 and 1911. He was twice ranked just behind the successful candidates for the president and vice president in terms of ballots they received from the annual elections of 1909 and 1910. Moreover, the two successive vice presidents of the Shanghai GCC in 1910 and 1911, Shao Qintao and Bei Runsheng, were both Jiangsu natives and leading elite merchants in foreign trades, and neither they nor Chen had strong official connections as Yan Xinhou and Zhou Jinbiao once had.[58] Thus, their entry into the major leadership of the Shanghai GCC reflected the decline of Ningbo dominance and the rise of elite merchant leaders from other regional groups and the business world. To be sure, the Ningbo elite merchants still had strong influence in the Shanghai GCC, but they henceforth had to rely more on collaboration with leaders of other regional groups, and they would not be able to take back major leadership until their provincial fellows dominated the Shanghai government after the 1911 Revolution.

Like the Shanghai GCC, the Hangzhou GCC also experienced continual reshuffles in its top leadership. In particular, annual elections gradually replaced its early leaders of gentry origin with elite merchants from the most important businesses. When this general chamber appeared in late 1906, its first president, Fan Gongxu, was a former metropolitan official, a gentry manager of charities, and a promoter of reformist institutions in Hangzhou, while the first vice president, Gu Hongzao, was a holder of the prestigious *daotai* title. However, neither Fan nor Gu were deeply involved in business activities. In 1907 and 1908, Fan and Gu's positions were taken over by, respectively, Jin Yuesheng, a salt merchant, and Pan Chiwen, a native banker. Like Fan, both Jin and Pan were leading philanthropists. Moreover, Jin Yuesheng could keep his position of president for two years partly because his brother was an official in charge of the Hangzhou branch of the Qing State Bank (Da-Qing yinhang).[59]

In early 1909, Jin's leadership became increasingly unpopular because he had helped Gao Fengde, the president of the Gongchenqiao ACC, to avoid paying back official loans and merchant investments in a cotton mill managed by the latter. Thus, in the election of March 1909, Jin presented his resignation in advance but actually tried to renew his tenure through the support of his associates. At the electoral meeting, the full members first elected new directors, who were supposedly to vote for president and vice president. However, before the election for the directors was over, Jin was reelected by his associates. This fake election was challenged by a bank manager, and Jin had to relinquish the position. Thereafter, Pan Chiwen became the new president, and the vice president, Gu Songqing, in turn replaced Pan in 1910. Although Gu held the low degree of licentiate (*xiucai*), he had started his business career as a small fan merchant and had been a guild leader in both the salt and foreign goods trades. The new vice president, Wang Xirong, was also a holder of the licentiate degree but worked as a pawnshop manager.[60] Thus, the Hangzhou GCC gradually came under the control of leaders with wider connections in the merchant community.

Both the Ningbo and Jiangning GCC experienced similar personnel and relational changes in their major leadership positions. The Ningbo GCC appeared in early 1906 with Wu Chuanji, a former prefect, as its president. Its first vice president, Gu Zhao, was a local manager of the semiofficial enterprise, the China Merchants' Steam Navigation Company. However, their respective successors, Qin Yunbing and Zheng Xianzi, were merchant holders of purchased titles. The former managed two business establishments in Ningbo and Shanghai, and the latter was a guild leader in the paper trade. As a business partner of Gu Zhao and other chamber directors in a cotton mill, Zheng went on to become president in 1909.[61] Similarly, the first president of the Jiangning GCC in 1904 and 1905, Liu Shihang, was the official director of the Jiangnan General Bureau of Commerce.[62] In contrast, the third president of this general chamber in 1909 and 1910, Song Enquan, was the manager of a native bank and a guild leader in that trade. Song lacked official connections because he could not handle the document formalities in communications with the government, but his native bank had twenty-four branches within and outside of the Lower Yangzi region. One of its branches was in Shanghai, and the branch manager, Ding Jiahou, was a director of the Shanghai GCC from 1907 to 1910.[63]

Unlike the four aforementioned general chambers of commerce, the Suzhou GCC and Tong-Chong-Hai GCCC were under long leadership of their first presidents, You Xianjia and Zhang Cha, but the two long-tenured leaders still underwent profound changes in their social relations. In fact, You and Zhang came from gentry and official backgrounds, respectively. In addition to gentry prestige and official connections, the two leaders could

SZ + TCH GCC- long tenured presidents
b/c of close business relations

repeatedly win merchant support in annual elections and enjoyed unusually long tenures because they had skillfully used their positions to develop close relations with the business world, especially with other chamber leaders of merchant origin.

The Suzhou GCC in 1905 initiated the rule limiting the tenure of its major leaders to three consecutive years, but its first president, You Xianjia, probably kept his position longer than any of his counterparts in the Lower Yangzi region. You had been the president of the Suzhou GCC from 1905 to 1912, except in 1909 when he followed the governmental rule to vacate the position in favor of a merchant titleholder, Zhang Lüqian, for one year.[64] Thus, You and Zhang served as the two only presidents of the general chamber in the late Qing period, although they came from different backgrounds.

You Xianjia had pursued an official career through civil service examinations until the age of forty but received only the title of provincial graduate and a secretarial position in the Grand Secretariat (Neige). At his father's instruction, You stayed in Suzhou as a gentry manager of local public affairs and let his younger brother handle all the family businesses in the silk fabric and other trades. Thus, his gentry reputation in public affairs rather than his business experience made him a founder and first president of the Suzhou GCC in 1905. By contrast, Zhang Lüqian was the owner of a pawnshop and a major investor in the Suzhou Silk Filature (Sujing sichang) and the Suzhou Cotton Mill (Sulun shachang). Nevertheless, he had become a close merchant associate of You in local public affairs,[65] and they even led other chamber leaders around Suzhou in an effort to take control of the two industrial enterprises.

The Suzhou Silk Filature and Suzhou Cotton Mill started in 1896 with funds from both the Qing government and merchants including Zhang; these merchants originally received annual dividends at a rate of 7 percent of their investment. However, the two mills were unprofitable until 1903, when a gentry merchant suite of Sheng Xuanhui, the associate imperial commissioner of commerce, contracted the two mills for five years and reduced the dividend rate to 3 percent. Zhang and the other shareholders were resentful of the dividend reduction, and on their behalf, You in 1906 led the Suzhou GCC to petition the Ministry of Commerce for permission to transfer the two mills into the hands of Zhang and other merchant shareholders.[66]

In order to get official approval, You and other leaders of the Suzhou GCC promised to fund local business schools with an annual contribution of 10,000 taels from the profits of the two enterprises. Their effort received strong support from Zeng Zhu, the president of the Shanghai GCC, because this general chamber also included merchant investors in the two enterprises. However, these chamber leaders did not realize their plan until 1908, when the Suzhou GCC gathered shareholder representatives from chambers of commerce in five nearby prefectures for a public meeting and decided to have the two enterprises managed by themselves. They first selected Zhou Tingbi, a long-term director of the Shanghai GCC and first president of the Wuxi-Jinkui ACC, as general manager of the two mills. In 1909, You, Zhang, and other leaders of the Suzhou GCC replaced Zhou with Wang Tongyu, an honorary member of the general chamber, and they filled other managerial positions in the two mills. Thus, under You's leadership, the Suzhou GCC not only brought the two enterprises into its membership and put them under the collective domination of its leaders but also turned the two business ventures into new links with other chambers of commerce around Suzhou.[67]

The first president of the Tong-Chong-Hai GCCC, Zhang Cha, also kept an unusually long tenure from 1904 to 1909 because he had developed close relations with local elite merchants. After his brother, Zhang Jian, left the Beijing court for the local textile industry in the mid-1890s, Zhang Cha followed suit, resigned from his position of county magistrate, and managed a succession of textile, reclamation, and other enterprises around Tongzhou. The success of these enterprises made the Zhang brothers more influential than local officials, and thus Zhang Cha naturally became a major founder and leader of the Tong-Chong-Hai GCCC.[68]

Through this general chamber, the Zhang brothers built new relations with elite merchants in nearby counties and in Shanghai and further linked local businesses to the Zhangs' textile empire. No sooner had the Tong-Chong-Hai GCCC come into being in late 1904 than Zhang Cha, together with the presidents of its three affiliated chambers and the major leaders of the Shanghai GCC, petitioned the Ministry of Commerce to regulate the cotton and cotton cloth markets centered around Shanghai. Then the leaders of the Tong-Chong-Hai GCCC and its affiliated chambers asked the Jiangnan General Bureau of Commerce in Jiangning for extensive rights to supervise local cotton and cotton cloth trades. Clearly, the Zhang brothers and other chamber leaders around Tongzhou effectively used the new chamber networks to expand their relations and dominance into the business world beyond their local area.[69]

As for the affiliated and branch chambers of commerce in small cities and market towns, their major leaders went through annual elections and personnel changes similar to those in the aforementioned general chambers.

Available data from *Shangwu guanbao* (Gazette of Commercial Administration) show that very few of these chamber leaders were able to keep their tenures longer than the three-year limit by claiming difficulty in finding suitable successors or making other excuses.[70] Although details about these chamber leaders are hard to find, the records of one power struggle in the Kunshan-Xinyang ACC and another in its branch chamber in the town of Lujiabang provide rare insights into the personnel and relational changes among the elite merchant leaders at the grass-roots level of chamber networks. In particular, the two cases demonstrate how power struggles intensified personnel changes among these chamber leaders and prompted them to seek alliances beyond the chasm between their native-place groups, the difference between their gentry and merchant backgrounds, and the geographical limits of their cities and towns.

The twin-county city of Kunshan and Xinyang was near Suzhou, and its native gentry and sojourning merchants had long mingled in local trades. Thus, they jointly founded an affiliated chamber in 1906 and elected a merchant titleholder of Ningbo origin, Li Qingzhao, as its president. As the major leader of the Kunshan-Xinyang ACC, Li played an active role in the construction of roads, improvement of the local police, the sponsorship of business schools, and the installation of street lights. However, Li annoyed a few native merchants with his partiality to Ningbo natives in handling business disputes, and he further offended native gentry with his attempt to transfer the newly created local police from their hands to merchant management. From late 1907, a few native gentry and their merchant associates lodged a succession of complaints against Li. In particular, they charged him with directing his shop clerk to weave bamboo articles in the county temple for Confucius, thereby profaning the sacred building. The two magistrates of Kunshan and Xinyang counties found Li innocent, but they still requested that the Jiangsu governor and the Ministry of Agriculture, Industry, and Commerce dismiss Li from the post of chamber president.[71]

This power struggle seemed to pit a Ningbo merchant leader against native gentry, but Li was able to use his chamber network to rally supporters across regional and social divisions. His supporters included both native and nonnative elite merchants among the chamber directors, especially Fang Huan, a founder of the affiliated chamber and a native scholar with the degree of imperial college student. Fang persuaded Li to seek a compromise with the native gentry by donating 200 silver dollars for the temple, and he also prevented Li from the humiliating dismissal through communications with the Suzhou GCC. At his request, this general chamber petitioned the Jiangsu governor to let Li withdraw from reelection gracefully at the end of his tenure.[72]

Nevertheless, the Kunshan-Xinyang ACC in September 1908 still elected Li as president for a third term. The enraged native gentry resumed their attacks on Li's profaning of the temple for Confucius, filing a new lawsuit with the Jiangsu governor. Fang again came to Li's defense through personal contacts with the Suzhou GCC and a direct petition to the Jiangsu governor, although Li finally resigned from his position under the pressure. In December 1908, the Kunshan-Xinyang ACC held another election and chose Fang Huan as its president. Fang had engaged in local business through partnership with merchants, and his close relations with such merchant leaders as Li enabled him to keep his position until July 1911. By that time, Fang had already become an influential member of the Jiangsu Provincial Assembly (Jiangsu ziyiju) and had also entered the National Assembly (Zizhengyuan). Thus, he resigned from his position in the affiliated chamber, paving the way for Li to win the position back through a new election. This case shows how two chamber leaders from different geographical and social backgrounds shared power between them and further developed their sociopolitical relations from the county up to the national level.[73]

Under the Kunshan-Xinyang ACC, the branch chamber in the town of Lujiabang underwent a much longer-lasting power struggle among local elite merchant leaders, but the intensive rivalry similarly forced them to explore and expand their relations with elite individuals and institutions beyond the local society. In May 1907, the creation of the Lujiabang BCC was initiated by local tea and meat merchants after their clash over surcharges for new schools with Zhang Yugao, a school director who held the degree of supplementary government student (fusheng) and owned a wine shop. This branch chamber recruited eight representatives from different trades as its full members, including at least five holders of lower degrees. Its chief director, Chen Guojun, was a military government student (wusheng) in the firewood business. Chen claimed he would protect any merchants who had registered under the branch chamber and made a donation to it. In total, the branch chamber included more than twenty elite and nonelite merchants as its full and associate members, although Lujiabang had more than 100 shops.[74]

Unable to collect the school surcharge from the local merchants, Zhang incited other school directors in the town and the county city to lodge complaints about the Lujiabang BCC with the Suzhou GCC. But Chen and other chamber leaders received support from the Kunshan-Xinyang ACC under President Li Qingzhao. The affiliated chamber in the county city first dispatched Li's son and three other members to give supportive speeches at the inaugural meeting of the Lujiabang BCC and then helped Chen and other leaders obtain approval from the Ministry of Agriculture, Industry, and Commerce in June 1907. It also refuted Zhang's attack on the branch chamber in an investigation report submitted to the Suzhou GCC.[75] Thus, the Lujiabang BCC effectively used its relations with the Kunshan–Xinyang ACC to achieve success in this first round of the power struggle.

Nevertheless, after Chief Director Chen Guojun died in 1908, Zhang Yugao was able to expand his personal influence into the Lujiabang BCC because its new leader was related to Zhang by marriage through their children. In a new twist in the power struggle, the branch chamber in August 1909 elected as chief director Zhu Jinshou, a former gentry director of the adjacent town of Huajiaqiao and the rival of Zhang in a previous lawsuit. Zhu held a low-ranking official title, had investments in a rice and cloth shop, and also managed a local newspaper. His entry into the chamber leadership helped bring more merchant participants from the town of Huajiaqiao into the Lujiabang BCC, but his leadership immediately came under Zhang's attack.[76]

At the time, Zhang Yugao had become a member of the Kunshan–Xinyang Office for Self-Government Preparation (Kun–Xin choubei zizhi gongsuo) at the county level, and he incited members of this office to file a charge against Zhu with the Suzhou GCC. Because the new president of the Kunshan–Xinyang ACC, Fang Huan, shared Zhang's interest in new schools, he rendered support to Zhang and ordered the Lujiabang BCC to hold another election for chief director. The second election in October 1909 allowed all elite and common merchant participants in the branch chamber to cast votes equally, and a majority of them again elected Zhu as chief director. In the following month, Zhang pushed Fang to hold yet a third election in the Lujiabang BCC, and the former brought more than 100 supporters to the electoral meeting. However, this electoral meeting ended in an uproar among members of the Lujiabang BCC. Thereafter, Fang hatched a plan to assimilate the Lujiabang BCC into a new branch chamber representing several nearby towns, but the Lujiabang BCC rejected the plan and still petitioned for its survival to the Suzhou GCC on July 12, 1911. Incredibly, only two days later, Zhang suddenly won another election for chief director of the branch chamber. It is unclear how Zhang became the final winner of the four-year power struggle, but he undoubtedly benefited from his relations with Fang, who had moved into the political arena at both the provincial and national levels, as mentioned above.[77]

[handwritten annotation at top: power struggles → how Qing elites used new institutions to seek local dominance]

The power struggles around the Kunshan-Xinyang ACC and the Lujia-bang BCC reveal how the late Qing elites at the county and township levels used the new institutions to seek and strengthen their local dominance. Previous studies of these local elites have already indicated that they differed from urban reformist elites because the former faced fewer imperialist threats than the latter and thus were more prone to pursue personal rather than national interests.[78] In fact, the foregoing discussion demonstrates that chamber leaders pursued personal wealth and power in both large cities and market towns. The difference in their behaviors was attributable not only to their varied sociopolitical environments but also to the different degrees of institutional checks on their personal and cliquish dominance. Because the chamber networks experienced earlier and fuller development in large cities than in towns, their institutional devices, such as competitive elections and limited tenure, were more effective in checking the personal and cliquish oligarchy of elite merchants in metropolitan settings than in township societies, as the leadership changes in the Shanghai GCC and the Lujiabang BCC demonstrated.

In spite of the difference between the metropolitan and township chambers, they universally recruited increasingly diverse elite merchants through institutionalized personnel changes and even through power struggles in the form of periodic elections. Meanwhile, these elite merchants also used the chamber networks to expand their collective dominance and interrelations beyond their personal cliques and respective locales. It was through such personnel and relational changes that the Lower Yangzi chambers of commerce gradually encompassed and integrated heterogeneous merchant participants, especially elite merchants from large cities to market towns. They also promoted the general trend of social integration by expanding their relations and influence into other sociopolitical organizations and activities.

[handwritten notes at bottom:]
- chambers recruited diverse elite merchants through elections, power struggles
- elite merchants used chamber networks to expand influence
- LY CCs → heterogeneous merchants

4

The Expansion of Associational
Networks and Influences

[handwritten margin note: gov't support of SH CCA w/ foreign authority clashes / arrests]

The Lower Yangzi chambers of commerce expanded their concerns from their merchant constituencies to community and national issues from the beginning. As their forerunner, the Shanghai CCA had operated partly as an advisory body for Qing officials in the negotiations with foreign diplomats over commercial treaties, although its participation in this diplomatic issue faced various official restrictions.[1] It also entered in direct struggles with foreign authorities in the International Settlement because Chinese residents always suffered discrimination there. In particular, the settlement police often arrested Chinese businessmen in humiliating ways, gripping their queues (braids of hair) in public or chaining them together with burglars. Through petitions to the Qing government and negotiations with foreign authorities, the Shanghai CCA obtained the legal right to post bail for indicted "respectable" merchants and save them from disgraceful arrest and custody. It even planned to select twelve of its directors as a committee for the protection of Chinese "face" (*timian*) and other interests in the settlement.[2]

The Shanghai CCA set a precedent for other chambers of commerce in the Lower Yangzi region. As its successor, the Shanghai GCC led a citywide protest in January 1905 after a Russian sailor received only a four-year prison sentence from a Russian tribunal for killing a Ningbo worker. On January 14, the general chamber gathered leaders of various regional and occupational guilds for an emergency meeting. It demanded that the Qing and foreign authorities retry the Russian convict and resolved to achieve its aim by boycotting Russian goods. This protest forced the Russian consul to extend the sentence

[handwritten margin note: – clashes b/w foreign powers – influenced Russian consul]

for the convict to eight years, and it became a direct prelude to the anti-American boycott starting from mid-1905.[3]

In the boycott against American discriminatory policy toward Chinese, the Shanghai GCC played a crucial role in coordinating numerous Chinese organizations, especially merchant guilds and chambers of commerce, for collective actions both in the Lower Yangzi region and throughout the country. It also initiated a new trend for these chambers of commerce and other social organizations to collaborate in their efforts to found, reform, and control communal institutions in their cities and towns. As a result, these chambers expanded personnel and institutional relations with other professional associations in commerce, agriculture, and education, as well as with the new paramilitary forces, the merchant militias (*shangtuan*).

Actually, in terms of both chronological sequence and organizational influence, the Lower Yangzi chambers of commerce pioneered the development of many new professional associations even though they still relied on personal relations, such as kinship and the local fellowship of their elite merchant leaders, for network expansion.[4] More important, the chamber networks significantly institutionalized these personal ties and expanded more formal relations with diverse sociopolitical organizations. In the forefront of this network revolution, these chambers of commerce greatly promoted social integration in the nation, inside their cities or towns, and among different professions through their engagements in nationalistic, community, and professional activities beyond the boundary of their business world.

CCS → developed new professional associations

Network Development and Mobilization in the 1905 Boycott

– led anti-American boycott, 1905

The Shanghai GCC led the anti-American boycott of 1905 together with other organizations for merchants, intellectuals, students, women, and others. Previous studies have generally regarded such collective action in the boycott as a result of a national awakening or of broader social changes, such as the appearance of new media, communications, and associations.[5] These studies have also examined the respective activities of the Shanghai GCC, the native-place associations in the treaty port, the Chinese Empire Reform Association (Baohuanghui) overseas, as well as other intellectual and popular organizations.[6] What has been downplayed in previous scholarship and needs to be detailed in this study is how the Lower Yangzi chambers of commerce, especially the Shanghai GCC, served as the central nodes of interaction among the different sociopolitical forces, expanded relations with varied urban organizations, and helped bring them into a nationwide boycott.

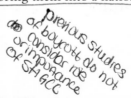
previous studies do of boycott do not consider role or importance of SH GCC

The seeds of this boycott had been sown in the United States decades before the 1905 boycott. From the mid-nineteenth century, Chinese and especially Cantonese immigrants had arrived in the American West to provide cheap labor for the gold rush, railroad building, and other economic activities. However, in the 1870s, the completion of the Central Pacific Railroad and the aggravation of economic depression intensified competition in the labor market and caused the trade unions of white laborers and a few racist groups to launch rallies, riots, and even massacres against Chinese immigrants. Consequently, the American government enacted a series of exclusion acts to prohibit Chinese labor immigration from 1882 and pressed the Qing court to accept these prohibitive measures through two successive treaties in 1880 and 1894. After the United States annexed Hawaii and the Philippines around 1898, the Chinese Exclusion Acts were further extended to the two archipelagos. Moreover, the American authorities subjected not only Chinese laborers but also scholars, students, merchants, and even diplomats to harsh and humiliating treatment in ports of entry.[7] In 1905, the decades of American racism finally triggered a Chinese boycott against renewal of the 1894 treaty governing labor migration from China to the United States, but the boycott also occurred because the newly formed chambers of commerce provided a concrete channel to merge the rising Chinese nationalism at home and abroad.

The call for an anti-American boycott was first issued by the Shanghai GCC at its meeting on May 10, 1905, an event that has received constant mention but little scrutiny in previous studies. This meeting merits reexamination because it gathered not only leaders of the general chamber and its affiliated guilds but also reporters of major Shanghai newspapers and the junior councilor of the Ministry of Commerce, Yang Shiqi. Moreover, it was not the major leaders of the Shanghai GCC but a director from the relatively small Fujian merchant group, Zeng Zhu, who delivered the opening speech at this meeting. Zeng was followed by an eloquent speaker, Ge Pengyun, a guild leader of silverware shops and an intellectual activist with an American education, but he was neither a director nor a full member of the general chamber.[8] The gathering of these merchants, intellectuals, and a metropolitan official, as well as the unusual meeting procedure, suggest that this boycott was a carefully planned movement from its beginning, rather than the decentralized and disorganized movement depicted by previous studies.[9]

The plans for the anti-American boycott first appeared in newspapers with overt or covert relations to the Chinese Empire Reform Association, which Kang Youwei established overseas after the failure of the 1898 Reform. In

1903, this association's newspaper in Honolulu, *Xin Zhongguo bao* (New China Daily), first proposed using a boycott against American goods to push for the repeal of the Chinese Exclusion Acts. This boycott proposal was later transferred to China through *Shibao* (The Eastern Times), a Shanghai newspaper with secret links to Kang.[10] Another major newspaper in Shanghai, *Shenbao* (Shanghai Daily), joined in propaganda for the boycott later on and became a major mouthpiece of the Shanghai GCC in the movement probably because its Chinese manager, Xi Zipei, was a full member of the general chamber, and its editors had recently decided to support Kang's reformist cause.[11] boycott promoted in newspapers

Meanwhile, Qing officials were also involved in the boycott plan and helped make the Shanghai GCC the leading organization in this movement. The Chinese minister in Washington, Liang Cheng, had started negotiations with the American government in 1903 for revision of the immigration treaty. After American officials rejected treaty revision with the excuse of pressure from trade unions, a communication from Liang to the Ministry of Foreign Affairs (Waiwubu) proposed breaking the diplomatic impasse through an anti-American boycott. He specifically suggested a boycott led by the newly formed chambers of commerce in China, which, like trade unions in the United States, were nonofficial organizations. Liang cautioned the Qing government not to offer public support to such a popular boycott so as to avoid any international confrontation. His letter reached the Ministry of Foreign Affairs in Beijing on January 12, 1905, less than four months before the Shanghai GCC launched the boycott. It undoubtedly affected the Qing court's policy in early May, when American minister William Rockhill was due to arrive in Beijing for direct treaty negotiations.[12] As detailed below, Qing officials in Beijing and Shanghai initially helped and handled the boycott exactly as Liang had suggested. *consion*

The Shanghai GCC launched the boycott after its leaders, especially Zeng Zhu, made contacts with Qing officials and the literati reformers under Kang Youwei's influence. In a letter dated June 7, 1905, Liang Qichao, a right-hand man of Kang, claimed that his fellows in *Shibao* had secretly contacted Zeng Zhu and other leaders of the Shanghai GCC in preparation for the boycott meeting of the general chamber on May 10. In the editorial office of *Shibao* in Shanghai, two staff members with the assumed names of Gao De and Gao Shan also sent a secret report to Kang Youwei on June 22, confirming that more than twenty leaders of the Shanghai GCC, including Zeng, had discussed the boycott plan beforehand. Meanwhile, *Shibao* contacted other newspapers, all of which promised to support the movement. The two "Gaos" even

[margin handwritten: ccs launched boycott in place of the Qing, to not cause an international affair]

[bottom handwritten: newspapers, Qing, KYW's reformers + GCC all together in anti-US boycott]

claimed to have brought Yang Shiqi and other higher officials in the Qing court into the secret plan in advance.[13]

Thus, the preparations for the boycott involved various elements ranging from reformist exiles to their political foes in the Qing court, but the Shanghai GCC served as a crucial link for their joint actions. On May 9, *Shibao* published an advance notice for the boycott meeting of the Shanghai GCC to be held the following day. On the morning of May 10, both the *Shibao* and *Shenbao* published an identical proclamation on behalf of an anti-American boycott, thereby further mobilizing public support for the imminent meeting of the general chamber. That afternoon, the Shanghai GCC held the boycott meeting that had already received wide attention through the two major newspapers in the city.[14] After Zeng Zhu and Ge Pengyun delivered impassioned speeches at the meeting, its participants were so moved that they unanimously endorsed Zeng's proposal to ban the use of American goods unless the American government modified its immigration acts within two months. However, the official attendee to the meeting, Yang Shiqi, opposed the usage of the term "ban" in the boycott resolution because it would imply a governmental embargo on American goods. Yang's opinion led to an hour of hot debates, and the meeting finally adopted another slogan: "Stop using American goods through mutual exhortation."[15]

The meeting then decided to telegraph its resolution to the Ministry of Commerce and the Ministry of Foreign Affairs, the Zhili and Liangjiang governors-general who respectively supervised treaty ports in northern and southern China, and chambers of commerce in twenty-one large cities. Yang again helped draft these telegrams, but he kept his involvement a secret so as to conceal official connections with the boycott. After the telegrams were drafted, the major leaders of the Shanghai GCC were still reluctant to send them out under their names. Zeng Zhu again stepped forward, voiced his determination to sacrifice himself for the public interest, and signed his name to the telegrams. This brave action won him thunderous applause.[16] Three days later, President Yan Xinhou and four other leaders of the Shanghai GCC joined Yang in sending out a secret telegram that further informed other chambers of commerce of the boycott plan.[17]

The boycott resolution of the Shanghai GCC received enthusiastic response at home and abroad, and this general chamber soon formed relations with various boycott-supporting organizations, especially those in Shanghai. Among its affiliated guilds, those of Guangdong and Fujian merchants held meetings on May 12 and 14. Both guilds vowed to follow the boycott resolution of the general chamber and developed more concrete measures that targeted

American companies, schools, and so on. Other merchant and literati organizations also followed the Shanghai GCC in holding public meetings. On
May 21, the Shanghai Study Society (Huxuehui), a group of leading scholars
and educated youths, and the Commercial Study Society (Shangxuehui), a
symbiotic organization of the Shanghai GCC, respectively held meetings to
support the boycott decision of the general chamber.[18] By May 21, when
new American minister Rockhill arrived in Shanghai, the general chamber
had received supportive telegrams from chambers of commerce and similar
organizations in Tianjin, Hankou, Canton, Hong Kong, and other cities.[19]

With such widespread support, the Shanghai GCC appeared as a key player
in the treaty negotiation between the Qing court and the United States, and
its leaders became increasingly assertive in front of both the Chinese and
American officials. Right after the Shanghai GCC's first boycott meeting on
May 10, junior and senior councilors of the Ministry of Commerce, Yang
Shiqi and Wang Qingmu, jointly sent a telegram from Shanghai to Beijing,
requesting that the Qing court postpone renewal of the immigration treaty
with the United States until the American government yielded to the Shanghai GCC's demands. Meanwhile, in an audience with President Roosevelt,
Minister Liang likened the boycott by Chinese chambers of commerce to
the anti–Chinese actions of American trade unions and claimed that the Qing
court, like the American government, could not intervene in such popular
movements. Consequently, the newly arrived Minster Rockhill and American
diplomats in Shanghai had to invite the leaders of the Shanghai GCC for a
direct talk.[20]

On the morning of May 21, Zeng and seven other leaders of the general
chamber, including its president, Yan Xinhou, and its vice president, Xu Run,
attended an unprecedented meeting between Chinese merchant leaders and
foreign diplomats. At the beginning of their meeting, the Americans promised a treaty that would prohibit only Chinese laborer immigration but provide courteous treatment to other Chinese travelers. However, they explained
that such a treaty would need the ratification of the Congress six months later.
In response, Zeng prescribed a two-month period starting from May 21, the
day of their meeting, for the American government to revise its exclusion
treaty or face a boycott.[21]

That same afternoon, the Shanghai GCC held a second boycott meeting with more than 200 attendees. Speakers at this meeting included former
students and travelers to the United States, their personal stories of suffering
from American mistreatments further arousing public indignation. Zeng
restated the determination to boycott after briefing the participants on his

meeting with American diplomats in the morning, but he also criticized the Qing court for its ignorance of public opinion in diplomatic negotiations with foreign governments. He then proposed a motion to telegraph Chinese Ministry Liang in Washington for accurate information about the treaty negotiation, and his motion received unanimous approval at the end of the meeting.[22]

After this meeting, Zeng successively sent two letters to the Ministry of Foreign Affairs, requesting it to sign the treaty reviewed by the Shanghai GCC and merchants in the city. He even asked the ministry to consult "gentry-merchants" as a routine practice in its future treaty negotiations with foreign powers. In his public letters to the major leaders of the general chamber, Zeng again criticized the conventional approach of the Qing government to treaty negotiations because it had never asked for merchant opinions. Thus, under his leadership, the movement gradually went beyond official expectations. Meanwhile, the Shanghai GCC conducted an investigation of American goods. It found that flour was the major American commodity and that Shanghai bakeries used most of the imported American flour. Under its pressure, the guild leader of this trade signed a pledge on June 10, promising to use only native flour thereafter.[23]

In response to the Shanghai GCC's call, scholars, students, women, and other urban residents also founded their own organizations and held public meetings to discuss the boycott issue, but they all collaborated closely with the general chamber.[24] On June 6, the Shanghai Study Society gathered representatives from twenty-six colleges, middle schools, women's schools, and other educational institutions as well as various intellectual organizations for a meeting. They decided to send delegates to the Shanghai GCC to serve as regular liaison so that they could continuously exchange opinions about boycott tactics with chamber leaders. The Shanghai GCC immediately accepted the suggestion for such cooperative action.[25]

In other treaty ports, large cities, and even overseas Chinese communities, numerous individuals and organizations, including chambers of commerce, also expressed support to the Shanghai GCC through telegrams, letters, and meetings. In the Lower Yangzi region, the newly formed chambers of commerce actively followed the Shanghai GCC's leadership in the boycott, and they in turn played the leading role in the movement within their own cities. The Jiangning and Zhejiang GCCs as well as the Tong-Chong-Hai GCCC, together with their affiliated chambers, quickly informed their local merchants of the boycott resolution and contacted the Shanghai GCC for the schedule and plans for future actions. Other social groups, including women's organizations, also responded quickly to the general chamber's call and took active part in the movement.[26]

In the face of a nationwide boycott in China, President Theodore Roosevelt on June 24 issued an executive order to American authorities, requiring them to "show the wisest and heartiest courtesy to all merchants, teachers, students, and travelers" as well as officials from China.[27] Meanwhile, both the American minister, Rockhill, in Beijing and the Zhili governor-general, Yuan Shikai, in Tianjin pressed the Qing government to ban the boycott. Qing officials in Beijing and Shanghai were also eager to moderate and even terminate the boycott. On June 29, the Ministry of Foreign Affairs in Beijing ordered provincial officials to dampen merchant animosity toward the American government and dissuade them from extreme actions. On July 4, Junior Councilor Yang in Shanghai responded to the telegram with a proposal to postpone the boycott for four months until the American Congress resumed its sessions and could revise the Chinese Exclusion Acts. Some of the Shanghai GCC's major leaders were prone to accept Yang's proposal, but Zeng and other boycott leaders were unwilling to do so. Zeng restated the resolution to carry out a boycott after the two-month waiting period, which would end on July 20, and he also declared that the Chinese people had the right to boycott American goods. Although the Qing government could ban people from public meetings, it could not force them to use American goods.[28]

Under Zeng's leadership, the Shanghai GCC eventually turned its boycott resolution into an actual movement through close collaboration with other elite and mass organizations. On July 19, just one day before the end of the two-month waiting period, the Shanghai Study Society held a meeting with more than 1,400 attendees, including delegates from new schools, intellectual associations, the Shanghai GCC, the Commercial Study Society, and sixteen guilds in the treaty ports, as well as representatives from inland cities. Speakers at the meeting praised the unprecedented unity of intellectual and merchant communities in this boycott, but they also raised the critical issue of whether to stop using or ordering American goods after the probationary period. Participants at the meeting finally decided to submit the issue to the Shanghai GCC for deliberation. The Commercial Study Society then gathered more than 1,000 people for another meeting at 2:00 P.M. on July 20, two hours before the Shanghai GCC's eye-catching conference. This meeting unanimously resolved to stop using American goods and thus offered support to Zeng and other radical activists in the subsequent discussion on boycott strategies.[29]

The two meetings helped push the movement to its climax, the long expected conference of the Shanghai GCC on the afternoon of July 20, but
they also foreshadowed a divergence of boycott strategies. At the preliminary meeting prior to the conference, leaders of the Shanghai GCC and its
affiliated guilds vetoed a motion of a native banker to stop ordering American goods immediately but to stop using these goods four months later so
that merchants could dispose of their stock. At 4:00 P.M., Zeng formally opened
the meeting with the call for a nationwide boycott of American goods, and
his speech was then echoed by Ge Pengyun's vehement condemnation of
American mistreatment of Chinese and by another speaker's motion to stop
using and ordering American goods simultaneously.[30]

However, at the end of the conference, major leaders of the Shanghai GCC
stepped forward and presented a moderate boycott strategy on behalf of the
merchants who had large stocks of American goods. Zhou Jinbiao, a senior
director of the Shanghai GCC, proposed to stop ordering American goods
immediately and requested large merchants in every business to voluntarily
sign a pledge to do so. Subsequently, guild leaders of nine businesses, most of
whom were directors and full members of the Shanghai GCC, signed the
pledge amid thunderous cheers and applause. The conference then resolved
to telegraph thirty-five large cities to announce the beginning of the nationwide boycott, although it was unable to reach agreement on whether to stop
using or ordering American goods immediately.[31]

The Shanghai GCC assembled guild leaders for another meeting on July
31, and this meeting confirmed the moderate boycott strategy of its major
leaders. It decided to investigate the American goods that had been ordered
by merchants in each trade before its July 20 conference and to give special
permissions for the sale of these goods. But those merchants who continued
to order American goods after July 20 would face a boycott by the two native
banking guilds in Shanghai. The Shanghai Study Society on August 6 also
held a meeting with more than 2,000 people in attendance, and its major
leader and leading educator, Ma Xiangbo, presented a more moderate proposal to boycott goods cleared by American customs from the day of this
meeting, and to allow the previously ordered goods to be sold with stamps
of approval issued by the Shanghai GCC. The general chamber quickly adopted this plan on August 9, and its advertisements in Shanghai's main newspapers called on merchants and guilds to report their stocks of American
goods and to obtain its stamps of approval for sale of these goods thereafter.[32]
On August 19, the Ministry of Commerce endorsed this moderate strategy,

and the Shanghai GCC then continued its registration of American goods in Chinese hands and issued its approvals for their sale until early September.[33]

Meanwhile, Zeng Zhu's call to stop using American goods received support mainly from radical intellectuals, petty merchants, workers, and women, all of whom anticipated little personal loss from the nationalist movement. The radical boycott movement reached a new high tide after August 11 when Zeng revealed an alleged plot against him and published a farewell letter that expressed his willingness to die for the boycott.[34] Meanwhile, Zeng also led the movement through concrete communications with other boycott activists and organizations. During the boycott, Zeng worked in the office of the general chamber every evening and received thirty to forty letters daily. He not only copied and compiled them for publication in Shanghai newspapers but also sent out numerous letters and telegrams as replies, encouragement, and advice to boycotters and their organizations.[35]

The Shanghai GCC also used its institutional relations with other chambers of commerce to coordinate the nationalistic movement in the Lower Yangzi region and the whole country. At least thirty-three chambers of commerce in other treaty ports, provincial capitals, and large cities as well as overseas Chinese communities made contact with the Shanghai GCC through the mail and telegrams. Among them were twelve general and affiliated chambers of commerce located in Lower Yangzi cities.[36] After the Shanghai GCC announced the commencement of the nationwide boycott on July 20, these chambers quickly took action, holding public meetings and mobilizing their merchant members to sign boycott pledges. The Zhejiang GCC, the predecessor of the Hangzhou GCC, dispatched the boycott notice to all shops in the provincial capital and also sent the notice to its affiliated chambers throughout the province. Among these affiliated chambers, the one in Shimen County had held four boycott meetings by August 28. The Tong-Chong-Hai GCCC listed all brands of American goods in a public notice and called on its affiliated guilds and merchants to stop selling or buying these goods.[37]

The boycott resolution of the Shanghai GCC also received responses from elite individuals and organizations in dozens of Lower Yangzi towns and inspired their protest activities at the township level. Boycott meetings were repeatedly held in towns like Xiashi in northern Zhejiang, and one such meeting in Nanxun, another town in northern Zhejiang, attracted as many as 2,000 participants on July 20. In Nanxiang, a satellite town of Shanghai, merchant leaders of the boycott used the movement as an opportunity to found one of the earliest township chambers in the Lower Yangzi region.[38]

This boycott eventually exceeded the limits of official tolerance. Due to the official fear of popular radicalization and American reaction, the Qing court on August 31 issued an edict banning the boycott. This edict dealt a fatal blow to the movement, but Zeng Zhu continued his boycott activity. On December 15, 1905, he still led more than 1,000 people from twenty-one provinces in a petition to the Ministry of Foreign Affairs, calling for rejection of the immigration treaty with the United States. Although Minister Rockhill repeatedly pushed the Qing court to punish Zeng, the Qing government dared not take such action and risk a popular riot. In November 1905, Zeng won the election for president of the Shanghai GCC and successfully received recognition from the Ministry of Commerce in January 1906.[39] Under his leadership, this general chamber further expanded its networks and influence in the urban community, as did other chambers of commerce in the Lower Yangzi region.

Leadership in Communal Organizations and Activities

After the Shanghai GCC launched the anti-American boycott, the first urban nationalistic movement in modern Chinese history, its elite merchant leaders also helped create the earliest modern municipal government in late Qing China. Other chambers of commerce in the Lower Yangzi region followed suit to provide new municipal services or to reform the existing communal organizations in their cities and towns. Their community involvement reinforced the tendency of guild leaders and other elite merchants to manage charities and other public projects. However, as chamber leaders, they brought new institutional norms and influence into the communal organizations and changed the long-established gentry oligarchy in communal activities.

While the anti-American boycott was still going on in late 1905, the Shanghai GCC became involved in another nationalistic protest, the Mixed Court Riot. The Mixed Court had operated in the International Settlement since 1869, and it had originally allowed the Chinese magistrate to hear all Chinese cases and to work with foreign assessors in handling legal disputes between Chinese and foreigners. However, foreign assessors had long encroached on the magistrate's jurisdiction. On December 8, 1905, interference by the British assessor in the trial of a Cantonese woman by Magistrate Guan Jiongzhi led to a skirmish between the settlement police and Guan's runners and to forcible custody of the female suspect by the foreign police force.[40]

Magistrate Guan reported the incident first to the Shanghai *daotai* and then to the Shanghai GCC because the latter had long fought for Chinese legal rights in foreign concessions and was leading the anti-American boycott at that time. The enraged chamber leaders held a protest meeting with thousands of participants on December 9. This meeting not only demanded the dismissal of the British assessor and the assurance of Chinese rights in the Mixed Court but also requested Chinese representation on the municipal council of the International Settlement.[41] On December 18, protesters enforced a general strike in the International Settlement and set fire to a police station. The settlement police responded by firing at the protesters, killing at least eleven Chinese and injuring dozens of others.[42] At the time, the Shanghai GCC still called for a solution through official negotiations with the foreign powers, and the leaders of the general chamber and its affiliated guilds played the role of key mediators between the Qing and settlement authorities. As a result, the municipal council in February 1906 had to accept a "Chinese merchant consultative committee" (*Huashang gongyihui*) as the representative body of the Chinese, and the Shanghai GCC was able to depute sixteen of its twenty-one directors to sit on this committee. Unfortunately, the settlement's Ratepayers' Association rejected this Chinese committee.[43]

Despite this setback in the foreign concession, the leaders of the general chamber successfully worked with other urban elites and obtained local official permission to establish the General Works Board of Shanghai and Its Suburbs (Shanghai chengxiang neiwai zonggongcheng ju) in the Chinese districts. Previous studies have depicted this new communal organization not only as the earliest Chinese creation of modern municipal administration but also as "the first formally democratic political institution" in modern China.[44] However, its institutional and interpersonal relations with the Shanghai GCC have not received much attention in previous literature, including two Chinese monographs on the general chamber itself.[45]

After Zeng Zhu used the Shanghai GCC to launch the anti-American boycott in May 1905, he and other urban elites made a special contact with Shanghai Daotai Yuan Shuxun. They expressed apprehension for the growth of foreign power and the loss of national sovereignty in the Chinese districts of Shanghai due to the Qing government's failure to maintain streets, roads, and rivers there. With encouragement from the *daotai*, Zeng further consulted Li Zhongjue (Pingshu), an important figure in both local officialdom and gentry society. Li had lost his official position of magistrate because of his resistance to French intrusion near Canton and returned to Shanghai as a manager of the Jiangnan Arsenal (Jiangnan zhizaoju) and the Imperial Bank of China, but he also established new schools and reformist associations together with other urban elites. Zeng and Li brought more Shanghai elites into a petition to Daotai Yuan for the General Works Board on September 20, and they received Yuan's permission to organize this new institution for managing "all matters concerning main roads, electric lights and police."[46]

The plan for this new communal institution was praised by one foreign newspaper in Shanghai as the "first attempt at purely Chinese municipal representative government."[47] Indeed, the regulations of the General Works Board for the first time in Chinese history specified a separation between executive and policy-making branches. The Executive Committee (Canshihui) comprised one leading general director (*lingxiu zongdong*), four general managing directors (*banshi zongdong*), and heads of several district bureaus and administrative departments. It directly controlled a police force and a court. In contrast, the Deliberative Council (Yihui) consisted of thirty-three councilors (*yishi jingdong*) who could decide the annual budget and make other resolutions, but its decisions were to be implemented by the Executive Committee and its administrative departments. These departments, together with the police and court, performed varied functions pertaining to household registration, tax collection, public works, street sanitation, social security, and other matters.[48]

Despite the influence of Western models of representative government, the General Works Board was based mainly on indigenous organizations ranging from guilds and charitable halls to the Shanghai GCC. In particular, it shared many elite merchant leaders with the general chamber. In late 1905, the General Works Board held its first election to select candidates for its leadership positions among gentry directors of charitable halls, classic academies, and so on. It then held a second election among the merchant leaders of different guilds. The remaining candidates came from "nomination by public opinion." The short list of seventy-six candidates was then submitted to Daotai Yuan for formal appointment. As a result of these elections, both the new president and vice president of the Shanghai GCC, Zeng Zhu and Zhu Baosan, became two of the four earliest general managing directors on the General Works Board.[49] Zeng was especially influential on the board because he and Li Zhongjue, its leading general director, shared "great ambition and lofty ideas," as Li recollected later on.[50] Although the thirty-three councilors on the board included only two full members of the Shanghai GCC, Shi Zhaoxiang (Shanqi) and Zhang Lejun, many of the remaining councilors were leaders of guilds affiliated with the general chamber. For example, the speaker (*yizhang*) of the Deliberative Council, Yao Wennan, was a major leader of both local educational organizations and the rice guild affiliated with the Shanghai GCC.[51]

SH GCC dominate GW Board through relations

After the South Shanghai BCC appeared in 1906, its leaders and those of the Shanghai GCC further dominated the General Works Board through personnel and institutional interpenetration. In 1907 the board opened its primary election for directors and councilors to all local residents who were over twenty-five, had lived in the city over five years, and paid more than 10 silver dollars of local tax annually. However, an electoral college (*xuanjuju*) composed of representatives from the two chambers and other urban elite organizations would make the final choice from among the successful candidates in the primary election. Then the list of the newly elected directors would receive official approval rather than appointment.[52] On the new Executive Committee, the four general managing directors included the incumbent president of the Shanghai GCC, Li Houyou, and the major leader and a full member of the South Shanghai BCC, Wang Zhen and Yu Pinghan (Huaizhi). Li Zhongjue remained the leading general director and later became a director of the South Shanghai ACC. Among the thirty-three councilors of the board, at least six were directors or full members of the South Shanghai BCC around 1908.[53] Although the Shanghai GCC sent fewer representatives to the Deliberative Council than did the branch chamber, its former president, vice president, and a full member, Zeng Zhu, Zhu Baosan, and Zhang Lejun, became three newly established honorary directors, who would "participate in discussions of important issues."[54]

In addition to these personnel and institutional connections, the two chambers and the General Works Board collaborated closely to provide public services for the urban community. When flooding of the Yangzi River in June 1906 led to rice shortage in Shanghai, the Shanghai GCC and the General Works Board borrowed 100,000 *dan* (approximately 100,000 hectoliters) of rice from the government and let merchants sell the rice in local markets at a price set by the board. In July they purchased more rice from Hong Kong, Thailand, and other places and set up ten stations in the city and twenty others in its suburbs to sell the purchased rice to both urban and rural residents at a reduced price. Their joint operation lasted for nearly two months from August 9 to October 7, 1906. The South Shanghai BCC also helped the General Works Board in dealing with many municipal issues. In 1907 it received a special request from the board to nominate a police chief, and its nominee was readily accepted by the board. On the basis of the support of the two chambers and other elite organizations, the General Works Board significantly transformed the Chinese districts of Shanghai through its management of public construction, education, charity, and other municipal services before the Qing court launched the self-government reform around 1909.[55]

The two chambers of commerce in Shanghai also kept close relations with other communal organizations, especially those with a concern for municipal reforms. By 1908 the aforementioned chamber leaders and members including Li Houyou, Wang Zhen, Yu Pinghan, and Lin Jingzhou had founded or joined the Study Society for Local Self-Government (Difang zizhi yanjiuhui), the Study Society for Local Public Welfare (Difang gongyi yanjiuhui), the Urban Federation of Southeastern Neighborhoods (Dongnancheng difang lianhehui), the Urban Federation of Northwestern Neighborhoods (Xibeicheng difang lianhehui), and the Study Society for Family Reform (Jiazheng gailiang yanjiuhui). Among these five organizations, the first four and the two Shanghai chambers were institutional members of the electoral college of the General Works Board in 1907. The Study Society for Family Reform involved the wives of chamber leaders, such as Shen Manyun, and its periodic meetings repeatedly called for the eradication of sexism and superstition, for the promotion of female education, and for the reform of familial rituals.[56]

When Zeng Zhu became the president of the Shanghai GCC at the end of the 1905, he also founded the Society for Martial Exertion (Zhenwu zongshe) under the general chamber and used it to launch an anti-opium campaign nearly a year before the Qing court issued its own anti-opium edict. According to a report of the Shanghai GCC in 1906, this society had about 600 branches and 30,000 members, maintained surveillance over the opium market, and effectively persuaded many people to stop smoking opium. Its branches appeared not only in nearby cities, including Songjiang, but also spread to other provinces, such as Anhui and Hunan, and influenced young students and coal miners there. They vowed to clean up China's ill reputation as the "sick man of East Asia" (*Dongya bingfu*) and to revitalize a valiant spirit among Chinese people.[57]

Clearly, the two chambers of commerce in Shanghai extended their relations and influence deeply into the General Works Board and other community associations in this treaty port, and these organizations in turn promoted social reforms from the community to the familial and individual levels. Other Lower Yangzi cities and towns did not form new municipal institutions similar to those in Shanghai before the Qing government launched the self-government reform around 1909. Nevertheless, the chambers of commerce in these cities and towns still took on new municipal services as their own responsibilities or made attempts to reform the preexisting charitable halls after the model of the General Works Board in Shanghai. The links between the chambers and these community institutions provided their interlocking leaders with a powerful network to rally progressive elites from different social circles and to break up the community oligarchies based on gentry pedigree and official connections.

Under the Shanghai GCC, the affiliated chamber in the prefectural city of Songjiang expanded its activities into many aspects of urban life. According to its report in 1906, this affiliated chamber opened a tuition-free evening school that offered shop clerks classes in Chinese, English, commerce, geography, mathematics, calligraphy, and law, as well as ethical and physical training. It also organized an anti-opium association that persuaded its 200 members to stop smoking opium and helped cure poor opium addicts by selling medicine to them at reduced price. Through collaboration with local charitable halls, the Songjiang ACC formed a firefighting association with fifty members and three new engines, and it installed street lights for the benefit of pedestrians and to prevent crimes. Moreover, the affiliated chamber organized a mercantile physical training corps that included forty members and maintained local security, and it even subsidized a rice shop that sold rice to residents at reduced prices during periods of food shortage.[58]

The affiliated chamber in the prefectural city of Changzhou provided an even wider range of municipal services. When the Changzhou ACC came into being in 1905, it began to employ cleaners for urban sanitation and to install kerosene lamps on all downtown streets. Its leaders also created a new police force for local security, although they quickly lost it to official control. In 1907 this affiliated chamber turned an old academy into the first public park in the city and took charge of the maintenance work thereafter. Its first president, Yun Zuqi, who had long been a gentry manager of local public affairs, raised funds for a middle school in the same year. Another chamber leader of merchant origin, Yu Dingyi, founded a public library in 1904. With financial support from Yun and other elite merchants, Yu later erected a new building for the library in 1909. Moreover, the Changzhou ACC took charge of large-scale famine relief three times, in 1907, 1908, and 1911. Its leaders made large donations, raised funds from local elites, and worked closely with other chambers in Suzhou and Shanghai in these activities.[59]

Chamber leadership in Lower Yangzi cities and towns did not always incorporate the gentry managers of community affairs as in Changzhou but often challenged the latter in their community activities. They entered especially intensive competitions with local gentry for the control of the newly formed police forces in the twin-county city of Kunshan and Xinyang in southern Jiangsu as well as the county city of Shimen in northern Zhejiang between 1906 and 1908. In such power struggles, chamber leaders often used their new institutional resources, especially their chamber networks, to gain the upper hand over their gentry opponents, even though the latter usually enjoyed official support.[60] *Comp. blw CCs and local gentry over community affairs*

In the county of Fenghua, in eastern Zhejiang, for instance, the magistrate in 1909 appointed two gentrymen to manage local police, but the managing director of the Fenghua ACC, Wang Yudian, strongly demanded merchant management of police surcharges on local businesses. When a servant of the affiliated chamber was arrested after a quarrel with a policeman, Wang at first pushed for the release of the servant by the magistrate but failed. Dozens of merchants then created a disturbance in the police bureau. At that moment, a shop clerk was brought into the bureau by police for having urinated in the road, and he was slapped by the police inspector after his cheer for the merchant uproar. The enraged merchant protesters then broke all the lights and pulled out newly planted trees around the bureau; the protest finally forced the magistrate to release the arrested chamber servant and shop clerk and to dismiss the police inspector. After the owner of an herbal pharmacy clashed with a policeman and again caused turmoil in the police bureau, the two gentry managers of the local police had to resign and asked the affiliated chamber to take over the police force.[61]

The affiliated chamber in Nanxiang, a town east of Shanghai, was involved in more intensive and dramatic struggles with the established gentry managers of community institutions. This case deserves detailed analysis because it exemplifies how the new chamber networks helped rally varied elite reformers and changed local society at the township level.[62] In this town, the Nanxiang Study Society (Nanxiang xuehui) first appeared in 1903 and began to manage new schools. Its leaders included both literati reformers and merchant titleholders, such as Li Shuxun. In August 1905, the Nanxiang ACC also appeared with the endorsement of more than 170 merchants, and it incorporated Li Shuxun and other elite merchants from the study society into its leadership. Its president, Wang Weitai, was an imperial student, and he was more active in the new schools of Songjiang Prefecture and Shanghai than in local businesses. His younger brother, Wang Weiliang, was also a director of the Nanxiang Study Society.[63]

Thus, the Nanxiang ACC and Nanxiang Study Society shared quite a few elite merchant leaders, and these elites quickly joined together in a struggle for control of public projects in the town and for the reform of two local charitable institutions, the Fondling Hall (Yuyingtang) and the Morality Promotion Hall (Zhendetang). In fact, the two charitable halls had also been under the interlocking leadership of fewer than ten gentry managers. The families of these gentry managers had monopolized positions in the two halls generation after generation simply because of their commercial wealth, achievements in the civil service examinations, and official connections.[64]

As the first challenge to these gentry managers, Wang Weitai in late 1905 led the Nanxiang ACC to demand merchant participation in a river-dredging project that had been controlled by the two charitable halls. These gentry managers had planned the project from 1903 and had already begun to impose surcharges on merchants for that plan from 1904. However, by late 1905, they had not yet started work on the rivers that linked the town with the county city of Jiading and the two large cities of Suzhou and Shanghai. Without any response from the two charitable halls, Wang submitted a petition to the Jiading magistrate, arguing that merchant participation in such a public project was in accordance with the imperial edicts regarding chambers of commerce.[65] *gentry vs. merchants over community affairs*

The leaders of the two charitable halls continued to ignore Wang's demand and instead asked the magistrate's permission to hire two "urban gentry directors" from the Jiading county seat as managers of the project. They also tried to levy an additional surcharge on local merchants but refused to answer the affiliated chamber's question as to why the previously collected funds were not enough for the project. As a result, Wang and eighteen directors of the affiliated chamber lodged a complaint about the charitable managers' corruption to the magistrate and again demanded the opportunity to participate in the river-dredging project.[66]

The magistrate was anxious to quell the dispute between the gentry managers of the charitable halls and the elite merchant leaders of the Nanxiang ACC and to see the project completed in the winter of 1905. Thus, he gave both the chamber leaders and the two "urban gentry directors" permission to manage the project. The charity managers in Nanxiang, however, still tried to change the magistrate's mind through petitions from their merchant associates. One of the urban gentry directors, Gu Zhongying, also attempted to keep the Nanxiang ACC out of the project. He first contracted out the dredging work at a high cost and then declared a postponement of the project. However, Wang and other chamber leaders foiled all these schemes, started the project in December 1905, and completed it by themselves in the winter of 1906.[67]

After this initial success, the affiliated chamber further cooperated with the Nanxiang Study Society in an effort to reform and control the two charitable halls. In January 1907, twenty-one local elites, who were mainly leaders of the two associations, submitted a petition to the Jiading magistrate,

Nanxiang ACC merchant gentry dispute

demanding that an election be held to vote on the charity managers in the town. They argued that a few gentry families had monopolized the two charitable halls for generations and had excluded merchants from such public institutions. Their petition called for an election based on the principle of majority rule, and it also laid down electoral regulations. According to these regulations, the leadership of the charitable halls would be expanded to include one general director, eight directors, and twelve councilors. These directors and councilors would have tenures of one year and could keep their positions only if they continued to win in annual elections. The electors would be limited to members of the Nanxiang ACC and the Nanxiang Study Society, the managers of the two charitable halls, other local gentry directors, graduates of normal and middle schools, and merchants who made a significant amount of yearly donation to the two charitable halls.[68]

Clearly, these elites were trying to reform the charitable halls along the line of the General Works Board in Shanghai and to acquire local community leadership through the reform. Because the magistrate relied increasingly on new elite associations for the management of public projects and the promotion of local reforms, he consented to their petition. Zhou Chengshi, the leading gentry manager of the two charitable halls, had no other option but to accept the proposal for an election. However, these charity managers still used their merchant associates to submit another petition to the magistrate, opposing merchant involvement in the election.[69]

At the same time, the Nanxiang ACC and the Nanxiang Study Society successively held two meetings to mobilize qualified voters. As a result of their efforts, an electoral meeting was successfully held in the afternoon of January 31, 1907. It attracted approximately 150 people and lasted for three hours, with sixty-two electors casting votes. Because the gentry managers of the two charitable halls and their supporters boycotted the election, the elected directors and councilors were mostly from the Nanxiang ACC and Study Society, including Li Tingbang, concurrently leader of the two new associations and of the two charitable halls. He and Li Shuxun received an equal number of votes, thirty-nine each. Thus, they were respectively declared general director and one of the directors for the two charitable halls. Moreover, four chamber leaders, including Wang Weitai, were among the remaining seven directors. Among the twelve elected councilors, three were also leaders of the Nanxiang ACC. Moreover, at least three leaders of the Nanxiang Study Society, including Wang Weiliang, won election as directors or councilors.[70]

The election results quickly received approval from the magistrate, but the original charity managers still refused to accept the fait accompli and threatened to stop making donations to the two charitable halls. Li Tingbang tried to strike a compromise between the two factions through his relations with both sides. He presented the magistrate with his resignation from the new position, but his true intention was to assume the post of vice general director and to retain Zhou Chengshi, one of the original gentry managers of the two charitable halls, as the general director. Zhou went along with the plan, and he and Li Tingbang even attempted to get all the original gentry managers to work with only five of the newly elected directors and councilors in the two charitable halls. Although the magistrate refused to endorse their plan, Zhou and Li made it difficult for the newly elected leaders to take over the accounting books and other managerial powers from the previous gentry managers of the charitable halls.[71]

After the first election for the two charitable halls failed to achieve its original purpose, the leaders of the Nanxiang Study Society called not only for new elections but also for the reform of managerial regulations in the two public institutions. In late 1907, Li Shuxun succeeded Wang Weitai as president of the Nanxiang ACC. In 1909, Li's leadership in both the Nanxiang ACC and Nanxiang Study Society helped him win election as general director of the two charitable halls. Under his leadership, these two halls played active roles in local public affairs ranging from the construction of streets, roads, and bridges to the promotion of self-government reforms.[72]

The Nanxiang case exemplified how the Lower Yangzi chambers of commerce worked with other elite reformist organizations and brought new or reorganized community institutions under their joint leadership. In Nanxiang, the chamber networks and reformed charitable halls not only integrated local merchant leaders with other elite reformers at the township level but also developed interpersonal relations with municipal institutions in Shanghai. Among the new leadership of the two charitable halls, the two brothers Wang Weitai and Wang Weiliang were, respectively, the first president of the Nanxiang ACC and a councilor of the General Works Board of Shanghai and Its Suburbs. One of their nephews, Wang Nashan, was also a departmental director on the General Works Board.[73] Although such community institutions had not yet established formal relations from the township to the metropolitan level before self-government institutions mushroomed after 1909, many chambers developed links with varied professional associations and controlled merchant militias. Such interrelations especially integrated reformist elites across professional lines.

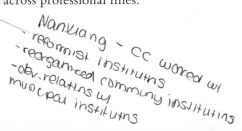

Nanxiang - CC worked w/
- reformist institutns
- reorganized communy institutns
- dev. relatns w/ municpal institutns

Links with New Professional Associations and Merchant Militias

Late Qing chambers of commerce led the trend for social elites to organize themselves into specialized groups along professional lines, but they also formed varied relations with other professional associations through their institutional influence, interlocking leaderships, overlapping memberships, and common reformist pursuits. In quite a few cities and towns, chambers of commerce promoted physical training among young merchants and other urban youths with the purpose of providing social security and reviving a martial spirit on behalf of national salvation. By the end of the Qing period, many of these physical training corps had become armed merchant militias under the command of chamber leaders. *CC-armed militias by late Qing*

In the Lower Yangzi region, elite merchants in a few large cities formed both chambers of commerce and commercial study societies within their professional circle. Although the commercial study societies were mainly concerned with research on business issues, they were often symbiotic or subsidiary organizations of chambers of commerce because of their institutional and personnel links with the latter. In 1904, two sibling entrepreneurs, Sun Duosen and Sun Duoxin, together with Vice President Xu Run and other leaders of the Shanghai GCC, initiated the Shanghai Commercial Study Society for discussion and research on business matters. This society also included Liu Shihang, president of the Jiangning GCC, and it formed closer relations with the Shanghai GCC after Sun Duosen gained the position of vice president of the general chamber in 1907.[74] The commercial study society established similar relations with the South Shanghai BCC because they shared a major leader, Wang Zhen, around 1908. As a result of these close ties, the Shanghai Commercial Study Society provided strong support for the Shanghai GCC during the anti-American boycott, as mentioned before, and it also helped the latter in the famine relief of 1906 with a financial donation and concrete suggestions.[75]

In 1907, the Ministry of Agriculture, Industry, and Commerce began to promote commercial study societies throughout the country, and it also criticized chambers of commerce for their failure to research and revitalize business.[76] Actually, the true purpose of the ministry was to create these commercial study societies as its new subordinate bodies and to separate them from chambers of commerce. When the Hangzhou Commercial Study Society (Hangzhou shangxue gonghui) came into being in 1909, Zhejiang provincial authorities specifically compelled it to "make a clear break with chambers of commerce." The society then held a meeting to revise its regulations, which distinguished the society from chambers of commerce by stressing that its goal was to explore and exchange commercial learning. In fact, its chairman (*huizhang*), Gao Peiqing, and three of its four vice chairmen, Zhou Xiangling, Wang Xirong, and Hu Zaoqing (Huan), were all directors of the Hangzhou GCC. Moreover, its fifteen directors included both President Pan Chiwen and Vice President Gu Songqing of the general chamber.[77]

The interest of these chamber leaders in commercial learning, including commercial schools, further led them and the literati into joint efforts to form new professional associations in the educational field. This phenomenon does not mean that "merchants occupied dominant positions" in these educational associations.[78] Rather, it further evinces the interpersonal and institutional fusion of merchant and literati elites within guilds, charitable halls, chambers of commerce, and these new educational associations. Because the Lower Yangzi chambers of commerce had already incorporated such hybrid elites and established hierarchical networks, their elite merchant leaderships and network structures deeply influenced the late-coming educational associations. Links w new educational associations

Indeed, chamber leaders of both merchant and literati origins were active organizers and promoters of these new associations for educational reforms. After a reformist society for private schools appeared in Suzhou in 1905, literati and merchant elites in Shanghai soon incorporated it into a larger association, the General Association for Private School Reforms (Sishu gailianghui). Its founders and directors included leaders of the Shanghai GCC, such as Li Houyou, Zeng Zhu, and Chen Runfu. Their major purpose was to advocate modernization of the numerous old-style private schools, but their propaganda campaign of public speeches also aimed at stopping opium smoking and the foot-binding custom. The General Association for Private School Reforms later generated more than forty branches in Jiangsu Province.[79]

In the same year, Zhang Jian, a leading gentry entrepreneur and educational reformer, established the office of educational affairs (*xuewu gongsuo*) to promote new schools in Tongzhou independent department and its nearby counties. After the Qing court abolished the civil service examinations in September 1905, an honorary member of the Suzhou GCC, Wang Tongyu, also initiated the Suzhou Office of Educational Affairs (Suzhou xuewu gongsuo), which basically used the regulations for chambers of commerce to develop its own organizational structures. The directors of this office later included Wang and other chamber leaders in Suzhou, such as You Xianjia, Zhang Lüqian, Pan Zuqian, and Peng Fusun, who controlled local educational resources in the name of promoting educational reforms.[80] Similar offices of educational affairs appeared in Shanghai and other cities, although they eventually became semi-official institutions renamed "bureaus to encourage education" (*quanxuesuo*).[81]

Meanwhile, chamber leaders and literati reformers also organized study societies to manage local educational resources and new schools, eventually turning these societies into leading professional associations in the educational field. In October 1905, a major leader of the Changzhou ACC, Yun Zuqi, initiated the Jiangsu Study Society (Jiangsu xuehui) together with other chamber leaders and literati reformers in Jiangsu Province, such as the aforesaid Zhang Jian of Tongzhou and Wang Tongyu of Suzhou. They soon reorganized it as the Jiangsu General Association for Educational Affairs (Jiangsu xuewu zonghui).[82] The founders of this new educational association admitted that they had "followed the rules of chambers of commerce" for the establishment of its leadership, membership, electoral procedures, and so on.[83]

This new educational association quickly met with censure from provincial officials in Jiangning because it was located in Shanghai rather than in the provincial capital, but its title implied its authority over educational affairs in the entire province. In 1906, the Jiangsu General Association for Educational Affairs twice received instructions from the Jiangsu provincial authorities in Jiangning, ordering it to move its office to the provincial capital. However, its leaders effectively used the precedent of the Shanghai GCC to justify its location in Shanghai and its jurisdiction over other educational associations in the province. Although the title of this organization was eventually changed to the Jiangsu General Association for Education (Jiangsu jiaoyu zonghui) in November 1906, as the Ministry of Education (Xuebu) had required, its Shanghai office remained the headquarters for educational associations in Jiangsu Province, and its new leadership included more chamber leaders of merchant origin, such as President Zeng Zhu and Director Zhou Tingbi of the Shanghai GCC.[84]

The Jiangsu General Association for Education stated in its regulations that it would promote educational research, new schools, and a martial spirit among students and would advance agriculture, industry, and commerce through vocational education. Such broad goals were established in order to attract both professional educators and other elite reformers, including elite merchant activists. Thus, this educational association recruited not only leaders of study societies and school managers but also leaders and members of the chambers of commerce. In addition to the aforementioned chamber leaders in this provincial educational association, its membership around 1909 also included other former and incumbent presidents of general and affiliated chambers in Jiangsu Province, such as You Xianjia of Suzhou, Zhou Shunian of Yangzhou Prefecture, Xu Dinglin of Haizhou independent department, Liu Xiejun of Haimen subprefecture, Zhang Zhenxiang of the town of Meili, and Zhu Yilie of the town of Luodian.[85]

In Jiangsu Province, educational associations at the prefectural and county levels usually grew out of local study societies, and they formed subsidiary relations with the Jiangsu General Association for Education in much the same way that affiliated chambers had operated under general chambers. Around 1909, quite a few of their chairmen were former or incumbent presidents of local chambers. Examples of such interlocking leadership include Sha Yuanbing of Rugao County, Zhu Tinghua of Jiangyin County, Fang Huan of Kunshan-Xinyang counties, and Ren Xifen (Xiaoyu) of Yixing-Jingxi counties. They were generally the major leaders in chambers of commerce first and then expanded their power into the local educational associations.[86]

The educational associations in Zhejiang did not leave behind records of personnel data for detailed analysis, but available information shows that a leading scholar and first president of the affiliated chamber in Ruian County, Sun Yirang, was a major founder and first president of the provincial educational association. The first president of the affiliated chamber in Dinghai subprefecture, Ding Zhongli, was also chairman of the local educational association around 1909.[87] Through such interlocking leadership, chambers of commerce and educational associations formed parallel yet interconnected networks from large to small cities.

Among the new professional organizations, agricultural associations (nonghui) emerged relatively late, and thus their development owed even more to the previously established chamber leadership. Many chamber leaders were interested in agricultural reform because they were not only rich merchants but also agricultural entrepreneurs or large landlords. The president of the Tong-Chong-Hai GCCC, Zhang Cha, together with his brother Zhang Jian, had already launched a reclamation company along the local seacoast with the purpose of producing cotton for their textile industry and providing a reliable livelihood for the salt producers on the saline land. Thus, after the Ministry of Agriculture, Industry, and Commerce in late 1907 issued rules for agricultural associations and encouraged them to promote agricultural production, Zhang Cha quickly gathered local elites for a meeting in September 1908, formed the Tongzhou Affiliated Association for Agriculture (Tongzhou nongwu fenhui), and used the Tong-Chong-Hai GCCC to gain official approval for it. This agricultural association was located in the same office as the general chamber, and its president was also Zhang Cha. It had generated six branches in nearby towns by January 1909 and formed networks similar to those of the Tong-Chong-Hai GCCC.[88]

The Suzhou GCC also included merchant leaders who had large land-holdings. Its two successive presidents, You Xianjia and Zhang Lüqian, owned 6,000–7,000 mu (990–1155 acres) and 4,000–5,000 mu (660–825 acres) of land, respectively, and their rent incomes were almost equal to if not more than their commercial profits. As early as June 1907, they had planned an agricultural and industrial association under the general chamber and tried to use it for rent collection. In view of the land reclamation achievements of the Tongzhou Affiliated Association for Agriculture, Suzhou chamber leaders in 1909 petitioned the Jiangsu governor to form a similar organization for the cultivation of wasteland around the city of Suzhou. They not only obtained official permission to establish the Suzhou General Association for Agriculture (Suzhou nongwu zonghui) in 1910 but also helped it formulate its regulations and establish leadership over affiliated agricultural associations in southern Jiangsu. Thereafter, the Suzhou General Association for Agriculture was able to claim ownership of uncultivated land from local governments, and its experimental farm even obtained improved varieties of rice from overseas Chinese chambers of commerce in Southeast Asia.[89]

Among the affiliated chambers of commerce in Jiangsu Province, the former president of the Wuxi-Jinkui ACC, Zhou Tingbi, directly founded an affiliated agricultural association in 1908 and became its first president, as did the incumbent president of the Baoying ACC, Bao Youke, in the next year. The Ministry of Agriculture, Industry, and Commerce reluctantly permitted Bao to hold the concurrent posts, though it restated its disapproval of interlocking leadership between local chambers and agricultural associations.[90] Nevertheless, such governmental intervention did not cut the close relations between these professional associations from the local to the national level.

In Rugao County, Sha Yuanbing was both president of the affiliated chamber and chairman of the educational association from 1906, and he further became president of the local agricultural association in 1909. In Jiading County, the local agricultural association was located in the same office as the affiliated chamber. Due to the influence of the chamber networks, a three-level hierarchy composed of general, affiliated, and branch agricultural associations appeared first in the Lower Yangzi region. In 1910, the National Federation of Agricultural Associations (Quanguo nongwu lianhehui) also came into being in Jiangning and selected Zhang Cha as its chairman.[91]

The development of chambers of commerce and other new professional associations, together with their concern for social security and national survival, also gave birth to varied exercise societies (*ticaohui*). In order to foster a martial spirit for national salvation, the Shanghai Study Society first founded an exercise society in 1904. For the same purpose, Yu Pinghan, a member of the Shanghai GCC, and Zeng Zhu, president of the general chamber, each organized a merchant study society to promote physical training. Other chamber leaders and elite reformers, such as Wang Zhen, initiated two more exercise societies before 1907.[92] After the General Works Board of Shanghai and Its Suburbs under Zeng and Li Zhongjue pushed the Shanghai *daotai* to enforce the anti-opium edict and close all opium dens by June 1907, it faced a possible rebellion by opium addicts and gangsters and thus called on the five exercise societies to patrol the streets. In September 1907, Zeng and Li began to organize the South Shanghai Merchant Militia (Nanshi shangtuan gonghui), which was composed of selected members from the five exercise societies and located in the same office as the South Shanghai BCC.[93]

In March 1908, Li further established the Shanghai Merchant Militia Federation (Shanghai shangtuan gonghui) to incorporate the aforementioned five exercise societies and others subsequently formed in different trades, districts, and the like. The new militia federation continued to share the office of the South Shanghai BCC. As social unrest in southern Shanghai increased toward the end of the Qing dynasty, local governments had to provide these militias with weapons for patrolling the streets, and the number of their militiamen reached more than 2,000. These militiamen were drawn from industrial, commercial, and educational circles, although they were usually from merchant families.[94] According to the recollection of one former participant in the Spare-Time Study Society for Commercial Learning (Shangyu xuehui), its 300 militiamen were mostly owners of shops and factories. Up to 1911, the six successive chairmen of the Shanghai Merchant Militia Federation, Li Zhongjue, Zeng Zhu, Su Benyan, Wang Zhen, Zhang Lejun, and Ye Zengming, were all leaders of the Shanghai GCC and the South Shanghai BCC or ACC.[95] Thus, these militias included both young elite merchants and other educated youth, and they shared many leaders with the two chambers of commerce in the city.

Another merchant militia in Shanghai, the Chinese Merchant Exercise Society (Huashang ticaohui) appeared in the International Settlement in 1906 and maintained similar relations with the Shanghai GCC because its major founder, Yu Qiaqing, and its honorary chairman (*mingyu huizhang*), Zeng Zhu, were, respectively, a director and the president of the general chamber. This militia force joined the foreign Volunteer Corps in the International Settlement in 1907 and then restricted its members to "respectable merchants," such as the incumbent president, Li Houyou, and many directors and full members of the Shanghai GCC. In 1909 the Shanghai GCC began to recruit seventeen "superior graduates" from this militia as special associate members, using them as its security guards.[96] The chamber leaders in Shanghai would further try to unite all the merchant militias in the treaty port and the entire country on the eve of the 1911 Revolution, as is discussed in Chapter 6.

The Suzhou GCC also helped found merchant militias under its elite merchant leadership. In late 1906, a few chamber leaders and members in Suzhou led a petition to the Qing government for a merchant exercise society. Their petition especially stressed the urgent need to strengthen the nation, protect merchants, improve personal health, maintain social order, and provide public welfare through such an exercise society. This petition went through the Suzhou GCC to the Jiangsu governor and Ministry of Commerce and quickly obtained official approval. The Suzhou Merchant Exercise Society (Sushang tiyuhui) then came into being, and nearly half of its nineteen founders were leaders of the Suzhou GCC. It received its funds from the general chamber from the beginning. Between 1906 and 1911, the commander of the merchant militia was first Hong Yulin and then Zou Zongqi, two directors of the Suzhou GCC.[97]

Like its Shanghai predecessors, the Suzhou Merchant Exercise Society comprised merchants, students, and other urban youth, but all its members needed to have merchant guarantors and had to pay one silver dollar in monthly membership fees. Thus, it mainly included well-to-do merchants or youths from these merchant families, although there were also a few shop clerks among its membership by 1911. Its members first received physical training and then turned to military training in 1907. Through the Suzhou GCC, this merchant militia received weapons from the local government, and it also provided help for the campaign against opium dens in the city. By the end of 1911, the Suzhou Merchant Exercise Society expanded to include about 145 members and hundreds of new members in its six branches, but it remained under the control of the Suzhou GCC.[98]

In Zhejiang Province, the provincial governor tried hard to prohibit such exercise societies and prevent them from engaging in military training until 1907, but a merchant militia still appeared in the silk and silk fabric trades of Hangzhou in September 1908. Later, the Hangzhou GCC was able to control a merchant militia and used it to maintain social order in the entire city.[99] The Tong-Chong-Hai GCCC also established a merchant exercise society of 160 members in December 1910, and it quickly formed another "worker" exercise society with 120 members in June 1911. Both militias required their members to have decent occupations, and their three major leaders included the first and second presidents of the Tong-Chong-Hai GCCC, Zhang Cha and Liu Guixin.[100]

Among affiliated chambers of commerce, those in the prefectural city of Songjiang and the town of Minghang were under the direct influence of the Shanghai GCC, and thus they formed merchant exercise societies as early as 1906. Moreover, the Wuxi-Jinkui and Changzhou ACCs established merchant exercise societies successively in 1908 and 1909. Like their forerunners in Shanghai, these merchant exercise societies included both shop clerks and students and received weapons from their local governments for military training.[101] In the last years of the Qing dynasty, social unrest allowed more affiliated chambers to form and arm merchant militias with official permission. In 1910 the chamber leaders in the town of Xiashi in the northern Zhejiang Province followed the model of the South Shanghai Merchant Militia to organize their own merchant militia with more than 130 shop clerks. This militia received military training from retired officers and was able to arm itself with weapons from both provincial and county governments.[102] *militias included shop clerks, students*

These merchant militias also tried to keep in touch with each other as did chambers of commerce and other professional associations. In October 1906, merchant exercise societies in Shanghai not only sent large number of members to attend the inaugural ceremony of their Suzhou counterpart but also donated 100 silver dollars as a portion of its initial funds. In return, the Suzhou Merchant Exercise Society maintained communications with its counterparts in Shanghai through two representatives residing there. It also organized its members for periodic trips to nearby cities, including Wuxi and Changzhou, holding meetings or even exercises with their peers there. In a typical case, the South Shanghai Merchant Militia issued the order for a trip to the town of Xiashi on March 19, 1910. Its members received a warm welcome in the town by local chamber and militia leaders together with 3,000 people, and its commanders delivered patriotic speeches in return. In addition to sightseeing, the Shanghai militiamen also drilled in Xiashi.[103]

This episode reflected the fact that the Lower Yangzi chambers of commerce and other new associations such as merchant militias not only pursued personnel and institutional interpenetration but also expanded their intertwined networks from large cities into market towns. Such network devel-

militias help expand influence

opment enabled these chambers to mobilize different social classes in the nationwide boycott of 1905 and maintain more prolonged relations with their community institutions and other social organizations within and beyond the business world. In particular, the chamber networks enabled their elite merchants to achieve an unprecedented level of social integration and take collective action in commercial and industrial affairs.

CCS – new educational associations
        community associations
        militias

↓

helped extend networks from cities to town

– enabled ccs to mobilze boycott of 1905 nationwide

5

Political Maneuvers in Commercial
and Industrial Affairs

The network expansion of the Lower Yangzi chambers of commerce increased their sociopolitical influence beyond their merchant constituencies, but it increasingly alarmed Qing officials. In October 1906, Jiangsu Governor Chen Kuilong reported to the Qing court that chambers of commerce and other new associations had meddled in public affairs and even rallied people against officials. Newspapers, the telegraph, and public meetings also allowed a few persons to hold inappropriate discussions on state policies, to circulate telegrams in the name of literati and merchants as a whole, and to intimidate the government. Thus, the governor proposed enforcing legal control over newspapers, the telegraph, meetings, and especially the newly formed associations.[1] *gov't proposed controlling political speech*

Consequently, the Qing court in 1907 ordered the Ministry of Civil Affairs (Minzhengbu) to issue a set of new rules for these associations and their meetings and prohibited "gentry, merchants, scholars and the masses" from interfering in political affairs. In response to a complaint about the Hangzhou GCC, and especially to the charge that it was intervening in governmental affairs, the Ministry of Agriculture, Industry, and Commerce in 1909 stressed that chambers of commerce were merely commercial associations and not allowed to engage in political activities.[2]

Contrary to the repeated official injunctions, the Lower Yangzi chambers of commerce had already politicized many commercial and industrial issues by that time, and they either clashed or collaborated with the government, depending on the contradiction or conformity of their elite merchant inter-

how bad a thing at govt shape policy from

ests to governmental policies. These chambers frequently took concerted actions against the official increase of tax burdens on merchants, especially on elite merchants. However, they also helped the government stabilize local markets at the expense of small merchants because of the common concern of the elite merchants and officials for social security. Through collective engagement in modern industries, such as the Jiangsu and Zhejiang railroads, chamber leaders and members pursued personal profit together with provincial and national interests, and they formed their first regional alliance against both Qing official and foreign intrusion into their railroads. Yet such clashes did not prevent them from working with the Qing government on other financial and industrial issues and even with foreign capital for international economic cooperation and nongovernmental diplomacy.

CCs clashed w/ officials on political issues despite injunctions but still worked w/ them

Thus, these chambers led a relational revolution in the business world not only because they institutionalized, diversified, and expanded the social relations among their merchant participants, especially the elite ones, but also because they brought the private and public interests of the latter into multiform interactions with the state's commercial and industrial policies. As a result, these elite merchants gradually used the chamber networks to relate their business interests with public politics from the local, provincial, and regional levels to the national level. Thus, the Lower Yangzi chambers of commerce could claim to represent both the merchant community and the larger society in their interactions with the state and foreign powers, despite the increase of class tensions between their elite participants and the populace at the local level. This kind of public representation in turn increased their influence on the state's policies regarding commercial and industrial issues.

CCs claimed to represent merchants and the wider community

Elite Merchants and Popular Welfare in Commercial Markets

The Lower Yangzi chambers of commerce generally represented their merchant communities in the face of the Qing government, but they always gave priority to elite merchant interests in commercial issues. In their responses to the increase of commercial taxes and the devaluation of copper coins during the last years of the Qing dynasty, these chambers repeatedly led merchant protests against the tax policies of the Qing government, but their collaboration with officials on the monetary issue also reflected elite merchant apprehensions for social unrest and caused economic losses to small merchants. Thus, there was still class tension between chamber leaders and common mer-

CCs always gave priority to elite merchant interests

chants in local markets, although the former always claimed to act on the interests of the entire merchant community and even local society in their management of the markets. *claimed to be supporting local merchants but gave elites priority*

The tax burden on the populace dramatically increased from 1906 as a result of surcharges for the New Policy reforms and the depreciation of copper coins.[3] Apart from the peasants, merchants were the main targets of these tax surcharges, and they also became victims of the currency depreciation, an issue to be discussed later. In Jiangsu Province, most surcharges for local reforms in Jiangning around 1908 came from urban merchants, especially from those in the silk and satin trades. In the same year, a report from the nearby Zhenjiang Prefecture indicated that the operating expenses for ordinary shops had doubled in the previous three or four years because the local government had imposed surcharges to support girls' schools, new police forces, and so on. In Zhejiang Province, new police forces in prefectures and counties also obtained their operating funds mostly from surcharges on merchants.[4] Although tax increases affected the merchant community as a whole, the Lower Yangzi chambers of commerce launched large-scale anti-tax movements mainly in those trades where elite merchants were concentrated.

The Suzhou GCC led chambers of commerce in southern Jiangsu Province into their first large-scale protest against the increase in the soy sauce tax because its leaders included influential elite merchants in this trade. For instance, one of its founders and long-term directors, Pan Zuqian, was from the powerful Pan lineage in the soy sauce trade. In fact, all soy sauce shops in Suzhou and southern Jiangsu Province tended to be owned by prestigious elite merchants and had powerful salt merchants as their guarantors because they used state-monopolized salt for soy sauce production.[5]

The soy sauce merchants originally paid an annual tax on only one of every five sauce-making vats, but this tax had gradually grown from approximately 2,000 *wen* of copper coin in 1904 to 4,560 *wen* around 1906, not to mention other irregular "contributions" merchants were expected to make to the government. In October 1906, the Jiangsu governor planned to further increase the soy sauce tax with the alleged purpose of raising funds for "various reform projects" and thus imposed a tax of 2,625 *wen* of copper coin on every vat, or a total of 13,125 *wen* for every five vats. Because of this sudden increase in tax by nearly 190 percent, the sixty-two soy sauce merchants around Suzhou first united under their own guild to petition the magistrates of Wu, Changzhou, and Yuanhe counties for a waiver of the new tax, but their petition met with flat rejection. Next they held a joint meeting with the soy sauce merchants of six other counties of Suzhou Prefecture and then submitted another

[margin notes: merchants and peasants most affected by tax surcharges in 1906 ↓ led to large protests; 1st in Suzhou GCC on soy sauce tax ↳]

petition to the Suzhou prefect and Jiangsu governor. In this new petition, they argued that their shops used only one out of every five vats to make sauce and that the remaining four were for storage and should be exempted from the tax. After this petition again was rejected, the Suzhou soy sauce merchants made a concession to the local government and agreed to pay 1,750 *wen* of copper coin in addition to the original 4,560 *wen* tax on every five vats. In other words, they would pay 6,310 *wen* tax for every five vats, accepting only a 38 percent increase in their tax burden.[6]

The Suzhou GCC began to contact its affiliated chambers in southern Jiangsu Province on this issue in early 1907. The affiliated chamber in Liyang County submitted a plan that called for all the chambers in southern Jiangsu to adopt uniform measures. It suggested that soy sauce merchants should jointly elect several leaders in Suzhou and Shanghai and collect funds to cover expenses for their joint actions. They should also rely on the chambers to lodge their complaints to the Ministry of Agriculture, Industry, and Commerce and gain support from the powerful salt merchants. If the government adopted repressive measures to take their leaders into custody, all merchants would voluntarily offer to be arrested, and a metropolitan official from southern Jiangsu would report the issue to the throne directly. As an ultimate play, all soy sauce merchants in southern Jiangsu would return their licenses to the government and launch a de facto strike.[7]

The chambers of commerce in southern Jiangsu did not put the whole plan into practice, but they did provide leadership, protection, and communications for soy sauce merchants in the anti-tax movement. In May 1907, the magistrates of Wu, Changzhou, and Yuanhe counties ordered all soy sauce merchants around Suzhou to submit their account books within three days so as to check whether their shops had really used only a portion of their vats to make sauce. In response, ninety-two soy sauce shops in nine counties of Suzhou Prefecture launched a joint complaint to the Ministry of Agriculture, Industry, and Commerce, using the state-issued commercial laws to defend their legal right to keep the information in their account books confidential. The Suzhou GCC forwarded this complaint, together with a supportive telegram, to the ministry. Through the Shanghai GCC, the Suzhou GCC also sent the soy sauce merchants' complaint to newspapers in Shanghai, publishing it under the name of the general chamber.[8]

With the support of these chambers of commerce, soy sauce merchants became more assertive. When provincial officials in Suzhou ordered them to reveal the author of the complaint submitted to the ministry, they claimed that their plea had been discussed at a joint meeting in their guildhall and

decided by a majority vote taken in the office of the Suzhou GCC. Through
the chamber networks and leadership, soy sauce merchants in Suzhou Prefecture also expanded the anti-tax alliance to include their counterparts in
Songjiang, Changzhou, and Zhenjiang prefectures as well as the Taicang independent department, and their total number increased from ninety-two in
Suzhou Prefecture to 265 throughout southern Jiangsu. In September 1907,
the 265 soy sauce shops again gained help from the Suzhou GCC to submit
another petition to the Ministry of Agriculture, Industry, and Commerce,
in which they directly attacked the Jiangsu governor for his neglect of merchant hardships and his interference with the salt taxation.[9]

Around Suzhou, the magistrates of Wu, Changzhou, and Yuanhe counties continued the high-handed policy until November 1907, threatening to
dismiss and arrest the guild leaders in the soy sauce trade if they continued
their resistance to a tax increase. Meanwhile, these local officials also tried to
appease Suzhou soy sauce merchants with a proposal to increase the tax by
3,500 *wen* of copper coin for every five vats. In other words, the government
would raise the soy sauce tax on every five vats from 4,560 to 8,060 *wen*, rather
than the originally designated 13,125 *wen*. The major guild leader in the Suzhou soy sauce trade and director in the Suzhou GCC, Pan Tingcong, rejected
the official proposal on the pretext of pressure from other soy sauce merchants
in southern Jiangsu. However, he secretly contacted chamber leaders in Wuxi
and other cities, calling for continuation of the protest. The Suzhou GCC
protected Pan from official arrest by protesting to the Liangjiang governor-
general and thus helped the soy sauce merchants withstand official pressure.
Eventually, in July 1908, the Liangjiang governor-general had to exempt the
soy sauce trade from a tax increase. Thus, this anti-tax movement, which
lasted for more than a year, ended with the complete success of the soy sauce
merchants under chamber leadership.[10]

At almost the same time, the chambers of commerce around Suzhou and
Shanghai led another large-scale protest against an increase in the brokerage
tax, a movement that affected more numerous merchants, especially commercial brokers in many chambers of commerce of southern Jiangsu Province. In the Qing period, brokerage houses in the different trades generally
needed to obtain licenses from their local governments, and the Jiangsu
provincial authorities in 1878 had limited the holders of brokerage licenses
to only well-to-do merchants. Thus, many brokers were rich merchants
who paid relatively low taxes until 1907, the annual taxes for the four different ranks of brokerage houses being only 0.5, 1, 1.5, and 2 taels.[11]

Among the chambers of commerce around Suzhou, many of the directors and full members representing different businesses were actually brokers in their trades. In 1906 the affiliated chamber in the town of Meili appeared with a pig broker as its president, while its two directors and three full members were also brokers in the pig, timber, bean cake, and brick/tile/lime trades. In 1907 the eleven directors of the affiliated chamber in the town of Shengze included at least five brokers in the silk and silk fabric trades, while ten of the remaining twenty full members were also brokers in the rice, silk, and silk fabric trades. Their dominance in the Shengze ACC was later confirmed by a complaint from weavers of silk cloth in the town.[12] Similarly, both the first and third presidents of the Wuxi-Jinkui ACC, Zhou Tingbi and Xue Nanming, owned large numbers of brokerage houses in the cocoon trade, and Zhou was also a long-term director of the Shanghai GCC.[13] It was natural that these chambers would take an active part in protesting against an increase in the brokerage tax.

After the Jiangsu governor decided to increase the brokerage tax by ten times in late 1906, the Zhenjiang ACC first forwarded a petition from local brokers to the Ministry of Commerce, demanding withdrawal of the decision. The Changzhou and Wuxi-Jinkui ACCs quickly contacted the Zhenjiang ACC concerning joint action. Then the Suzhou and Shanghai GCCs, together with the Wujiang-Zhenze, Shengze, and Meili ACCs, made a joint complaint about the tax increase to the Ministry of Agriculture, Industry, and Commerce in January 1907. These chambers argued that the brokerage taxes had already risen by three times in recent years because of the silver inflation and other surcharges and that the new official decree would actually raise the tax by thirty times according to the original base. Thus, they requested that the ministry contact the Jiangsu governor about a more moderate tax increase. Meanwhile, the two general chambers in Suzhou and Shanghai brought the Tong-Chong-Hai GCCC into a similar petition to the Jiangsu governor.[14]

Although the Jiangsu governor and the Ministry of Agriculture, Industry, and Commerce rejected the requests from these chambers, the Changzhou, Jiangyin, Zhenjiang, and Wuxi-Jinkui ACCs continued to send petitions to the ministry in early 1907. Under the leadership of President Yun Zuqi, the Changzhou ACC twice lodged complaints against the tax increase with the ministry. Meanwhile, it actively sought for countermeasures through communications with seven other affiliated chambers in Changzhou, Zhenjiang, and Suzhou prefectures and urged the Suzhou and Shanghai GCCs to lead a concerted action. Through such contacts, the chambers in Suzhou, Songjiang, Changzhou, and Zhenjiang prefectures as well as Taicang independent department decided to discuss the brokerage tax issue at a general conference in Suzhou in late 1907.[15] *← ex of institutional networks*

One week before this general conference, the affiliated chamber in Danyang County submitted to the Suzhou GCC a letter with a plan for protesting against new brokerage tax just as the Liyang ACC had done in the simultaneous struggle against the increase in the soy sauce tax. The Danyang ACC proposed launching complaints against the tax increases in both the brokerage and soy sauce trades through newspapers and through collective petitions to the Ministry of Agriculture, Industry, and Commerce. It also suggested calling on metropolitan officials of Jiangsu origin to report the two issues to the throne, but its letter stressed that the real key to the anti-tax struggles was the unity of all chambers and their persistence under governmental pressure.[16] The chambers of commerce in southern Jiangsu basically followed this plan in the anti-tax movement. *↓ meeting of 22 ccs to petition govt on br. tax*

On October 1, 1907, twenty-two chambers of commerce from the aforementioned four prefectures and one independent department held their joint meeting, after which the Suzhou GCC led a collective petition to the Ministry of Agriculture, Industry, and Commerce for an increase in the brokerage tax of five rather than ten times. These chambers also pursued the strategy of using their informal connections with metropolitan officials in their fights against the tax increase. *used for informal connections w/ metropol. officials to fight br. tax* Indeed, an official of Zhenjiang origin, together with three other metropolitan officials in the Qing court, sent a personal letter to the Jiangsu governor, requesting a moderate tax increase in both the brokerage and soy sauce trades. Moreover, Yun Yuding, a member of the National Academy (Hanlinyuan) and nephew of President Yun Zuqi of the Changzhou ACC, petitioned the throne about the tax increase in the Jiangsu brokerage trade and suggested the same rate that the chambers of commerce had demanded. Under pressure from both the chambers of commerce and metropolitan officials of Jiangsu origin, the Ministry of Agriculture, Industry, and Commerce and the Jiangsu provincial authorities finally made a concession. In late August of 1908, the Liangjiang governor-general agreed to an increase of the brokerage tax by five times while completely waiving the proposed tax increase in the soy sauce trade.[17] *← br. tax protest success in Jiangsu*

In addition to the protests against tax increases in the brokerage and soy sauce trades, the Suzhou and Hangzhou GCCs led merchant struggles against the official imposition of a new stamp tax (*yinhuashui*) on all commercial documents in 1909, in which they, too, achieved success. The general chamber in

protest against stamp tax → success

Suzhou also helped local merchants fight against heavy taxes in the flower nursery, foreign goods, and other trades between 1906 and 1909.[18] Such anti-tax activities did not involve the mobilization of the wider chamber networks, but they directly represented the interests of common merchants. In contrast, the Lower Yangzi chambers of commerce in the copper coinage crisis helped the Qing government maintain its currency policy but sacrificed the interests of small merchants in the effort. It merits special attention, however, that the chamber leaders still claimed to have protected popular consumers in the monetary issue.

The Qing government had begun to issue ten-*wen* copper pieces as token coins in 1853, when a shortage of copper made it difficult to mint copper coins in the form of one-*wen* pieces. During the last decade of the Qing dynasty, the ten-*wen* copper coins became the major currency among the urban and rural poor. Because the face value of a ten-*wen* copper piece was much higher than the actual value of the copper it contained, both the central and provincial governments' mints recklessly issued such coins to realize profit, but local officials refused to accept them for tax payment. Private mints, too, produced a large amount of counterfeit coins, putting them into the market illegally and thus aggravating the depreciation of all such copper coins.[19] In the county of Yin in eastern Zhejiang, the populace had to pay both tax and rent in silver dollars rather than in the ten-*wen* coins. According to the official rate of currency exchange, one silver dollar was valued at 960 *wen* of copper coin in the ten-*wen* pieces, but its actual value in the local market had risen to 1,360 *wen* by late 1909. Thus, the populace suffered a loss of 400 *wen* of copper coin for each dollar of tax and rent owed. Small merchants were also victims of the official currency exchange rate because they had to pay wholesalers in silver dollars and accept the devalued coins in business deals with the poor populace.[20] Although they demanded a change in the government's currency policy, their requests did not always receive support from chambers of commerce.

In many counties and prefectures of Zhejiang Province, the ten-*wen* copper coin had actually depreciated to 80–90 percent of its face value in early 1908, but many chambers of commerce were still reluctant to accept the fait accompli in local markets because their elite merchant participants used only silver dollars in business transactions and feared mass riots that might be triggered by an official coinage devaluation. In mid-1908 the affiliated chambers in Shimen County and the town of Tangqi did devalue the ten-*wen* coins in their local markets by 10 percent under the pressure of small merchants. However, after the coinage devaluation caused a serious riot in the town of Wangjiangjing in Xiushui County in late June 1908, the affiliated chamber in this county immediately followed local official instruction to maintain the face value of the debased coins. The next month, the branch chamber in the nearby town of Xincheng made the same decision after the county magistrate objected to the discounting of coins in the local markets.[21]

In the provincial capital of Zhejiang, the Hangzhou GCC gathered more than ninety guild leaders and other elite merchants to discuss the issue on June 7, 1908, and most of its directors expressed concern about potential mass riots rather than the financial loss that would be suffered by small merchants. The participants in the meeting called on the government to accept a certain percentage of the ten-*wen* copper coins in its tax collection and to stop issuing and importing such coins. But this call received official support only in word and not in deed. Less than three months later, the provincial government imported 200 chests of ten-*wen* copper coins from the official mint in Fujian Province. The Hangzhou GCC immediately held an emergency meeting on September 15 and tried to stop officials from putting the large amount of debased copper coins into the market, but it was still hesitant to accept the depreciation of the coins in the urban market. Consequently, the coinage crisis in Hangzhou reached its height in April 1909, when the rate of exchange between silver dollars and ten-*wen* coins rose from 1:1200 to 1:1400, and many shops closed their doors.[22] devaluation of coin crisis

gov't continued to add copper coins to market despite CC

The coinage crisis was more serious in southern Jiangsu, and even the three magistrates in Wu, Changzhou, and Yuanhe counties, around Suzhou, proposed discounting the coins in markets from 1906. However, both the Suzhou and Shanghai GCC rejected the three magistrates' proposal and still pushed the Jiangsu provincial authorities to maintain the face value of the ten-*wen* copper coins until 1908. The leaders of the two general chambers indicated that the poor segment of the populace had already suffered from the rise in prices for daily necessities and could not afford further devaluation of the ten-*wen* copper coins. They also expressed their worry about disturbance and even strikes in Suzhou if local officials announced a coinage devaluation.[23]

However, neither the two general chambers nor the Jiangsu provincial authorities were able to offer any concrete solution to the coinage crisis and especially the economic losses of small merchants. The Suzhou GCC simply urged the provincial government to prohibit the illegal minting of the ten-*wen* copper coins and to limit their importation from adjacent provinces. Other chambers of commerce in southern Jiangsu basically followed the decisions of the Shanghai and Suzhou GCCs, and none of them challenged the official policy of sustaining the unrealistic coin value. However, the branch

CCS → not able to offer concrete solutions in coin crisis

and affiliated chambers in the towns of Lujiabang, Luodian, and Shengze, as well as in the twin counties of Wujiang-Zhenze, tended to include more small merchants among their memberships, and thus their letters to the Su-zhou GCC requested that it lead a joint petition to the government for the acceptance of the ten-*wen* token coins in tax payments.[24]

Meanwhile, small merchants had already enforced a coinage discount in a few towns and had launched strikes in protest against the governmental currency policy. In Zhujing, a market town near Shanghai, more than ten merchants in May 1909 pushed the local chamber president to announce the devaluation of the ten-*wen* coins by 20 percent. Although their request was rejected by the chamber leader, these merchants discounted the coins in their own shops. After their clerks were involved in quarrels and scuffles with customers, nearly half of the shops in the town closed their doors, initiating a merchant strike. Meanwhile, the local chamber president pursued the county government to prohibit coinage discounting through a public notice, and he and local officials personally pushed all shops to open their doors. However, in the face of continuous merchant protest, the chamber president later had to submit his resignation to the Shanghai GCC.[25]

While the Shanghai GCC was sending one of its members to investigate the riot in the town of Zhujing, the coinage agitation further spread to the towns of Tinglin, Zhangyan, and Yexie within the adjacent Huating County in May 1909. In Tinglin merchants first discounted the ten-*wen* copper coins by themselves. After enraged customers destroyed two of the shops that accepted the token coins only as debased currency, all shops in the town closed their doors. In Zhangyan furious rioters also demolished five shops after local merchants enforced the coinage devaluation by themselves.[26] In late May of 1909, Yexie saw the most violent riot and a direct clash between the mass rioters and the local chamber leaders. After the rioters destroyed six shops that discounted the ten-*wen* copper coins, all local merchants stopped their business activities. The president of the local affiliated chamber called on local police to arrest the riot leader, but rioters rescued their leader from a police boat by force. The mass protest then continued even though the local township headman had called in two military boats from the local Qing army to restore order. Meanwhile, poor consumers led a similar riot in the town of Zhenze, near Suzhou, causing a merchant strike there.[27]

In June 1909, the Shanghai GCC sent to the Ministry of Agriculture, Industry, and Commerce an emergency telegram about the riots and strikes in Zhujing, Tinglin, Yexie, and other towns. It still opposed any official coinage devaluation and again warned the government of market unrest after such

[handwritten annotation at top: gov't agreed to accept debased coins in tax collection and stop minting coins — after CC urged them. Suzhou GCC helped officials pacify crisis]

an announcement. However, its telegram also urged the government to solve the coinage crisis through the acceptance of the debased coins in tax collection. In view of the mass riots and merchant strikes in the Lower Yangzi region, the Ministry of Finance (Duzhibu) eventually adopted the proposal from this general chamber, and it also ordered provincial governments to stop minting the ten-*wen* copper coins. Meanwhile, the Suzhou GCC made more active efforts to help local officials pacify the coinage crisis in a nearby town, Zhouzhuang. It induced dozens of its own merchant participants in that town to follow the official order and instructed the Wujiang-Zhenze ACC to investigate and discipline the merchants who had already discounted the ten-*wen* copper coins. Moreover, this general chamber urged the magistrate of Yuanhe County to issue a public notice, prohibiting merchants in other towns from following the Zhouzhuang example.[28]

The management of the copper coinage crisis by these chambers of commerce may seem to differ from their anti-tax activities because they actually allied with the Qing government against small businesses in the monetary issue. In fact, the involvement of these chambers in both kinds of commercial issues reflected their primary pursuit of elite merchant interests and their broader concern for local society. In coinage crisis, their effort to prevent small merchants from discounting the ten-*wen* copper coins not only reflected elite anxiety for social stability but also benefited popular consumers. In particular, the Shanghai GCC eventually used the popular protests to push the Qing government into acceptance of the devalued coins in tax collection and thus alleviated the monetary crisis in favor of small merchants as well as popular consumers. As these chambers of commerce expanded their economic activities into railroad construction in Jiangsu and Zhejiang provinces, their elite merchants found even more common interests with small merchants and the populace as such large-scale public projects went beyond class tensions in local markets.

[handwritten annotation: reflects CCs elite merchant interests & concern for societal stability]

Elite, Provincial, and National Interests in the Railroad Movement

The chambers of commerce in Zhejiang and Jiangsu successively engaged in the construction of provincial railroads because such large-scale industrial projects combined the economic interests of elite merchants with their public concern for their native provinces and for the national sovereignty under foreign encroachment. Thus, these chambers provided both institutional and personnel resources for their provincial railroad companies. In particular, they first helped the two companies obtain merchant support and gov-

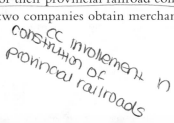

[handwritten annotation: CC involvement in construction of provincial railroads]

ernmental approval and then joined in agitations against both Qing official and British interference. Although the late Qing railroad movement in the Lower Yangzi region has previously received scholarly scrutiny, its crucial relations with the chambers of commerce in the region and with their political mobilization still deserve analysis beyond the past literature.[29]

Shanghai merchants of Ningbo origin had entered competition with foreign companies for railroad construction in Zhejiang Province from the late 1890s. However, in 1898, the Qing government signed a preliminary contract with Jardine, Matheson, and Company, which represented the Hongkong and Shanghai Banking Corporation and the British and Chinese Corporation, granting the British the right to build a railroad from Suzhou to Ningbo via Hangzhou.[30] After Fan Gongxu, the would-be president of the Hangzhou GCC, led a protest of Zhejiang elites against an American plan for another railroad in the province in 1905, leading literati reformers in Zhejiang, notably Tang Shouqian, contacted President Yan Xinhou of the Shanghai GCC and other Zhejiang elite merchants there, proposing to build the railroad with provincial capital. Yan then called on Zhejiang natives for a discussion of the railroad issue in the office of the Shanghai GCC on June 24, 1905. Although the meeting was later postponed to July 24 because of the late arrival of Zhejiang students from Japan, it attracted more than 160 gentry, merchants, metropolitan officials, and student representatives of Zhejiang origin. They decided to organize the Zhejiang Railroad Company (Zhejiang tielu gongsi) and selected Tang Shouqian as its president.[31]

The Zhejiang Railroad Company quickly obtained recognition from the Ministry of Commerce, and it also received endorsement from many elite merchant participants in the chambers of commerce within Shanghai and Zhejiang Province. Its nineteen identifiable founders and first officers in 1906–1907 included Yan Xinhou, Li Houyou, and eight other leaders and full members of the Shanghai GCC, as well as Fan Gongxu and Sun Yirang, who were presidents of the Hangzhou GCC and Ruian ACC, respectively.[32] An election at the first shareholders' meeting of the Zhejiang Railroad Company on October 26, 1906 produced eleven directors, including other identifiable chamber leaders, such as Wang Dafu (Wenxian) and Hu Zaoqing from the Hangzhou GCC.[33]

Chamber leaders and other wealthy merchants could occupy such important positions in the Zhejiang Railroad Company because its 1905 regulations stipulated that large shareholders owning more than 5,000 silver dollars of stock would not only receive yearly dividends at the rate of 7 percent of their investment but also met the qualifications for directors and auditors as well as voters in the company's elections and decision-making meetings.[34] Indeed, the Zhejiang merchant leaders of the Shanghai GCC, such as Yan Xinhou, Li Houyou, Yu Qiaqing, Su Baosen, Zhu Baosan, Chen Ziqin, and Yang Xinzhi, all made investments ranging from 5,000 to 10,000 silver dollars. So did other chamber leaders, including Wang Zhen of the South Shanghai BCC and Li Kai of the Huzhou ACC. By 1908 the relatively large shareholders (those who purchased stock from 100 to 10,000 silver dollars) numbered 7,305, accounting for 70 percent of the total 10,422 investors. They provided 4,773,600 silver dollars out of the total 4,899,500 silver dollars of investment in the company, thereby holding 97 percent of the railroad stock.[35] Thus, like the Lower Yangzi chambers of commerce, the Zhejiang Railroad Company mainly included elite merchants, and it also shared many leaders with these chambers. CC investors in ZRC

In Jiangsu Province, the railroad movement resulted more directly from the initiative of chamber leaders. Under the influence of Zhejiang elites, the Suzhou GCC in October 1905 also asked Jiangsu provincial authorities to petition the Qing court for the abolishment of its preliminary agreement with the British over the Suzhou-Hangzhou-Ningbo railroad. This general chamber further proposed building the railroad in southern Jiangsu with provincial capital. Thereafter, two leaders of the Suzhou GCC, You Xianjia and Wang Tongyu, made a special trip to Shanghai. Their discussion with Shanghai elite merchants and Tang Shouqian, the president of the Zhejiang Railroad Company, led to a plan for a merchant-owned railroad company in southern Jiangsu. After the Ministry of Commerce received their plan in February 1906, it encouraged the Suzhou GCC to make preparations to set up the Jiangsu Railroad Company (Susheng tielu gongsi), which would be responsible for railroad construction in the entire province.[36]

More gentry and elite merchants from Jiangsu soon joined the leaders of the Suzhou GCC as founders of the Jiangsu Railroad Company. They included the president of the Shanghai GCC, Zeng Zhu; vice president of the Tong-Chong-Hai GCCC, Liu Guixin; and presidents of many affiliated chambers in Jiangsu Province, such as Yun Zuqi of Changzhou Prefecture, Zhou Tingbi of Wuxi County, and Sha Yuanbing of Rugao County. The president of the Jiangsu Railroad Company was Wang Qingmu, the senior councilor of the Ministry of Commerce who had supervised chambers of commerce in Shanghai but was on mourning leave from his official duties. The three vice presidents were Zhang Jian, a close associate of many chamber leaders; Wang Tongyu, an honorary member of the Suzhou GCC; and Xu Dinglin, who

leaders of other GCCs join ZRC

would become president of the Haizhou-Ganyu ACC the following year. Under their leadership, the Jiangsu Railroad Company quickly received the endorsement of more than 200 metropolitan officials of Jiangsu origin and subsequently obtained approval from the Ministry of Commerce and the throne in May 1906.[37]

The Jiangsu Railroad Company also received financial support from chamber leaders and members. In its capital-raising appeal of 1906, the company stated that it was organized by the chambers of commerce in all the prefectures, departments, and counties of Jiangsu Province.[38] Among its large shareholders, with investments ranging from 2,500 to 5,000 silver dollars, there were many elite merchants from the chambers of commerce in the province, such as Wang Tongyu, Hang Zuliang (Xiaoxuan), Wang Jialiu (Li'ao), and Zhang Lüqian from the Suzhou GCC; Zhou Tingbi and Chen Youxiang from the Shanghai GCC; Gu Xinyi from the South Shanghai BCC; and Ren Xifen from the Yixing-Jingxi ACC. Other large shareholders included prestigious gentry entrepreneurs, such as Zhang Jian, and one former grand councilor, Wang Wenshao.[39] Actually, the gentry, elite merchant, and official shareholders from the three cities of Suzhou, Shanghai, and Beijing provided about two-thirds of the total three million silver dollars of capital investment in the Jiangsu Railroad Company by late 1907. Similar to their Zhejiang peers, the shareholders in the Jiangsu Railroad Company were to receive annual dividends of 7 percent on their investment, and those with more than 500 silver dollars of stock were allowed to cast one vote each at annual meetings of the railroad company and in the elections of its directors.[40]

Thus, the chamber leaders and other elites in Jiangsu and Zhejiang provinces formed their respective railroad companies with the similar purpose of pursuing profit and power in the new industrial projects. However, the two railroad companies could still claim to be public-spirited institutions, not only because they assembled shareholders from each prefecture and county in their respective provinces and received support from varied social organizations, including chambers of commerce, but also because they sought to protect the two provinces as well as Chinese sovereignty from foreign economic intrusion. This nationalistic purpose led the two railroad companies to work closely with the Qing government at the outset. On September 23, 1905, an imperial edict rendered full support to the Zhejiang elite effort to build their provincial railroads and ordered Sheng Xuanhuai, the signer of the preliminary agreement regarding the Suzhou-Hangzhou-Ningbo railroad, to negotiate with the British for the annulment of this agreement. As Qing officials admitted later on, the Ministry of Commerce realized that this agreement had granted the British the right to build this railroad, but it still supported the Zhejiang and Jiangsu elites in order to recover railroad concessions from foreign powers through popular pressure.[41]

In early 1906, the Qing court realized that the British would not yield easily, and it instead tried to redeem the railroad concession. By October 1907, the Ministry of Foreign Affairs had negotiated with the British to offset the previous concession over the Suzhou-Hangzhou-Ningbo railroad with a British loan to the Jiangsu and Zhejiang railroads. Although the new agreement pledged other revenues rather than those from the two provincial railroads as security for this loan, it mandated the repayment of the loan from the profits of the Zhejiang and Jiangsu railroads . On October 20, 1907, an imperial edict announced not only this loan agreement but also the governmental plan to make official appointments of the managers of railroad projects in Zhejiang and Jiangsu provinces.[42]

This imperial edict immediately provoked protests from Jiangsu and Zhejiang elites because it honored the preliminary agreement with the British but broke previous imperial promises to grant them the right to build and control the provincial railroads. In their eyes, acceptance of the British loan and the imperial edict could lead to both foreign and Qing official control over their provincial railroads. In fact, chamber leaders and directors of the Zhejiang and Jiangsu railroad companies had been sending protest telegrams to the Ministry of Foreign Affairs, the Ministry of Agriculture, Industry, and Commerce, and the Ministry of Posts and Communications (Youchuanbu) from October 6, 1907, when they first received information about the negotiations over the loan agreement.[43] After the announcement of the imperial edict, an anti-loan movement soon started in Zhejiang and Jiangsu provinces; chambers of commerce and their elite merchants played leading roles in the movement.

The earliest responses to the imperial edict included protest telegrams from individual gentry, merchants, students, and stockholders, as well as schools, educational associations, railroad companies, and especially chambers of commerce in Jiangsu and Zhejiang provinces. Among the 209 protest telegrams sent from the two provinces between late October and early December of 1907, at least forty were from chambers of commerce. These telegrams came mainly from the chambers with large shareholders or from those within cities and towns along the projected railroad line, such as the general chambers in Shanghai, Suzhou, Hangzhou, and Tongzhou, as well as the affiliated chambers in Songjiang, Jiaxing, and Shaoxing prefectures, Wuxi-Jinkui and Wujiang-

Zhenze counties, and the towns of Shengze and Pingwang. Their protests forced the Qing court to propose a dialogue with the presidents of the Jiangsu and Zhejiang railroad companies.[44]

The Shanghai GCC led the telegram protests because its incumbent president, Li Houyou, and other leaders and members had made heavy investment in either the Zhejiang or Jiangsu railroad company. In its first telegram to the Ministry of Agriculture, Industry, and Commerce on October 28, 1907, Li and Sun Duosen, vice president of the general chamber, headed the list of protesters. They indicated that the loan deal with the British and the governmental plan for official supervision of the railroads in Jiangsu and Zhejiang contradicted the previous imperial promises and would destroy merchant confidence in the government. In the face of such indictments, the Ministry of Foreign Affairs sent a telegram in reply, denying the possibility of British interference through the loan agreement and any governmental plan for official control over railroads in the two provinces, but this telegram failed to quell the protests.[45]

On November 15, 1907, the Shanghai GCC under Li's leadership sent out its second protest telegram to the Ministry of Agriculture, Industry, and Commerce. The unusually long telegram reviewed Li's previous engagement in the competition with the British over railroad construction in Zhejiang from 1903. It bitterly criticized the court for keeping its promises with foreigners rather than with its own people and openly denounced the official quibble that the loan deal would not result in British control of the railroad. After the Ministry of Foreign Affairs and the Liangjiang governor-general invited representatives from the Zhejiang and Jiangsu railroad companies for a discussion in Beijing, the Shanghai GCC on November 16 sent a third protest telegram to the governor-general. This telegram refused to send any representatives into a discussion trap set by the Qing government in Beijing. The general chamber later agreed to do so only because Jiangsu elites insisted on sending representatives to Beijing as a way of rejecting the British loan.[46]

The chambers of commerce in Jiangsu and Zhejiang also helped organize many anti-loan meetings and associations. On October 22, 1907, a protest meeting in Hangzhou led to the formation of the Anti-Loan Public Society of Zhejiang Citizens (Zhejiang guomin jukuan gonghui), which further sought to assemble representatives of gentry, merchants, students, and soldiers from all prefectures and counties of Zhejiang Province for a protest conference on November 25. Chambers of commerce in many Zhejiang cities and towns responded to this call, established their own anti-loan associations, and made preparations for this provincial conference.[47]

On October 27, 1907, the Ningbo GCC held a joint meeting with the local educational association, and it then telegraphed the Ministry of Foreign Affairs to protest the loan agreement. On November 1, more than 400 gentry, merchants, and students gathered in the office of the Ningbo GCC to hold the first large-scale protest meeting in the prefecture. This conference gave birth to an anti-loan association in Ningbo and elected the president of the general chamber, Wu Chuanji, as the chairman of the new association. Meanwhile, the Ningbo GCC contacted the Shanghai GCC, the Zhejiang Railroad Company, and the Anti-Loan Public Society of Zhejiang Citizens in Hangzhou for cooperative action.[48] The affiliated chambers of commerce in Jiaxing and Huzhou prefectures, Dinghai subprefecture, the town of Xiashi, and other places also held protest meetings, organized anti-loan associations, and selected delegates for the planned provincial conference. This conference was eventually held in Hangzhou on November 25 and drew more than 2,000 protesters from the whole Zhejiang Province.[49]

In Jiangsu Province, one of the earliest anti-loan meetings was held in the office of the Suzhou GCC on October 29, 1907. It produced the Suzhou Anti-Loan Society (Suzhou jukuanhui) and planned a mass protest meeting for October 31. About 1,000 gentry, merchants, and students attended the mass meeting, deciding to use the Suzhou Anti-Loan Society to support and supervise the Jiangsu Railroad Company during the railroad movement. The meeting also elected twenty-seven leaders for the Suzhou Anti-Loan Society, including You Xianjia, the president of the Suzhou GCC, and four other chamber leaders in the city, Wang Tongyu, Peng Fusun, Ni Kaiding, and Hang Zuliang. Thereafter, the Suzhou Anti-Loan Society repeatedly used the office of the general chamber to hold its protest meetings. The affiliated chambers in Songjiang Prefecture, Jiading County, and the town of Shengze also established their own anti-loan associations.[50]

The center of the anti-loan movement was Shanghai, and the Shanghai GCC also became a key link for protest organizations and activities in Jiangsu and Zhejiang provinces. Between November 1 and November 15, at least eight anti-loan meetings were held in Shanghai by the Jiangsu and Zhejiang railroad companies, the Jiangsu Railroad Association (Jiangsu tielu xiehui), and Zhejiang native-place organizations, and all of them drew chamber leaders from the two provinces.[51] Elite activists of the two provinces eventually held their first joint meeting in Shanghai on November 19 and elected delegates to directly petition the imperial court for rejection of the British loan. These delegates included Wang Tongyu and Xu Dinglin, the leaders of the Suzhou GCC and the Haizhou-Ganyu ACC. This meeting also established the Jiangsu–Zhejiang Federation (Jiang-Zhe xiehui) as the representative organ of citizens in both provinces for the movement. Later on, the Jiangsu and Zhejiang railroad companies further formed the Jiang-Zhe Railroad Directors' Federation (Su-Zhe tielu dongshiju lianhehui) to communicate with their delegates to Beijing.[52]

From early November of 1907, the railroad movements in both Zhejiang and Jiangsu provinces adopted a new strategy: to reject the British loan by raising more railroad capital. This strategy made chambers of commerce more important for the success of the movement. On November 10, representatives of eleven Zhejiang prefectures held a meeting in Shanghai and pledged more than 22 million silver dollars for their provincial railroad company. The Jiangsu Railroad Company held a similar meeting in Shanghai on November 13, with delegates from six prefectures of southern Jiangsu making a commitment to 13.4 million silver dollars of stock. One week later, Yangzhou Prefecture in northern Jiangsu pledged to purchase another million silver dollars of stock. After the two stock-subscribing conferences in Shanghai, many chambers of commerce in the two provinces held meetings to fulfill the pledges made by their prefectural representatives and to allocate portions of the pledged amount to their affiliated guilds.[53]

One veteran leader of the Shanghai GCC, Zhou Jinbiao, represented his home prefecture of Ningbo at the Shanghai conference of Zhejiang delegates, promising to purchase seven million silver dollars of railroad stock, the largest amount pledged by any prefectural delegate in the province. In order to achieve that goal, the Ningbo GCC and the local educational association took responsibility for stock-selling activities and loan-resisting propaganda, respectively. Thereafter, the general chamber selected nineteen merchant members as directors of stock-selling agencies, and its affiliated chamber in Fenghua County in turn sent out agents to promote stock purchases in the eight townships of the county. At the Shanghai conference, the delegates of Hangzhou, Jiaxing, and Huzhou also promised that each of their prefectures would contribute one to five million silver dollars of railroad capital. Thus, the Hangzhou GCC and its affiliated chambers in Yuhang County as well as those in Huzhou and Jiaxing prefectures actively mobilized their guilds and merchant members to purchase railroad stocks through public meetings or other measures.[54]

In Jiangsu Province, leaders of the Suzhou GCC and the Suzhou Anti-Loan Society rallied urban residents to purchase railroad stock on a ward by ward basis after their prefectural delegates promised to raise three million silver dollars of railroad stock at the Shanghai meeting. Meanwhile, Changzhou

Prefecture pledged two million silver dollars of railroad capital, and the affiliated chambers in the prefectural city and county cities, such as Wuxi, either subscribed directly for large amount of stocks or had their guilds accept portions of the stock. After Zhenjiang Prefecture made a commitment of one million silver dollars of railroad stock, the affiliated chamber in the prefectural city undertook to raise 400,000 silver dollars from its guilds and portioned out the remaining 600,000 silver dollars to other affiliated chambers in Liyang, Jintan, and Lishui counties. Around Shanghai and Suzhou, the affiliated and branch chambers in the towns of Luodian, Minhang, Meili, Shengze, Pingwang, and Zhenze also fulfilled their apportionments by pushing merchant subscription to railroad stocks at their public meetings.[55]

It was largely through such organized efforts that the Jiangsu Railroad Company collected 620,682 silver dollars of additional capital by 1908, and the Zhejiang Railroad Company issued 3,400,117 silver dollars of new stocks by 1909.[56] The anti-loan movement did not alter the elite merchant dominance of the two railroad companies, but it did make them appear more like public enterprises and more representative of the populace through the stock-purchasing campaigns. In early November 1907, more than 2,000 porters in Hangzhou contributed about 1,000 silver dollars as railroad capital, and sedan bearers in this city and Suzhou quickly followed suit. In Shanghai, beggars, actors, and dockers also joined the movement in mid-November and purchased railroad stock. In the town of Shuanlin, the anti-loan movement under the leadership of local branch chamber even involved waiters, maids, and water carriers in the stock-purchasing activities. When the delegates of the Jiangsu and Zhejiang railroad companies left Shanghai for Beijing on December 10 for direct negotiations with the Qing court over the British loan, hundreds of workers joined a crowd of more than 1,000 to see them off and shouted: "Don't borrow money!"[57]

Thus, the railroad movement linked chamber participants and other elite investors with the populace not only through their shared provincialism and nationalism but also through concrete economic interest. As a result of this movement, the total number of shareholders in the Zhejiang Railroad Company rose from 10,422 in 1908 to 67,691 in 1912. In particular, the number of its small stockholders with less than 100 silver dollars of investment skyrocketed from 3,117 to 51,361, or from 30 to 76 percent of all shareholders. Meanwhile, the total stock capitalization of the Zhejiang Railroad Company increased from 4,899,500 to 10,248,660 silver dollars, and the stock value of small shareholder increased from 125,900 to 1,284,045 silver dollars, or from 2.6 to 12.5 percent of the company's total stock.[58]

The two companies did not collect as much capital as the stock subscribers had pledged during the anti-loan movement mainly because the movement failed to achieve its original goal. After the delegates of the Jiangsu and Zheji-ang railroad companies arrived in Beijing, their negotiations with the Ministry of Foreign Affairs resulted in a compromise. According to their agreement with officials, this ministry would sign a loan agreement with the British and secure the loan with the earnings from the Imperial Railroad of North China, and then the two companies would accept the loan from the Ministry of Posts and Communications via another agreement, so that the British would not be able to interfere directly in the two provincial railroads.[59]

[margin handwriting: Compromise loan was signed but company accepted thru Chinese ministry not directly]

After this compromise, conflicts between the two railroad companies and the Qing government continued over the implementation of their agreement. By mid-1908, the president of the Zhejiang Railroad Company, Tang Shouqian, still refused to use the monies loaned by the British through the Ministry of Posts and Communications. The Hangzhou GCC and other anti-loan associations actively supported him and continuously pushed all stock subscribers to hand in their pledged capital. In April and July of 1909, the Jiangsu and Zhejiang railroad companies twice made joint petitions to the Ministry of Posts and Communications, asking to return the first installment of the British loan and to cancel the loan agreement. The conflict escalated after August 23, 1910, when the imperial court dismissed Tang Shouqian from his position in the Zhejiang Railroad Company because he had openly attacked Sheng Xuanhuai, the incumbent vice minister of posts and communications, for the latter's mismanagement of the Suzhou-Hangzhou-Ningbo railroad issue.[60] The court's arbitrary decision resulted in a new wave of protests in Zhejiang, and the Hangzhou GCC again played a leading role in the movement.

[margin handwriting: ZRC still refused to accept money loaned by British]

Immediately after Tang's dismissal, the Hangzhou GCC successively held three emergency meetings to discuss the issue on August 27–28 and September 5, 1910, and these meetings attracted both merchants and literati. On October 1, this general chamber gathered representatives from all chambers of commerce in Zhejiang for a general conference, and attendees at this conference again included chamber leaders and literati elites. The meeting decided to challenge the government's right to dismiss Tang by invoking the Qing commercial laws and sending delegates to Beijing to directly petition the Qing court.[61] The vice president of the Hangzhou GCC, Wang Xirong, and the former president of the Shanghai GCC, Li Houyou, later joined other delegates of the Zhejiang Railroad Company in the petition in Beijing. Wang also submitted to the Ministry of Agriculture, Industry, and Commerce a separate petition in the names of the Hangzhou and Ningbo GCCs as well as the affiliated and branch chambers of Zhejiang Province. This petition argued that the government's imposition of the loan agreement and dismissal of Tang had violated the Qing commercial laws and asked whether the Qing court would adhere to its laws regarding merchant-owned companies and chambers of commerce. In response to the petitions, the Qing court had to affirm merchant ownership of the Zhejiang Railroad Company, and it eventually transferred the British loan to another railroad just before the outbreak of the 1911 Revolution.[62] *Qing eventually transferred ZRC loan*

The railroad movement in Jiangsu and Zhejiang provinces undoubtedly alienated Lower Yangzi elites, including chamber leaders, from the Qing government. However, the question remains whether this movement led these elites and their organizations toward a complete break with the imperial state and ended in their acceptance of the anti-Qing revolution, as previous scholarship has argued.[63] Actually, the railroad movement in the Lower Yangzi region reached its climax in late 1907 rather than thereafter, and even at its climatic moment Tang Shouqian still warned the Hangzhou GCC against its proposal to withhold tax payments as capital for the Zhejiang Railroad Company.[64] At the beginning of 1908, when the railroad movement was still going on, one major leader of the movement, President Fan Gongxu of the Hangzhou GCC, returned to the officialdom that he had left more than two decades earlier. In 1909 two other leaders of the railroad movement, Honorary Director Wang Tongyu of the Suzhou GCC and President Wang Qingmu of the Jiangsu Railroad Company, also resumed their official careers. As the vice president of the Shanghai GCC in 1907, Sun Duosen was once involved in the railroad protest, but he, too, became a provincial official around 1909.[65]

Actually, in the railroad movement, the leaders of these chambers and the two railroad companies had collaborated closely with the Qing court before clashing with the latter over the British loan from 1907. Even during the confrontation, their anti-loan movement still won sympathy and support from provincial bureaucrats, including Manchu officials, in Jiangsu and Zhejiang provinces. In early December 1907, the Manchu Liangjiang governor-general, Duanfang, even contributed part of his salary to the Jiangsu Railroad Company and then forced all officials in the Jiangsu provincial government to follow suit. When the Hangzhou GCC led the protest against the dismissal of Tang Shouqian in early October of 1910, its protest meeting was actually presided over by a leading general of the Manchu banner garrison in Hangzhou, Gui Hanxiang.[66]

[left margin handwritten note: RR- did not cause break blw Qing & elite merchants]

Clearly, most elite leaders of the Lower Yangzi chambers of commerce and the Jiangsu and Zhejiang railroad companies did not choose to break with the Qing government during the railroad movement because their associational networks had effectively protected their personal, provincial, and national interests by bringing them into more varied and effective interactions with officials than would uncompromising showdown. While there were still repercussions of the anti-loan movement after its climax in 1907, chamber leaders in the Lower Yangzi region actively collaborated with the Qing government in other financial and industrial affairs.

[margin note: CC still collaborated w/ Qing in other affairs despite RR movement]

Financial Crises, the Nanyang Expo, and Sino–American Joint Ventures

It seems counterintuitive that the Lower Yangzi chambers of commerce continued to protest against the official imposition of the British loan deal on their provincial railroads after 1907 while simultaneously looking for financial help from the Qing government and foreign banks during market crises. At the same time, they were also helping the Qing government to organize the largest production fair in late Qing China and trying to strengthen Chinese diplomatic relations with the United States through joint ventures with American chambers of commerce. The explanation for the bewildering phenomenon is that the widespread chamber networks provided a common ground for elite merchants to work and make business deals with the Qing government and foreign capital beyond the aforesaid conflicts over the railroad issue.

Shanghai was a center of the Lower Yangzi railroad movement around 1907, but it repeatedly faced financial crises thereafter. Thus, the two chambers in the city had to look for official help to obtain huge loans from governmental and foreign banks for the rescue of the financial market, including the native banks of their elite merchant participants. In late 1908, the Shanghai financial market experienced a serious shortage of silver currency as a result of economic depression in Western countries. In particular, a few Shanghai comprador merchants went bankrupt, prompting foreign banks to retrieve about five million taels of loans from Chinese native banks. In order to stabilize the financial market, President Zhou Jinbiao and Vice President Li Houyou of the Shanghai GCC, the two major leaders of the railroad agitation against the British loan, made a desperate bid to obtain official help for a loan deal with the British-owned Hongkong and Shanghai Banking Corporation. After the Shanghai *daotai* agreed to serve as a guarantor and two governmental

[margin note: financial crisis in Shanghai; merchants need official help – loans]

banks and a Ningbo merchant bank put up their property deeds as security, the general chamber received a total of 2,300,000 taels in foreign loans, as well as a loan of 400,000 silver dollars from the Jiangsu provincial government. These foreign and governmental loans were then distributed to native banks through the Shanghai GCC and thus helped the urban market avoid imminent disaster.[67] *SH GCC obtained foreign + gov loans in crisis* [67]

However, new financial crisis quickly struck Shanghai after the collapse of the rubber stock market there in 1910, which brought the Shanghai GCC into another financial deal with the Qing government and foreign banks. The rubber stock fervor engulfed the Shanghai stock market from 1909, when Western industries, especially the American auto industry, faced a shortage in their rubber supplies. Consequently, there appeared a rush for investment in the rubber industry, and the face value of its stock skyrocketed from about 60 taels per share to 1,000 taels. By early 1910, more than forty foreign firms had sold rubber stocks at a total value of 25 million taels in Shanghai, and the Chinese and foreigners in the city purchased 80 and 20 percent of these stocks, respectively. Shanghai native banks not only invested heavily in this stock speculation but also received large numbers of rubber stock as pledges of security on loans. The inflated rubber stock market collapsed in July 1910, and eight Shanghai native banks immediately declared bankruptcy during the three days between July 21 and 24.[68]

SH GCC had to make deal w/ Qing and foreign banks in rubber-crisis

The Shanghai GCC quickly contacted Shanghai Daotai Cai Naihuang for a plan to save the financial market. On the evening of July 24, its president, Zhou Jinbiao, and Daotai Cai took a special train for Jiangning and personally requested that the Liangjiang governor-general petition the Qing court for financial assistance to Shanghai native bankers. As a result of their discussion, the Shanghai *daotai* again served as a guarantor for Chinese native bankers to borrow 3.5 million taels from nine foreign banks. The vice president of the Shanghai GCC, Shao Qintao, was to supervise these native banks to ensure that they would pay back their debts to the creditors.[69]

The repercussions of the rubber stock collapse and the resultant financial crisis in Shanghai, however, were far from over. On October 8, 1910, the Yuanfengrun Remittance Shop in Shanghai and its seventeen branches in other large cities declared bankruptcy, leaving a debt of more than twenty million taels. As one of the largest native banking institutions in Shanghai and late Qing China, this shop had been founded by Yan Xinhou, the first president of the Shanghai GCC, and inherited by his son, Yan Yibin, the former vice president of the general chamber. Its bankruptcy aggravated the financial crisis in Shanghai and brought down additional native banks in Tianjin, Beijing, and other large cities.[70] Thus, the financial crisis affected late Qing society far beyond Shanghai.

Immediately after the bankruptcy of the Yuanfengrun Remittance Shop, the Shanghai GCC assembled guild leaders from all businesses for a special meeting and sent three identical telegrams to the Qing court, the Liangjiang governor-general, and the Jiangsu governor. In these emergency telegrams, the general chamber predicted the possible expansion of the financial disaster in the city, the danger of a business standstill, and unemployment of 200,000–300,000 laborers, as well as the collapse of social security. However, the Ministry of Finance instructed the Qing State Bank to transfer only one million taels to Shanghai, and the Qing court simply ordered the Liangjiang governor-general to visit Shanghai and save its financial market through other means.[71]

Through the help of the Liangjiang governor-general, the Shanghai GCC and the South Shanghai ACC negotiated another loan of two million taels from the Hongkong and Shanghai Banking Corporation. According to the harsh terms set by the British bank, this loan was not only guaranteed by Shanghai *daotai*, together with thirty directors and the presidents of the two chambers, but was also secured on the properties of individual merchant recipients. Vice President Shao Qintao of the Shanghai GCC, President Wang Zhen of the South Shanghai ACC, and a director of both chambers, Shen Manyun, were elected as chamber representatives who would help Chinese merchants raise mortgages from the British bank.[72]

In addition to the chambers of commerce in Shanghai, the Suzhou GCC and other chambers in the Lower Yangzi region played important roles in maintaining the stability of local financial markets, but it became increasingly hard for them to get help from the Qing government during financial upheavals.[73] Nevertheless, these chambers of commerce still provided the Qing government with crucial help for the organization of the Nanyang Expo (Nanyang quanyehui, literally meaning "Nanyang industry-promoting exhibition") in 1910, even though they had already experienced financial difficulty by that time.

The Nanyang Expo was promoted by Liangjiang governor-general Duanfang in his jurisdiction because he held the concurrent post of *Nanyang dachen*, or imperial commissioner for treaty ports in southern China. In fact, this exhibition was a national fair that received imperial endorsement from the beginning, and its organizers also requested support from all provinces.[74] The official plan for such a national fair attracted the Lower Yangzi chambers of commerce because it promised its elite merchant sponsors both fame and fortune and also merged merchant and official interest in the development of national industries.

The official initiator of the Nanyang Expo, Duanfang, was a Manchu official famed as a connoisseur in curios and an opportunist in political reforms. In 1908 he came up with the idea of opening a botanical exhibition in the public park of Jiangning.[75] The officials subordinate to him quickly expanded the idea into a grand plan for a national exhibition. They further proposed turning this exhibition into a joint venture of officials and merchants and to have the Shanghai and Jiangning GCCs subscribe half of the 500,000 silver dollars of stocks. Governor-General Duanfang then submitted this plan to the Qing court for approval, claiming that this exhibition would vitalize "practical businesses" and enlighten people's minds.[76]

In June 1908, Duanfang invited President Zhou Jinbiao and seven directors of the Shanghai GCC to a meeting in Jiangning and promised to pay merchant investors high dividends of 8 percent and to make up any possible loss in their investment from the official share of the stock. Thus, the Shanghai chamber leaders readily subscribed 150,000 silver dollars for the Nanyang Expo and let the Jiangning GCC purchase the remaining 100,000 silver dollars of merchant stock. In 1909, official organizers of the exhibition found that the budget of 500,000 silver dollars was far from enough and decided to issue another 200,000 silver dollars of new stock. Their call for additional merchant investment received only symbolic support from the Suzhou GCC and other Lower Yangzi chambers of commerce because of the aggravation of financial market at that time. However, the Shanghai GCC used its relations with Chinese chambers of commerce in Southeast Asia, helping the officials raise sufficient merchant capital from that quarter.[77]

The Lower Yangzi chambers of commerce also joined in the preparatory organizations and activities for the Nanyang Expo. By March 1909, the major leaders of the exhibition included one chairman, five vice chairmen, and thirteen directors. The chairman was the Liangjiang governor-general himself, while the vice chairmen were all incumbent and former officials, with the exception of Yu Qiaqing, a former director of the Shanghai GCC. Moreover, all thirteen directors were elite merchants from Shanghai and Jiangning, including such chamber leaders as Zhou Jinbiao, Yan Yibin, and Ding Jiahou of the Shanghai GCC, as well as Song Enquan of the Jiangning GCC. More chamber leaders joined other preparatory organizations, including the exhibition-assisting associations (*xiezan hui*) in provincial capitals and major treaty ports, exhibit-providing associations (*chupin xiehui*) in these large cities and a few major trades, and staple-displaying associations (*wuchanhui*) in all prefectures of Jiangsu, Anhui, and Jiangxi provinces that were under the direct jurisdiction of the Liangjiang governor-general.[78]

In Jiangsu Province, exhibition-assisting associations appeared in Shanghai, Jiangning, Suzhou, and other large cities, and there were a dozen exhibit-providing associations or staple-displaying associations in these cities and other prefectural capitals. Some counties in southern Jiangsu also established exhibit-providing branches (*chupinsuo*). Most of these associations were not only dominated by chamber leaders but were also located in the chamber premises. Local governments provided either part or most of the funds for these associations to organize preparatory exhibitions at the prefectural level. The chambers of commerce in these cities usually bore the remaining costs, led merchants to provide staples for local displays, and helped select local exhibits through communications with branch chambers of commerce at the township level.[79]

Through the preparatory works for the Nanyang Expo, the chambers of commerce in Jiangsu mobilized their urban communities beyond their merchant constituencies. On April 11, 1909, the inaugural meeting of the exhibition-assisting association in Shanghai attracted more than 200 officials, merchants, literati, and other elites. President Zhou Jinbiao of the Shanghai GCC first called on all his compatriots to make concerted efforts to realize the Nanyang Expo. Then an official speaker further excited the audience by comparing the exhibition to a school for Chinese merchants, an advertisement for national commodities, an examination of commercial civilization, and a clock for national progress. In Jiangning, the exhibition-assisting association even recruited officers from New Army units to collect military equipment as exhibits. The staple-displaying association in Suzhou held the first prefectural exhibition in Jiangsu Province in late August 1909, attracting more than 7,000 visitors over eight days despite turning away many poor residents of the city because of the high admission fees.[80]

The chambers of commerce in Zhejiang also mobilized their associational networks to provide support for the Nanyang Expo. In August 1909, the Hangzhou GCC invited fourteen affiliated chambers of commerce in the province to discuss preparatory works for the exhibition, and they resolved to organize an exhibition-assisting association and an exhibit-providing association. At the meeting they also decided that the provincial government and chambers of commerce would each raise half of the 50,000 silver dollars in funds required by the two associations. The affiliated chambers in Jiaxing, Huzhou, and Shaoxing prefectures likewise organized exhibit-providing associations or staple-displaying associations as had their counterparts in Jiangsu.[81]

Further support for the Nanyang Expo came from chambers of commerce in other provinces and the overseas Chinese communities. Liangjiang governor-general Duanfang originally planned staple-displaying associations in twenty-seven prefectures within Anhui and Jiangxi provinces, many of which were, indeed, formed by local chambers of commerce. At the provincial level, exhibition-assisting associations also came into being in Anhui, Jiangxi, Guangdong, Guangxi, Zhili, Hubei, Hunan, Fujian, and Guizhou provinces. Because the plan for the exhibition included a special hall for Southeast Asia, the Chinese chambers of commerce there also took responsibility for providing exhibits.[82] *Support from other province's ccs*

The Nanyang Expo eventually opened on June 5, 1910, and ended on November 29, a run of nearly six months. Its inaugural ceremony was attended by more than 5,000 guests, and the representative of the Shanghai GCC received a special invitation to give a complimentary address. The exhibition site occupied about 3.5 square kilometers in the northern part of Jiangning city, and more than thirty exhibition halls displayed exhibits from the imperial capital of Beijing, eighteen provinces, the overseas Chinese communities, and a dozen sectors ranging from agriculture and industry to education and the military. There were also a zoo, a garden, a circus troupe, a movie theater, a racecourse, and many shops inside the exhibition site. The exhibits included a total of about one million items. At the end of the exhibition, five ranks of medals were awarded to 5,269 exhibits. Visitors to the exhibition totaled about 200,000, including Chinese from home and abroad as well as American, Japanese, and German delegations.[83]

The Nanyang Expo, the largest national fair in late Qing China, was primarily a joint venture of the Lower Yangzi chambers of commerce and the Qing government. However, its preparatory work did not always bring chamber leaders and Qing officials into harmonious collaboration. From the outset, the Qing government intended to levy tax on all items brought to the exhibition by merchants, and the tax was waived only after Governor-General Duanfang made repeated petitions to the throne on behalf of the merchants. The exhibition also disappointed merchant investors because it did not make any profit, as Duanfang had expected, but lost more than 100,000 silver dollars. Most merchant investors in the exhibition barely recouped their investments after a Chinese merchant from Southeast Asia contributed 100,000 silver dollars to the exhibition and purchased all the exhibition halls with an additional 200,000 silver dollars.[84]

One leading merchant sponsor of the Nanyang Expo, President Zhou Jinbiao of the Shanghai GCC, soon suffered a political setback as he was dismissed by the Qing court during the financial crisis in early December 1910. As late as October 1911, a former director of the Shanghai GCC and a vice chairman of the exhibition, Yu Qiaqing, was still complaining about his personal loss in this joint venture with officials. Interestingly, many chamber leaders in the Lower Yangzi region, including Zhou, were still trying to get official support for their joint ventures with American chambers of commerce around the same time and were also attempting to help the Qing government build close relations with the United States through such business deals.[85] *some CCS complained @ of loss in N Expo*

American diplomats in Shanghai first suggested contacts between chambers of commerce in the United States and late Qing China because the American government was anxious to expand its commercial interests in China at that time. In October 1908, the American consul-general in Shanghai, Charles Denby, sent a letter to the Shanghai GCC, urging it to invite delegates of American chambers of commerce on the Pacific coast for a visit to China after their stay in Japan in late October. Denby's letter stressed that this visit could increase American understanding of Chinese markets and help develop China's export trade with the United States. In a reply letter, the Shanghai GCC expressed its willingness to welcome the American visitors. It also decided to investigate Chinese products for export and asked the Suzhou GCC and other chambers along the Yangzi River to bring sample goods to Shanghai for its research on the export trade.[86] *US wanted to link American + Qing CCs*

Only one member of the American chamber delegation to Japan, Robert Dollar, arrived in China in November 1908 because the delegation had received the Chinese invitation too late. Dollar, however, arrived in Shanghai because he had been engaged in business in China from 1901. He paid a special visit to the Shanghai GCC, and his successive meetings with chamber leaders in Shanghai and Hankou persuaded them to issue a joint invitation to American chambers of commerce for a visit to China. On February 18, 1909, the Shanghai GCC, together with the chambers of commerce in Jiangning, Canton, Xiamen, Fuzhou, and Wuzhou, formally invited leaders of American chambers of commerce on the Pacific coast for a visit to Shanghai in late April. They not only entrusted Consul-General Denby to deliver their invitation letters but also asked the Chinese minister in Washington, D.C., and the Chinese consul-general in San Francisco to render assistance in this matter.[87] *1909 SH + other GCCs formally invite American CCs to visit SH*

Before the American chambers of commerce were ready to send a delegation to China, the Shanghai WGCC in July 1909 contacted the Shanghai GCC, revealing that the Honolulu Chamber of Commerce was also hoping to join the delegation. Meanwhile, the American consul-general in Shanghai returned home via Hawaii, and in a letter to the Shanghai GCC reiterated that hope. On the Chinese side, fifteen other chambers of commerce in April 1910 joined the Shanghai GCC and the five aforementioned chambers to send a new invitation to American chambers for a visit. They included general chambers in Beijing, Tianjin, Suzhou, Hangzhou, and Ningbo, as well as three affiliated chambers in the Lower Yangzi region, the South Shanghai, Wuxi-Jinkui, and Zhenjiang ACCs. Meanwhile, the Shanghai GCC persuaded the Ministry of Agriculture, Industry, and Commerce as well as the Ministry of Foreign Affairs to subsidize reception of the American guests. The Qing government later provided the Americans with special trains and steamships for free trips from Shanghai to Wuhan and Beijing.[88]

The American chamber delegation set out from San Francisco on August 23, 1910. It eventually included twenty-three representatives from chambers of commerce in San Francisco, Los Angeles, Seattle, Tacoma, Spokane, Portland, Oakland, San Diego, and Honolulu, as well as the men's wives, three secretaries, and a historian. On September 15, 1910, this group arrived in Shanghai and met a reception committee led by Zhou Jinbiao, the president of the Shanghai GCC.[89] Thereafter, the delegation entered "a six weeks' season of banquets, receptions, trade conferences and investigations, and visits to commercial establishments, educational institutions, government buildings, theaters, gardens, palaces and prisons."[90]

Between September 15 and 27, the American delegation visited large cities in the Lower Yangzi region, including Shanghai, Hangzhou, Suzhou, and Jiangning, and it also made stopovers in smaller cities, including Jiaxing, Wuxi, Changzhou, and Zhenjiang. In the large cities the Americans were met with a "storm of hospitality" from chamber leaders and Qing officials, ranging from the Shanghai *daotai* to the Zhejiang and Jiangsu governors, as well as the Liangjiang governor-general.[91] Even in smaller cities, "there were decorations, fireworks, refreshments, speeches and gifts."[92]

The grandiose welcome at first puzzled the American visitors because the anti-American boycott and the railroad agitation against the British loan were still recent memories. Their reflection on the visit to Hangzhou, the capital of Zhejiang Province, is especially interesting:

> To those who have studied the anti-foreign spirit in China and have followed the doings of the Hangzhou [General] Chamber of Commerce recently, its attitude on this occasion was perplexing. . . . We were aware early in the visit that our reception was being carried beyond an appropriate welcome to the delegates of foreign commercial bodies. . . . So we went on, from demonstration to demonstration, not like a company of western business men but like the President of the United States and a selected group of cabinet officials.[93]

Likewise, a Shanghai foreign newspaper indicated that "never had there been a visit of this kind since China had had dealings with foreigners. . . . [It] was not ordered by the government, but was given spontaneously and heartily by the people."[94]

In fact, the leaders of the Lower Yangzi chambers and other elites regarded the American visit as an opportunity to develop not only international business but also nongovernmental diplomacy between China and the United States. Zhang Jian, the president of the newly formed Jiangsu Provincial Assembly, entertained the American delegation in Jiangning after its visit to the Nanyang Expo on September 25, regarding the reception as the "starting point of people's diplomacy."[95] This reception ended with a business meeting between the American delegates and leading Chinese merchants who had gathered in Jiangning for the exhibition. They planned a future conference to discuss how to increase trade between China and the United States.[96]

Thereafter, the American delegates went on to visit Wuhan, Beijing, Tianjin, Yantai, Fuzhou, Xiamen, Canton, and Hong Kong, and its members even had an audience with Prince Regent Zaifeng and attended a party at the Ministry of Foreign Affairs in Beijing. On November 11, 1910, they returned to Shanghai and held a business meeting with leaders of the Shanghai, Jiangning, Tianjin, Canton, and Hankou GCCs as well as with those of the South Shanghai and Zhenjiang ACCs. This meeting gave birth to four agreements: (1) the establishment of a Sino-American bank with capital of ten million Mexican dollars to be subscribed by Chinese and American merchants equally; (2) the organization of a Sino-American steam navigation company that would be composed of seven steamships owned by Robert Dollar and one ship purchased by Chinese merchants; (3) the opening of a Chinese commodity exposition in the United States and an American one in China; and (4) the dispatch of an American commercial investigator to China and a Chinese counterpart to the United States.[97]

Early in 1911, the Shanghai GCC set up a special office to prepare to found the Sino-American steam navigation company and called on other chambers of commerce to invest in it. Meanwhile, the Shanghai, Tianjin, Hankou, and Canton GCCs entrusted Zhang Jian to petition the Qing court for financial assistance for the planned Sino-American bank and steamship company. In response, the minister of finance, Zaize, notified Zhang that the Qing court would make an under-the-table loan to the chambers of commerce for their business ventures with American merchants.[98]

Zhang's motive, however, was not only to develop business partnerships with American chambers of commerce but also to help the Qing government

develop closer ties with the United States. In his audience with Prince Regent
Zaifeng on June 13, 1911, Zhang stressed that China should give top priority
to Sino-American relations in its foreign policy. However, he worried that a
third nation might stand in the way of developing formal relations between
the two governments. Thus, he believed that informal cooperation between
the chambers of commerce of the two countries would be easier and more
reliable. Meanwhile, the Shanghai, Jiangning, Suzhou, and Hangzhou GCCs,
together with the general chambers in Tianjin, Hankou, Canton, Fuzhou, and
other large cities, petitioned the Qing court for 200,000 taels of subsidy to
underwrite their reciprocal visit to the United States. In response, the Ministry of Finance and the Ministry of Agriculture, Industry, and Commerce in
late June 1911 promised to provide a maximum of two million taels for joint
ventures between Chinese and American chambers of commerce.[99] However,
the outbreak of the Republican Revolution in October 1911 interrupted the
plan.[100] *Qing plan to finance ventures interrupted by Revolution*

Although the collaboration of these chamber leaders with the Qing government in Sino-American contacts lasted until the eve of the 1911 Revolution, it did not become an obstacle to their participation in the anti-Qing
revolutionary movement because they had never stopped clashing with the
imperial state over commercial taxes, provincial railroads, and other issues
during this period. They had long entered different forms of interactions
with Qing officials for the pursuit of their business and public interests, and
such pursuits in turn strengthened their claim to represent public interests
while expanding their political influence in commercial and industrial affairs from the local to the national level. Similarly, in the constitutional and
revolutionary movements, the Lower Yangzi chambers of commerce also increased their influence through their network expansion and multiform interactions with Qing officials and other political forces.

• merchant clashes w/ Qing

– anti-tax movements : soy sauce, brokerage, stamp, etc

– anti-loan Railroad movement

– conflict over devaluing the ten-wen copper coin

in many of these CCs fought for elite merchant
interest & wider pop./ social stability, not for small
merchants

• merchant + Qing support

– Nanyang Expo
– loans in financial crises
– US-China cc trip and business ventures

6

Joint Actions in the Constitutional and Revolutionary Movements

The Lower Yangzi chambers of commerce acquired an unprecedented opportunity for political participation after the Qing court formally committed itself to constitutional reform. On September 1, 1906, an imperial edict promised a "constitutional polity, which would keep fundamental power in the court but open various policies to public discussion."[1] The Shanghai GCC quickly passed this exciting news to other chambers of commerce in the Lower Yangzi region and to those in Fujian, Guangdong, and other provinces. It also urged them to celebrate the government's decision. On September 9, the general chamber and the General Works Board of Shanghai and Its Suburbs respectively held celebrations and sent supportive telegrams to the Qing court. The merchant exercise societies in southern Shanghai, the future merchant militias there, also gathered for the celebration. They set off tens of thousands of firecrackers and fired a twenty-four gun salute at the ceremony. After the Qing national flag was raised, all the people in attendance took off their hats, shouted loud slogans, cheerfully hailed the speeches, and then marched to the office of the South Shanghai BCC.[2]

Interestingly, the most active leaders of the Shanghai chambers and merchant militias in the constitutional reform also played crucial roles in the Republican Revolution against the Qing dynasty in 1911, as did the radical constitutionalists in other Lower Yangzi cities. Previous research on these chamber leaders and other social elites has usually explained their turn from constitutional to revolutionary movements mainly through their increasing

[margin note: ccs had opportunity to participate in Qing constitutional reform]

[margin note: cc members, elite merchants active role in the Republican Revolution]

conflicts with the Qing court over their bourgeois interests, elite reformism, or public activism.[3]

In this chapter, my network analysis of the political activism of the Lower Yangzi chambers of commerce in the constitutional reform and the Republican Revolution goes beyond the focus on their conflicts with the Qing court. It reveals how they promoted both constitutional and revolutionary movements through their multiform interactions with varied political forces ranging from the Qing government to revolutionary parties. In alliance with other constitutional organizations, these chambers repeatedly pressed the Qing government for more radical reforms, and they significantly changed the power structures ranging from commercial legislation to local administration. Driven by such interactive dynamics, many chamber leaders in the Lower Yangzi region, especially in the regional core, eventually endorsed the 1911 Revolution by joining revolutionary parties in military uprisings or by pushing the Qing officials to seek peaceful independence from the Qing court. While these elite merchants helped lead the revolutionary movement to success, their chamber networks also provided various types of support, especially social legitimization, for the newly formed political powers.

Thus, the associational networks of the Lower Yangzi chambers of commerce enabled their elite merchant leaders to take joint actions with other elite reformers, revolutionary partisans, and cooperative Qing officials from the constitutional reform up to the 1911 Revolution. In this sense, the network revolution led by these chambers provided both a foundation and the dynamics for drastic change in the last years of Qing politics, including a political revolution.

Reformist Initiatives in Business Legislation and Jurisdiction

Before the Qing court formally launched constitutional reform, chamber leaders and other reformist elites in the Lower Yangzi region had already formed a variety of constitutional organizations. They had also initiated constitutional reform in the sphere of commercial legislation and jurisdiction, although the Qing government still tried to hold onto such lawmaking and juridical power as official prerogatives. Thus, these chambers were not simply the "legally sanctioned associations" stressed by previous studies.[4] They also used their associational networks, especially their links with other constitutional organizations, to challenge and change the legal and juridical systems in business administration.

One of the earliest and most influential constitutional organizations in late Qing China, the Society for Constitutional Preparation (Yubei lixian gonghui), appeared in December 1906, and it was located in the same office as the Shanghai Commercial Study Society, a companion of the Shanghai GCC. Its major founders were a few high-profile reformers of literati origin, such as its president, Zheng Xiaoxu, and its two vice presidents, Zhang Jian and Tang Shouqian. But its eighteen earliest directors included at least seven chamber leaders, namely, Li Houyou, Zhou Jinbiao, and Zhou Tingbi of the Shanghai GCC, Wang Zhen of the South Shanghai BCC, Wang Tongyu of the Suzhou GCC, Zhang Guang'en of the Jiaxing ACC, and Xu Dinglin of the Haizhou-Ganyu ACC. In the register of this society, nine of its members recorded their relations with chambers of commerce in Jiangsu and Zhejiang provinces, and they included five chamber presidents, You Xianjia of Suzhou, Gao Baoquan of Jiaxing Prefecture, Liu Xiejun of Haimen subprefecture, Xu Guangpu of the town of Xiashi, and Zhang Di of the town of Wangdian. Many other elite merchants joined this constitutional organization without indicating their chamber affiliations, but their number was over a dozen in the Shanghai GCC alone.[5]

Due to such close interrelations, the Society for Constitutional Preparation naturally expressed a special interest in commercial affairs. In May 1907, it presented to the Shanghai GCC and the Shanghai Commercial Study Society a proposal to draft new commercial laws to replace the extant laws earlier issued by the Qing court. The Shanghai GCC quickly accepted this proposal and called on all Chinese chambers of commerce to hold a general conference in Shanghai on the law-drafting issue. The three elite associations justified their law-drafting activities by arguing that the Qing court had issued the few existing commercial laws without consultation with merchants or concern for commercial customs. Thus, merchants still lacked legal protection in business activities and especially in trades involving foreigners.[6]

In response to the Shanghai GCC's call, about eighty chambers of commerce from fourteen provinces and six chambers from overseas Chinese communities in Singapore, Nagasaki, Vladivostok, and other foreign cities dispatched delegates to attend the general conference in Shanghai on November 19 and 20, 1907. More than thirty chambers of commerce also sent letters endorsing the conference. Among the 151 delegates at the meeting, 105 were from sixty general, affiliated, and branch chambers in Jiangsu and Zhejiang provinces. Moreover, two general chambers in Southeast Asia appointed Zeng Zhu and Li Houyou, the former and incumbent presidents of the Shanghai GCC, respectively, as their delegates. Thus, leaders from the Lower Yangzi chambers of commerce constituted the overwhelming majority at the conference.[7] *national meeting of CCs*

The first national meeting of these chambers lasted for only two days, but it was an epoch-making event for Chinese merchants, for the development of their associational networks and for their participation in constitutional politics. On behalf of the Shanghai GCC, Li Houyou delivered the opening speech, declaring this gathering to be the beginning of Chinese merchant efforts to pursue associational solidarity and the public interest at home and abroad. Zheng Xiaoxu, the president of the Society for Constitutional Preparation, then called on all chambers of commerce to make joint efforts to investigate their local commercial customs and to complete a set of commercial laws for the legal protection of Chinese business from foreign encroachments. Zhou Jinbiao, the vice president of the Shanghai Commercial Study Society and a director of the Shanghai GCC, praised the meeting as the effort of public associations to promote public interest in business development and constitutional preparation. He especially emphasized the necessity for all chambers of commerce to maintain regular communications in law-drafting efforts.[8] *est. editorial office in SH for work on commercial laws*

In fact, from August 1907, the three sponsoring organizations had already established an editorial office in Shanghai to conduct joint work on the commercial laws. Based on the proposal of this office, participants at this meeting decided to draft commercial laws in seven comprehensive categories: companies, contracts, bankruptcy, commercial transaction, vouchers, sea-borne trade, and general principles, even though the Qing court had already issued laws regarding companies, bankruptcy, and so on. It also called on all chambers to investigate and report commercial customs in their cities and towns and required them each to select a reviewer of the laws to be drafted by the editorial office. When one participant in the meeting raised the question of whether the law-drafting plan should be reported to the Ministry of Agriculture, Industry, and Commerce, all delegates resolved that the draft laws should first be endorsed by all chambers of commerce before being submitted to the ministry for approval.[9]

participation on multiple levels

In order to ensure long-term collaboration following this first national meeting, these delegates unanimously adopted a proposal to form a national union of Chinese chambers of commerce and to publish a journal for their communications on law drafting and other issues. They entrusted Li Houyou and Zhou Jinbiao with the task of drafting a set of concise bylaws for this national union. In addition, the participants in the meeting decided that all chambers would keep regular contact with the aforesaid editorial office in

- national union of CCs - happens in 1912
- journal for communications

Shanghai through periodic letters. The unprecedented unity of chamber leaders especially excited one participant, Ma Xiangbo, a leading educator, eloquent speaker, and temporary delegate for the Sijing ACC. His speech at the end of the general conference extolled the public discussion of these chamber leaders as the basis of Chinese constitutionalism and called for the establishment of a national federation of Chinese citizens.[10]

This meeting indeed initiated a new trend for the late Qing chambers of commerce to unite and fight together for their legal rights. At the second Shanghai conference of these chambers in December 1909, Li and Zhou represented the Shanghai GCC and presented a set of bylaws for the national union of Chinese chambers of commerce. In their view, such an organization would bring together general, affiliated, and branch chambers of commerce, as well as other Chinese merchant organizations at home and abroad, so that all Chinese merchants could work in unison to advance their common interests. By that time, the Shanghai GCC had already begun publishing a journal to facilitate communications among chambers of commerce. After the second Shanghai meeting, the editorial office of this journal formally set up the Preparatory Office of the Union of Chinese Chambers of Commerce (Huashang lianhehui banshichu).[11]

Such a national union would not appear until 1912, but the two Shanghai conferences greatly strengthened the interrelations among the Lower Yangzi chambers of commerce. After the first Shanghai conference of 1907, many of the Lower Yangzi chambers either appointed delegates or used the mail to maintain regular contact with the Shanghai GCC. By March 1908, sixteen chambers of commerce in the Lower Yangzi region had paid membership dues to their national union, even though it was still in the planning stage.[12] Thus, through the two conferences, these chambers of commerce further strengthened their associational networks in the Lower Yangzi region, and such networks in turn increased their influence over commercial legislation.

At the suggestion of the Society for Constitutional Preparation, the Shanghai GCC also worked closely with the Shanghai Commercial Study Society to push for merchant participation in the negotiation of commercial treaties between the Qing and foreign governments. Their joint meeting in July 1907 reached a decision to petition the Qing court for merchant discussions on and approval of all commercial treaties drafted by the government. The Shanghai GCC and the Shanghai Commercial Study Society held another meeting in late August and then submitted to Sheng Xuanhuai, the official in charge of commercial treaty negotiations, a joint petition that had received endorsement from all Chinese merchant organizations in Shanghai. In this petition, they demanded that their delegates be allowed to investigate and discuss the issues to be raised in commercial treaty negotiations. By the end of 1907, their petition had received Sheng's approval.[13]

The joint efforts of these chambers of commerce, the Society for Constitutional Preparation, and the Shanghai Commercial Study Society led to the first draft of the *Company Law* (Gongsifa) in early 1909. Upon its publication, major Shanghai newspapers unanimously hailed this work as a monumental document in Chinese history. They applauded the law-drafting work of the chambers as the first step taken by the people to regain their legislative rights from the autocratic Qing government and by the nation to change from a society ruled by officials to one ruled by laws. These newspapers pushed the Qing court to accept the *Company Law*, stating that the government's decision on this matter would be a touchstone for testing its true attitude toward public opinion.[14]

With the support of public opinion, the Shanghai GCC and the Society for Constitutional Preparation presented the draft of the *Company Law* to the second general conference of chambers of commerce in December 1909. Delegates from seventy-six chambers reviewed this draft and passed it with some revisions, and a total of 140 chambers endorsed the draft law through either the mail or their delegates. The draft of the *General Principles of Commercial Law* (Shangfa zongze) was also distributed to the delegates for their review. Eventually, two representatives selected by the second Shanghai conference submitted to the Ministry of Agriculture, Industry, and Commerce the two draft laws on behalf of all the chambers of commerce. The ministry readily accepted it and passed it to the provisional National Assembly for ratification in 1910. Because the Qing rule was soon to come to an end, the Republican government later enacted the drafts into laws in 1914.[15]

The law-drafting activities also led the chambers of commerce into collective discussions about commercial jurisdiction, another major issue between them and the Qing government. At the first Shanghai conference in 1907, the delegate from the Qingjiangpu ACC of northern Jiangsu proposed that chambers of commerce should establish adjudicative offices for commercial disputes (*shangye caipansuo*) so that they could avert official interference in commercial affairs. Delegates at the meeting either rendered support to the proposal or expressed the worry that the government would not grant such adjudicative power to the chambers of commerce. Yet they all agreed that chambers of commerce should have the right to mediate merchant disputes.[16]

Actually, the Lower Yangzi chambers of commerce had long formalized the mediatory practices of traditional guilds, and some of them had even seized adjudicative power in business lawsuits. As early as 1902, the Shanghai CCA had stipulated that its leaders would mediate business disputes through special meetings. This stipulation was later codified in the regulations of the Lower Yangzi chambers of commerce and approved by the Ministry of Commerce. According to the rules for chambers of commerce issued by the ministry in 1904, chamber presidents and directors were to mediate merchant disputes periodically before such cases went to court.[17]

Chambers of commerce in the Lower Yangzi region duly performed the mediatory role.[18] Some of them went on to develop formal procedures for their mediation of business disputes. For instance, the two general chambers in Shanghai and Hangzhou as well as the affiliated chamber in Luodian all designated some of their directors to handle business disputes.[19] In Shanghai, both the Chinese county government and foreign authorities in the International Settlement relied heavily on the mediation of the Shanghai GCC "as a more customary form of settling complicated commercial disputes."[20]

The Suzhou GCC also stipulated procedures for mediation, by which two of its designated directors would first have hearings with the disputing parties, then question witnesses, and finally decide how to settle each dispute. During the first fifteen months following its formation in November 1905, this general chamber successfully settled more than 70 percent of the seventy business disputes it handled. During the period from 1905 to 1911, it accepted and handled a total of 393 business cases. This general chamber could conduct effective mediation between merchant disputants because it both exercised its authority granted by the government and followed the mediatory practices of traditional guilds. Sometimes it also requested official sanctions to enforce its mediatory decisions.[21]

More important, the Lower Yangzi chambers of commerce made effective use of their associational networks in their mediation of business disputes. In 1906, the Hangzhou GCC and its affiliated chambers in Jiaxing Prefecture and the town of Wangdian jointly settled a dispute between a pawnshop in the town and its creditors in Hangzhou before the case went to court. In 1907 the Hangzhou GCC handled a more complicated business dispute between a silk merchant in Shaoxing Prefecture and another one in Tongxiang County of Jiaxing Prefecture. This dispute had remained unsettled from 1905 because the Shaoxing merchant got support from a local official and tried to extort 9,000 silver dollars from the Tongxiang merchant. After a thorough investigation of the case by the Hangzhou GCC, the president of this general chamber and the major leaders of its three affiliated chambers in Shaoxing, Jiaxing, and Tongxiang held a joint mediatory meeting and successfully persuaded the Shaoxing merchant to accept only 900 silver dollars as compensation, thus ending the two years of dispute.[22]

The Qing government, however, did not give these chambers of commerce a free hand in settling business disputes. In 1906, the Ministry of Commerce ordered all chambers of commerce to record their handlings of business cases in standardized reports and to submit their annual reports to the ministry for review. Moreover, it repeatedly instructed chambers of commerce to mediate only merchant disputes and not to adjudicate business lawsuits (*duan'an*), which remained the prerogative of local officials.[23] In spite of the official warnings, chambers of commerce in the Lower Yangzi region did not give up their attempts to extend their authority from mediation in merchant disputes to adjudication of business lawsuits.

In 1909, the newly formed Wukang ACC directly listed adjudicative and interrogative duties in its regulations and submitted its regulations for official approval. In response, the Zhejiang governor rebuked this affiliated chamber for encroaching on official power and prohibited it from handling any commercial lawsuits. In commenting on this event, one commercial journal ridiculed the governor's reaction, stating that most chambers of commerce had already handled business lawsuits by that time.[24] Indeed, chambers of commerce in the Lower Yangzi region not only demanded equal rights with officials but also challenged official jurisdiction in commercial matters.

In particular, these chambers of commerce adroitly used their associational networks to increase their power at the expense of local governments in the adjudication of business lawsuits. In 1906, the magistrate of Changzhou County used an unauthorized deposit receipt as evidence to convict a silk fabric shop of swindling 50 silver dollars from the widow of a former clerk. The shop refused to accept the official judgment and presented the case to the Suzhou GCC. The general chamber soon contacted the Shanghai GCC for support, called all guild leaders in Suzhou for a special meeting, and invited the director of the provincial bureau of commerce to preside over this meeting. Consequently, the desperate magistrate repeatedly visited the leaders of the Suzhou GCC and requested the latter to take over the case rather than hold a special meeting. Thus, the Suzhou GCC achieved total success while the magistrate suffered a major humiliation.[25]

In another dramatic case, the Agricultural, Industrial, and Commercial Bureau of South Jiangsu Province (Susheng nonggongshangwu ju) in 1909 established an adjudicative office to deal with business lawsuits and then ordered the Suzhou GCC to submit annual reports about its handling of such cases. However, this general chamber refused to submit any "reports" on the grounds that it was not a subsidiary office of the provincial bureau. By using the Ministry of Agriculture, Industry, and Commerce's 1908 rules for chamber-government relations (see Chapter 2), the Suzhou GCC insisted on the use of the neutral term "communication" in addressing correspondence to the bureau and demanded a mutual exchange of records about handling merchant disputes and lawsuits. The defiant attitude of the general chamber forced the provincial bureau to deny any intention of increasing its own authority over that of chambers of commerce in judicial matters.[26]

Some chamber leaders obviously abused their new power by interfering not only in business lawsuits but also in civil cases. In 1910 the former president of the Jiaxing ACC, Gao Baoquan, became a defendant in a homicide trial after he allegedly mishandled a case of liability and pressured an innocent merchant to commit suicide. When the Jiaxing prefect summoned Gao to court, the affiliated chamber held a meeting and decided that Gao need not appear in the court as he was a former chamber president. When it attempted to force the decision on the prefect with help from the Ministry of Agriculture, Industry, and Commerce, the ministry angrily called upon the Jiaxing ACC to specify which law would allow Gao to be excused from such a trial.[27]

However, in the same year, the Jiaxing ACC also led a legal fight for chambers of commerce in Zhejiang Province. In mid-1909, all chambers in the province received an order (*zha*) in red ink from Dong Jiyou, the Zhejiang *daotai* for industrial affairs. In this order, Dong claimed that the Ministry of Agriculture, Industry, and Commerce had granted him the authority to supervise all chambers of commerce in Zhejiang Province. Hence their regular correspondence with the ministry would now have to pass through his office. All chamber leaders in Jiaxing Prefecture expressed indignation over Daotai Dong, claiming that they had always received official orders in black rather than red ink. In fact, these chamber leaders were upset mainly because they feared that this provincial official would control their organizations and obstruct their direct communication with the ministry. In an open letter to Daotai Dong and to the Hangzhou and Ningbo GCCs, the Jiaxing ACC accused Dong of attempting to disconnect the chambers of commerce from the central government through the use of bureaucratic formalities and to turn respectable chamber leaders into governmental runners. The letter urged the two general chambers of commerce to immediately oppose the *daotai*'s order or to develop countermeasures through a general conference of chambers of commerce of the whole province.[28]

This case clearly shows the attempt of these chamber leaders to institutionalize their newly acquired power and pursue equal relations with officials in business administration through the mobilization of their associational networks. Zhang Zhenxiang, the president of the affiliated chamber in the town of Meili, near Suzhou, in 1909 had already submitted to the Ministry of Agriculture, Industry, and Commerce a set of draft rules, requesting that the ministry clarify the authority of chambers of commerce in business jurisdictions. According to Zhang's draft rules, chambers of commerce must receive official notice of all business lawsuits and make investigations of such cases before local governments dispatched runners to arrest the accused merchants. Under the draft rule, the chambers could ask the ministry to punish officials who had allowed local gentry to bail out defendants in business cases pursued by these chambers. Zhang even demanded that the ministry delimit the areas under the jurisdiction of all chambers and that it allow general and affiliated chambers to operate in a hierarchical system as did the different levels of governments.[29]

Although Zhang Zhenxiang's petition did not receive governmental approval, it expressed a common aspiration of the chamber leaders because the first Shanghai conference of chambers of commerce for commercial law drafting in 1907, in which Zhang was a participant, had already raised the issues included later in his petition.[30] The collective struggles of these elite merchants for lawmaking and juridical power challenged the existing power relations because their chambers did not merely rely on state legalization for recognition but also initiated constitutional reform of the legal system by themselves. Such activities had already touched upon the fundamental issue in the constitutional reform before the reformist movement formally started.

Associational Activism and Alliance in Constitutional Reform

Reformist elites had been enthusiastically discussing constitutionalism for years, but the Qing court eventually issued its own nine-year program for constitutional reform on August 27, 1908. It envisaged the election of a parliament, or *yiyuan*, in 1916, the last year of the projected nine-year program. However, provincial assemblies, or *ziyiju*, would be elected by 1909, and a provisional national assembly, or *zizhengyuan*, would be convened in 1910. Moreover, the elections for self-government institutions in cities, towns, and rural townships as well as counties, departments, and prefectures would be completed by 1914.[31]

Previous studies of the constitutional reform have either stressed that the Qing court's sincere intentions were foiled by conservative officials and elites or have argued that its sham reform increasingly frustrated radical elite reformers. Nevertheless, scholars have generally agreed that the state-led re-formist movement failed because it intensified the clashes between the Qing government and social elites and even drove the latter into the revolutionary camp.[32] Recent works on constitutional reform have given more credit to the state-led reformist movement, but none of them has paid special attention to the role of the late Qing chambers of commerce.[33] Thus, it is necessary to examine how the chambers and other constitutional organizations mobilized their associational networks and used multiform interactions with the Qing officials to accelerate reforms involving local self-government, provincial as-semblies, and a national parliament.

The Qing court first launched the constitutional reform at the provincial level. On October 19, 1907, an imperial edict began to call for the formation of provincial assemblies. However, in July 1907, the Shanghai GCC and the South Shanghai BCC had already initiated discussion on this issue together with ten other elite organizations and had quickly produced a set of draft regulations for a provincial assembly in Jiangsu. This set of regulations was a harbinger of similar documents drafted by reformist elites and officials in Anhui, Guangdong, and other provinces. In January 1908, it was formally sub-mitted to the Qing government.[34]

Under such elite pressure, the Qing court in July 1908 issued its own rules for provincial assemblies and for the elections of assemblymen. This official set of rules allowed provincial assemblies to discuss only budgets, taxes, loans, and other issues, and their decisions on these issues had to be approved by governors and governors-general or submitted by the latter to the National Assembly for deliberation. According to the electoral rules for provincial as-semblymen, the voters and candidates must be natives of the province and adult males over the ages of twenty-five and thirty, respectively. They also had to have been managers of local schools or other public affairs for over three years; recipients of middle-school diplomas or academic degrees issued by governments; former officials of at least the seventh rank in civil service or the fifth rank in military service; or owners of at least 5,000 silver dollars' worth of business or immovable assets. By contrast, nonnative voters and candidates had to have been residents locally for over ten years and to own more than 10,000 silver dollars' worth of capital or property in their host areas.[35] Such rules were unfavorable for chambers of commerce because many of their par-ticipants were nonnative merchants who were afraid of potential tax increases after declarations of their wealth.

Nonetheless, the Lower Yangzi chambers of commerce still took an active part in preparations for the elections of provincial assemblies. In late September

1908, President Zhou Jinbiao of the Shanghai GCC and other sojourning Zhejiang elites in the treaty port submitted to the governor of their home province a detailed plan for registration of qualified voters and pushed for timely elections of provincial assemblymen in early 1909. Their plan specifically put chamber leaders and other elites in charge of the preparatory work for local elections. Inside Zhejiang Province, the Ningbo GCC in December 1908 offered its building as the office for the preparatory work in the prefecture, and its leaders actively joined other local elites in the mobilization and registration of local electors.[36]

In Jiangsu Province, many chamber leaders attended a meeting in Shanghai on September 19 and 20, 1908, and pledged to compile electoral rolls for the election without waiting for local official action. Thereafter, the South Shanghai BCC not only helped register qualified electors and launched special investigations of nonnative merchant voters but also helped merchant militiamen to fight for their electoral rights. The chamber's petition to local authorities argued that these militiamen had received graduate certificates from local officials for their physical training, had served the public interest in their militia activities, and thus deserved the same electoral rights as graduates from new schools and managers of public institutions.[37]

The Changzhou ACC was especially active in the preparatory work. On September 23, 1908, it held a meeting to organize a preparatory office for the local election. The meeting also selected President Yun Zuqi and other leaders of the affiliated chamber as the director, assistant director, chief of staff, and secretaries of the preparatory office. Yun, together with the affiliated chamber and the local educational association, raised funds for the office. These elite organizations decided to register all qualified electors through a house-to-house survey and to mobilize voters through weekly lectures in each town. In particular, the Changzhou ACC urged merchants to register for the election without worrying about exposure of their wealth.[38]

The chambers of commerce in southern Jiangsu also demanded official relaxation of the residence requirement for nonnative merchant voters because the Qing court by late 1908 still regarded all residents from neighboring prefectures or counties as "sojourners" (jijuren) in a local jurisdiction. In November 1908, the affiliated chamber in the town of Shengze first complained to the Suzhou GCC that the strict residence requirement would exclude a majority of nonnative merchants from local elections. In Suzhou, the prefectural seat of Changzhou, and the twin-county seats of Kunshan-Xinyang and Yixing-Jingxi, chamber leaders also petitioned the Jiangsu governor to change the strict residence requirement for voters. They argued that their host cities were the seats of two or even three counties, and thus the residents of different counties were indistinguishable. Finally, the Qing court granted both natives and sojourners in any subprovincial units equal rights in local elections if they were from the same province.[39]

As a result of their active involvement in the provincial elections, the Lower Yangzi chambers of commerce helped place quite a few elite merchants in the Jiangsu and Zhejiang provincial assemblies, although only some of the chamber leaders and members could be identified. Among the 125 provincial assemblymen in Jiangsu, there were no fewer than eight chamber leaders or honorary members. Similarly, the 111 provincial assemblymen of Zhejiang included at least eight incumbent and former presidents as well as an honorary member of chambers of commerce.[40] Such personnel overlap enabled the Lower Yangzi chambers of commerce to work closely with the two provincial assemblies in their activities from the local to the national level.

Indeed, both the Jiangsu and Zhejiang provincial assemblies provided political leadership for these chambers of commerce and in return received strong support from the latter. The Jiangsu Provincial Assembly quickly mobilized chambers of commerce in the province to reform *lijin*, the most onerous levy on merchants during the late Qing period. In November 1909, its first session specially discussed the proposals for *lijin* reform submitted by the Rugao and Shengze ACCs, and participants in the meeting resolved to replace the official collection of *lijin* with a merchant tax-collecting (*renjuan*) system. In response, the Jiangning GCC and a majority of its twenty-eight affiliated chambers in northern and western Jiangsu endorsed this resolution at their annual conference in March 1910. Meanwhile, in southern Jiangsu, the provincial assembly contacted thirty-nine chambers through its investigators or the mail, and its resolution received support from thirty-five of them.[41] The joint effort of the provincial assembly and chambers of commerce in the *lijin* reform failed later on because provincial authority sabotaged the reform with a scheme to impose a more exorbitant consolidated tax (*tongjuan*). Nevertheless, by the end of this movement, elite merchants in this province were able to found the Southern Jiangsu Coalition of Chambers of Commerce (Sushu shanghui lianhehui) in Shanghai in July 1911.[42]

Meanwhile, the Zhejiang Provincial Assembly (*Zhejiang ziyiju*) also made an unsuccessful attempt to promote *lijin* reform through collaboration with chambers of commerce, but their joint actions over the provincial railroad issue were more successful. After the Qing court dismissed President Tang Shouqian from his position in the Zhejiang Railroad Company on August

23, 1910, the Zhejiang Provincial Assembly held an emergency meeting on August 26 and 27 and sent a protest telegram to Beijing. Meanwhile, the Hangzhou GCC led both merchant and literati protests in the city through its successive meetings from late August to early September 1910. Their pressure forced the Zhejiang governor to petition the throne to restore Tang's post. After the governor received an imperial rebuke and refused to submit another petition on behalf of Tang, the Zhejiang Provincial Assembly suspended its second annual session for ten days in October 1910 and forced the governor to submit another petition.[43] At the same time, its president and members joined chamber leaders throughout the province for a meeting and decided to send petitioners directly to Beijing. Thereafter, a provincial assemblyman, Zhu Zhen, and the vice president of the Hangzhou GCC, Wang Xirong, led the petition.[44] The protests of the elite associations in Zhejiang and their petitions in Beijing eventually forced the Qing court into concession, as discussed in Chapter 5.

The alliance between provincial assemblies and chambers of commerce in the Lower Yangzi region also extended to constitutional reform at the national level. In October 1910, the National Assembly convened in Beijing. It comprised 196 members, half of whom were appointed by the throne and the other half elected by provincial assemblies. Three of the elected national assemblymen were chamber leaders and members from Jiangsu and Zhejiang: Fang Huan, Xu Dinglin, and Shao Xi. One veteran director of the Shanghai GCC and former president of the Wuxi-Jinkui ACC, Zhou Tingbi, also entered the National Assembly as one of ten large taxpayers, though they had received imperial appointment.[45] As a result of these personal links and common political purposes, the Lower Yangzi chambers, their two provincial assemblies, and the National Assembly entered into close collaboration in the constitutional movement, especially in nationwide petitions for the early convening of a parliament.

In fact, under the leadership of Zhang Jian and other reformist elites in the Lower Yangzi region, the Society for Constitutional Preparation in June 1908 had already led constitutional associations from nearly nine provinces to petition the Qing court to convene a parliament within two years, and these reformist elites had persuaded many leaders in chambers of commerce and other organizations to endorse their petitions. Xu Dinglin, the former president of the Haizhou-Ganyu ACC, was one of the petitioners from Jiangsu Province. Meanwhile, the Hangzhou GCC prepared a special handbill on the parliamentary issue and distributed it among merchants throughout Zhejiang Province, urging them to sign onto the petition.[46] Nevertheless,

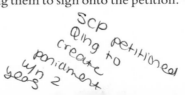

the Qing court's nine-year plan for constitutional reform, which was issued in August 1908, still put off the election of a parliament to 1916 and its convocation to the following year. After Zhang Jian became the chairman of the Jiangsu Provincial Assembly in late 1909, he held a special discussion with Xu Dinglin and other assemblymen in this province, and they together decided to mobilize all provincial assemblies to petition once again for the early opening of the parliament. Three provincial assemblymen in Jiangsu, including President Fang Huan of the Kunshan-Xinyang ACC, took on the tasks of visiting different provincial assemblies and keeping contact with them on the issue.[47]

At Zhang's invitation, delegates from sixteen provincial assemblies held a joint meeting in Shanghai in December 1909. This meeting concluded that a national parliament was imperative to save China from imperialist partition and revolutionary violence, and thus it decided to petition the Qing court for the convening of a parliament within two years. Thirty-three members from all the provincial assemblies formed a petition delegation, which included Fang Huan and another chamber leader from Changzhou, Yu Dingyi.[48]

The first petition for the early opening of a parliament was presented to the Qing court by the delegation on behalf of all provincial assemblies on January 26, 1910, but it received a flat-out rejection. After this petition failed, its promoters realized the inadequacy of mobilizing only provincial assemblies for their movement and began to call for the involvement of chambers of commerce, educational associations, and other organizations in a second petition. They directly appealed to the chambers of commerce in Jiangsu, Guangdong, Hubei, and Zhili provinces to join the petition movement, and Yu Dingyi returned from Beijing with the special mission of mobilizing the chambers of commerce in southern Jiangsu Province.[49]

In response, the general chambers in Shanghai, Suzhou, and Jiangning as well as the affiliated chamber in Changzhou by May 1910 had selected Shen Manyun, Hang Zuliang, and other representatives for the second petition. Meanwhile, the chambers of commerce in Zhejiang Province had also selected representatives and led the local mobilization for a new petition. Under the leadership of the former president of the Shanghai GCC, Li Houyou, the Preparatory Office of the Union of Chinese Chambers of Commerce issued a long proclamation calling all merchants at home and abroad to join in the second petition. It also drafted a long petition for the delegates who would represent chambers of commerce and other merchant organizations.[50]

In the second petition, Shen Manyun, Hang Zuliang, and twenty-four other delegates represented chambers of commerce in twelve provinces and twenty-six Southeast Asian cities. On June 16, 1910, the petitioners presented the Qing court with ten pleas for the early convening of a parliament on behalf of ten different kinds of organizations. Shen submitted a petition on behalf of nationwide chambers of commerce. He and Hang also made a special plea as representatives of the chambers of commerce in Jiangsu Province. Moreover, they signed two other pleas along with delegates of provincial assemblies, educational associations, constitutional organizations, and the like. Although the second petition effort again met with a negative reply from the Qing court, its participants did not give up but resolved to petition for a third time.[51]

In the third petition, submitted on October 22, 1910, Shen acted again as the leading petitioner for the nationwide chambers of commerce. From the first to the third petitions, the petitioners tried to persuade the Qing court with increasingly urgent warnings: only a parliament could ensure genuine constitutional reform, enable China to survive domestic trouble and foreign invasion, and bring about an effective government under a responsible cabinet. Pleas from the chambers of commerce further argued that only a parliament could save Chinese business from complete collapse because it would be able to oversee a national banking system and state commercial and tax policies. In particular, the third petition warned the Qing court of its likely downfall if it continued its sham constitutional reform without convening a parliament.[52]

The third petition received the support from the newly opened National Assembly and even from dozens of governors and governors-general, but it resulted only in a promise by the throne to convene a parliament in 1913, four years earlier than the court's nine-year plan had prescribed. Petitioners from provinces such as Sichuan and Hubei expressed disappointment with the imperial edict, but those from Jiangsu and Zhejiang appeared ready to accept a compromise with the Qing government. In telegrams to the National Assembly, both the Jiangsu and Zhejiang provincial assemblies hailed this new imperial promise as a victory. The Suzhou GCC took the lead in holding a three-day celebration in the downtown area of the city.[53]

Certainly, the elite merchant leaders and members of the Lower Yangzi chambers and provincial assemblies did not unanimously accept the compromise. Shen Manyun, a leading petitioner and a director of both the Shanghai GCC and the South Shanghai ACC, together with a few relatively young leaders in the two chambers, soon turned to the anti-Qing revolution. Nevertheless, even revolutionary converts like Shen still joined other chamber leaders and members in the local self-government movement within their cities and towns. Thus, they continued to promote constitutional reform at the local level until the end of the Qing period.[54]

Chamber leaders and other reformist elites in the Lower Yangzi region had originally planned local self-government institutions as the basis of constitutional reform. From September to October 1907, the Shanghai GCC, the South Shanghai BCC, and ten other elite organizations drafted not only the aforementioned regulations for a provincial assembly in Jiangsu but also a set of regulations for self-government institutions in subprefectures, departments, and counties in the province. Meanwhile, local elites in Jiangsu Province planned and formed dozens of self-government organizations with different titles, but these organizations received from the provincial authorities only permission to investigate and study local issues. In Beijing, the Ministry of Civil Affairs also attempted to impose central control over the movement. It issued self-government regulations for cities, towns, and rural townships in January 1909, as well as for prefectures, subprefectures, departments, and counties in February 1910. In a telegram to officials in southern Jiangsu in June 1909, the ministry insisted on its own schedule for elections of all self-government institutions between 1912 and 1914.[55]

Reformist elites in many cities and towns of southern Jiangsu, including local chamber leaders, quickly pushed provincial authorities to advance the schedule for self-government and successfully established new community administrations under their collective dominance. As one of the earliest municipal institutions in late Qing China, the General Works Board of Shanghai and Its Suburbs directly changed its name to the Self-Government Office of Shanghai City (Shanghai cheng zizhi gongsuo) in February 1910 and adopted self-government rules in its due election for directors and councilors around that time. The new Self-Government Office of Shanghai City continued to include leaders of the Shanghai GCC and the South Shanghai ACC, and its jurisdiction was expanded from the three urban districts into the northern and southwestern suburbs around the foreign concessions. Moreover, chamber leaders including Lin Jingzhou and other urban elites also founded self-government organizations in a few urban neighborhoods, such as the aforementioned Urban Federation of Southeastern Neighborhoods and the Urban Federation of Northwestern Neighborhoods. These grassroots self-government organizations, which had begun to appear from 1905, later formed a citywide federation in 1912.[56]

The Suzhou GCC, together with other local elite organizations, also promoted self-government in that city ahead of official plans. Jiang Bingzhang, an important figure in the general chamber and the local educational association, was a major founder and leader of the Local Self-Government Investigation and Study Society of Jiangsu Province (Susheng difang zizhi diaocha yanjiuhui), which appeared in March 1907. This society invited all members of the Suzhou GCC to participate in its elections and other activities. In July 1909, the president of the Suzhou GCC, Zhang Lüqian, began to make preparations for a self-government office in Suzhou. This office eventually grew out of a local election in April 1910, and both its executive board and deliberative council included major leaders from the Suzhou GCC, such as its president, You Xianjia; its former president, Zhang Lüqian; its vice president, Ni Kaiding; and a veteran director, Pan Zuqian.[57]

After a fire destroyed seventeen stores in downtown Suzhou in May 1909, Ni and Shi Ying, a full member of the general chamber, further initiated the Urban Residents' Association of Guanqian Street (Guanqianjie shimin gongshe) to prevent fires, maintain sanitation, build roads, and provide security for residents. These chamber leaders and members, as well as representatives from other elite organizations, held their inaugural meeting on June 28, 1909, expressing a common ambition to build this urban neighborhood organization as the foundation of self-government and a new municipal administration. Their petition for this urban residents' association quickly received local official approval by way of the Suzhou GCC.[58]

The Urban Residents' Association of Guanqian Street included about 100 members in 1909, and most of its members, especially its leaders, were store owners. Such rich merchants also contributed the bulk of its initial funds and monthly fees. Thus, this association was evidently a well-to-do merchant organization like the Suzhou GCC, and its major leaders included Shi Ying, Ni Kaiding, and other elite merchants from the general chamber.[59] From 1910 to 1912, there appeared three other urban residents' associations in Suzhou's downtown areas around Dusengqiao, Jinchang xiatang, and Daoqian streets. Like their Guanqian Street predecessor, all three associations gained local official approval through the Suzhou GCC, and their leaders also included elite merchants from the general chamber. In September 1910, Suzhou officials tried to bring these urban residents' associations under their direct control. Nevertheless, the newly formed associations continued to submit their regulations and membership lists to the general chamber because they considered it the "leading institution for commerce and merchants."[60]

In the provincial capital of Zhejiang, both the Hangzhou GCC and the local educational association for the two satellite counties, Renhe and Qiantang, played a leading role in the self-government movement. In late 1908, a study society for self-government appeared in the office of the educational association, but its four initiators included Jin Yuesheng and Pan Chiwen, the president and vice president of the general chamber, as well as Hu Zaoqing, an honorary member of the latter. In the northeastern suburb of Hangzhou, one of the earliest self-government offices was founded mainly by Wu Enyuan, president of the Gongchenqiao ACC, in March 1910. It also shared the office of the affiliated chamber.[61]

In a few prefectural and county cities, self-government institutions appeared even earlier than in the aforementioned provincial capitals. The Tong-Chong-Hai GCCC had helped organize the election of a local self-governing society (zizhihui), including a deliberative council and an executive board, by September 1908, almost one and a half years before the Qing court issued its self-government regulations for such new institutions.[62] In Jiading, a county near Shanghai, the first president of the local affiliated chamber, Zhou Shiheng, helped found a self-government office as early as 1907, although its function was limited by officials to investigation and study of the local situation. By April 1911, Jiading County had produced thirty-four self-government offices in local towns and rural townships. In one of its market towns, Nanxiang, chamber leaders directly initiated and controlled self-government institutions.[63] In southern Jiangsu as a whole, self-government offices, including elected councils, numbered approximately twenty-seven in prefectural and county cities and more than 420 in towns and rural townships by September 1911, and many of them included chamber leaders.[64]

In Zhejiang Province, 1,021 cities, towns, and rural townships had elected their local councils by September 1911, and 810 of them had also selected their executive boards or directors. In the town of Xiashi, the first and second presidents of the affiliated chamber, Xu Guangpu and Wu Zhaopei, were the only two directors of the local self-government office, while Wu Qing, who had founded with Xu a merchant militia, was the chairman of the deliberative council in the office.[65] The domination of the self-government institutions by such local elites has long drawn scholarly criticism for their use of the constitutional reform to seek power and profit at the expense of the populace.[66] Indeed, Xu and a few chamber leaders in the Lower Yangzi region were among the targets of popular protests against self-government reform, especially against the tax surcharges for funding such local reforms. In 1908, Xu's sauce and pickle shop in Xiashi was destroyed along with new schools, police bureaus, and the like in a dozen nearby towns during a peasant protest against tax collection.[67] This kind of popular protest certainly confirms the previous discovery of strained class relations between the local elites and the populace during the constitutional reform.

Nevertheless, such class analysis cannot negate the fact that the associational activism and alliance of chamber leaders and other reformist elites in the Lower Yangzi region also brought about progressive changes in their interrelations and especially in their interactions with the larger society and the imperial state. In the case of the town of Xiashi, Xu Guangpu and other local chamber leaders were not simply a group of parochial, conservative, and selfish elite merchants. Rather, Xu was actively involved in the nationalist movement around the Suzhou-Hangzhou-Ningbo railroad, in various reformist organizations such as the Zhejiang Provincial Assembly, and even in the anti-Qing uprising in Hangzhou in 1911.[68] Clearly, the class conflicts of chamber leaders and other elite reformers, such as Xu, with the populace over local self-government reform did not prevent them from representing and protecting the larger society, including the masses, in their struggles with foreign imperialism and the Qing government.

Therefore, in the last years of the Qing period, the Lower Yangzi chambers of commerce indeed faced popular protests against the negative effects of their reformist activities at the local level. However, these chambers mainly played a positive role in the constitutional movement because they helped build local self-government offices, provincial assemblies, and the National Assembly, which not only transformed the local dominance of social elites but also linked their personal pursuits with public interests and reformist causes at the provincial and national levels. These chambers and the newly formed political institutions also accelerated the constitutional reform through their varied interactions with the Qing government. Such interactive movement inevitably influenced the 1911 Revolution.

The Power of Elite Associational Networks during the 1911 Revolution

The Republican Revolution erupted with the Wuchang uprising in the Middle Yangzi valley on October 10, 1911, but its climax was the establishment of the new Republican government in the Lower Yangzi region thereafter. Previous studies have noticed the differences in the revolutionary experiences, including those of chambers of commerce, between the core and peripheral areas of the Lower Yangzi region. In the regional peripheries, chamber leaders could hardly reach consensus with the rampant bandits, secret societies, and local troops during the revolutionary chaos, and they played no more than the role of peacekeepers there. However, in the core area of the Yangzi Delta and especially in large cities, such as Shanghai, chamber leaders and other urban elites took an active part in the anti-Qing uprisings and made significant contributions to the revolutionary movement.[69] Actually, even in the regional core, the chambers of commerce also played two different roles in the 1911 Revolution: they either supported revolutionary parties in military uprisings or pressured Qing officials to declare peaceful independence from the Qing court.

These chambers of commerce entered the two different kinds of anti-Qing revolutionary movement just as they had long engaged in multiform interactions with the Qing government for the private and public interests of their elite merchants. The expansion of their networks by late 1911 also brought many of their elite merchant leaders into direct or indirect contact with Sun Yat-sen's Revolutionary Alliance (Tongmenghui) and the Restoration Society (Guangfuhui), the anti-Qing organization led by Zhejiang revolutionaries.[70] The interactions of these chambers with these different sociopolitical forces around 1911 typically displayed their network power.

Chambers of commerce in Shanghai, coastal Jiangsu, and northeastern Zhejiang became supporters of revolutionary parties in 1911 because many of their leaders had developed various relations with the latter beforehand, and the new revolutionary powers soon gave local elites hope for political opportunities and social stability. One major leader of the Revolutionary Alliance in the Lower Yangzi region, Chen Qimei, returned from Japan to Shanghai in 1908 and first got a teaching job in the city through the help of a Huzhou prefectural fellow and a director of the Shanghai GCC, Yang Xinzhi. Before the 1911 Revolution, Chen and other partisans had recruited at least six former and incumbent leaders of the Shanghai GCC and South Shanghai ACC, Shen Manyun, Wang Zhen, Yu Qiaqing, Ye Huijun, Gu Xinyi, and Li Houyou. Li's brother, Li Zhengwu, an individual associate member of the Shanghai GCC, had also joined the Revolutionary Alliance by 1911.[71]

In early 1911, the Tokyo headquarters of the Revolutionary Alliance decided to establish a national volunteer corps (*guominjun*) and a national association (*guominhui*) as its peripheral organizations. In response, Shen, Ye, and other revolutionaries in Shanghai actively developed these organizations as their links with chamber leaders in the Lower Yangzi region. In March 1911, they founded the National Federation of Merchant Militias (Quanguo shangtuan gonghui) with the proclaimed purpose of promoting military training for national salvation and invited Song Jiaoren, a major leader of the Revolutionary Alliance, as a speaker at their inaugural meeting. However, they elected Li Zhongjue, a director of the South Shanghai ACC and the leading general director of the Shanghai Self-Government Office, as the commander of this new militia force, although he was not a revolutionary. This organization unified many merchant militias in Shanghai and quickly received endorsements from the merchant militias in Tongzhou independent department of northern Jiangsu and in the town of Xiashi in northern Zhejiang.[72] Later on, leaders of local chambers and merchant militias in Tongzhou and Xiashi would also respond quickly to the revolutionary uprisings in Shanghai and Hangzhou, respectively.

In June 1911, Shen Manyun and a few members of the Revolutionary Alliance in Shanghai further founded the headquarters of the Chinese National Association (Zhongguo guomin zonghui), and Shen was elected as its chairman. This association then formed branches in Jiaxing Prefecture of Zhejiang Province and in the provincial capital of Hangzhou through the help of Chu Fucheng, an underground revolutionary partisan, the president of the Jiaxing ACC, and a member of the Zhejiang Provincial Assembly.[73] The Hangzhou GCC also called on its affiliated chambers in Zhejiang Province to help this organization establish merchant militias. Thus, this revolutionary-led organization quickly formed branches in Huzhou, Ningbo, and other prefectures of Zhejiang. Its Huzhou branch was mainly initiated by local chamber leaders and was even located in their office, and these elite merchants also took this opportunity to plan a merchant militia.[74] Thus, either purposely or unconsciously, these elite merchants served as links between their chambers and the Revolutionary Alliance prior to the 1911 Revolution.

After the anti-Qing uprising broke out in Wuchang on October 10, Chen Qimei and his Revolutionary Alliance soon used Shen Manyun as an intermediary to contact Li Zhongjue and other leaders of the two chambers of commerce and the self-government office in Shanghai and brought them into a plan for joint action. On the afternoon of November 3, the Shanghai uprising began after Chen's "dare-to-die" corps launched an attack on the Jiangnan Arsenal. Meanwhile, Li used merchant militias to take over the offices of local officials and maintain order in the Chinese districts of Shanghai. After Chen lost the battle around the arsenal and was captured by the Qing defense force inside, Li Zhongjue and Wang Zhen still maintained contact with the Qing commander in the arsenal while trying to bail Chen out under the auspices of the South Shanghai ACC and the Self-Government Office of Shanghai City. After this attempt failed, they mobilized merchant militias to attack the arsenal again. Their joint action with the insurrectionary police and army forces commanded by Li Xiehe, a leader of the Restoration Society, eventually defeated the Qing army inside the arsenal in the early morning of November 4 and freed Chen from imprisonment.[75]

The support of the leaders of the chambers of commerce and other Shanghai elite organizations was crucial not only for the military uprising but also
for the subsequent power struggle between the Revolutionary Alliance and
the Restoration Society. Although Li Xiehe and his Restoration Society first
formed a military government and asked the Shanghai GCC to keep order
in the urban market, Li failed to get support from Shanghai elites and was
not even invited by the elites to a meeting for the election of another military government. Li Zhongjue and other leaders of the chambers of commerce, self-governing office, merchant militia, and firefighting corps held the
meeting together with followers of Chen Qimei and his Revolutionary Alliance for the establishment of a new military government because of their
closer relations before and during the Shanghai uprising. Participants in the
meeting selected Chen Qimei as military governor (*dudu*) of this new government. Moreover, leaders of the two chambers and self-government office
in Shanghai, such as Li Zhongjue, Shen Manyun, and Wang Zhen, soon entered this new government as its ministers of civil affairs, finance, transportation, and the like. Former president and vice president of the Shanghai GCC,
Zhou Jinbiao and Zhu Baosan, also joined the military government later on.[76]

These elite merchants made generous donations and organized various
fund-raising activities for the new revolutionary government. Shen Manyun
alone lent over 300,000 silver dollars to the new government from the Xincheng
Bank, which was under his management and owned by Zhou Tingbi, another
director of the Shanghai GCC. They also helped organize the Chinese Bank
(Zhonghua yinhang) as the financial organ of the military government. The
South Shanghai ACC held a special meeting to urge merchants to support
this bank by accepting its notes and depositing money there. The Shanghai
GCC also helped Chen's military government borrow more than three million silver dollars from local merchants to cover its enormous expenses. Chen's
popularity among Shanghai elites forced Li Xiehe to move his preexisting
military government to the town of Wusong, Shanghai's port on the Yangzi
River. The president of the Wusong ACC participated in this separate revolutionary government.[77]

Both Chen's and Li's governments dispatched revolutionary troops to
nearby prefectures and counties to take over local administrations. Such military takeovers usually enjoyed the collaboration of local elites, especially chamber leaders. For instance, Li's army was well received by the Tong-Chong-Hai-
Tai GCC, and its commander established a military government together
with the former president of this general chamber, Zhang Cha. In places near
Shanghai or Tongzhou, such as Songjiang Prefecture and Rugao County,

chamber leaders and other elites also cooperated closely with local revolutionaries or with the revolutionary forces from Shanghai and Wusong in the
military takeover of their local governments.[78]

The precedent of military uprising in Shanghai was followed by Hangzhou late in the night of November 4; the members of the Revolutionary
Alliance in both cities, including those in the Zhejiang New Army, had
planned a mutiny together. They also brought Chu Fucheng, the president
of the Jiaxing ACC and a revolutionary partisan himself, into the conspiracy. Chu in turn used his position in the Zhejiang Provincial Assembly to
involve its major leaders in the preparatory work. Meanwhile, Chu and his
fellow partisans contacted two leaders of the affiliated chamber and merchant
militia in the nearby town of Xiashi to borrow 4,000 rounds of ammunition
from their militia for the Hangzhou uprising. Thus, the revolutionary uprising in Hangzhou received critical support from chamber leaders and other
elite reformers around the provincial capital. After its success on November
5, chamber leaders and other local elites in Xiashi and nearby towns immediately raised revolutionary flags in response, and the merchant militia from
Xiashi even joined revolutionary troops in fights with the Qing armies in
Jiaxing prefectural city and the provincial capital of Jiangning later on.[79]

Although the Hangzhou GCC did not join the revolutionary uprising in
the provincial capital, it remained indispensable to the newly formed military
government. Before the uprising, the Hangzhou GCC had already worked
with the Zhejiang Provincial Assembly to plan a provincial militia bureau.
When the plan failed to receive official approval, the general chamber formed
its own merchant militia with six branch offices under a headquarters. This
militia force began to patrol streets with rifles after the Hangzhou uprising
and effectively ensured merchant and public security during the political
chaos. In late November of 1911, the new military government sank into serious financial crisis, and it could neither pay its troops nor prevent its soldiers
from blackmailing pawnshops. At this critical moment, the Hangzhou GCC
made repeated efforts to stave off a merchant strike. Moreover, it helped solve
the financial crisis by taking responsibility for issuing military bonds in the
urban market and organizing a new bank for the military government.[80]

Close collaboration between chamber leaders and revolutionary partisans
also influenced the 1911 Revolution in Ningbo of coastal Zhejiang. In this
city, major leaders of the Ningbo GCC had already helped the local members
of the Revolutionary Alliance to form a branch of the Chinese National Association in July 1911 and then served as its honorary directors. In late October, they also provided financial support for a militia under the command of

the revolutionary partisans, and in turn received encouragement from the latter to establish a merchant militia. The alliance of these local elites and revolutionary partisans even won over the Han Chinese prefect of Ningbo and scared off the Manchu *daotai*. Subsequently, chamber leaders joined with revolutionary partisans and insurgent officials in a society for peace preservation (*baoanhui*), and they actually controlled local military and administrative affairs from the beginning of November 1911. On November 5, revolutionary partisans successfully used local militias to take over this city and then pushed for the formation of a new military government on the basis of the existing society for peace preservation. Following the pattern of its predecessor in Shanghai, this new government included leaders of the Ningbo GCC and the local self-government office. Such elite organizations provided not only militia force, financial support, and other resources but also social recognition for the revolutionary power.[81]

In addition to following Shanghai's pattern of military uprisings, leaders of the Suzhou GCC and other urban elite organizations as well as the Jiangsu provincial officials in that city initiated another type of revolutionary movement, the peaceful independence from the Qing court. The Suzhou pattern of peaceful independence influenced the anti-Qing revolution in many cities and towns in southern Jiangsu as well as other provinces in southern China.[82] In this kind of revolutionary movement, the insurgent Qing officials could hardly justify their actions against the old regime and legitimize their new powers as the revolutionary partisans did. Thus, they relied more on social legitimization from chambers of commerce and other social elite associations, not to mention the latter's support in other aspects.

Chambers of commerce around Suzhou were unable to join revolutionary uprisings because revolutionary partisans there were few and inactive before and during the 1911 Revolution. However, chamber leaders and other elite reformers shared a strong apprehension of violent revolution by the populace, and they had also formed close alliances with reformist officials against the Qing court during the constitutional movement. Zhang Jian, the chairman of the Jiangsu Provincial Assembly and a major leader of numerous reformist organizations in the province, personally witnessed the outbreak of the Wuchang uprising on the night of October 10, 1911, but his instant reaction was to push for official suppression of the revolutionary uprising so as to save the constitutional reform. On October 14–15, Zhang's successive meetings with the Qing officials in Jiangning failed to persuade them to send reinforcements to Wuchang. However, he still visited Jiangsu Governor Cheng Dequan in Suzhou on October 16 and helped him draft a petition to the Qing court, urging it to reform its cabinet, proclaim a constitution, and thus stem the revolutionary tide. The cold reaction from the court eventually disenchanted Zhang and Cheng, the latter of whom had also become resentful of the court's discrimination against Han Chinese officials and its centralization of power in the constitutional reform.[83]

Meanwhile, the Suzhou GCC had repeatedly received reports about rice riots from its affiliated and branch chambers around the city from September 1911, and it also faced financial and social crises inside the city after the Wuchang uprising. Large groups of unemployed silk weavers had threatened to take militant action, and urban residents began to flee from the city as revolutionary revolts spread from the middle toward the Lower Yangzi region in late October.[84] The Shanghai uprising on November 3 further shocked elites and officials in this city, and on the following day about fifty revolutionary soldiers arrived from Shanghai to mobilize the new army in Suzhou for a mutiny. At this critical moment, Suzhou elites held a special meeting inside a local academy, the outcome of which was that all participants advocated peaceful independence from the Qing court. The president of the Suzhou GCC, You Xianjia, together with other leaders of the local educational association and self-government office, met with Governor Cheng three times on the same day. They not only advised Cheng to adopt expedient measures to avoid plunging Jiangsu people into an abyss of misery but also helped the governor make arrangements for provincial independence. When Governor Cheng presented the plan for Jiangsu independence at a meeting of officials in Suzhou, there were few objections. Fan Gongxu, the former president of the Hangzhou GCC and the incumbent commissioner of education (*tixueshi*) in Jiangsu, rendered support to Cheng on behalf of other officials in attendance.[85]

On the eve of Jiangsu independence, the Suzhou GCC deployed its merchant exercise corps to patrol the streets and maintain social order on that crucial night. On the morning of November 5, New Army units in Suzhou moved from the suburbs into the city to support Cheng as the new military governor, and he inaugurated the new military government under the revolutionary flag of the "Chinese Republic" (Zhonghua minguo). Because the political transition in Suzhou was even more peaceful than the reformist elites and officials had expected, they deliberately broke several tiles on the roof of the governor's office to show the "violence" required of their revolutionary action. At a more symbolic ceremony that afternoon, leaders from the Suzhou GCC and local self-government office formally signed a pledge endorsing this new government.[86]

The Suzhou pattern of peaceful independence soon influenced revolutionary movements in southern Jiangsu after Cheng Dequan, now the new military governor of Jiangsu, sent out a public telegram to all his former subordinate officials, ordering them to immediately declare independence of their prefectures and counties.[87] Leaders of chambers of commerce, self-government offices, and other local elite organizations actively pushed their local officials to follow Cheng's suit. In some cases, they even worked with former Qing officials for peaceful independence and opposed militant actions by local revolutionary partisans. Such political activities reflected their concerns for personal interests and community safety, but their support was invariably important for the political change during the local revolution and for the new governments led by insurgent officials or revolutionary partisans.

In Changzhou Prefecture, Yun Zuqi had been a major leader of the local affiliated chamber and other elite organizations. After Yun received the aforesaid telegram from Jiangsu Military Governor Cheng on November 5, he immediately persuaded the Manchu prefect to transfer his power to a Han Chinese magistrate and began to organize a new government with the support of the local defense army. However, the leaders of the local agricultural association had already contacted revolutionary partisans in Shanghai and decided to take over the prefectural city with their peasant militias (*nongtuan*) from the countryside. They also planned a new government under the leadership of a revolutionary partisan but excluded Yun, his merchant militia, and local defense army from the revolutionary conspiracy. On the night of November 7, at a meeting in a middle school, these leaders resolved to take action the next day.[88]

Meanwhile, Yun decided to take preemptive measures. He ordered local merchants to immediately raise white flags that night and announced Changzhou independence before his partisan competitors could realize their plan. In two telegrams to the military government in Suzhou, Yun claimed that "local bandits" in the middle school had banned merchants from hanging out white flags and asked for permission to drive these "bandits" out of the city. He even deployed the Qing defense force to attack the middle school, although his request to Suzhou had received no response. After the revolutionary-led elites and their peasant militias held the middle school and withstood the attack of the local defense force for the whole night, Yun had to flee to Shanghai. Thereafter, a new government appeared in Changzhou with a revolutionary partisan as its major leader. However, the new revolutionary government soon met with strong protests from the Changzhou ACC because it enforced merchant contributions to the local military budget. Its troops almost became embroiled in a military clash with the merchant militia of the affiliated chamber. The militant protests of the Changzhou ACC protected merchant interests and later caused the dismissal of the revolutionary partisan from the leadership of the new government.[89]

Chamber leaders in the nearby capital of Zhenjiang Prefecture protected their urban community and achieved peaceful independence in a more dangerous situation. In this prefectural city, revolutionary partisans from Shanghai and those in the local New Army units had planned a military uprising, but the Manchu banner force there was determined to resist any revolutionary takeover. The commander of the Manchu banner, however, had maintained intimate relations with leaders of various elite organizations in the city, including Wu Zhaoen and Yu Dingyuan, the former and incumbent presidents of the Zhenjiang ACC as well as the major leaders of the local self-government office. Thus, these elite leaders did not flee the city as did most of its residents; instead they actively searched for a peaceful solution. After Jiangsu Military Governor Cheng Dequan's order for independence arrived in Zhenjiang, these local elites held a special meeting with the commander of the Manchu banner and other Qing officials on November 6, at which it was resolved to follow the Suzhou precedent in peaceful revolution. The Zhenjiang ACC and local self-government office presented a written pledge ensuring the safety of all the Manchus in the city and thus persuaded the banner commander to agree to a peaceful surrender.[90]

After these local elites actually pushed the Qing officials into peaceful independence, they also obtained the agreement of revolutionary partisans on November 7, when the New Army had already received the order to bombard and attack the city the following day. As president of the Zhenjiang ACC, Yu Dingyuan later helped the city avoid another war disaster after the New Army commander ordered the bombardment of the Manchu garrison as retaliation for an unsuccessful bomb attack on his office. Yu argued with the commander for a whole night and eventually had him retract the order. Moreover, Yu was also instrumental in arranging peaceful independence in the capital of Yangzhou Prefecture across the Yangzi River.[91]

During the Zhenjiang revolution, Yu Dingyuan had kept up frequent contact with the president of the Yangzhou ACC, Zhou Shunian, because they were also close relatives. On November 7, Zhou's representatives arrived in Zhenjing and invited Xu Baoshan, a Qing military officer and former salt smuggler who had just joined the revolution forces, to lead the peaceful independence of Yangzhou. On the same day, a self-proclaimed revolutionary partisan called Sun Tiansheng got the support of the local Qing troops in Yangzhou and seized the city. While Sun released prisoners, plundered governmental treasures, and created other disturbances, the Manchu salt controller in the city mounted cannons in his office for self-defense.[92]

At this critical moment, Zhou Shunian sent another delegate to Zhenjiang to ask for help. On November 9, Xu Baoshan's army entered Yangzhou together with a revolutionary partisan and a delegate from the Zhenjiang ACC. After Xu suppressed Sun Tiansheng's force and inaugurated a new administration in Yangzhou, both Zhou and his younger brother joined the government. Thereafter, Xu's army received invitations from affiliated chambers of commerce and other elite organizations in the nearby Taizhou and Xinghua counties, suppressed mutinous troops there, and helped local elite organizations declare peaceful independence. In another county of northern Jiangsu, Dongtai, chamber leaders also worked with the Qing officer of the local defense force and achieved independence on November 23, 1911.[93]

More county cities and even market towns in southern Jiangsu declared peaceful independence at the initiative of chamber leaders, other local elites, and opportunist officials. In Jiangyin County, the president of the affiliated chamber and other local elites had formed a public league (*gongtuan*) to control financial, police, judicial, and other affairs after the Wuchang uprising. Thus, they naturally declared peaceful independence on November 8, but the new government still retained the former magistrate as its chief of civil administration. In Kunshan County, the major leader of the local affiliated chamber, Fang Huan, was a member of the Jiangsu Provincial Assembly and the National Assembly, and he controlled the local defense force after the Manchu magistrate took refuge in his home. On November 6, Fang formed a new government under his own leadership but pushed the few local revolutionaries out.[94]

Even in Jiading, a satellite county of Shanghai, leaders of the affiliated chamber, merchant militia, self-government office, and the like continued to work closely with the Qing officials to maintain social order after the Shanghai uprising. They later declared independence on November 6, following the Suzhou precedent. Under the order of Shanghai Military Governor Chen Qimei, Jiading County finally formed a branch of his military government on November 8. However, in one of its towns, Nanxiang, chamber leaders and other reformist elites had already established an office of civil affairs (*minzheng shiwusuo*) by themselves two days earlier and had elected a former president of the affiliated chamber and a major leader of the study society and local self-government office, Li Shuxun, as the mayor (*shizhang*).[95] Li and other Nanxiang

elites were able to build a new political power after a peaceful revolution
because their chamber of commerce and study society already controlled such
community institutions as charitable halls by 1909, and their associational
networks had further expanded to include the local self-government office
thereafter, as mentioned before.

Clearly, from Shanghai and other Lower Yangzi cities to local towns, such
as Nanxiang, chamber leaders and other social elites provided crucial support for either militant or peaceful revolution and also helped build the new
political powers on the basis of their associational networks. Their involvement in the construction of the new powers under the Republican flag was
a culmination of their previous efforts to secure a share of official authority
in business legislation and jurisdiction and to seek political influence through
local self-government offices, provincial assemblies, and an unrealized parliament in the constitutional reform. Thus, the political participation of the
Lower Yangzi chambers of commerce in the constitutional and revolutionary
movements was significant not merely because they eventually turned from
reform to a revolution that ended the Qing imperial system and its claim to
the mandate of heaven. They also helped create the republican polity that
based its legitimacy on social organizations and the society in general. Such
sociopolitical transformation in the economic heartland of China was destined
to influence societal-state relations at the national level.

— Clashes w/ gov over control over judicial matters
- Constitutional movement
      - provincial assemblies
      - national assemblies
      - petitions for Qing parliament
      - self - government

- revolutionary movement
      → provided support for militant or peaceful
        revolutions
      - helped build new political powers on
        base of associational networks

7

Nationwide Chamber Networks
and the Republican Governments

[handwritten annotation: └ CC's expanded networks and influence to the national level]

As China was moving from the imperial into the Republican era in the course of the 1911 Revolution, the Lower Yangzi chambers of commerce further expanded their associational network and political influence toward the national level. Such a trend marked a great upsurge of the network revolution during this watershed period because it helped integrate the nationwide merchant community and brought the latter into more intensive interactions with the varied Republican governments in the early twentieth century. Through such interactive movements, these Lower Yangzi chambers provided dynamics for historical changes in the larger society and state politics that extended far beyond their elite merchant strata and the regional arena.

The 1911 Revolution basically ended Qing rule in the Lower Yangzi region on December 2, 1911, when the Jiangsu-Zhejiang Allied Army (Jiang-Zhe lianjun) occupied Jiangning, soon to be renamed Nanjing. Thereafter, representatives of both provincial assemblies and military governors in the independent provinces decided to establish the Nanjing Provisional Government (Nanjing linshi zhengfu) and elected Sun Yat-sen, the veteran revolutionary leader, as its provisional president on December 29.[1] The Lower Yangzi chambers of commerce initially endorsed Sun's government in Nanjing and the revolutionary powers under its authority for both political protection and advancement. But they soon withdrew their support as a result of their conflicts with these revolutionary powers over the economic and political interests of their merchant community, especially those of their elite merchants.

[handwritten annotation: CC leaders began to clash w/ Sun's govt over economic interests]

The primary source of the discord between these chambers and the revolutionary governments was the latter's insatiable demands for merchant contributions to cover military and administrative expenses. The Jiangning GCC bore the brunt of these financial burdens after the Jiangsu-Zhejiang Allied Army drove the Qing military forces out of the city in early December 1911. This general chamber had warmly welcomed the allied army with meat, wine, and a poetic eulogy that praised the revolutionary soldiers as "the most lovely compatriots."[2] Less than a month later, however, it had to raise 200,000 silver dollars to have the "lovely" army leave Nanjing without creating further disturbances.[3]

The Shanghai GCC encountered especially onerous demands from the military government under the control of the Revolutionary Alliance. Its merchant leaders and members even became targets of coercive fund-raising measures implemented by the military governor, Chen Qimei. In order to obtain the Qing government's remaining deposits from the native banks, Chen shocked the local merchant community by placing Zhu Wulou, a director of the Shanghai GCC and a leading native banker, under house arrest. The military government did not release Zhu until thirty-one native banks extended a huge loan to it. Chen also attempted to seize the assets of the Shanghai branch of the Qing State Bank by kidnapping its manager, Song Hanzhang, another member of the general chamber of commerce. This kidnapping soon aroused merchant protest, but Chen still refused to allow the Shanghai GCC to bail Song out. Moreover, Chen's military government was unable to repay the Shanghai GCC's three million silver dollars of merchant loans before that government's demise in 1912.[4]

Such financial burdens quickly dampened the elite merchants' support for the military government. After Chen's government came into being on November 6, 1911, chamber leaders including Li Zhongjue, Wang Zhen, Shen Manyun, and Zhu Baosan joined it with enthusiasm. Only one month later, Shen resigned from the post of minister of finance after the Xincheng Bank under his management had extended outstanding credits to the government and had become bankrupt. Zhu succeeded Shen and over the next two months raised nearly 600,000 silver dollars for the military government. In February 1912, he too left the government together with another chamber leader, Wang Zhen, the minister of commerce. Meanwhile, Li repeatedly handed in his resignation but was pressed to stay on by military governor Chen.[5] Moreover, in November 1911, Zhu had founded the Shanghai Commercial Association (Shanghai shangwu gongsuo) for the purpose of replacing the Qing-legitimized Shanghai GCC and working with the Republican government. When he left the military government in February 1912, his pro-revolution association assimilated the old Shanghai GCC and basically renamed itself after the latter. The new Shanghai GCC soon joined ten other elite organizations to oppose the grain tax (*mimaishui*) that had been recently imposed by the Shanghai military governor.[6]

The revolutionary powers further alienated these chambers of commerce because they failed to maintain social order. In early 1912, the Nanjing Provisional Government appointed a pro-revolution politician to replace the Jiangsu military governor, Cheng Dequan, the former Qing official who had led the provincial independence in Suzhou. But the new governor did not enjoy the confidence of local elites or the military garrison in this city. On March 27–28, hundreds of lawless soldiers launched a large-scale mutiny in Suzhou, killing seven persons, severely injuring another one, looting 331 business establishments, and causing more than 730,000 silver dollars' worth of losses to local merchants. This mutiny directly widened the political chasm between the Suzhou GCC and the revolutionary governments in the city itself and in Nanjing.[7]

The Nanjing Provisional Government lost the support of the Lower Yangzi chambers of commerce for similar reasons. No sooner had this government taken shape on January 1, 1912, than it faced a financial crisis and sought to force the chambers of commerce in Nanjing and other Lower Yangzi cities to donate 500,000 silver dollars. This plan did not materialize because of opposition from Zhang Jian, the minister of industry in this government and a long-time patron of chambers of commerce. Nevertheless, the Nanjing GCC still paid the aforementioned 200,000 silver dollars in late January 1912, and it then shouldered the heavy load of cashing the military bonds issued by the Nanjing Provisional Government so as to avoid a merchant strike. Although this government urgently needed merchant support, it did not grant chambers of commerce representative powers in return. In March 1912, the Shanghai GCC appealed to the provisional president, Sun Yat-sen, to send three chamber representatives to the Provisional Senate (Linshi canyiyuan). It received a negative reply and failed to secure even the representation it had gained in the National Assembly under Qing rule.[8]

As a result, chamber leaders and other elites in the Lower Yangzi region were ready to side with Yuan Shikai's military power in Beijing for peaceful national unification after Yuan reached a political deal with the Nanjing Provisional Government and forced the Qing court to abdicate in February 1912. According to the deal, Sun Yat-sen surrendered his presidential post to Yuan Shikai. However, Sun and other revolutionary leaders insisted that

Yuan assume the presidency in Nanjing, so they could separate him from his power base in Beijing. In regard to this critical issue, the Shanghai GCC and South Shanghai ACC did not endorse Sun's demand. In a public telegram addressed to Sun, Yuan, the Provisional Senate in Nanjing, and all military governors and provincial assemblies on March 9, 1912, the two chambers of commerce called for the early unification of China without further disputes over the location of the capital.[9] CCS - call for early unification

Historians in mainland China have usually interpreted this telegram as a passive political choice by the Shanghai capitalists for the sake of their own class interest or even as evidence of their collusion with Yuan against Sun's revolutionary party.[10] Actually, in this telegram, the Shanghai chamber leaders placed the same hope on Yuan for establishing a unified republic as did revolutionaries at that time, and their stance on the capital issue actually reflected general public opinion in the country as a whole.[11] Thus, these chambers of commerce first supported and then shunned the new revolutionary power for both their elite merchant interest and their general public concern.

More important, these Lower Yangzi chambers of commerce did not simply endorse Yuan Shikai's regime but engaged in clashes with it from the beginning. In particular, they collectively challenged its Ministry of Industry and Commerce (Gongshangbu) at the National Conference of Industry and Commerce between November 1 and December 5, 1912. The ministry called the meeting to discuss statutes, policies, and strategies regarding commercial and industrial development. In response, more than seventy representatives from forty-five chambers of commerce at home and abroad attended the meeting, including eighteen delegates from about ten chambers of commerce in the Lower Yangzi region. Also attending were representatives of other commercial and industrial groups as well as a few officials and special delegates.[12] The chamber leaders from the Lower Yangzi region not only accounted for nearly 26 percent of the chamber delegates from the whole country but also brought their own agenda to the meeting.

As early as July 1912, the Shanghai GCC had contacted the Hankou GCC concerning its plan to organize a national union of chambers. It then telegraphed the plan to other chambers throughout the country and received positive responses from most of them. After the leaders of the Shanghai and Hankou GCCs presented the plan to the Beijing meeting, they received unanimous support from other chamber representatives. Their collective action on this issue directly challenged the Ministry of Industry and Commerce because its rules permitted the establishment of only provincial chamber federations at that time. Nevertheless, the chamber delegates passed a set of bylaws for the

plan to organize National Union of CCs

National Union of Chinese Chambers of Commerce (Zhonghua quanguo shanghui lianhehui) in November 1912. Through the joint petition of the Shanghai and Hankou GCCs, this union received the ministry's approval on December 20, 1912. Although its nominal headquarters (*benbu*) were located in the national capital of Beijing, its general office (*zongshiwu suo*) was the Shanghai GCC itself.[13] Thus, this general chamber actually controlled the national union.

[margin note: national union controlled by SH GCC]

Chamber delegates at the Beijing meeting also clashed with the Ministry of Industry and Commerce over its draft law for chambers of commerce. Through this law, the ministry tried to revoke the official seals granted earlier to all chambers of commerce, eliminate the distinctions between "general" and "affiliated" chambers in their titles, and place them under the administration of local governments. Its purpose was obviously to cut the vertical connections among the general, affiliated, and branch chambers and to divide and rule them through the local governments. All the chamber delegates strongly opposed this draft law and even planned a boycott against the ministry's motion to discuss the draft law at this conference. As a result, Yuan Shikai's regime was unable to issue a law for chambers of commerce after this meeting.[14]

[margin note: Clashes wi BJ govt]

The conflicts between the chamber delegates and Yuan's government at the Beijing conference further expanded into a political issue about merchant rights in the first national election for the House of Representatives (Zhongyiyuan) and about chamber representation in the Senate (Canyiyuan). Yuan's government had issued electoral laws in August 1912, but it seriously limited the merchant franchise in the election by excluding payment of commercial taxes from the qualifications for voters. In collaboration with the Tianjin GCC and other chambers in northern China, the Shanghai GCC led petitions by the general chambers in Suzhou, Nanjing, Hankou, and other cities of southern China, demanding amendment of the electoral law in favor of merchants. The chamber representatives from the Lower Yangzi region, including those from Jiangdu, Jiangpu, and Wuxi counties, directly joined their counterparts from other provinces in a petition in Beijing.[15]

The Shanghai GCC further proposed to elect ten nonvoting delegates from the national union of chambers to the Senate, who might attend all of its sessions regarding commercial affairs and have the right to ratify its relevant resolutions. In response, chamber delegates presented this demand to the Beijing conference, and they even threatened to stop paying commercial taxes if their demand was met with refusal. Unfortunately, their fight for merchant representation in the state legislature was not as successful as their efforts regarding their national union and the draft law for chambers of commerce.[16]

By leading these three contests with Yuan Shikai's regime at the Beijing conference, the Lower Yangzi chambers of commerce achieved their aims of forming associational networks at the national level and of foiling the government's attempt to impose legal limitations on their interconnections. However, they still failed in their struggles for political representation in the national legislature. Because the Parliament seriously limited the participation in its activities of elite associations such as the chambers of commerce, not to mention the populace, it failed to check the rise of Yuan Shikai's dictatorship even though the national elections in December 1912 and January 1913 ended with victory of the Nationalist Party (Guomindang), the successor of the Revolutionary Alliance. After Yuan defeated the Nationalist Party in its "Second Revolution" of 1913, he dissolved the Parliament, the provincial assemblies, and all self-government institutions in early 1914.[17]

However, Yuan's regime was not able to dismantle chambers of commerce and similar associations. In September 1914, it tried again to impose a new law for chambers of commerce, hoping to use the law to dissolve the National Union of Chinese Chambers of Commerce, remove the title "general chamber," and reduce the number of other chambers. The government's scheme immediately met with strong protests from chambers of commerce nationwide, and the Shanghai GCC not only used repeated petitions to delay official imposition of the law but also called an emergency meeting of the national union of chambers for concerted action. Under such pressure, Yuan's government in December 1915 issued a revised *Law for Chambers of Commerce* (Shanghuifa) that basically accepted the chambers' demands.[18] When Yuan's clique launched the monarchical movement for him from August 1915, it specifically pressed the National Union of Chinese Chambers of Commerce and its chamber members for endorsements. However, of the approximately 1,000 chambers of commerce in the country, only twenty-four yielded to the political pressure and reluctantly sent out supportive telegrams for the monarchical movement by mid-September of 1915. By contrast, many chambers actively joined the nationwide resistance to the imperial restoration and helped defeat Yuan's monarchical movement in early 1916.[19]

Clearly, these chambers of commerce retained their associational networks and political vitality after Yuan dissolved the Parliament, provincial assemblies, and self-government offices, and they even achieved success in the battle over the *Law for Chambers of Commerce* at the peak of Yuan's dictatorship. In this legal battle, the concession by Yuan Shikai's dictatorship to these chambers showed that their power derived more from their social legitimacy than from state legalization. The reliance of Yuan's monarchical movement on the chambers' endorsement further revealed that any ruling government in the post-imperial era, even the briefly restored monarchy, had to seek its political legitimacy from such social organizations. Thus, their political performance under Yuan's dictatorship indicated that they had significantly institutionalized their network power and permanently transformed sociopolitical relations in modern China. rulers now sought legitimacy from social orgs

Certainly, even at the apex of Republican democracy around 1912, these chambers of commerce still failed to get their associational representatives into the Parliament. Thus, they were unable to prevent the turn of the national polity toward Yuan's dictatorship and then toward warlord rule. Nor could such new elite associations expand their networks into the vast countryside and impose institutional checks on the local bullies or what Prasenjit Duara calls the state's "entrepreneurial brokers" in the rural society.[20] However, from the beginning of the Republican era to the warlord period (1916–1928), the chambers of commerce retained their network power, as a foreign observer testified in 1920:[21]

> Chinese chambers of commerce have become, within their city-wide territories, probably the most autocratic [authoritative?] trades-unions in the world. The advantages of being a member of the Chamber are such that no business of any consequence can afford to stay out.
>
> The official position of the Chinese Chamber is that of middleman between the national Ministry of Commerce and provincial Commissions of Industry on one hand and the merchant class on the other. . . . Chambers are given the power to recommend the enactment, amendment or repeal of laws regulating manufactures, industry and trade.
>
> In cases of great exigency or public calamity the power of the Chamber of Commerce over the merchant class is extended to cover the entire population. . . . They constitute the only organized power in China today which is able to stand up against the military cliques, and the students have been able to influence and purify public affairs in such measure as they have won the support of the Chambers.
>
> The Chambers are representative bodies, which, unlike most existing institutions in China, are in actual working order, and as such, constitute a living germ of democracy of great promise for China's political future.

The chambers of commerce failed to live up to the Western scholar's wishes for leading democratization thereafter largely because of the failure of the overall political system of Republican China. However, they still brought significant changes to Chinese society during national unity or division and to the Chinese polity, whether of an authoritarian or democratic nature. As the quotation shows, these chambers of commerce had entrenched their associational networks in their constituencies and in the larger society and become an indispensable force in government-business relations and even in interactions between popular organizations and the military powers.

After the Nationalist Party launched its campaigns against warlords and founded the Nanjing government in April 1927, it immediately reorganized the Shanghai GCC. In December 1927, the party further planned to dissolve all Chinese chambers of commerce and replace them with the Merchant Associations (Shangmin xiehui), which were under its control. In order to foil this plan, the Shanghai GCC called chambers of commerce from the whole country to a meeting in November 1927, and the National Union of Chinese Chambers of Commerce led repeated petitions to the Nanjing government thereafter. This struggle lasted until mid-1929, with the chambers of commerce eventually winning the right to keep their titles and organizations, but they had to go through a reorganization process and actually came under governmental control.[22]

Most previous studies on Chinese chambers of commerce wind up their narratives around this historical moment and conclude that these chambers reflected the failure of Chinese modernization and exemplified the trend toward the ascendancy of state power over merchant activism in the twentieth century.[23] In a case study of Canton during the early twentieth century, Michael Tsin best summarizes this line of scholarship with the argument that the late Qing social organizations, including chambers of commerce, achieved little substantive change in their relationship with the state because they mainly embodied a cyclical rise of nonofficial organizations in a period of weakened government.[24]

To some extent, the relations of the chambers of commerce with the late Qing and the successive Republican governments indeed reflected such cyclic change in Chinese history. From the late Qing to the early Republican period, the state's inability to deal with foreign and domestic challenges allowed elite merchants and their social peers to expand their sociopolitical power. Thus, as a key part of the elite associational networks, chambers of commerce played a leading role in reformist, revolutionary, and nationalistic movements as well as commercial and industrial developments, as preceding chapters have shown.

However, the interaction of these chambers of commerce with the Republican governments up to the late 1920s showed not merely the resurgence of state authority over social elites, as what happened under a new, strong, and centralized dynasty in imperial China. In fact, it significantly broke the cyclic change in the society-state relationship because these chambers and other social organizations retained both legally sanctioned status and their associational networks, which perpetually provided an institutional foundation for elite merchants and other social leaders to rally themselves and even the populace, to challenge the authority of the state, or to provide social legitimacy for the latter. It is in this sense that the network revolution led by the chambers of commerce and other state-legitimized associations brought about institutionalized and irreversible change in the sociopolitical relationship of modern China.

Non Hamocratic Revoluntury
Sun + CCs

- party did not maintain social order
- policies not in interests of elite merchants

Republican
CCs → back Yuan/Beijing

- govt attempted to limit CC power,
  disband national union

- ended with state control over CCS

• CCs maintand status + associational
  networks - could challenge or
  provide legitmacy for a State

Conclusion

This study has used the concept of associational networks to analyze the development of Chinese chambers of commerce in Lower Yangzi cities and towns in the early twentieth century, as well as the expansion of their relations and influence from local urban and township societies to national politics. This concept reflects the interconnected reality of interpersonal and institutional relations among the chamber networks, and it also offers new insights into their drastic change toward relational institutionalization, expansion, diversification, and interaction in this historical period. Such relational change showed revolutionary significance because it not only triggered the abrupt development of state-legitimized associations and their intertwined networks across the merchant community and other social circles but also influenced sociopolitical transformation in the whole country starting in the early twentieth century.

At the beginning of this century, Chinese chambers of commerce first appeared in the Lower Yangzi region because of long-term relational changes in the business world and society at large, especially the relational institutionalization and expansion among guild leaders and other elite merchants. In the institutional contexts of guilds, semi-official enterprises, and bureaus of commerce, the interactions of elite merchants with officials also became increasingly intensive and resulted directly in the development of the earliest Chinese chambers of commerce in this region. The rise of these chambers inaugurated a series of new institutional norms and links, such as formal leadership, membership, periodic meetings, competitive elections, and network hierarchy, which had made only sporadic appearances in the preexisting guilds, charitable halls, study societies, and other social organizations.

As contemporary sociology indicates, social institutions are characterized by their ability to replicate themselves with particular types of structures and to organize relatively stable patterns of human activities.[1] The institutional development of these chambers of commerce naturally allowed them to reproduce and expand their associational networks at a faster speed and on a larger scale than had previously been seen in the history of Chinese social organizations. Thus, the Lower Yangzi chambers provided an institutional model and pivotal linkage for their counterparts throughout the country and for new associations in agriculture, education, and other social circles. These new associations fundamentally transformed Chinese social networks with new institutional frameworks, and their network expansion also nurtured more stable social relations among the merchant community and the larger society.

The Lower Yangzi chambers of commerce brought about such social change not only through their network institutionalization and expansion but also through their relational diversification. These chambers used multi-level memberships, meetings, elections, and other hierarchical systems to incorporate increasingly heterogeneous merchants, especially elite ones, rather than a small bourgeois class.[2] Their personnel and organizational interpenetration with more numerous and diverse institutions within and beyond the business world also helped integrate social elites across professional lines when local reforms in education, self-government, and other issues intensified power struggles among these elite groups.[3] Such interrelated associational networks further led a revolutionary trend toward general social integration because they helped bring the elites and masses together in their national or regional struggles with foreign powers and the late Qing government, as was shown by the nationwide boycott of 1905 and the Jiangsu and Zhejiang railroad movements around 1907.

The interactions of these chambers with both the populace and the state became more intensive and complicated because of the expansion and diversification of their institutionalized networks, and such interactive movements reflected the most dynamic and significant aspect of their network revolution starting from the late Qing period. Indeed, the development of the chamber networks in the progressively expanded social arenas enabled their elite merchants to find more common ground with the populace and offered them more opportunities to pursue personal power and wealth in line with the public interest of the larger society. In the last years of the Qing period, these

chambers expanded their relations from local markets into new business ventures up to the national level, including the Nanyang Expo and the Sino-
American joint ventures. Such institutional relations combined the fundamentally private interests of chamber participants, namely, their drive for business
profit, with their public concern for national interests, including their push
for nongovernmental diplomacy between China and the United States. In
these politicized business activities, chamber leaders and members either con-
fronted or collaborated with the Qing government for the sake of their private and public interests. In most cases, they successfully advanced their elite
merchant interests and simultaneously enhanced their claim of public representation because their chamber networks effectively mobilized elites and
even the general populace into collective actions.

In the late Qing reform and revolution, the Lower Yangzi chambers of
commerce further boosted their elite merchant power and public representation through their multiform interactions with the Qing officials and other
sociopolitical forces. Both their response and their challenge to state-led constitutional reform accelerated the reformist programs for business legislation,
self-government, provincial assemblies, and so on. Chamber leaders in many
Lower Yangzi cities and towns also expedited the 1911 Revolution through
their joint actions with revolutionary partisans in the anti-Qing uprisings or
with opportunist Qing officials in the move toward peaceful independence
from the Qing court.

In short, the network revolution led by these chambers of commerce and
other new associations in late Qing and early Republican China constituted
one of the most substantial and significant parts of sociopolitical change. It
helped integrate elite merchants and more diverse social forces, including the
populace, through the expansion of increasingly institutionalized networks
and enabled these social forces, especially new elite associations, to exercise
unprecedented influence on state politics through multiform interactions with
the latter. Such a relational revolution was quieter than the 1911 Revolution,
but it lasted much longer and left deeper impacts on the sociopolitical landscape of China, especially on its lower-level society. However, its significance
has not received sufficient attention in previous scholarship.

In a classic study of the 1911 Revolution, Joseph W. Esherick concludes that
the revolution was "politically progressive and socially regressive" because
urban reformist elites turned their frustration with the Qing court into a radical revolution, but the elites as a whole, especially those in local towns and
rural townships, strengthened their dominance over the populace.[4] Edward
J. M. Rhoads's analysis of the Republican Revolution around Canton pre-

sents a similarly pessimistic view of the social regression in the class relations between local elites and the masses.[5] Such scholarly viewpoints reflect the historical limitations of the 1911 Revolution, but they cannot fully explain the social dynamics for the revolutionary movement that ended both the Qing dynasty and the entire imperial system.

This study also pays attention to the increasing dominance of chamber leaders and members as well as other late Qing elites and to their class clashes with the masses in local markets and reforms, but it further reveals how the widespread chamber networks changed the social dominance of elites and the society as a whole. The network development among the chambers and other new associations expanded the social relations of these elites, especially the progressive ones, beyond their personal cliques and local arenas and linked their pursuit of power and wealth with public interests in community and national affairs. It also led these elite merchants, other social elites, and the populace into unprecedented interconnections and even social integration in an era full of cliquish strife and class tensions. Such social transformation enabled these chambers of commerce to act on behalf of their local merchant communities and the larger society in business and politics, but it did not prevent them from taking a flexible stance in the interactions between society and the state.

In society-state relations, the Lower Yangzi chambers of commerce partly performed the traditional function of middleman between officials and merchants, as guild leaders had before, and they greatly institutionalized and expanded such intermediary roles, as Philip C. C. Huang's notion of a "third realm" suggests.[6] Nevertheless, these chambers were more animated associational networks of elite merchants than a neutral third realm between society and the state, and they played more varied roles than a mere institutional mediator between the two sides, as previous chapters have demonstrated.

A focus on the complicated relations between these chambers of commerce and other sociopolitical forces, especially the state, can also advance the scholarly discussions on the public sphere and civil society in Chinese studies. The development of such chambers from the late Qing period on did not contribute merely to constant contention between the public sphere and official administration, nor did it lead to complete autonomy of civil society from the state.[7] Rather, these chambers enhanced their public representation by leading different social forces into more diverse interactions than mere contention with the state. What the chambers actually achieved was the aforesaid "structural autonomy" because they entered into more intensive interactions with the late Qing and successive Republican governments than had the guilds and other preexisting social organizations, but such interactive relations reduced their dependence on precarious official patronage and increased their influence on state politics.

Indeed, as the earliest state-legitimized nonofficial associations, the chambers started the trend for social organizations to interact with the government within a legal framework and further pushed for institutional reform of the legal and political systems in the late Qing reform, the 1911 Revolution, and early Republican politics. As a result, these chambers developed more formal relations with the state than the personal contacts of guild leaders and other social elites with local officials, and their multiform interactions with the bureaucratic hierarchy also expanded from the local to the national level. In the new society-state relations of Republican China, the chambers of commerce and other social associations not only relied on governmental legalization but also became a new institutional base for elites and the populace to seek social solidarity and even constituted a major source of legitimacy for any political regime.[8] In this sense, the network revolution triggered by the Lower Yangzi chambers of commerce not only transformed government-business relations but also helped institutionalize, expand, and diversify the interactive relationships among different social forces and between them and the state in modern China.

From the early Republican to the Nationalist era, chambers of commerce came under increasingly tighter state control, but they did not totally lose their institutionalized network power, as is shown by the foregoing analysis of their interactions with the various Republican regimes until the late 1920s. The most striking evidence of their network vitality and resilience comes from the People's Republic of China, the most centralized political power in modern Chinese history. After the Chinese Communist Party (Zhongguo gongchandang) defeated the Nationalist Party and established the People's Republic of China in October 1949, it ordered all chambers of commerce in mainland China to reorganize and rename themselves as "unions of industry and commerce" (gongshangye lianhehui). However, after mainland China entered the era of economic reform, the unions of industry and commerce began to rename themselves chambers of commerce from 1988 onward.[9]

With remarkable similarity to what had happened in the late Qing period, chambers of commerce reemerged in the Lower Yangzi region through multiform interactions between the new generation of business elites and the communist government, and they quickly developed new networks within and beyond this region. As a forerunner in nationwide economic reform, the city of Wenzhou in costal Zhejiang produced the first chamber of commerce for private, foreign, and Sino-foreign joint ventures in 1988. By the late 1990s, dozens of chambers of commerce had appeared in different trades in Wenzhou and even in other provinces where Wenzhou natives operated their businesses. In 1997, Shanghai, Wenzhou, Canton, and Xiamen became the four cities in the governmental experiment to promote chambers of commerce throughout the country.[10]

When I first conducted my field work for this book in Shanghai, Suzhou, Hangzhou, Nanjing, and other Lower Yangzi cities in 1995, the signboards of chambers of commerce also appeared in front of many governmental buildings, hanging side by side with those of the so-called democratic parties and groups (*minzhu dangpai*). The regeneration of Chinese chambers of commerce in the late twentieth century was not a mere repetition of what happened in the late Qing period. Rather, it developed on the basis of the preexisting chamber networks and reflected a new stage of relational revolution in contemporary China.

Reference Matter

Appendix 1

General Chambers of Commerce in the Lower Yangzi Region, 1904–1911

Location and rank of seat	Founding year	President	Vice president
Shanghai: treaty port	1904	Yan Xinhou (1904–1905)	Xu Run (1904–1905)
		Zeng Zhu (1906)	Zhu Baosan (1906)
		Li Houyou (1907)	Sun Duosen (1907)
		Zhou Jinbiao (1908–1910)	Li Houyou (1908)
			Yan Yibin (1909)
			Shao Qintao (1910)
		Chen Runfu (1911)	Bei Runsheng (1911)
Suzhou: provincial capital	1905	You Xianjia (1905–1908)	Ni Sijiu (1905)
			Wu Ligao (1906–1908)
		Zhang Lüqian (1909)	Ni Kaiding (1909)
		You Xianjia (1910–1911)	Wu Ligao (1910–1911)
Jiangning (Nanjing): provincial capital	1904	Liu Shihang (1904–1905)	Zhu Zhongxuan (1904–1908)
		Su Xidai (1906–1908)	
		Song Enquan (1909–1910)	Zhang Zilin (1909–?)
		Su Xidai (1911–?)	
Tongzhou: prefectural city	1904	Zhang Cha (1904–1908)	Liu Guixin (1904–1906)
		Liu Guixin (1909–?)	Lin Shixin (1907–?)
Hangzhou: provincial capital	1906	Fan Gongxu (1906–1907)	Gu Hongzao (1906–1907)
			Pan Chiwen (1907–1908)
		Jin Yuesheng (1908)	
		Pan Chiwen (1909)	Gu Songqing (1909)
		Gu Songqing (1910–?)	Wang Xirong (1910–?)

(continued)

Location and rank of seat	Founding year	President	Vice president
Ningbo: treaty port	1906	Wu Chuanji (1906–1907)	Gu Zhao (1906)
		Qin Yunbin (1908–?)	Zheng Xianzi (1907–1908)
		Zheng Xianzi (1909–?)	Qin Jihan (1909–?)

Sources: NGST: I, 4:b–5a, 7a–b; NGST: II, 4A:22a–24b; SZZZ, 1:94–5; SSDC, 46–58, 380; HSLB, no. 11 (1909): haineiwai shanghui tongrenlu 4–6, no. 16 (1909): haineiwai shanghui tongrenlu 3–4, no. 20 (1909): haineiwai shanghui tongrenlu 1–3; SWGB 29 (1909): 9b.

Note: This table does not include information on the Shanghai CCA, the predecessor of the Shanghai GCC, or the short-lived Zhejiang and Jiaxing GCCs. For such information, see Chapter 2. Shanghai and Ningbo were two of the earliest treaty ports, and they formed general chambers of commerce in spite of their low administrative status. Other late-coming treaty ports in the Lower Yangzi region are not specified in this and the following tables.

Appendix 2

Affiliated Chambers of Commerce in the Lower Yangzi Region, 1904–1911

Location	Rank of seat[a]	Prefecture[b]	Founding year[c]
1. Baoying	county	Yangzhou	1906
2. Changshan	county	Quzhou	1907
3. Changshu-Zhaowen	county	Suzhou	1906
4. Changxing	county	Huzhou	1909
5. Changzhou	prefecture	Changzhou	1905
6. Chenmu	town	Suzhou	1911
7. Chongming	county	Taicang	1904
8. Chuansha	county	Songjiang	1906
9. Chun'an	county	Yanzhou	1909
10. Chuzhou	prefecture	Chuzhou	1908
11. Cixi	county	Ningbo	1906
12. Dangshan	county	Xuzhou	1909
13. Danyang	county	Zhenjiang	1907
14. Deqing	county	Huzhou	1907
15. Dinghai	prefecture	Dinghai	1907
16. Dongba	town	Jiangning	1908 [1906]
17. Dongtai	county	Yangzhou	1907
18. Dongtangshi	town	Suzhou	1909 [1906]
19. Dongyang	county	Jinhua	1909
20. Feng	county	Xuzhou	1907
21. Fenghua	county	Ningbo	1907
22. Fuyang	county	Hangzhou	1909
23. Gaoyou	county	Yangzhou	1910
24. Gongchenqiao	prefecture-province	Hangzhou	1906
25. Haian	town	Yangzhou	1908
26. Haimen	prefecture	Haimen	1904
27. Haiyan	county	Jiaxing	1909
28. Haizhou-Ganyu	prefecture	Haizhou	1906
29. Huabu	town	Quzhou	1908

(continued)

Location	Rank of seat[a]	Prefecture[b]	Founding year[c]
30. Huai'an	prefecture	Huai'an	1907
31. Huzhou	prefecture	Huzhou	1907
32. Jiading	county	Taicang	1905
33. Jiande	county	Yanzhou	1910
34. Jiangpu	county	Jiangning	1907
35. Jiangyan	town	Yangzhou	1909 [1908]
36. Jiangyin	county	Changzhou	1906
37. Jiashan	county	Jiaxing	1908
38. Jiaxing	prefecture	Jiaxing	1907 [1905]
39. Jingjiang	county	Changzhou	1908
40. Jinhua	prefecture	Jinhua	1908
41. Jintan	county	Zhenjiang	1906
42. Jurong	county	Jiangning	1908
43. Kunshan-Xinyang	county	Suzhou	1907
44. Lanqi	county	Jinhua	1905
45. Leqing	county	Wenzhou	1908
46. Linghu	town	Huzhou	1908
47. Linpu	town	Shaoxing	1910
48. Lishui	county	Jiangning	1908
49. Liuhe	town	Taicang	1906
50. Liyang	county	Zhenjiang	1906
51. Longquan	county	Chuzhou	1911
52. Longyou	county	Quzhou	1910
53. Luhe	county	Jiangning	1907
54. Luodian	town	Taicang	1908
55. Luoshe	town	Huzhou	1907
56. Luqiao	town	Taizhou	1908
57. Meili	town	Suzhou	1906
58. Minhang	town	Songjiang	1906
59. Nanhui	county	Songjiang	1909
60. Nanqiao	town	Songjiang	1908
61. Nanxiang	town	Taicang	1906
62. Ninghai	county	Taizhou	1908
63. Peixian	county	Xuzhou	1909
64. Pinghu	county	Jiaxing	1907
65. Pingwang	town	Suzhou	1906
66. Pingyang	county	Wenzhou	1909
67. Pingyao	town	Hangzhou	1909
68. Pujiang	county	Jinhua	1910
69. Qingjiangpu	town	Huai'an	1906
70. Qingpu	county	Songjiang	1909
71. Qingtian	county	Chuzhou	1909
72. Quzhou	prefecture	Quzhou	1906
73. Rugao	county	Tongzhou	1906
74. Ruian	county	Wenzhou	1907
75. Ruichang	county	Chuzhou	1909
76. Shangbai	town	Huzhou	1908
77. Shanggang	town	Huai'an	1908
78. Shangyu	county	Shaoxing	1907
79. Shanyin-Kuaiji	county-prefecture	Shaoxing	1906
80. Shendang	town	Jiaxing	1908
81. Shengxian	county	Shaoxing	1910
82. Shengze	town	Suzhou	1906
83. Shimen	county	Jiaxing	1905

Location	Rank of seat[a]	Prefecture[b]	Founding year[c]
84. Shipu	town	Ningbo	1907
85. Shouchang	county	Yanzhou	1911
86. Shuyang	county	Haizhou	1909
87. Sian	town	Huzhou	1911
88. Sijing	town	Songjiang	1906
89. Songjiang	prefecture	Songjiang	1906
90. Songyang	county	Chuzhou	1908
91. South Shanghai	county	Songjiang	1909 [1906]
92. Suining	county	Xuzhou	1910
93. Suqian	county	Xuzhou	1907
94. Taicang	prefecture	Taicang	1908 [1908]
95. Taixing	county	Tongzhou	1906
96. Taizhou	county	Yangzhou	1906
97. Tangqi	town	Hangzhou	1907
98. Tiantai	county	Taizhou	1909
99. Tonglu	county	Yanzhou	1909
100. Tongxiang	county	Jiaxing	1907
101. Tongzhou	prefecture	Tongzhou	1904
102. Waisha	town	Taicang	1908
103. Wangdian	town	Jiaxing	1908
104. Wenzhou	prefecture	Wenzhou	1906
105. Wujiang-Zhenze	county	Suzhou	1906
106. Wukang	county	Huzhou	1909
107. Wuqing	town	Huzhou	1907
108. Wusong	town	Taicang	1909
109. Wuxi-Jinkui	county	Changzhou	1905
110. Wuyi	county	Jinhua	1909
111. Xiaguan	town	Jiangning	1911
112. Xiangshan	county	Ningbo	1907
113. Xiaofeng	county	Huzhou	1907
114. Xiaoshan	county	Shaoxing	1908
115. Xiaoxian	county	Xuzhou	1908
116. Xiashi	town	Hangzhou	1907
117. Xincheng	county	Hangzhou	1906
118. Xincheng	town	Jiaxing	1911
119. Xinghua	county	Yangzhou	1908
120. Xinshi	town	Huzhou	1907
121. Xinzhuang	town	Songjiang	1907
122. Xuzhou	prefecture	Xuzhou	1908
123. Yangzhou	prefecture	Yangzhou	1908
124. Yaowan	town	Xuzhou	1909
125. Yexie	town	Songjiang	1908
126. Yiqiao	town	Shaoxing	1910
127. Yiwu	county	Jinhua	1909
128. Yixing-Jingxi	county	Changzhou	1906
129. Yizheng (Yangzi)	county	Yangzhou	1907
130. Yongkang	county	Jinhua	1909
131. Yuhang	county	Hangzhou	1908
132. Yuqian	county	Hangzhou	1907
133. Yuyao	county	Shaoxing	1907
134. Zhangyan	town	Songjiang	1905
135. Zhaowen	county	Suzhou	1905
136. Zhapu	town	Jiaxing	1907

(continued)

Location	Rank of seat[a]	Prefecture[b]	Founding year[c]
137. Zhenhai	county	Ningbo	1906
138. Zhenjiang	prefecture	Zhenjiang	1906
139. Zhongxing	town	Huai'an	1908
140. Zhoupu	town	Songjiang	1906
141. Zhouxiang	town	Shaoxing	1909
142. Zhuanghang	town	Songjiang	1906
143. Zhuji	county	Shaoxing	1907
144. Zhujiajiao	town	Songjiang	1909
145. Zhujing	town	Songjiang	1906

Sources: NGST: I, 4:18a–20a, 21a–b, 25a–32a, 36b–38a, 41a–43a; NGST: II, 4A:10b–12b, 15b–17b; Nongshangbu zongwuting tongjike, Zhonghua minguo yuannian, 180–81, 184–85; SSDC, 185, 193–94; SWGB, 11(1907):10a; 7 (1909):7b, 8a; 15 (1909):10b; 19 (1909):9b; 20 (1909):11b; 21 (1909):9a; 22 (1909):9b; 23 (1909):8a; 24 (1910):10a; 25 (1909):11a–b; 27 (1909):10a; 30 (1909):7b; 25 (1910):9a; HSLB 7 (1909): haineiwai shanghui jishi 11; Hangzhou shangye zazhi, 1 (1909): diaochalu 1–4; Xinwen bao, December 8, 1908; Nanhui xian xuzhi, 3: 9a.

[a] For the classification of county and prefectural seats, see the caption for the map. The phrase "county-prefecture" or "prefecture-province" denotes that a county shared its seat with a prefecture or a prefecture shared its capital with a province.

[b] An independent department or independent subprefecture is regarded as a prefecture.

[c] This table dates the founding of a few affiliated chambers according to NGST: I, NGST: II, and SWGB if other sources give different information about their founding years. Some affiliated chambers evolved from branch chambers that appeared in the years noted in brackets, but the Jiaxing ACC originated from the Jiaxing GCC, which appeared in 1905. See Chapter 2 for details.

Appendix 3

Branch Chambers of Commerce in the Lower Yangzi Region, 1906–1911

Location	Rank of seat	Prefecture[a]	Founding year[b]
1. Anchang	town	Shaoxing	1909
2. Anting	town	Taicang	1906
3. Bacheng	town	Suzhou	1907
4. Beiche	town	Suzhou	1908
5. Beishe	town	Suzhou	1908
6. Cangtang	town	Shaoxing	1910
7. Chonggu	town	Songjiang	1909
8. Dagang	town	Zhenjiang	1908
9. Daqiao	town	Yangzhou	1907
10. Dongshan	town	Suzhou	1908
11. Doumen	town	Shaoxing	1910
12. Duhang	town	Songjiang	1907
13. Fengjing	town	Songjiang	1910
14. Fenglichang	town	Tongzhou	1908
15. Fotang[c]	town	Chuzhou	1910
16. Fushan	town	Suzhou	1907
17. Guazhou	town	Yangzhou	1909
18. Haimen	town	Taizhou	1909
19. Hengshan	town	Suzhou	1908
20. Hujiaqiao	town	Songjiang	1907
21. Jieshou	town	Yangzhou	1910
22. Jinhuiqiao	town	Songjiang	1909
23. Jinze	town	Songjiang	1910
24. Keqiao	town	Shaoxing	1910
25. Liantang	town	Suzhou	1908

(*continued*)

Location	Rank of seat	Prefecture[a]	Founding year[b]
26. Lili	town	Suzhou	1908
27. Linze	town	Yangzhou	1910
28. Lujiabang	town	Suzhou	1907
29. Lüsi	town	Tongzhou	1906
30. Luxu	town	Suzhou	1908
31. Maqiao[d]	town	Songjiang	1910
32. Mashan	town	Shaoxing	1910
33. Meiyan	town	Suzhou	1908
34. Nandu	town	Ningbo	1909
35. Nanma	town	Suzhou	1908
36. Nanyang'an	town	Huaian	1910
37. Neishabao	town	Taicang	1908
38. Pingwang	town	Suzhou	1908
39. Puyuan	town	Jiaxing	1906
40. Ruanxiang	town	Songjiang	1909
41. Sanduo	town	Yangzhou	1910
42. Sanlintang[d]	town	Songjiang	1907
43. Shaobo	town	Yangzhou	1908
44. Shenta	town	Suzhou	1908
45. Shimenwan	town	Jiaxing	1908
46. Shuanglin	town	Huzhou	1907
47. Songyin	town	Songjiang	1907
48. Sunduan	town	Shaoxing	1909
49. Taiqiao	town	Ningbo	1909
50. Tairiqiao	town	Songjiang	1909
51. Tangwan[d]	town	Songjiang	1911
52. Tingxia	town	Ningbo	1909
53. Tongli	town	Suzhou	1908
54. Tudian	town	Jiaxing	1909
55. Wujiang	county	Suzhou	1908
56. Xiannümiao	town	Yangzhou	unknown
57. Yiling	town	Yangzhou	unknown
58. Zhenze	town	Suzhou	1908
59. Zhouzhuang	town	Suzhou	1908

Sources: NGST: I, 4:3b, 4b, 7b, 18a, 26a, 28a, 38a; SWGB, 17 (1906): 9a; 27 (1906): 13a; 9 (1907): 16a; 12 (1907): 9a; 16 (1907): 11b; 17 (1907): 7b; 29 (1907): 10a; 1 (1908): 11a; 15 (1908): 10b; 33 (1908): 11a; 22 (1909): 9a; 24 (1909): 11a; SSDC, 111, 160, 184–85; *Hangzhou shangye zazhi*, 1 (1909): 2; HSLB, no. 7 (1909): haineiwai shanghui tongrenlu 4, haineiwai shanghui jishi 10; no. 8 (1909): haineiwai shanghui jishi 3; no. 16 (1909): haineiwai shanghui tongrenlu 9; *Huashang lianhehui bao*, 3 (1910): haineiwai shanghui jishi 1b; *Nanyang shangbao*, 4 (1910): wendu 2; *Quan-Zhe gongbao*, July 7, 1909; *Shenbao*, February 9, 1911; *Jiangdu xian xuzhi*, 5:1b. *Qingpu xian xuzhi*, 3:6a; *Puyuanzhi*, 7:4a; *Sanxu Gaoyou zhou zhi*, 1:108b–109a; *Shanghai xian xuzhi*, 2:51b–52a; *Shuanglin zhenzhi*, 8:4a–b.

Note: This table excludes branch chambers that became affiliated chambers later on.

[a] An independent department or independent subprefecture is regarded as a prefecture.

[b] The founding years of some branch chambers are the years in which they first appear in historical records.

[c] The Fotang BCC evolved from the Fotang ACC that appeared in 1910 but immediately suffered demotion in status.

[d] The branch chambers in Maqiao, Sanlintang, and Tangwan are all recorded as affiliated chambers by *Shanghai xian xuzhi*, 2:51b–52a, but they were actually branch chambers. See SWGB, 16 (1907): 11b; *Huashang lianhehui bao*, 4 (1910): haineiwai gongdu 2a.

Notes

Preface

1. Yu, *Shanghui yu Zhongguo zaoqi xiandaihua*, 76–84.
2. Gold, Guthrie, and Wank, "An Introduction to the Study of *Guanxi*," 5–17.
3. Ma and Zhu, *Chuantong yu jindai de er'chong bianzou*, 107–17; Yu, *Shanghui yu Zhongguo zaoqi xiandaihua*, 117–20. For two recent examples of this scholarly tendency, see Ying, *Tianjin shanghui zuzhi wangluo yanjiu*, esp. 35, 309–11, and Li Peide, *Jindai Zhongguo de shanghui wangluo ji shehui gongneng*.
4. For definitions of these terms, see Scott, *Social Network Analysis*.
5. Wellman, Chen, and Dong, "Networking *Guanxi*," 232.
6. Hinde, *Towards Understanding Relationships*, 14–15, 37–38, cited by Perlman and Vangelisti, "Personal Relationships," 3.
7. Thelen and Steinmo, "Historical Institutionalism in Comparative Politics," 2.
8. Gordon, "Social Networking in Pre-Modern Asian History," 16.
9. Ikegami, *Bonds of Civility*, 10. For a definitional discussion on varied revolutions and an analysis of the late Qing "quiet" revolution of intellectual and institutional structures, including the commercial law reforms concerning chambers of commerce, see Reynolds, *China*, 12–14, 184–85.
10. Apart from the chambers of commerce in Shanghai and Suzhou, their counterparts around Tinjian have also received systematic examination in Song, *Jindai Tianjin shanghui*. Song's book (pp. 153–56) shows that the chambers around Tianjin formed only two-level networks in the early twentieth century, but the chamber networks in the Lower Yangzi region quickly developed their three-level hierarchy during the same period, as is shown in Chapter 2.

Introduction

1. Yu, *Shanghui yu Zhongguo zaoqi xiandaihua*, 74–87, 92–109, 276–95, 341–46. Yu indicates that 998 chambers of commerce appeared in China between 1902 and 1912,

and 151 of them were in the Jiangsu and Zhejiang provinces. My statistical analysis shows that the two provinces had at least 210 chambers of commerce by 1911; see Appendixes 1–3.

2. Jiangsu sheng shangyeting and Zhongguo di'er lishi dang'anguan, *Zhonghua minguo shangye dang'an ziliao huibian*, 1:166–68.

3. Chan, *Merchants, Mandarins, and Modern Enterprise in Late Ch'ing China*, 216–21; Ma Min, *Guanshang zhijian*, 80–147.

4. For a review of previous literature on this subject, see Feng, "Zhongguo shanghuishi yanjiu zhi huigu yu fansi," 148–67. One exception to the previous scholarship is Linda Grove's book *A Chinese Economic Revolution*, which includes detailed discussion on the chamber of commerce in Gaoyang, a county of northern China, in the early twentieth century.

5. For a discussion of the core-periphery difference in the Lower Yangzi and other macroregions during the late Qing period, see Skinner, "Regional Urbanization in Nineteenth-Century China," 211–49. In this study, the Lower Yangzi region largely overlaps with the corresponding macroregion of Skinner's framework. However, its boundary is redrawn along the provincial borders of Jiangsu and Zhejiang for the analysis of chambers of commerce that developed interconnections mainly within the two provinces, especially in their joint core area around the Yangzi Delta.

6. Murphey, *Shanghai*; Brunnert and Hagelstrom, *Present Day Political Organization of China*, 398–401.

7. For the different cities at the county and prefectural levels, see the caption for the map of the Lower Yangzi region in the late Qing period. The number of these cities is from Liu Jinzao, *Qingchao xu wenxian tongkao*, 4:10555, 10579.

8. Tōa dōbunkai, *Shina shōbetsu zenshi*, 13:23, 36, 42, 55, 84–176; 15:36, 74, 97, 104, 140–223. Wang Shuhuai indicates that the Japanese records of urban population in many Jiangsu cities were too low, and he presents demographic figures for twenty-seven Jiangsu cities between 1905 and 1916. But his data are still from Japanese surveys or other estimates. See Wang, *Zhongguo xiandaihua de quyu yanjiu*, 482–89.

9. Chang, *The Chinese Gentry*, xviii–xix, 102–11, 132–41, and *The Income of the Chinese Gentry*, 149–88, 282–84; Ma Min, *Guanshang zhijian*, 45–63.

10. Chan, *Merchants, Mandarins, and Modern Enterprise in Late Ch'ing China*, 21–25, 49–63, 69–74, 214–19.

11. Chu, *Reformer in Modern China*, 9–52; Köll, *From Cotton Mill to Business Empire*, 58–80.

12. Zhang Jian, *Zhang Jian quanji*, 2:11; 6:855.

13. Shen, "Wei Ningbobang kailu de Yan Xinhou," 65–70.

14. SZZZ, 1:42, 45.

15. Zhu, *Xinhai geming shiqi xinshi shangren shetuan yanjiu*, 1–2, 5–9; Yu, *Shanghui yu Zhongguo zaoqi xiandaihua*, 76–84, 99.

16. Wellman, Chen, and Dong, "Networking *Guanxi*," 224. Emphases are in the original.

17. Wellman, "Structural Analysis," 20; Wasserman and Faust, *Social Network Analysis*, i.

18. Liang, *Zhongguo wenhua yaoyi*, 86; Fei, *From the Soil*, 20, 65; Wellman, Chen, and Dong, "Networking *Guanxi*," 221–41.

19. Redding, *The Spirit of Chinese Capitalism*; Hamilton, *Asian Business Networks*.

20. Perry, *Shanghai on Strike*; Goodman, *Native Place, City, and Nation*.

21. Mayfair Mei-hui Yang, *Gifts, Favors, and Banquets*; Yan, *The Flow of Gifts*; Kipnis, *Producing Guanxi*.

22. Eastman, *The Abortive Revolution*; Nathan, *Peking Politics*; Geisert, *Radicalism and Its Demise*. Nathan also presented a theoretical analysis of this issue in his article, "A Factionalism Model for CCP Politics." But this model has been criticized by Tang Tsou for its neglect of institutional constraints; see Tsou's "Prolegomenon to the Study of Informal Groups in CCP Politics," 102. For a further critique of Nathan's model, see Dittmer, "Chinese Informal Politics," 2–5.

23. Duara, *Culture, Power, and the State*; Cochran, *Encountering Chinese Networks*.

24. Yeh, "Huang Yanpei and the Chinese Society of Vocational Education in Shanghai Networking," 28.

25. Dillon and Oi, "Middlemen, Social Networks, and State-Building in Republican Shanghai," 7.

26. Szonyi, *Practicing Kinship*, esp. 5–6, 197–98; Goodman, *Native Place, City, and Nation*, esp. 29–38; Fuma, *Chūgoku zenkai zendoshi kenkyū*, 246–49.

27. In the mid-1890s, literati reformers developed "study societies" (*xuehui*) with formal membership, leadership, and other institutional norms, but these organizations never received recognition from the imperial government and were outlawed after the failure of the 1898 Reform. See Zhang Yufa, "Wuxu shiqi de xuehui yundong," 5–26.

28. Knoke, "Networks of Elite Structure and Decision Making," 290.

29. Negishi, *Shanhai no girudo*, 27–29, 341–42, 379; Garrett, "The Chambers of Commerce and the YMCA," 216–19.

30. Chan, *Merchants, Mandarins, and Modern Enterprise in Late Ch'ing China*, 213; Rankin, *Elite Activism and Political Transformation in China*, 202–11. Quite a few scholars, especially those in mainland China, have also stressed that Chinese chambers of commerce resulted from the rise of a bourgeois class, which Rankin treats as a part of the social elites. This issue will be explored in the subsequent discussion.

31. Esherick and Rankin, *Chinese Local Elites and Patterns of Dominance*.

32. Ma and Zhu, *Chuantong yu jindai de er'chong bianzou*, 122–40.

33. Feng, "Zhongguo shanghuishi yanjiu zhi huigu yu fansi," 156–57.

34. Ma and Zhu, *Chuantong yu jindai de er'chong bianzou*, 61, 134–35; Ma Min, *Guanshang zhijian*, 108; Zhu, *Zhuanxing shiqi de shehui yu guojia*, 121.

35. Du and Zhou, "Summary of Studies of the Bourgeoisie since 1949," 115–16; Xu and Qian, *Shanghai zongshanghui shi, 1902–1929*, 24, 138, 166; Ma and Zhu, *Chuantong yu jindai de er'chong bianzou*, 259–80, 406–9; Yu, *Shanghui yu Zhongguo zaoqi xiandaihua*, 27–29, 279–95.

36. Bergère, "The Role of the Bourgeoisie," 241, 279, 295, and *The Golden Age of the Chinese Bourgeoisie*, 191–99.

37. Rhoads, *China's Republican Revolution*, 80–81; Chan, *Merchants, Mandarins, and Modern Enterprise in Late Ch'ing China*, 213–34, esp. 216; Ma Min, *Guanshang zhijian*, 97–108, 205–13.

38. Esherick and Rankin, "Introduction," 10–11.

39. Kuhn, *Rebellion and Its Enemies in Late Imperial China*, 217n44; Rankin, *Elite Activism and Political Transformation in China*, 4.

40. Ichiko, "The Role of the Gentry," 301–4, 312; Rhoads, *China's Republican Revolution*, 80–81, 224, 262, 276–77.

41. Du and Zhou, "Summary of Studies of the Bourgeoisie since 1949," 114–18; Feng, "Zhongguo shanghuishi yanjiu zhi huigu yu fansi," 158–59.

42. Rankin, *Elite Activism and Political Transformation in China*, 15–33, 206–11, 269, 283.

43. Rowe, *Hankow: Conflict and Community in a Chinese City*; Strand, *Rickshaw Beijing*.

44. Rowe, "The Problem of 'Civil Society' in Late Imperial China," 141; see also Rankin, "Some Observations on a Chinese Public Sphere," 158–59, 170–77.

45. Zhu, *Zhuanxing shiqi de shehui yu guojia*, 162, 216–62.

46. Shils, "The Virtue of Civil Society," 3–20.

47. Habermas, *The Structural Transformation of the Public Sphere*.

48. Huang, "'Public Sphere'/'Civil Society' in China?" 224–32; Xiaobo Zhang directly uses Huang's notion in his dissertation, "Merchant Associational Activism in Early Twentieth-Century China," 33.

49. Kohama, *Kindai Shanhai no kōkyōsei to kokka*, 8–12, 327.

50. Xiaoqun Xu, *Chinese Professionals and the Republican State*, 18, 272.

51. Knoke, "Networks of Elite Structure and Decision Making," 290.

Chapter 1

1. Williams, *The Middle Kingdom*, 2:87–88.

2. Pusey, *China and Charles Darwin*, 62–66, 107–9.

3. Chen Baoliang, *Zhongguo de she yu hui*.

4. Goodman indicates that all merchant organizations in Shanghai were more or less based on native-place relations, even though the titles of many guilds, especially those of natives, referred only to their trades. See Goodman, *Native Place, City, and Nation*, 29–32. Nevertheless, many common-trade guilds mentioned in the following discussion undoubtedly relaxed their regional exclusiveness and laid more stress on the occupational principle.

5. Morse, *The Gilds of China*, 31, 43–44.

6. For an incomplete list of guilds in late imperial China, see ZGHS, 2:999–1048.

7. He Bingdi, *Zhongguo huiguan shilun*, 13–14.

8. Peng, "Daolun," 15–16. Peng's article, like early Chinese and Japanese studies of guilds in China, traces them to the late eighth century. That viewpoint still needs to be verified through further research; see Golas, "Early Ch'ing Guilds," 555.

9. Golas, "Early Ch'ing Guilds," 556–59; Lü, "Ming-Qing shiqi de huiguan bingfei gongshangye hanghui," 66–79.

10. Kwang-ching Liu, "Chinese Merchant Guilds," 2, 14.

11. MacGowan, "Chinese Guilds or Chambers of Commerce and Trades Unions," 133–39.

12. Negishi, *Shanhai no girudo*, 341, 378; Garrett, "The Chambers of Commerce and the YMCA," 218–19; Soda, "Shōkai no setsuritsu," 43–47, 55; Kurahashi, "Shinmatsu no shōkai to Chūgoku burujoajī," 117–19.

13. Yu, *Shanghai yu Zhongguo zaoqi xiandaihua*, 37–39, 45–51, 148–49.

14. Rowe, *Hankow: Commerce and Society in a Chinese City*, 279–83, 299, 389n80. Rowe uses Negishi Tadashi's research on Chinese guilds, especially the multiplex Cantonese provincial guild in Shanghai, to infer a trend toward guild confederation in this city during the late Qing period. But Negishi's examples of guild confederations in Shanghai, including the multiplex Cantonese provincial guild, mainly came from the Republican period; see Negishi, *Chūgoku no girudo*, 38–42; Goodman, *Native Place, City, and Nation*, 231, 295n83.

15. SBZX, 259–60; ZGHS, 2:906–7, 913.

16. Tōa dōbunkai, *Shina keizai zensho*, 2:544, 564–66, 573–78; Xu Dingxin, "Shanghai gongshang tuanti de jindaihua," 518–22; SBZX, 430; Jones, "The Ningpo Pang and Financial Power at Shanghai," 77–78, 84–85; ZGHS, 2:906–7.

17. Tōa dōbunkai, *Shina keizai zensho*, 2:564–65.

18. Many Ningbo merchant leaders joined the Shanghai CCA as representatives of specific businesses and semiofficial enterprises, but none of them formally represented their prefectural guild in the first Chinese chamber of commerce. See Tōa dōbun shoin, *Shinkoku shōgyō kanshū to kinyū jijō*, 1:109, 115–20.

19. ZGHS, 2:878; Tōa dōbun shoin, *Shinkoku shōgyō kanshū to kinyū jijō*, 1:116–19; Leung, "Regional Rivalry in Mid-Nineteenth Century Shanghai," 29–43.

20. ZGHS, 2:878–79; Xu Dingxin, "Shanghai gongshang tuanti," 518; Tōa dōbun shoin, *Shinkoku shōgyō kanshū to kinyū jijō*, 119; Xu Run, *Xu Yuzhai zixu nianpu*, 14a–15a, 49a–b, 212a–b.

21. Goodman, *Native Place, City, and Nation*, 55–56; SBZX, 68, 325, 359, 507–13.

22. SBZX, 249–52, 275–79; *Shanghai xian xuzhi*, 3:6a, 18:47a–b; Tōa dōbun shoin, *Shinkoku shōgyō kanshū to kinyū jijō*, 1:119.

23. Tōa dōbun shoin, *Shinkoku shōgyō kanshū to kinyū jijō*, 1:115, 120; SBZX, 332–45; ZGHS, 2:856–57.

24. SBZX, 196–202; *Shanghai xian xuzhi*, 2:22a–b, 3:1a–b, 18:15a–b, 18b.

25. *Shanghai xian xuzhi*, 3:5a–b; SBZX, 201; Tōa dōbun shoin, *Shinkoku shōgyō kanshū to kinyū jijō*, 1:119; Zhongguo renmin yinhang Shanghai shi fenhang, *Shanghai qianzhuang shiliao*, 734–37.

26. SBZX, 281–82, 304–7, 362–64; ZGHS, 2:791–95; *Shanghai xian xuzhi*, 3:6b; Tōa dōbun shoin, *Shinkoku shōgyō kanshū to kinyū jijō*, 1:115–19.

27. SBZX, 282–83, 364–66; ZGHS, 2:793–94, 797–99; *Shanghai xian xuzhi*, 3:9b; Tōa dōbun shoin, *Shinkoku shōgyō kanshū to kinyū jijō*, 1:119.

28. Zhongguo renmin yinhang Shanghai shi fenhang, *Shanghai qianzhuang shiliao*, 9, 11, 31–35, 645–46, 731, 769–70; SBZX, 256–57, 400–402; Tōa dōbun shoin, *Shinkoku shōgyō kanshū to kinyū jijō*, 1:115–17.

29. *Shanghai xian xuzhi*, 3:8a; ZGHS, 2:766–69, 777.

30. *Shanghai xian xuzhi*, 3:8a; Tōa dōbunkai, *Shina keizai zensho*, 2:299; Xu Run, *Xu Yuzhai zixu nianpu*, 14b, 16b, 102a, 212a.

31. SBZX, 204, 355, 361, 402, 409; ZGHS, 2:815; *Shanghai xian xuzhi*, 3:8b–9a, 12b; Zhongguo renmin yinhang Shanghai shi fenhang, *Shanghai qianzhuang shiliao*, 34, 743; Jiangsu sheng bowuguan, *Jiangsu sheng Ming-Qing yilai beike ziliao xuanji*, 508–9.

32. ZGHS, 2:907–9; Rowe, *Hankow: Commerce and Society in a Chinese City, 1796–1889*, 138; SZZZ, 1:94.

33. *Shanghai xian xuzhi*, 2:31a–39a, 7:9a–10b; *Shanghai Tongren Fuyuantang zhengxinlu*, 1a, 10a–b, 62a–b.

34. Jing, *Jing Yuanshan ji*, 19, 36–38, 326–27; Zheng, *Shengshi weiyan houbian*, 14:13b, 24a–25b.

35. Rankin, *Elite Activism and Political Transformation in China*, 15, 142–47.

36. Jing, *Jing Yuanshan ji*, 276, 286, 326–27.

37. Xu Run, *Xu Yuzhai zixu nianpu*, 14b–15a, 16b; *Shanghai renjitang zhengxinlu*, 1a–3a, 6a–23b; Tōa dōbun shoin, *Shinkoku shōgyō kanshū to kinyū jijō*, 1:109, 115; SZZZ, 1:50–51, 94.

38. Ma and Zhu, *Chuantong yu jindai de er'chong bianzou*, 50–51.

39. Lü, "Ming-Qing shiqi Suzhou de huiguan he gongsuo," 10–12. The provincial guild of Guangdong is missed by Lü's article; see *Wuxian zhi*, 30:5b–6b.

40. Jiangsu sheng bowuguan, *Jiangsu sheng Ming-Qing yilai beike*, 340–50; SZZZ, 1:94. For other connections between the Chaozhou guilds in Suzhou and Shanghai, see Goodman, *Native Place, City, and Nation*, 56–57.

41. Fan, *Ming-Qing Jiangnan shangye de fazhan*, 286–94.

42. For nonnative elite merchants in the Suzhou GCC, see SSDC, 49–52, 67.

43. Gu, *Wumen biaoyin*, 63.

44. MQSG, 11–15, 19–22, 45–46; Jiangsu sheng bowuguan, *Jiangsu sheng Ming-Qing yilai beike*, 389, 661.

45. MQSG, 28–29. "Qixiang" (seven moves) refers to the daily movements of Vega, the star of Weaving Goddess in Chinese legends.

46. Wang and Tang, *Ming-Qing yilai Suzhou shehuishi beikeji*, 298–300; MQSG, 27; Jiangsu sheng bowuguan, *Jiangsu sheng Ming-Qing yilai beike*, 29.

47. MQSG, 26, 28–29.

48. Wu Qin, "Guanyu You Xianjia shiliao yize," 146–47; SSDC, 2, 12, 50.

49. Gu, *Wumen biaoyin*, 122–23.

50. Bao, *Chuanyinglou huiyilu*, 13–16, 79.

51. MQSG, 260–61; Du, "Translocal Lineage and the Romance of Homeland Attachment," 37–41; Ma and Zhu, *Chuantong yu jindai de er'chong bianzou*, 285.

52. MQSG, 260–61, 321–23; Jiangsu sheng bowuguan, *Jiangsu sheng Ming-Qing yilai beike*, 193; *Wuxian zhi*, 23B:19a–21a; SSDC, 2, 46–47.

53. *Shangwu bao*, 8 (1904): 27; *Nanyang shangwubao*, 1 (1906): guilü 3a; *Baoshan xian xuzhi*, 6:31a–32b.

54. Fuma, *Chūgoku zenkai zendoshi kenkyū*, 545–47, 557–58, 563–83.

55. Zhejiang tongxianghui ganshi, *Zhe-Gan tielu shijian*, 12; *Zhongwai ribao*, October 21, 1906.

56. MacGowan, "Chinese Guilds or Chambers of Commerce and Trades Unions," 138.

57. *Yinxian tongzhi*, part 2, 1522–23, part 4, 2637.

58. China: Imperial Maritime Customs, *Decennial Reports*, 2:80; Qiu, "Wenzhou shanghui zhi chuangli yu yange," 156–58.

59. MQSG, 355–57.

60. Fan, *Ming-Qing Jiangnan shangye de fazhan*, 286–88, 294; MQSG, 42–43; *Shanghai renjitang zhengxinlu*, 18a; SSDC, 119–21.

61. *Shuanglin zhenzhi*, vol. 8:1b–2b, 32:9b; Cai, *Shuanglin zhenzhi xinbu*, 718.

62. Cai, *Shuanglin zhenzhi xinbu*, 717–18; *Shuanglin zhenzhi*, 30:37b.

63. Eitel, *Europe in China*, 24–35; Fairbank, *Trade and Diplomacy on the China Coast*, 1:48–51, 78–79.

64. Arnold, *China*, 378–79.

65. Eitel, *Europe in China*, 67; Arnold, *China*, 379; Wu Yixiong, "Guangzhou waiqiao zongshanghui yu Yapian zhanzheng qianxi de Zhong-Ying guanxi," 91–116.

66. Shanghai [Western] General Chamber of Commerce, *Annual Report for 1876*, appendix, 1; *Report of the Committee of the Shanghai General Chamber of Commerce for the Year Ended 31 December 1904*, 9–10.

67. Shanghai [Western] General Chamber of Commerce, *Minutes of the Annual General Meeting, November 26, 1869*, 3.

68. Shanghai [Western] General Chamber of Commerce, *Annual Report for 1868–69*, 5; *Minutes of a General Meeting, December 31, 1869*, 4; *Annual Report for 1891*, 2; *Annual Report for 1892*, 3; *Annual Report for 1896*, 3.

69. "Shanghai xishang zonghui zhangcheng," 17a–25b. The original English version of the regulations is not available. However, this Chinese version of the original rules was more influential among late Qing merchants and officials because of its appearance in the Shanghai-based *Shiwubao* (The Chinese progress), a widely circulated reformist journal. This Chinese translation was later reprinted in *Hubei shangwubao*, 23 (1899): 17a–25b.

70. Shanghai [Western] General Chamber of Commerce, *Report of the Committee of the Shanghai General Chamber of Commerce for the Year Ended 31 December 1904*, 51.

71. Shanghai [Western] General Chamber of Commerce, *Minutes of the Annual General Meeting, November 26, 1869*, 2.

72. Ibid., 2; *Minutes of a General Meeting, December 31, 1869*, 3–4.

73. Arnold, *China*, 379.

74. Shanghai [Western] General Chamber of Commerce, *Annual Report for 1868–69*, 2; *Annual Report for 1869–70*, 2.

75. Shanghai [Western] General Chamber of Commerce, *Annual Report for 1897*, 1; *Minutes of the Annual General Meeting on March 31, 1898*, 1.

76. Zhongguo renmin yinhang Shanghai shi fenhang, *Shanghai qianzhuang shiliao*, 21–23.

77. For Zhong's biography and thought, see Zhong Xiangcai, "Zhong Tianwei sixiang lunyao," 261–69.

78. Zhong Tianwei, "Kuochong shangwu shitiao," 4a–b. Zhong did not date his petition, but it was included in Ge Shirui, ed., *Huangchao jingshiwen xubian*, in 1888. I infer that Zhong made his proposal in 1884 because it mentions the Shanghai financial crisis in the "last year." Prior to 1888, Shanghai experienced its most serious financial crisis in 1883.

79. Zhang and Wang's writings are quoted in Wang Er'min, "Zhongguo jindai zhi gongshang zhifulun yu shangmao tizhi zhi xihua," 127, 130.

80. Ch'en, *State Economic Policies of the Ch'ing Government, 1840–1895*, 215.

81. Xia, *Zheng Guanying ji*, 225–26.

82. Ibid., 593, 604–8, 611–17.

83. Ibid., 588, 606, 616–17.

84. Zhongguo shixuehui, *Wuxu bianfa*, 2:146, 154–66, 4:130.

85. For a detailed discussion about these radical reformers' opinions on chambers of commerce, see Zhongping Chen, "The Rise of Chinese Chambers of Commerce in Late Qing," 1102–8.

86. "Ni Zhongguo jianli shangye zonghui zhangcheng."

87. Tang, *Wuxu shiqi de xuehui he baokan*, 115–25.

88. Zhang Jian, *Zhang Jian quanji*, 1:37, 2:11–12.

89. Ibid., 2:11.

90. Zhongguo shixuehui, *Wuxu bianfa*, 3:133–35, 139–42.

91. Tang, *Wuxu shiqi de xuehui he baokan*, 425–34. For information about Wang Dajun, see Shanghai tushuguan, *Wang Kangnian shiyou xinzha*, 591–613.

92. Tang, *Wuxu shiqi de xuehui he baokan*, 434–36.

93. Ibid., 121, 483–89. The Asiatic Society appeared in Japan in 1880, and its Chinese branch was promoted by Japanese diplomats with an imperialist ambition. However, most Chinese participants joined this study society with the sincere intention of reforming

late Qing politics with Japanese help and of vitalizing Asia through collaboration among Asian nations.

Chapter 2

1. Owen Hong-hin Wong, *The First Chinese Minister to Great Britain*, 152–59.
2. Guo, *Lundun yu Bali riji*, 183, 273, 347, 590, 825.
3. Ma Jianzhong, *Shikezhai jiyan*, 31.
4. Ma and Zhu, *Chuantong yu jindai de er'chong bianzou*, 41–42, 231–59; Yu, *Shanghui yu Zhongguo zaoqi xiandaihua*, 70; Xu and Qian, *Shanghai zongshanghui shi, 1902–1929*, 35.
5. Feuerwerker, *China's Early Industrialization*, 98–99, 189–241; Tōa dōbun shoin, *Shinkoku shōgyō kanshū to kinyū jijō*, 1:109, 115–16.
6. Zhang Guohui, *Yangwu yundong yu Zhongguo jindai qiye*, 148–65; Feuerwerker, *China's Early Industrialization*, 99–128, 150–57, 190–241.
7. Chan, *Merchants, Mandarins, and Modern Enterprise in Late Ch'ing China*, 3, 80–153.
8. Sheng, *Yuzhai cungao*, 1:6b–7b, 14a–15b, 90:24b.
9. Ibid., 90:24b.
10. Zhongguo renmin yinhang Shanghai shi fenhang jinrong yanjiushi, *Zhongguo diyijia yinhang*, 74, 92, 96–98.
11. Feuerwerker, *China's Early Industrialization*, 230–34.
12. Zhongguo renmin yinhang Shanghai shi fenhang jinrong yanjiushi, *Zhongguo diyijia yinhang*, 84, 102.
13. Zhang Zhidong, *Zhang Wenxianggong quanji*, 46:3b–9a; Feuerwerker, *China's Early Industrialization*, 232.
14. Zhongguo renmin yinhang Shanghai shi fenhang jinrong yanjiushi, *Zhongguo diyijia yinhang*, 107; Xu and Qian, *Shanghai zongshanghui shi, 1902–1929*, 43–45. Feuerwerker's book provides general background for these directors, but it mistakes Yan Xinhou for his son, Yan Yibin, and inaccurately includes Wang Wei and Chen Gan on the first board of directors. See Feuerwerker, *China's Early Industrialization*, 234–35.
15. Zhang Zhidong, *Zhang Wenxianggong quanji*, 37: 29b–30a, 148:8a–b.
16. Ibid., 42:11b–12b; 43:15b–16b; 78:27a–33a; 148:18a–b; Köll, *From Cotton Mill to Business Empire*, 63–80.
17. Zhang Zhidong, *Zhang Wenxianggong quanji*, 43:13b–16a; 78:27a–b; 148:18a–b, 23b–24b.
18. Zhongguo shixuehui, *Wuxu bianfa*, 2:399–400; Chan, *Merchants, Mandarins, and Modern Enterprise*, 199–200.
19. Liu Kunyi, *Liu Kunyi yiji*, 2173–74, 2177–78, 2185.
20. Zhongguo shixuehui, *Wuxu bianfa*, 2:17, 43, 64; 4:151.
21. Ibid., 2: 48, 54; Guojia dang'anju Ming-Qing dang'anguan, *Wuxu bianfa dang'an shiliao*, 389–90.
22. *Gongshang xuebao*, 3 (1898): gongdu 4b–6a; *Hubei shangwu bao*, 36 (1900): jufa wendu 1a.
23. Liu Kunyi, *Liu Kunyi yiji*, 1056, 1088, 1154, 1413; *Jiangnan shangwu bao*, 1 (1900): gongdu 1a–b; 2 (1900): gongdu 5b–6a.
24. *Jiangnan shangwu bao*, 1 (1900): gongdu 1a; 2 (1900): gongdu 5b–6a.

25. *Jiangnan shangwu bao*, 1 (1900): gongdu 1a–2a; 5 (1900): gongdu 1b; 7 (1900): gongdu 1a; 9 (1900): gongdu 1a; Zhongguo renmin yinhang Shanghai shi fenhang jinrong yanjiushi, *Zhongguo diyijia yinhang*, 107; Xu and Qian, *Shanghai zongshanghui shi, 1902–1929*, 43–45.

26. *Jiangnan shangwu bao*, 2 (1900): gongdu 5b–6a; 14 (1900): gongdu 1a–b; Yang Fangyi, "Zhenjiang shanghui shimo," 8–9; *Shibao*, April 16, 1907; Wang Junshi, "Huaiyin shanghui zuzhi jiankuang," 140.

27. *Shangwu bao*, 7 (1904): 26–27; 8 (1904): 27; *Jiaxing xian shanghui diyiqi baogao*, 1.

28. *Jiangnan shangwu bao*, 1 (1900): gongdu 1a–4b.

29. Ibid., 3 (1900): gongdu 1a–1b; 9 (1900): gongdu 1a; 15 (1900): gongdu 1b; Fuma, *Chūgoku zenkai zendoshi kenkyū*, 558.

30. Sheng, *Yuzhai cungao*, 3:61b.

31. Zhang Zhidong, *Zhang Wenxianggong quanji*, 221:12b–13b.

32. *Shenbao*, February 22, 1902.

33. *Zhongwai ribao*, February 22, 1902.

34. SZZZ, 1:45.

35. Ibid., 1:45–46, 49.

36. Ibid., 1:46–48.

37. Tōa dōbun shoin, *Shinkoku shōgyō kanshū to kinyū jijō*, 1:109, 115–20.

38. *Xinwen bao*, February 22, 1902; Tōa dōbun shoin, *Shinkoku shōgyō kanshū to kinyū jijō*, 1:109; *Shenbao*, May 4, 1905; Xu and Qian, *Shanghai zongshanghui shi, 1902–1929*, 43–47. Mao was a provincial graduate from 1893. Xu and Qian assume that he was an official appointee, but their sources could not identify his official position until he received an official appointment in August 1903.

39. SZZZ, 1:48–50.

40. Ibid., 1:46–47.

41. Yu, *Shanghui yu Zhongguo zaoqi xiandaihua*, 75–76.

42. Chan, *Merchants, Mandarins, and Modern Enterprise in Late Ch'ing China*, 158–59.

43. Shiyebu, *Da-Qing fagui daquan*, 7:1a–3b.

44. Ibid., 7:1b–3b.

45. *Dongfang zazhi*, 2, no. 2 (1905): jiaoyu 41; SZZZ, 1:62; Feuerwerker, *China's Early Industrialization*, 73–75.

46. SZZZ, 1:62, 69–79; Chan, *Merchants, Mandarins, and Modern Enterprise in Late Ch'ing China*, 218–19.

47. *Xinwen bao*, March 13, 1904; *Shenbao*, July 16, 1905; *Nanyang shangwubao*, 1 (1906): guilü 3a.

48. *Zhongwai ribao*, March 22, April 24, May 21, June 10, July 23, 1905; May 3, 1906.

49. "Suzhou shanghui dang'an," 3:25; SSDC, 5, 8.

50. SSDC, 2–4.

51. *Shibao*, July 7, 1905; SSDC, 4, 12–17, 46.

52. Zhang Jian, *Zhang Jian quanji*, 3:771–72; 6:524. According to Zhang's diary in the cited collection, he received the ministry's instruction on January 30, 1904, but his reply letter was probably misdated 1905.

53. NGST: I, 4:4b; Bian and Tang, *Minguo renwu beizhuanji*, 257.

54. "Tong-Chong-Hai shangwu zonghui bing Tongzhou fenhui shiban zhangcheng," 1a–4b. In the cited draft regulations, the general chamber had not linked its title to cotton trade yet.

55. *Shangwu bao*, 7 (1904): 26–27; 8 (1904): 27; 11 (1904): 35; *Zhongwai ribao*, July 5, August 17, 1905; April 8, 1906. The provincial bureau of commerce in Zhejiang was incorporated into the general bureau for agriculture, industry, commerce, and mines (*nong-gong-shang-kuang wu zongju*) around 1904.

56. *Zhongwai ribao*, July 5, July 15, July 16, August 17, September 11, 1905; *Shenbao*, July 22, 1905.

57. Zhejiang tongxianghui ganshi, *Zhe-Gan tielu shijian*, 12–13; Woqiu Zhongzi, *Jindai mingren zhuan*, 163. For biographical information about Fan, also see Rankin, *Elite Activism and Political Transformation in China*, 177, 228.

58. Zhejiang tongxianghui ganshi, *Zhe-Gan tielu shijian*, 16, 24, 41; *Zhongwai ribao*, August 17, September 11, September 21, 1905.

59. *Zhongwai ribao*, September 21, 1905; March 11, April 8, October 21, 1906.

60. *Zhongwai ribao*, September 11 and 17, 1905; NGST: I, 4:7a.

61. *Jiaxing xian shanghui diyiqi baogao*, 2–3; *Zhongwai ribao*, February 17, 1905; February 6, 1906.

62. *Zhongwai ribao*, June 3, August 1, August 6, August 29, November 9, December 7, 1906.

63. NGST: I, 4:18a–20a, 21a–b, 25a–b, 30b–31a.

64. *Xinwen bao*, April 9, 1904; *Shenbao*, May 27, July 21, 1905; *Zhongwai ribao*, July 18, 1905; February 12, May 18, 1906; Yang Fangyi, "Zhenjiang shanghui shimo," 8–9.

65. *Shenbao*, June 15, 1905; *Zhongwai ribao*, June 29, 1905.

66. *Shenbao*, April 22, July 17, 1906.

67. *Zhongwai ribao*, February 6, 1906; NGST: I, 4:31a.

68. Qiu, "Wenzhou shanghui zhi chuangli yu yange," 156–58; NGST: I, 4:30b.

69. *Zhongwai ribao*, February 18, 1905; May 9, November 21, 1906.

70. SSDC, 71–72.

71. The Ministry of Commerce absorbed part of the old Board of Works (Gongbu) and became the Ministry of Agriculture, Industry, and Commerce in November 1906; see Brunnert and Hagelstrom, *Present Day Political Organization of China*, 153.

72. SSDC, 17, 23, 75–81, 120–21, 140–41.

73. *Shenbao*, October 30, 1908; *Xinwen bao*, February 17, 1909.

74. SWGB, 17 (1906): 9a; SSDC, 73.

75. SSDC, 72–73.

76. Ibid., 187–93.

77. Ibid., 118, 187–93; *Shanghai xian xuzhi*, 2: 51b–52a; *Zhenyang xianzhi*, appendix 16a–b.

78. *Xuzuan Taizhou zhi*, 9:1–2; NGST: I, 4:27a, 38a; NGST: II, 4A: 12a.

79. *Nanyang shangbao*, 4 (1910): wendu 2.

80. *Zhejiang guanbao*, 15 (1909): wendulei 137b; 36 (1910): wendulei 357a–b; *Huashang lianhehui bao*, 6 (1910): haineiwai shanghui jishi 2a.

81. *Shuanglin zhenzhi*, 8:4a–b.

82. HSLB, 8 (1909): haineiwai shanghui jishi 3–4; 20 (1909): haineiwai shanghui jishi 4; *Huashang Lianhehui bao*, 3 (1910): haineiwai shanghui jishi 1b.

83. SSDC, 110–11; *Shanghai xian xuzhi*, 2:51b–52a; HSLB, 7 (1909): haineiwai shanghui tongrenlu 4.

84. *Jiangdu xian xuzhi*, 5:1b; *Sanxu Gaoyou zhouzhi*, 1:108b–109a; HSLB, 16 (1909): haineiwei shanghui tongrenlu 8–9.

85. *Xinwen bao*, January 21, 1904; SSDC, 36–38. For a discussion about the different types of documents in official communications, see Fairbank and Teng, "On the Types and Uses of Ch'ing Documents," 76, 78, 88, 100.

86. Zhang Yufa, *Qingji de lixian tuanti*, 90–143, 312.

Chapter 3

1. Shiyebu, *Da-Qing fagui daquan*, 7:1b–2b.

2. SSDC, 70–71; *Zhejiang Quanye Gongsuo diyijie chengji baogaoshu*, 18a–b.

3. Shiyebu, *Da-Qing fagui daquan*, 7:1b, 2b.

4. SZZZ, 1:70.

5. SZZZ, 1:70, 72–74, 83, 85, 115–16; Shanghai tongshe, *Shanghai yanjiu ziliao xuji*, 192.

6. SZZZ, 1:71–72, 80, 84, 115; Shiyebu, *Da-Qing fagui daquan*, 7:1b.

7. SZZZ, 1:76.

8. SSZT: 1906. The titles of these elite merchants are classified into ranks 1–9 according to the standard provided by Xu Daling, *Qingdai juanna zhidu*, 80–81.

9. Jiang, "Xu Run," 266–69; SSZT: 1906, 1b; SZZZ, 1:94; SSZT: 1910, 10a.

10. SSZT: 1908; SSZT: 1911. The leading, individual, and special associate members are not included in Table 4 because they rarely existed in the Lower Yangzi chambers other than the Shanghai GCC.

11. *Shenbao*, May 9, 1905; May 10, 1906; HSLB, 10 (1909): haineiwei diaocha conglu 9–12.

12. SSZT: 1908, 4b, 8b; SSZT: 1909: 4b; SSZT: 1910, 3b; SSZT: 1911, 3a, 6a–b.

13. SSDC, 18–26, 46–47; "Tong-Chong-Hai shangwu zonghui bing Tongzhou fenhui shiban zhangcheng," 2a–10b; SZZZ, 1:71; *Zhongwai ribao*, October 21, 1906.

14. SSDC, 16, 44, 46–47, 68, 203; "Suzhou shanghui dang'an," 29:1a–6a.

15. SSDC, 46, 49–52, 58; Bian and Tang, *Minguo renwu beizhuanji*, 239–41.

16. HSLB, 16 (1909): haineiwai shanghui tongrenlu 3–4; *Hangzhou shangye zazhi*, 1 (1909): diaochalu 6.

17. HSLB, 11 (1909): haineiwai shanghui tongrenlu 4–6; 20 (1909): haineiwai shanghui tongrenlu 1–3.

18. SSDC, 76–78. The Meili ACC's regulations in 1906 initially stipulated only ten directors and one president as its leaders.

19. Ibid., 102–4, 120–21, 124, 133, 139–41.

20. Ibid., 83–84, 105–6, 131–33, 143–45, 199; HSLB (the section "haineiwai shanghui tongrenlu" in each issue), 12 (1909): 5–6; 16 (1909): 4–10; 18 (1909): 3–4; 21 (1910): 5–10, 12–16; 22 (1910): 11–14. The fifteen other affiliated chambers were located in the prefectural capitals of Huzhou and Jiaxing; the county seats of Baoying, Fenghua, Qingpu, Ruian, Shanyin-Kuaiji, and Wuxi-Jinkui; and the towns of Dongba, Jiangyan, Linghu, Luodian, Xinshi, Zhoupu, and Zhujing.

21. SSDC, 40, 72–73, 116–17; *Nanyang shangbao*, 4 (1910): wendu 2.

22. Nongshangbu zongwuting tongjike, *Zhonghua minguo yuannian diyici nongshang tongjibiao*, 1:180–81, 184–85.

23. SZZZ, 1:117, 125–26.

24. Gao and Yan, *Jindai Wuxi cansiye ziliao xuanji*, 31–37; ZGHS, 2:922–30; SZZZ, 1:51, 94–95, 125; NGST: I, 4:19a; TSDH, 1:761–63.

25. Wang Jingyu, *Zhongguo jindai gongyeshi ziliao, 1895–1914*, 2:958–60; SZZZ, 1:51, 94–95, 113; NGST: I, 4:19a; ZGHS, 2:922–30; SSDC, 46, 56.

26. "Suzhou shanghui dang'an," 4:37; 29:171; SSDC, 102–3, 110–11.

27. "Tong-Chong-Hai shangwu zonghui bing Tongzhou fenhui shiban zhang-cheng," 2a; SSZT: 1906, 1b; SWGB, 28 (1908): 9b; Zhongguo diyi lishi dang'anguan, "Qingmo gesheng sheli shanghui shiliao," 59–60.

28. HSLB, 20 (1910): haineiwai shanghui tongrenlu 1; Shen, "Wei Ningbobang kailu de Yan Xinhou," 67; *Shibao*, March 12, 1907.

29. HSLB, 17 (1909): haineiwai shanghui jishi 4; *Nanyang shangbao*, 4 (1910): jishi 2–3.

30. SSDC, 100–6, 112–14, 143–45, 157–58.

31. SSZT: 1906; SSZT: 1911. The average ages are calculated according to the actual ages rather than the nominal ages (one year older than actual) recorded in Chinese sources. For year-by-year analysis of the different age groups among the directors and full members of the Shanghai GCC, see Zhongping Chen, "Business and Politics," 151.

32. SSDC, 94–95, 124–26, 131–33, 143–45, 157–58; HSLB (the section "haineiwai shanghui tongrenlu" in each issue), 11 (1909): 4–6; 12 (1909): 3–6; 16 (1909): 3–10; 18 (1909): 3–4; 21 (1909): 5–9, 12–16; 22 (1909): 11–14; The eighteen affiliated chambers were located in the prefectural capitals of Huai'an, Huzhou, and Jiaxing; the county seats of Baoying, Fenghua, Huating-Lou, Ruian, and Shanyin-Kuaiji; and the towns of Dongba, Haian, Jiangyan, Linghu, Luodian, Pingwang, Shipu, Xinshi, Zhoupu, and Zhujing. For a detailed analysis of the averages ages of their directors, see Zhongping Chen, "Business and Politics," 152.

33. Jones, "The Ningpo Pang and Financial Power at Shanghai," 90–91; Chan, *Merchants, Mandarins, and Modern Enterprise*, 218–19; Goodman, *Native Place, City, and Nation*, 177–78.

34. HSLB, 1 (1909): haineiwai gongdu 6–8; supplemental issue (1909): haineiwai tongxin 1.

35. SSZT: 1911, 6a–10b.

36. SWGS, section 2, 4–6; *Hunan Shangwu Fenhui baogao timingce*, section 4.

37. SSDC, 49–52, 76–77, 94–95, 105–6, 143–45, 148, 199; HSLB (the section "haineiwai shanghui tongrenlu" in each issue), 11 (1909): 4–6; 12 (1909): 3–6; 16 (1909): 3–10; 18 (1909): 3–4; 20 (1909): 1–3; 21 (1909): 5–10, 12–16; 22 (1910): 11–14. The twenty-three affiliated chambers were located in the prefectural capitals of Huai'an, Huzhou, and Jiaxing; the county seats of Baoying, Fenghua, Huating-Lou, Kunshan-Xinyang, Qingpu, Ruian, Shanyin-Kuaiji, Wujiang-Zhenze, and Wuxi-Jinkui; and the towns of Dongba, Haian, Jiangyan, Linghu, Luodian, Meili, Pingwang, Shipu, Xinshi, Zhoupu, and Zhujing. "Natives" in the chambers of provincial and prefectural capitals include merchants from the counties surrounding the provincial and prefectural capitals. In township chambers of commerce, "natives" comprise only people from the counties in which the towns were located. For more detailed data about the percentages of natives and nonnatives in these general and affiliated chambers, see Zhongping Chen, "Business and Politics," 139–40.

38. Feng, "Zhongguo shanghuishi yanjiu zhi huigu yu fansi," 158.

39. Xu and Qian, *Shanghai zongshanghui shi, 1902–1929*, 61; SZZZ, 1:68. Xu's data come from Tōa dōbunkai, *Shina keizai zensho*, 4:69–76. For a critique of the unreliable data, see the note for Table 4.

40. SSZT: 1911, 6a–10b.

41. SSZT: 1908, 4b, 6a; Sun Choucheng et al., "Yu Qiaqing shilue," 104, 112.

42. NGST: I, 4:3b; SSZT: 1906, 1b, 2b, 4b–5b; SSZT: 1908, 3a–b; SSZT: 1909, 3a–b; SSZT: 1910, 3a; SSZT: 1911, 3a.

43. SSZT: 1906, 2a, 3a, 4a, 5a; SSZT: 1908, 3b; SSZT: 1909, 3a; SSZT: 1910, 3a; SSZT: 1911, 3a.

44. SSZT: 1906, 1b–3a; SSZT: 1911, 1b, 3a; SZZZ, 1:94.

45. SSDC, 53–56; HSLB (the section "haineiwai shanghui tongrenlu" in each issue), 11 (1909): 4–6; 16 (1909): 3–4; 20 (1910): 1–3. For more detailed statistical analysis of the business backgrounds of these chamber directors, see Zhongping Chen, "Business and Politics," 143.

46. Ma and Zhu, *Chuantong yu jindai de er'chong bianzou*, 67–68; SSDC, 18, 44, 65.

47. Ma and Zhu, *Chuantong yu jindai de er'chong bianzou*, 67–68; SSDC, 65.

48. Changzhoushi minjian and Gongshanglian wenshi ziliao ban'gongshi, "Wujin xian shanghui ji gongshangye fazhan shiluo," 104–6; *Shenbao*, July 31, August 16, and August 28, 1907; SWGB, 26 (1906): 17b–18a; 11 (1910): 12a–b.

49. SSDC, 18, 20–21; SWGB, 24 (1909): 11b; 25 (1909): 11a.

50. SZZZ, 1:45, 50, 94–95, 110; SWGB, 4 (1908): 14b; SSZT: 1908, 2a, 3b; *Xinwen bao*, September 9, 1906.

51. NGST: I, 4:26a; 5:9a, 18a, 28a; SZZZ, 1:94; SSZT: 1906, 1a–b, 4b; HSLB, 20 (1910): haineiwei shanghui tongrenlu 2.

52. *Jiading xian xuzhi*, 11: 28a–b; Xu and Qian, *Shanghai zongshanghui shi, 1902–1929*, 90–91; *Shenbao*, September 22, 1906; NGST: II, 4B:6b; SWGB, 18 (1908): 11a.

53. SZZZ, 1:94–95; SSZT: 1906, 1b, 5a; SWGB, 20 (1908): 12a; *Nanyang shangbao*, 2 (1910): wendu 21–23; 3 (1910): wendu 1–2; "Shouxian Sunshi jingying Fufeng mianfenchang ji youguan caituan suoshu qiye shiliaogao."

54. SZZZ, 1:94–95; SSZT: 1908, 4a, 10a; SSZT: 1910, 6a; SSZT: 1911, 5b, 8a; Wang Suijin, "Zhenhai Xiaogang Lishi jiazu shilue," 130.

55. NGST: II, 4B:9b; SSDC, 46; SWGS, section 2, 4; TSDH, 1:727–29; 2:2180–86; HSLB, 1 (1909): xumu 1–4.

56. SZZZ, 1:94–95, 97–98; Tahara, *Shinmatsu minsho Chūgoku kanshin jimmei roku*, 225.

57. SZZZ, 1:94–95, 110; *Huashang lianhehui bao*, 1 (1910): haineiwai shanghui jishi 11; *Shibao*, December 4, 1910.

58. Xu and Qian, *Shanghai zongshanghui shi, 1902–1929*, 180; SZZZ, 1:51, 94–95, 97, 100, 102–3.

59. NGST: I, 4:7b; Rankin, *Elite Activism and Political Transformation in China*, 177; Zhejiang Tongxianghui ganshi, *Zhe-Gan tielu shijian*, 12; SWGB, 15 (1909): 8a; Cheng, "Jiushidai de Hangzhou shanghui," 122.

60. *Shenbao*, May 10, 1909; HSLB, 6 (1909): haineiwai shanghui jishi 1–4; 8 (1909): haineiwai shanghui jishi 1–2; Cheng, "Jiushidai de Hangzhou shanghui," 122–23.

61. NGST: I, 4:7a; HSLB, 20 (1910): haineiwai shanghui tongrenlu 1–3.

62. NGST: I, 4:4a; *Nanyang shangwubao*, 1 (1906): guilü 3a.

63. HSLB, 5 (1909): haineiwai shanghui jishi 6, 11 (1909): haineiwai shanghui tongrenlu 4; TSDH, 1:583–84; SZZZ, 1:94–95.

64. SSDC, 46–58; Ma and Zu, *Suzhou shanghui dang'an congbian, 1912–1919*, 22, 30.

65. Wu, "Guanyu You Xianjia shiliao yize," 147; SSDC, 53, 270.

66. SSDC, 267–70; Wang and Chen, *Qingmo yiding zhongwai shangyue jiaoshe*, 713.

67. SSDC, 53–57, 269–72, 276–77, 290–95; Wang and Chen, *Qingmo yiding zhongwai shangyue jiaoshe*, 713; *Shenbao*, May 5, 1908; SZZZ, 1:94–95; NGST: I, 4:19a.

68. *Nantong difang zizhi shijiunian zhi chengji*, section 1, shiye 71–72; Bian and Tang, *Minguo renwu beizhuanji*, 257; NGST: I, 4:4b; SWGB, 29 (1909): 9b.

69. HSLB, 5 (1909): haineiwai diaocha conglu 1–9.

70. SWGB, 30 (1908): 8a; 25 (1909): 11a.

71. SSDC, 139–42, 146–49, 151–52.

72. Ibid., 144–45, 147–52, 157.

73. SSDC, 152–59; Yangzhou shifan xueyuan lishixi, *Xinhai geming Jiangsu diqu shiliao*, 132; Zhang Pengyuan, *Lixianpai yu Xinhai geming*, 260, 314.

74. SSDC, 161, 163, 166, 169, 172, 175.

75. Ibid., 160–63.

76. Ibid., 166–70.

77. Ibid., 163–80.

78. Esherick, "1911," 166–68.

Chapter 4

1. Xu and Qian, *Shanghai zongshanghui shi, 1902–1929*, 54–57.

2. *Shanghai zongshanghui luyin cuoshang gongxie youdai Huashang cheng'an*, 1a–4b, 7b–9b.

3. *Shibao*, January 15, 1905. For detailed analysis of this incident in previous studies, see Goodman, *Native Place, City, and Nation*, 179–83, esp. 179n3.

4. Xiaoqun Xu denies the professional nature of the late Qing chambers of chambers because they retained local and familial ties. Nevertheless, these chambers still conform roughly to his definition for professional associations, which "strove to establish professional standards and obtain professional status and privileges recognized by the state and society at large." See Xu, *Chinese Professionals and the Republican State*, 3, 5, 11.

5. Major studies of this boycott include Field, "The Chinese Boycott of 1905"; Zhang Cunwu, *Guangxu sayinian Zhong-Mei gongyue fengchao*; Guanhua Wang, *In Search of Justice*; Wong Sin Kiong, *China's Anti-American Boycott in 1905*.

6. Xu and Qian, *Shanghai zongshanghui shi, 1902–1929*, 67–87; Goodman, *Native Place, City, and Nation*, 183–87; Larson, "The Chinese Empire Reform Association (Baohuanghui) and the 1905 Anti-American Boycott."

7. Wong Sin Kiong, *China's Anti-American Boycott*, 15–27. Wong's study stresses the extralegal mistreatment of the Chinese by American authorities as a major cause of the boycott.

8. Su, *Shanzhong ji*, 11, 482–84; *Shenbao*, May 11, 1905; Zhang Cunwu, *Guangxu sayinian Zhong-Mei gongyue fengchao*, 96, 101–2.

9. Field, "The Chinese Boycott of 1905," 67–68; Wang, *In Search of Justice*, 10, 88, 115, 166.

10. Zhang Cunwu, *Guangxu sayinian Zhong-Mei gongyue fengchao*, 27; Fang, *Kang-Liang yu Baohuanghui*, 113–14; Judge, *Print and Politics*, 32.

11. *Shenbao*, May 5, 1905; SZZZ, 1:110; SSZT: 1906, 7b; Xu and Xu, *Qingmo sishinian Shenbao shiliao*, 21, 36, 97–108.

12. Zhang Cunwu, *Guangxu sayinian Zhong-Mei gongyue fengchao*, 23, 29–32.

13. Fang, *Kang-Liang yu Baohuanghui*, 113–15, 321–22.

14. *Shibao*, May 9 and 10, 1905; *Shenbao*, May 10, 1905.

15. *Shenbao*, May 11, 1905; Su, *Shanzhong ji*, 11, 482–84.

16. *Shenbao*, May 11, 1905; Su, *Shanzhong ji*, 11, 27–28, 511–13.

17. TSDH, 2:1877.

18. *Shibao,* October 14, 1904; May 13, 15, and 22, 1905; *Shanghai xian xuzhi,* 11:15a; SZZZ, 1:94.

19. *Shibao,* May 16, 19, and 21, 1905.

20. Zhang Cunwu, *Guangxu sayinian Zhong-Mei gongyue fengchao,* 64–65; Su, *Shan-zhong ji,* 29.

21. Zhang Cunwu, *Guangxu sayinian Zhong-Mei gongyue fengchao,* 47–49; Su, *Shan-zhong ji,* 36.

22. *Shibao,* May 22, 1905.

23. Su, *Shanzhong ji,* 29–32, 474–75; *Shenbao,* June 10, 1905.

24. Su, *Shanzhong ji,* 11–15; He Zuo, "Yijiu lingwu nian fan-Mei aiguo yundong," 31–33.

25. *Shenbao,* June 7 and 8, 1905. This meeting is misdated May 27 in Zhang Cunwu, *Guangxu sayinian Zhong-Mei gongyue fengchao,* 51, 62n2, and in Wong Sin Kiong, *China's Anti-American Boycott,* 48–49.

26. Su, *Shanzhong ji,* 13–15, 44–45, 61, 73, 80, 102; *Shenbao,* July 19, 1905.

27. Quotation from Tsai, *China and the Overseas Chinese in the United States, 1868–1911,* 121–22.

28. Zhang Cunwu, *Guangxu sayinian Zhong-Mei gongyue fengchao,* 67–72, 82–84.

29. *Shenbao,* July 20–21, 1905.

30. *Shenbao,* July 21, 1905.

31. *Shenbao,* July 21, 1905.

32. *Shenbao,* August 3, 7, and 10, 1905.

33. Zhang Cunwu, *Guangxu sayinian Zhong-Mei gongyue fengchao,* 93, 154–55; *Shen-bao,* September 3, 1905.

34. He Zuo, "Yijiu lingwu nian fan-Mei aiguo yundong," 68–89; *Shenbao,* August 11, 1905; Zhang Cunwu, *Guangxu sayinian Zhong-Mei gongyue fengchao,* 159–65.

35. *Shenbao,* August 9 and 11, 1905; Su, *Shanzhong ji,* 28.

36. Su, *Shanzhong ji,* 42, 44–47, 49, 56, 73, 102, 105, 133, 136, 155, 164, 173, 186, 209, 236, 253.

37. Ibid., 20, 128, 131, 164, 195, 222.

38. Ibid., 15–24, 135, 143, 166, 180–81, 187–88, 211, 215, 246, 284; *Shibao,* July 25 and November 10, 1905; *Shenbao,* July 31, August 1, and August 4, 1905; NGST: I, 4: 25a.

39. Zhang Cunwu, *Guangxu sayinian Zhong-Mei gongyue fengchao,* 194–95, 202–3, 209–10, 212–13; SZZZ, 1:100.

40. Kotenev, *Shanghai,* 69–72, 127; Xi, "Da'nao gongtang'an," 417–19.

41. *Shibao,* December 9, 1905; *Shenbao,* December 10, 1905.

42. Xi, "Da'nao gongtang'an," 432; Goodman, *Native Place, City, and Nation,* 189–91.

43. *Shenbao,* December 18, 1905; Xu and Qian, *Shanghai zongshanghui shi, 1902–1929,* 132–33; Kuai, "Shanghai gonggong zujie Huaguwen hui de shizhong," 919–23.

44. Elvin, "The Gentry Democracy in Chinese Shanghai, 1905–1914," 41, and "The Administration of Shanghai, 1905–1914," 239–62.

45. Xu and Qian, *Shanghai zongshanghui shi, 1902–1929;* Zhang Huanzhong, *Shanghai zongshanghui yanjiu, 1902–1929.*

46. Li Pingshu, *Li Pingshu qishi zixu,* 40–44, 50–53; Yang Yi, *Shanghai shi zizhizhi,* dashiji A, 1a, gongdu A, 1a.

47. *North China Herald,* October 20, 1905.

48. Yang Yi, *Shanghai shi zizhizhi*, dashiji A, 1a–3b, 7a; guize guiyue zhangcheng A, 1a–7a; SSZT: 1906. For a detailed description of the board's structure, see Elvin, "The Administration of Shanghai, 1905–1914," 250–57, but he takes little notice of its personnel overlap with the Shanghai GCC.

49. Yang Yi, *Shanghai shi zizhizhi*, dashiji A, 1a–1b; SSZT: 1906, 1a.

50. Li Pingshu, *Li Pingshu qishi zixu*, 53.

51. Yang Yi, *Shanghai shi zizhizhi*, dashiji A, 1b; SSZT: 1906, 3b, 5a. On Yao, other guild leaders, and elite merchants on the General Works Board, see Shanghai tongshe, *Shanghai yanjiu ziliao xuji*, 143–55; Elvin, "The Gentry Democracy in Chinese Shanghai, 1905–1914," 43–45; SZZZ, 1:108.

52. Yang Yi, *Shanghai shi zizhizhi*, dashiji A, 7a–8a, gongdu A, 6a–7b, guize guiyue zhangcheng A, 3b–4a; Elvin, "The Gentry Democracy in Chinese Shanghai, 1905–1914," 53–54.

53. Yang Yi, *Shanghai shi zizhizhi*, dongshihui zhiyuanbiao, 1a–2a, yishihui zhiyuanbiao, 2a–6a; SZZZ, 1:94; SWGS, section 2, 4–5; *Hunan Shangwu Fenhui baogao timingce*, sections 4–5. On the Deliberative Council, the six identifiable directors and full members of the South Shanghai BCC were Cheng Ding (Ningyuan), Li Houyuan, Gan Cheng (Lanping), Gu Xinyi (Lügui), Shen Manyun (Maozhao), and Lin Jingzhou.

54. Yang Yi, *Shanghai shi zizhizhi*, dashiji A, 8b; SZZZ, 1:94.

55. *Shenbao*, June 9, 1906; Yang Yi, *Shanghai shi zizhizhi*, dashiji A, 4a, 6b; Elvin, "The Administration of Shanghai, 1905–1914," 257–60.

56. Shanghai tongshe, *Shanghai yanjiu ziliao xuji*, 155–57; SWGS, section 2, 19–22; Yang Yi, *Shanghai shi zizhizhi*, gongdu A, 6a; *Xinwen bao*, January 7, March 25, and May 27, 1907.

57. *Xinwen Bao*, November 11 and 13, 1905; August 8, 1907; SWGB, 10 (1906): 25b; 6 (1907): 18a; *Shanghai xian xuzhi*, 13:12a.

58. SWGB, 6 (1907): 18a–19a.

59. Changzhoushi minjian and Gongshanglian wenshi ziliao ban'gongshi, "Wujin xian shanghui ji gongshangye fazhan shiluo," 104–8.

60. SSDC, 148; *Zhongwai ribao*, August 17 and December 7, 1906.

61. *Shenbao*, August 23, 1909; HSLB, 14 (1909): haineiwai shanghui jishi 4–6.

62. For a more detailed analysis of the Nanxiang case in the context of the 1911 Revolution, see Zhongping Chen, "Beneath the Republican Revolution, Beyond Revolutionary Politics."

63. Zizhihui, *Nanxiang jinshi diaochalu*, section 2B, 8, 12, 18–21; section 3, 22–23; NGST: I, 4:25a; Jiading xian Nanxiang zhenzhi bianzuan weiyuanhui, *Nanxiang zhenzhi*, 458.

64. Zizhihui, *Nanxiang jinshi*, section 2B, 28; section 3, 2, 18, 28; *Jiading xian xuzhi*, 10:2b.

65. Zizhihui, *Nanxiang jinshi*, section 2A, 1–3; section 2B, 1, 5–7.

66. Ibid., section 2B, 1–2, 6–8.

67. Ibid., section 2B, 10–13, 17–18, 21–35; *Jiading xian xuzhi*, 4:17b.

68. Zizhihui, *Nanxiang jinshi*, section 3, 2–5.

69. Ibid., section 3, 1–3, 5–8.

70. Ibid., section 3, 6–13.

71. Ibid., section 3, 13–16, 27–30, 34–35; bulu 1.

72. Ibid., section 3, 34–35; NGST: I, 4:25a; SWGB, 25 (1909): 11a; *Liaotian yihe*, March 11, 1910.

73. Yang Yi, *Shanghai shi zizhizhi*, yishihui zhiyuanbiao 4b, geke banshi zhurenbiao, 2b; Jiading xian Nanxiang zhenzhi bianzuan weiyuanhui, *Nanxiang zhenzhi*, 459, 465.

74. *Zhongwei ribao*, April 9, 1904; *Shibao*, August 25 and October 14, 1904; SZZZ, 1:94, 106–10; SSZT: 1906, 5a; "Shouxian Sunshi jingying Fufeng mianfenchang ji youguan caituan suoshu qiye shiliaogao."

75. The Shanghai Commercial Study Society was also called the Public Society for Commercial Studies (Shangxue gonghui) around 1908. There was another little-known organization with the name Shangxuehui in Shanghai by that time. In order to avoid confusion, I will refer to Shangxue gonghui only as the Shanghai Commercial Study Society. For its personnel overlap with the two Shanghai chambers of commerce and its collaboration with the Shanghai GCC, see *Shangxue gonghui tongrenlu*; SWGS, section 2, 1–6, 22–23; *Xinwen bao*, October 2, 1906.

76. *Shenbao*, July 3, 1907.

77. Zhejiang sheng Xinhai geming shi yanjiuhui and Zhejiang sheng tushuguan, *Xinhai geming Zhejiang shiliao xuanji*, 7, 13; *Hangzhou shangye zazhi*, 1 (1909): diaochalu 5–6.

78. Zhu, *Xinhai gemin shiqi xinshi shangren shetuan yanjiu*, 225, 228.

79. *Zhongwai ribao*, May 29, 1905; *Jiangsu xuewu zonghui wendu*, bubian 12–13; SZZZ, 1:94.

80. *Nantong difang zizhi shijiunian zhi chengji*, section 2, 167; "Suzhou shanghui dang'an," 92:3, 5; SSDC, 46.

81. *Shanghai xian xuzhi*, 9:8a–9a.

82. *Xinwen bao*, October 9 and December 22, 1905; NGST: I, 4:19b; *Shanghai xian xuzhi*, 11:16a. At that time, Yun was also a senior accountant in the Shanghai office of Zhang Jian's cotton mills in Tongzhou; see Köll, *From Cotton Mill to Business Empire*, 142.

83. *Jiangsu xuewu zonghui wendu*, section A, 2.

84. Ibid., 9–10, 81–83; *Shibao*, November 7–8, 1906; SZZZ, 1:94.

85. *Jiangsu xuewu zonghui wendu*, section A, 3–5, 11. For information about the elite merchant participants in both the Jiangsu General Association for Education and chambers of commerce by 1909, see Jiangsu jiaoyu zonghui, "Jiangsu jiaoyu zonghui huiyuan xingming yilanbiao," 3a, 9a, 12a, 14a, 24b; NGST: I, 4:4b, 18b, 26a–b, 38a; *Baoshan xian xuzhi*, 6:31b.

86. Jiangsu jiaoyu zonghui, "Jiangsu jiaoyu zonghui huiyuan xingming yilanbiao," 10a, 12b, 20a–b; and "Jiangsu quansheng jiaoyuhui yilanbiao," 100–101, 104; *Yi-Jing xuzhi*, 5:2b.

87. *Shenbao*, August 30, 1907; *Xinwen bao*, August 13, 1908; Xuewu gongsuo, *Xuantong yuannianfen Zhejiang jiaoyu tongjibiao*, 7; NGST: I, 4:41b, 42b.

88. Bian and Tang, *Minguo renwu beizhuanji*, 257; Chu, *Reformer in Modern China*, 114–23; Köll, *From Cotton Mill to Business Empire*, 212–30; *Nantong difang zizhi shijiunian zhi chengji*, section 1, 77; NGST: II, 2:2b; *Xinwen bao*, September 12, 1908.

89. Ma Min, *Guanshang zhijian*, 162–64; *Xinwen bao*, June 18, 1907; "Suzhou shanghui dang'an," 73:5–37; Ma and Zhu, *Chuantong yu jindai de er'chong bianzou*, 115.

90. NGST: II, 2:2b; *Shenbao*, March 28, 1909; SWGB, 6 (1909): 8b.

91. NGST: I, 4:25b; Jiangsu jiaoyu zonghui, "Jiangsu quansheng jiaoyuhui yilanbiao," 100; SWGB, 18 (1909): 11b; *Jiading xian xuzhi*, 2:39a; Zhu, "Xinhai geming qian de nonghui," 19–20, 22–23.

92. *Shanghai xian xuzhi*, 13:12a; SZZZ, 1:94, 107, 122; *Xinwen bao*, July 22 and August 9, 1906; *Shanghai xianzhi*, 15:29.

93. *Shanghai xian xuzhi*, 13:12a; *Xinwen bao*, October 26, 1907; February 23, 1908; Yang Yi, *Shanghai shi zizhizhi*, gongdu A, 159a–122a.

94. *Shenbao*, March 3, 1908; *Shanghai xian xuzhi*, 13:12b–13b; Zhongguo shixuehui, *Xinhai geming*, 7:87.

95. Yang and Shen, "Shanghai shangtuan yu Xinhai geming," 109n1, 111; *Shanghai xian xuzhi*, 13:12b–13b; SZZZ, 1:94–95; SWGS, section 2, 4–6; *Hunan Shangwu Fenhui baogao timingce*, section 4.

96. *Xinwen bao*, May 21, 1906; Shanghai tongshe, *Shanghai yanjiu ziliao xuji*, 191–92; SSZT: 1906, 1a–2a; SWGS, section 2, 1–4, 12; SZZZ, 1:115–16.

97. Zhang, Zhu, Zu, and Ye, *Suzhou Shangtuan dang'an huibian, 1905–1911*, 1:1–14; 2:1068.

98. Ibid., 1:2–5, 16–21, 230–31; 2:479–580, 936–44; *Shibao*, April 16, 1911; *Xinwen bao*, July 28, 1911.

99. *Xinwen bao*, August 18, 1907; *Shibao*, September 6, 1908; Cheng, "Jiushidai de Hangzhou shanghui," 144–45.

100. *Nantong difang zizhi shijiunian zhi chengji*, section 1, 71, 73–74.

101. SWGB, 6 (1907): 18a–19a; 22 (1909): 10a; NGST: I, 4:25b; *Shenbao*, August 10, 1908; Changzhoushi minjian and Gongshanglian wenshi ziliao ban'gongshi, "Wujin xian shanghui ji gongshangye fazhan shiluo," 108.

102. Wu Xinmu, "Xinhai geming shiqi de Xiashi shangtuan he gongbing tiedao dadui," 170; NGST: I, 4:32.

103. Zhang, Zhu, Zu, and Ye, *Suzhou Shangtuan dang'an huibian*, 1:4; 2:230–32; *Xinwen bao*, January 9, 1908, and March 23, 1910.

Chapter 5

1. Gugong bowuyuan Ming-Qing dang'anbu, *Qingmo choubei lixian dang'an shiliao*, 1:149–51.

2. Ibid., 1:53–54; SWGB, 15 (1909): 8a.

3. Yeh-chien Wang, *Land Taxation in Imperial China, 1750–1911*, 121.

4. *Shenbao*, March 22, 1908; SWGB, 25 (1908): 25a; Jingji xuehui, *Zhejiang quansheng caizheng shuomingshu*, part two, section 3, 48–50.

5. Ma and Zhu, *Chuantong yu jindai de er'chong bianzou*, 49; Jingji xuehui, *Zhejiang quansheng caizheng shuomingshu*, part one, section 3, 43, 46; MQSG, 260–61.

6. SSDC, 1042–52, esp. 1045, 1048, 1050, 1052, 1176. Late Qing China used *wen* as the basic unit of copper currency. In eastern Zhejiang Province, local governments in 1906 stipulated that 1,000 *wen* of copper coin could be exchanged for one silver dollar.

7. Ibid., 1052–54.

8. Ibid., 1058–63; *Shibao*, June 14, 1907; *Xinwen bao*, June 14, 1907.

9. SSDC, 1069–72.

10. Ibid., 48, 1073–79.

11. *Shenbao*, February 9, 1878; SSDC, 1029.

12. SSDC, 76–77, 124–26; *Shenbao*, September 4, 1911.

13. Gao and Yan, *Jindai Wuxi cansiye ziliao xuanji*, 31, 34, 44–45.

14. *Shenbao*, November 14, 1906; SSDC, 1028–30.

15. SSDC, 1032–35; SWGB, 1 (1907): 14a; 8 (1907): 10b–12a; 10 (1907): 11b.

16. SSDC, 1033–34.

17. Ibid., 1031–32, 1034–35, 1039–41, 1079; *Shenbao*, August 22, 1907; Yun, *Yun Yuding Chengzhai riji*, 1:314, 316, 381.

18. Ma and Zhu, *Chuantong yu jindai de er'chong bianzou*, 349–53, 357–60; *Huashang lianhehui bao* 1 (1910): haineiwai shanghui jishi 5; Jingji xuehui, *Zhejiang quansheng caizheng shuomingshu*, part one, section 6, 5.

19. Morse, *The Trade and Administration of China*, 144–46; SSDC, 1177–78, 1187.

20. HSLB, 10 (1909): haineiwai jiwen 3.

21. SSDC, 1177, 1185; *Zhejiang ribao*, June 12, 19, 20, and 27, and July 19, 1908.

22. *Zhejiang ribao*, June 8, 1908; *Shenbao*, June 11 and 22 and September 3, 1908; April 26, 1909.

23. SSDC, 1175–76, 1179–83; *Xinwen bao*, July 25, 1908; *Shenbao*, July 11, 12, and 13, 1908; HSLB, 15 (1909): haineiwai gongdu 3.

24. SSDC, 1177–79, 1184–85.

25. *Shenbao*, May 14 and 16, 1909; HSLB, 15 (1909): haineiwai gongdu 3–4.

26. HSLB, 15 (1909): haineiwai gongdu 3; *Shenbao*, May 22, 1909.

27. *Shenbao*, May 22 and 27, 1909; *Xinwen bao*, May 26, 1909; HSLB, 7 (1909): haineiwai shanghui jishi 11.

28. *Dongfang zazhi*, 6, no. 6 (1909): jishi 161–63; HSLB, 8 (1909): haineiwai shanghui jishi 6–7, 10 (1909): haineiwai jiwen 3; SSDC, 1191–93.

29. Rankin's *Elite Activism and Political Transformation in China* (pp. 251–98) includes passing discussion about late Qing chambers of commerce in the railroad movement of Zhejiang Province. However, their relations with this movement have largely been ignored by other works in Chinese, Japanese, and English. See Zhao, "Su-Hang-Yong tielu jiekuan he Jiang-Zhe renmin de jukuan yundong"; Fujii, "Shimmatsu Kō-Setsu ni okeru tetsuro mondai to burujoa seiryoku no ichi sokumen"; Sun, "The Shanghai-Hangchow-Ningpo Railway Loan of 1908"; Lee, "The Chekiang Gentry-Merchants vs. the Peking Court Officials"; and Chi, "Shanghai-Hangchow-Ningpo Railway Loan."

30. Mo Bei, *Jiang-Zhe tielu fengchao*, 7–8, 29–31; Sun, "The Shanghai-Hangchow-Ningpo Railway Loan of 1908," 138.

31. Zhejiang tongxianghui ganshi, *Zhe-Gan tielu shijian*, 12, 16, 24; *Dongfang zazhi*, 2, no. 11 (1905): jiaotong 151; *Shenbao*, July 25, 1905.

32. Fu, *Jindai Zhongguo tielushi ziliao*, 3:1000–1001. Rankin's *Elite Activism and Political Transformation in China* (table 20 on pp. 254–55) identifies seven of the nineteen founders and officers of the railroad company as the members or leaders of the Shanghai GCC. Actually, Fan Shixun (Fen), Shi Zejing (Ziying), and Xie Lunhui, who are listed in Rankin's table, also came from the Shanghai GCC; see SSZT: 1906, 1b–3a.

33. *Shangban Zhejiang quansheng tielu youxian gongsi gudonghui diyici yishilu*, 13b–15b; *Shibao*, August 19, 1907.

34. *Dongfang zazhi*, 3, no. 3 (1906): jiaotong 80. The first shareholders' meeting of the Zhejiang Railroad Company in October 1906 lowered the requirement for one vote in the decision-making process to the possession of 100 silver dollars of stock; see *Shangban Zhejiang quansheng tielu youxian gongsi gudonghui diyici yishilu*, 5a–5b.

35. *Shangban Quan-Zhe tielu youxian gongsi Zhonghua minguo yuannianfen diqijie baogao*, 24–25. On November 15, 1907, this company reduced each share of railroad stock from ten silver dollars to five silver dollars. This change resulted in the division of old stockholders by late 1907 and new shareholders thereafter. See *Shenbao*, November 16, 1907.

36. Fu, *Jindai Zhongguo tielushi ziliao*, 3:962; SSDC, 48, 767–70, 777.

37. SSDC, 48, 771–78; SZZZ, 1:64, 94; NGST: I, 4:5a, 19a–b, 25b–26a; *Shibao*, April 12, 1909.

38. *Dongfang zazhi*, 3, no. 9 (1906): jiaotong 190.

39. "Sulu gongsi wubaigu yishang gudong mingdan." For the relations of these large shareholders with the chambers of commerce in Shanghai and Jiangsu province, see SSDC, 48; SSZT: 1906, 2a, 6a; SWGS, section 2, 4; NGST: I, 4:28b.

40. SSDC, 777; Mo Bei, *Jiang-Zhe tielu fengchao*, 410; *Dongfang zazhi*, 3, no. 9 (1906): jiaotong 189–90; 3, no. 11 (1906): jiaotong 225.

41. Fu, *Jindai Zhongguo tielushi ziliao*, 3:1004; Zhongyang yanjiuyuan jindaishi yanjiusuo, *Haifang dang*, 5:593.

42. Fu, *Jindai Zhongguo tielushi ziliao*, 2:842, 855–56; *Shibao*, October 27, 1907.

43. *Shibao*, October 6, 25, and 27 and November 17, 1907.

44. Rankin's *Elite Activism and Political Transformation in China* (p. 274) identifies twenty-four telegrams from the chambers of commerce in Zhejiang Province. For the sixteen telegrams from the chambers of commerce in Jiangsu Province, see Mo Bei, *Jiang-Zhe tielu fengchao*, 76–77, 81–83, 88, 91, 327, 332, 343–44, 347–48, 350; *Shenbao*, November 7, 1907.

45. *Shibao*, October 28 and November 17, 1907.

46. *Shenbao*, November 15 and 16, 1907; Mo Bei, *Jiang-Zhe tielu fengchao*, 413.

47. Mo Bei, *Jiang-Zhe tielu fengchao*, 95–97, 113–18, 122, 132; *Shibao*, November 1, 1907.

48. Mo Bei, *Jiang-Zhe tielu fengchao*, 78, 90–92, 124–25.

49. Ibid., 82, 86, 92, 135–36, 339, 369, 403; *Shibao*, November 29, 1907.

50. Mo Bei, *Jiang-Zhe tielu fengchao*, 119–24; *Shenbao*, November 2, 1907; SSDC, 48; *Shibao*, November 13, 23, and 30 and December 9, 1907.

51. Mo Bei, *Jiang-Zhe tielu fengchao*, 118–19, 124, 126–27, 139–40, 274, 381–82, 384–88, 409–13; *Shenbao*, November 16, 1907. For information about the Jiangsu Railroad Association, see *Shibao*, November 15, 1907.

52. *Shenbao*, November 20, 1909; *Shibao*, December 8 and 11, 1907.

53. Mo Bei, *Jiang-Zhe tielu fengchao*, 139–54, 357–428, esp. 385–87, 412; *Shibao*, November 20, 1907.

54. SZZZ, 1:94–95; Mo Bei, *Jiang-Zhe tielu fengchao*, 373, 394–98, 403, 420–21, 423; *Shenbao*, November 11, 13, 19, 21, and 22, 1907.

55. *Shenbao*, November 14, 23, 24, and 26 and December 3 and 22, 1907; *Shibao*, November 23 and December 29 and 31, 1907.

56. Fu, *Jindai Zhongguo tielushi ziliao*, 3:1008; *Xuantong yuannianfen shangban Quan-Zhe tielu youxian gongsi shouzhi zhanglue*, 1a.

57. *Shenbao*, November 10 and 17, 1907; *Shibao*, November 21, December 11, 12, and 14, 1907.

58. *Shangban Quan-Zhe tielu youxian gongsi Zhonghua minguo yuannianfen diqijie baogao*, 24.

59. *Dongfang zazhi*, 4, no. 12 (1907): zazu 29; 5, no. 6 (1908): jiaotong 95–99. For the texts of the two loan agreements, see Zhongyang yanjiuyuan jindaishi yanjiusuo, *Haifang dang*, 5:582–92, 620–26.

60. *Shibao*, April 28 and May 8, 1908; July 9, 1909; Fu, *Jindai Zhongguo tielushi ziliao*, 2:880–86.

61. Zhengxie Zhejiang sheng Xiaoshan shi weiyuanhui wenshi gongzuo weiyuanhui, *Tang Shouqian shiliao zhuanji*, 155, 163; *Shibao*, October 4, 1910.

62. *Dongfang zazhi*, 7, no. 10 (1910): Zhongguo dashiji buyi 77–79; *Zhelu daibiao lü-Jin shenshang feizhang baolü gongdu*, section 1, 1a–2a; *Zhelu Dongshiju baogao*, 2; Qi, "Lun Qingmo de tielu fengchao," 53, 59.

63. Rankin, *Elite Activism and Political Transformation in China*, 248–98, esp. 250–51.

64. *Shenbao*, November 14, 1907.

65. *Xinwen bao*, January 9, 1908; SSDC, 293; *Shibao*, October 28, 1907 and December 12 and 16, 1909; Tahara, *Shinmatsu minsho Chūgoku kanshin jimmei roku*, 721.

66. *Shibao*, December 8, 13, and 14, 1907; October 4, 1910; Zhejiang sheng Xinhai geming shi yanjiuhui and Zhejiang sheng tushuguan, *Xinhai geming Zhejiang shiliao xuanji*, 521–22.

67. Xu and Qian, *Shanghai zongshanghui shi, 1902–1929*, 115–16; *Shenbao*, October 10, 11, 12, and 15, 1908.

68. Zhongguo renmin yinhang Shanghai shi fenhang, *Shanghai qianzhuang shiliao*, 74–75; Ji, *A History of Modern Shanghai Banking*, 92–93; Xu and Qian, *Shanghai zongshanghui shi, 1902–1929*, 117–19.

69. Zhongguo renmin yinhang Shanghai shi fenhang, *Shanghai qianzhuang shiliao*, 75–78.

70. Ibid., 80–81; TSDH, 1:538–65.

71. Zhongguo renmin yinhang Shanghai shi fenhang, *Shanghai qianzhuang shiliao*, 81; *Xinwen bao*, October 18, 1910; *Shibao*, October 20, 1910.

72. *Shibao*, November 2, 1910; Zhongguo renmin yinhang Shanghai shi fenhang, *Shanghai qianzhuang shiliao*, 81–84; SZZZ, 1:95, 122, 125.

73. SSDC, 1291–306.

74. Ibid., 391.

75. *North China Herald*, January 8, 1902; SSDC, 384.

76. SSDC, 384–92.

77. *Shenbao*, June 19, 1908; SSDC, 416–17; HSLB, 22 (1910): haineiwai tongxin 1–3; SWGB, 12 (1910): 4b.

78. *Shenbao*, March 14, 1909; SSDC, 392–93, 396–401; *Quanyehui xunbao*, 3 (1910): gongdu 1b. The list of chairman, vice chairmen, and directors is cited in *Shenbao*. A slightly different list in SSDC (p. 416) is inconsistent with the regulations of the exhibition.

79. *Quanyehui xunbao*, 3 (1910): baogao 1a–5a; 4 (1910): baogao 1a–3b, 7a–9b; 6 (1910): baogao 1a–4a; 7 (1910): baogao 3b–5a; 8 (1910): baogao 1a–3b; 9 (1910): baogao 1a–4a; 10 (1910): baogao 1a–3b.

80. *Shibao*, April 12 and September 14, 1909; *Xinwen bao*, August 27, 1909.

81. HSLB, 14 (1909): haineiwai shanghui jishi 3–4; *Dongfang zazhi*, 6, no. 11 (1909): jishi 356; 6, no. 12 (1909): jishi 407; 7, no. 1 (1910): jizai disan 16.

82. SSDC, 385, 400–401; *Quanyehui xunbao* 3 (1910): gongdu 3a–b, zalu 1a–2a; 4 (1910): baogao 3b–6a; *Dongfang zazhi* 6, no. 11 (1909): jishi 355; 6, no. 13 (1909): jishi 463.

83. *Shibao*, June 8, 1910; Shangwu yinshuguan bianyisuo, *Nanyang quanyehui youji*, youlan xuzhi 2–19; SWGB, 12 (1910): 5a–6a; 24 (1910): 6a; 25 (1910): 5a; Ma Min, *Guanshang zhijian*, 295.

84. SSDC, 405–15; SWGB, 25 (1910): 4b–5b.

85. *Shibao*, December 4, 1910; *Xinwen bao*, October 2, 1911; SSDC, 355–56, 360.

86. *Shenbao*, October 19, 1908; *Xinwen bao*, May 26, 1909. The Shanghai GCC's letter to the Suzhou GCC in 1908 is included in SSDC (p. 353) but is misdated 1910. The letter mentioned that the American delegation would stay in Japan until November 1 on the

Gregorian calendar or the eighth day of the tenth month of the lunar calendar. The two dates coincided in 1908 but not in 1910.

87. Dollar, *Memoirs of Robert Dollar*, 28, 104–34; Associated Chambers of Commerce of the Pacific Coast, *A Visit to China*, title page; HSLB, 2 (1909): haineiwai tongxin 6–7.

88. *Xinwen bao*, July 15, 1909; September 11, 1910; TSDH, 1:1129–31.

89. Associated Chambers of Commerce of the Pacific Coast, *A Visit to China*, ii–iii, 33–34; *Dongfang zazhi*, 7, no. 9 (1910): jizai disan 267.

90. Associated Chambers of Commerce of the Pacific Coast, *A Visit to China*, 34–35.

91. Ibid., 33–56, esp. 34; *Dongfang zazhi*, 7, no. 9 (1910): jizai disan 267–68.

92. Associated Chambers of Commerce of the Pacific Coast, *A Visit to China*, 49.

93. Ibid., 46–49.

94. Quoted in ibid., 43.

95. Zhang Jian, *Zhang Jian quanji*, 6:872.

96. Associated Chambers of Commerce of the Pacific Coast, *A Visit to China*, 53–54.

97. Dollar, *Memoirs of Robert Dollar*, 168–90; SSDC, 355–58.

98. SSDC, 358–62; Zhang Jian, *Zhang Jian quanji*, 2:277; 6:649.

99. Zhang Jian, *Zhang Jian quanji*, 1:164; 6:651; SSDC, 380–82; *Shibao*, June 23, 1911.

100. The plan for joint ventures between Chinese and American chambers of commerce was partly realized after 1915. See Pugach, "Keep an Idea Alive"; Jia, *Zhong-Mei shangren tuanti yu jindai guomin waijiao, 1905–1927*.

Chapter 6

1. Gugong bowuyuan Ming-Qing dang'anbu, *Qingmo choubei lixian dang'an shiliao*, 1:43–44.

2. *Xinwen bao*, September 8, 10, and 11, 1906; *Shenbao*, September 10, 1906.

3. Zhang Kaiyuan, "The 1911 Revolution and the Jiang-Zhe Bourgeoisie"; Esherick, *Reform and Revolution in China*; Rankin, *Elite Activism and Political Transformation in China*.

4. Yu, *Shanghui yu Zhongguo zaoqi xiandaihua*, 76–92.

5. Zhejiang sheng Xinhai geming shi yanjiuhui and Zhejiang sheng tushuguan, *Xinhai geming Zhejiang shiliao xuanji*, 203, 208, 210–23; SWGS, section 2, 6, 22; SZZZ, 1:94; SWGB, 17 (1906): 9a; SSDC, 48; NGST: I, 4:26a; SSZT: 1906.

6. *Gesheng shanghui dahui jishi*, 10a–10b; *Shenbao*, July 30 and August 24, 1907.

7. *Gesheng shanghui dahui jishi*, 1a–9a, 10a; *Shibao*, November 21, 1907.

8. *Gesheng shanghui dahui jishi*, 10a–11b.

9. Ibid., 11b–12a, 13a–b.

10. Ibid., 5b, 12a–13a, 14a–15a. The proposal for the national union of Chinese chambers of commerce is in TSDH, 1:291–94.

11. Yu, *Shanghaui yu Zhonguo zaoqi xiandaihua*, 104–7. For this set of bylaws, see HSLB, 1 (1909): haineiwai gongdu 10–14.

12. *Gesheng shanghui dahui jishi*, 18b–21a; *Yubei lixian gonghui bao*, 3 (1908): 17a–17b.

13. *Shenbao*, July 30 and August 30, 1907; *Gesheng shanghui dahui jishi*, 25a.

14. *Yubei lixian gonghuibao*, 8 (1909): 19–21; 9 (1909): 19–21; 10 (1909): 17–19; 16 (1909): 19. This journal reprinted some editorials from major Shanghai newspapers.

15. *Shenbao*, December 23, 1909; Yu, *Shanghui yu Zhongguo zaoqi xiandaihua*, 206–7; Jiangsu sheng shangyeting and Zhongguo di'er lishi dang'anguan, *Zhonghua minguo shangye dang'an ziliao huibian*, 1:166–67.

16. *Gesheng shanghui dahui jishi*, 12b, 14b–15a, 19a, 21b. The difference between mediation and adjudication was that the former proceeded through informal hearings, while the latter involved formal interrogation. Decisions of mediators were to be accepted by disputants voluntarily, while judgments of adjudicators were to be enforced by the government or chambers of commerce.

17. SZZZ, 1:50, 70, 78; SSDC, 17, 27, 182, 186; Shiyebu, *Da-Qing fagui daquan*, 7:2b.

18. SWGB, 13 (1907): 13a; 14 (1907): 10a; 4 (1908): 9a; 5 (1908): 10b; 11 (1908): 9b.

19. SSZT: 1906, 2b–3a; HSLB, 16 (1909): haineiwai shanghui tongrenlu, 4; 21 (1909): haineiwai shanghui tongrenlu, 13.

20. Kotenev, *Shanghai*, 256.

21. SSDC, 521–22; Ma Min, "Shangshi caipan yu shanghui," 33–40.

22. *Shenbao*, August 21, 1906; *Xinwen bao*, May 20, 1907.

23. SSDC, 522–23; SWGB, 15 (1909): 8a.

24. HSLB, 15 (1909): haineiwai shanghui jishi 2–3.

25. *Shenbao*, August 14 and 25, 1906.

26. SSDC, 38–39.

27. "Suzhou shanghui dang'an," 202:1a–3a; SWGB, 14 (1910): 8b.

28. *Huashang lianhehui bao*, 6 (1910): haineiwai shanghui jishi, 1a–2a.

29. HSLB, 14 (1909): haineiwai gongdu, 1–4.

30. *Gesheng shanghui dahui jishi*, 6a.

31. Gugong bowuyuan Ming-Qing dang'anbu, *Qingmo choubei lixian dang'an shiliao*, 1:54–67.

32. For a relatively positive review of the Qing constitutional reform, see Cameron, *The Reform Movement in China, 1898–1912*. For a negative viewpoint on the Qing court's reform, see Esherick, *Reform and Revolution in China*.

33. Fincher, *Chinese Democracy*; Thompson, *China's Local Councils in the Age of Constitutional Reform, 1898–1911*.

34. Min, "The Late-Ch'ing Provincial Assembly," 150–54; Yang Yi, *Shanghai shi zizhizhi*, part 1, dashiji A, 7a–7b; *Xinwen bao*, October 21, 1907; January 21, 1908. For the text of the regulations, see *Zhengzhi guanbao*, 81 (1908): zalulei 17–19.

35. Gugong bowuyuan Ming-Qing dang'anbu, *Qingmo choubei lixian dang'an shiliao*, 2:667–77.

36. *Shenbao*, September 25, 1908; *Shibao*, December 20, 1908.

37. *Dongfang zazhi*, 5, no. 9 (1908): jizai 72–73; *Shibao*, November 13, 1908; March 13, 1909.

38. *Dongfang zazhi*, 5, no. 9 (1908): jizai 72–73; SSDC, 1233–34.

39. *Dongfang zazhi*, 5, no. 12 (1908): jizai 156–57; 6, no. 1 (1909): jizai yi 17–18; SSDC, 50, 126, 157, 1233; NGST: II, 4A:33b.

40. In the Jiangsu Provincial Assembly, the eight identifiable chamber leaders and members were Fang Huan, Jiang Bingzhang, Qian Yizhen, Sha Yuanbing, Wang Tongyu, Xu Dinglin, Yu Dingyi, and Zhou Shunian. The Zhejiang Provincial Assembly initially included at least six former and incumbent presidents of chambers as well as one honorary member, namely, Ding Zhongli, Huang Yan, Qian Yunkang, Rao Jiongzhang, Zhang Di, Zhu Qizhen, and Shao Xi. However, it later drew two more chamber leaders, Wu Enyuan and Xu Guangpu, as alternative assemblymen. See Zhang Pengyuan, *Lixianpai yu Xinhai geming*, 258–63, 270–74; SSDC, 54; NGST: I, 4:26a, 32a; NGST: II, 4A:15b, 16b–17a, 27b, 28a, 30b, 31b, 33a, 35a, 37a; Changzhoushi minjian and Gongshanglian wenshi ziliao ban'gongshi, "Wujin xian shanghui ji gongshangye fazhan shiluo,"

104; Zhejiang sheng Xinhai geming shi yanjiuhui and Zhejiang sheng tushuguan, *Xinhai geming Zhejiang shiliao xuanji*, 191–92; *Hangzhou shangye zazhi*, 1 (1909): diaochalu 6; *Haining zhou zhigao*, 41:1b; *Shibao*, July 12, 1910.

41. *Jiangsu ziyiju diyiniandu baogao*, 1:3a–4b; 3:54a; *Jiangsu sheng ziyiju lijin gaiban renjun wendu*, 9a–12a, 24a; SSDC, 844–47.

42. SSDC, 847–904, 980–1014, esp. 885–93.

43. *Zhejiang ziyiju di'erjie changnianhui yishilu*, 1:1a–b; 2:37a–39b; Zhengxie Zhejiang sheng Xiaoshan shi weiyuanhui wenshi gongzuo weiyuanhui, *Tang Shouqian shiliao zhuanji*, 152–59; *Dongfang zazhi*, 7, no. 10 (1910): Zhongguo dashiji buyi 75–77; 7, no. 11 (1910): Zhongguo dashiji buyi 94–95.

44. *Shibao*, October 4, 1910; *Zhelu daibiao lü-Jin shenshang feizhang baolü gongdu*, section 1, 4a; Zhejiang sheng Xinhai geming shi yanjiuhui and Zhejiang sheng tushuguan, *Xinhai geming Zhejiang shiliao xuanji*, 192.

45. Zhang Pengyuan, *Lixianpai yu Xinhai geming*, 84, 102n3, 314, 320; SSDC, 158–59; NGST: I, 4:19a, 26a; *Hangzhou shangye zazhi*, 1 (1909): diaochalu 6; SZZZ, 1:94–95. The National Assembly was supposed to include 200 members. Because Xinjiang Province did not have a provincial assembly and was unable to elect two members to the National Assembly, the positions of two imperially appointed assemblymen were not filled either. Thus, there were only 196 assemblymen.

46. Zhang Yufa, *Qingji de lixian tuanti*, 356; *Xinwen bao*, June 22, 1908; NGST: I, 4:26a; *Zhejiang ribao*, July 19, 1908.

47. Gugong bowuyuan Ming-Qing dang'anbu, *Qingmo choubei lixian dang'an shiliao*, 1:67; Zhang Jian, *Zhang Jian quanji*, 6:625; SSDC, 157.

48. *Dongfang zazhi*, 6, no. 12 (1909): jishi 394; 6, no. 13 (1909): jizai yi 446–48; Zhang Pengyuan, *Lixianpai yu Xinhai geming*, 63–64, 78n6; HSLB, 8 (1909): haineiwai shanghui jishi 2.

49. *Dongfang zazhi*, 7, no. 2 (1910): jizai disan 27–29; 7, no. 3 (1910): jizai disan 47–48; SSDC, 1258–62.

50. SSDC, 1262–64; Rankin, *Elite Activism and Political Transformation in China*, 292; *Shibao*, April 26 and May 1–3, 1910; *Huashang lianhehuibao*, 4 (1910): haineiwai shishi sheyan 1a–4b.

51. *Guohui qingyuan daibiao di'erci cheng Duchayuan daizoushu huilu*, 20–32, 42, 51; *Dongfang zazhi*, 7, no. 6 (1910): jizai diyi 84–86.

52. Zhang Pengyuan, *Lixianpai yu Xinhai geming*, 64, 73–75, 81n27; *Guohui qingyuan daibiao di'erci cheng Duchayuan daizoushu huilu*, 20–32.

53. *Dongfang zazhi*, 7, no. 11 (1910): lunshuo 265, jizai diyi 143–57; *Zhengzhi guanbao* 1091 (1910): shiyoudan 3–4; SSDC, 1275–77.

54. Xu and Qian, *Shanghai zongshanghui shi, 1902–1929*, 151–52; Yang Yi, *Shanghai shi zizhizhi*, dashiji B, 11a.

55. Yang Yi, *Shanghai shi zizhizhi*, dashiji A, 7a–b; *Xinwen bao*, September 15 and October 21, 1907; January 21, 1908; Thompson, *China's Local Councils in the Age of Constitutional Reform, 1898–1911*, 59–60, 73, 86, 111–12, 219n12.

56. SSDC, 1226; *Shanghai shi zizhizhi*, dashiji A, 12b–13b, dashiji B, 1a; SZZZ, 1:96, 123; *Xinwen bao*, November 10, 1905; January 14, 1912; SWGS, part 2, 4, 20–21.

57. *Xinwen bao*, May 28, 1907; Thompson, *China's Local Councils in the Age of Constitutional Reform, 1898–1911*, 61–62; SSDC, 48, 53, 56, 1213–17, 1222–24; Zhang Hailin, *Suzhou zaoqi chengshi xiandaihua yanjiu*, 190; Jiangsu sheng Sushu difang zizhi choubanchu, *Jiangsu zizhi gongbao leibian*, 144–45.

58. Suzhou shi dang'anguan, "Suzhou shimin gongshe dangan xuanji," 58–59, 87–89; *Shibao*, June 24, 1909; *Xinwen bao*, June 29, 1909; SSDC, 55.

59. Suzhou shi dang'anguan, "Suzhou shimin gongshe dangan xuanji," 61–62, 112–14, 183–84; SSDC, 53–57.

60. Suzhou shi dang'anguan, "Suzhou shimin gongshe dangan xuanji," 64–70, 89–93, 114, esp. 92.

61. *Zhejiang ribao*, July 8, 1908; March 30, 1910; *Hangzhou shangye zazhi*, 1 (1909): diaochalu 5–6; NGST: II, 4A:27b.

62. *Nantong difang zizhi*, section 4, zizhi 1–2.

63. *Jiading xian xuzhi*, 2:38a–b; 6:4a, 10a–12a; *Liaotian yihe*, April 10, 1910; *Minli bao*, June 4, 1911.

64. *Zhengzhi guanbao* 76 (1911): 233–34; Jiangsu sheng Sushu difang zizhi choubanchu, *Jiangsu zizhi gongbao leibian*, 143–61. The Qing court defined all self-government units at and above the county level as cities (*cheng*) and divided subcounty communities into towns (*zhen*) that had at least 50,000 residents each or rural townships (*xiang*) that had fewer inhabitants. See Thompson, *China's Local Councils in the Age of Constitutional Reform, 1898–1911*, 111.

65. *Zhengzhi guanbao*, 63 (1911): 209–10; *Haining zhou zhigao*, 41:4a, 6a; NGST: I, 4:32a; NGST: II, 4A:29a; Wu Xinmu, "Xinhai geming shiqi de Xiashi shangtuan he gongbing tiedao dadui," 170.

66. Ichiko, "The Role of the Gentry," 301–4, 312; Esherick, "1911," 166–68.

67. *Haining zhou zhigao*, 40:27a–b; Haining Xiashi zhenzhi banzuan weiyuanhui, *Haining Xiashi zhenzhi*, 6, 443.

68. Haining Xiashi zhenzhi banzuan weiyuanhui, *Haining Xiashi zhenzhi*, 443; *Haining zhou zhigao*, 41:1b; Zhongguo shixuehui, *Xinhai geming*, 7:130.

69. Schoppa, *Chinese Elites and Political Change*, 145–54; Bergère, *The Golden Age of the Chinese Bourgeoisie, 1911–1937*, 191–201.

70. For the activities of these two revolutionary parties in the Lower Yangzi region, see Rankin, *Early Chinese Revolutionaries*.

71. "Xinhai Shanghai guangfu qianhou," 10–11; Ding, "Shanghai Capitalists before the 1911 Revolution," 66–74; SZZZ, 1:94–95, 120, 125.

72. Kojima, "The Chinese National Association and the 1911 Revolution," 177–82; *Xinwen bao*, March 13, May 19, and July 13, 1911; SZZZ, 1:125; Yang Yi, *Shanghai shi zizhizhi*, donshihui zhiyuanbiao, 1a.

73. Ding, "Shanghai Capitalists before the 1911 Revolution," 70–71; *Mili bao*, June 11, 12 and 17, 1911; July 6, 1911; *Shibao*, July 12, 1910. For a short biography of Chu, see Rankin, *Elite Activism and Political Transformation in China*, 374n57.

74. *Shibao*, July 6, 1911; *Minli bao*, July 18, 1911; *Quan-Zhe gongbao*, July 8 and 11, 1911.

75. Li Pingshu, *Li Pingshu qishi zixu*, 58–59; Shanghai shehui kexueyuan lishi yanjiusuo, *Xinhai geming zai Shanghai shiliao*, 149–52, 203–5.

76. Shanghai shehui kexueyuan lishi yanjiusuo, *Xinhai geming zai Shanghai shiliao*, 136, 285–88, 307–9, 537, 617–20; Zhongguo shixuehui, *Xinhai geming*, 7:48–49; SZZZ, 1:95, 125; "Xinhai Shanghai guangfu qianhou," 7–8; Xu and Li, "Zhengduo Hu-jun dudu xianchang mujiji," 29–31. These sources date the electoral meeting to November 4 or 6, but the meeting was evidently held on November 6 because the election results appeared in Shanghai's newspapers on the following day. There are also disputes over whether Chen became the military governor because his fellows intimidated other attendees with weapons. The cited sources show that Chen was first elected as the commander

of military administration (*junzhengzhang*), and his fellows made him the military governor through intimidation at the end of the meeting. In any case, Chen's government enjoyed strong support from Shanghai elite merchants at its beginning.

77. Shanghai shehui kexueyuan lishi yanjiusuo, *Xinhai geming zai Shanghai shiliao*, 290, 414–16, 614–20, 624–25, 983; *Shenbao*, November 20, 1911; Xu and Qian, *Shanghai zongshanghui shi, 1902–1929*, 161; Zhongguo shixuehui, *Xinhai geming*, 7:45.

78. Shanghai shehui kexueyuan lishi yanjiusuo, *Xinhai geming zai Shanghai shiliao*, 154–55, 165; Yangzhou shifan xueyuan lishixi, *Xinhai geming Jiangsu diqu shiliao*, 217–19, 230–31; Li Pingshu, *Li Pingshu qishi zixu*, 58; NGST: I, 4:4b–5a, 25b.

79. Zhongguo shixuehui, *Xinhai geming*, 7:129–34, 154–56; Wu Xinmu, "Xinhai geming shiqi de Xiashi shangtuan," 170–73; NGST: I, 4:32a; *Haining zhou zhigao*, 40:28a.

80. Zhengxie Zhejiang sheng Xiaoshan shi weiyuanhui wenshi gongzuo weiyuanhui, *Tang Shouqian shiliao zhuanji*, 200–201; *Shenzhou ribao*, November 7, 1911; *Shenbao*, November 2, 5, 27, and 28, December 2–5 and 12, 1911.

81. Lin, "Ningbo guangfu qinliji," 175–80; Wei, "Xinhai Ningbo guangfu de huiyi," 205–17; Zhongguo shixuehui, *Xinhai geming*, 7:161–63.

82. For a discussion of the Suzhou-initiated pattern of peaceful revolution and its influence on other provinces, see Wang Laidi, "The 'Peaceful Independence' of the Constitutionalists and the 1911 Revolution," 4–15.

83. Yangzhou shifan xueyuan lishixi, *Xinhai geming Jiangsu diqu shiliao*, 127; Zhang Jian, *Zhang Jian quanji*, 1:175–7, 180; 6:658–61; Wang Laidi, "The 'Peaceful Independence' of the Constitutionalists and the 1911 Revolution," 8.

84. SSDC, 657–59, 1155–70, 1291–305; Ye, *Yuandulu rijichao*, 14:36b–38b; Zhang, Zhu, Zu, and Ye, *Suzhou Shangtuan dang'an*, 1:233.

85. Yangzhou shifan xueyuan lishixi, *Xinhai geming Jiangsu diqu shiliao*, 54–56, 123; Zhongguo shixuehui, *Xinhai geming*, 7:5–6; Zhang Guogan, *Xinhai geming shiliao*, 228–29.

86. Zhongguo shixuehui, *Xinhai geming*, 7:5–6; Yangzhou shifan xueyuan lishixi, *Xinhai geming Jiangsu diqu shiliao*, 117, 125; Ye, *Yuandulu rijichao*, 14:39a.

87. Zhongguo shixuehui, *Xinhai geming*, 7:8.

88. Changzhoushi minjian and Gongshanglian wenshi ziliao ban'gongshi, "Wujin xian shanghui ji gongshangye fazhan shiluo," 104, 110–11; Yangzhou shifan xueyuan lishixi, *Xinhai geming Jiangsu diqu shiliao*, 152–53, 157.

89. Changzhoushi minjian and Gongshanglian wenshi ziliao ban'gongshi, "Wujin xian shanghui ji gongshangye fazhan shiluo," 111, 118; Yangzhou shifan xueyuan lishixi, *Xinhai geming Jiangsu diqu shiliao*, 153–54, 159–61.

90. Yangzhou shifan xueyuan lishixi, *Xinhai geming Jiangsu diqu shiliao*, 266–68, 291–92; Bian and Tang, *Minguo renwu beizhuanji*, 232; Zhongguo shixuehui, *Xinhai geming*, 7:266.

91. Yangzhou shifan xueyuan lishixi, *Xinhai geming Jiangsu diqu shiliao*, 254–57, 261, 268–70, 278–79, 287; Bian and Tang, *Minguo renwu beizhuanji*, 232; Zhongguo shixuehui, *Xinhai geming*, 7:266–67.

92. Yangzhou shifan xueyuan lishixi, *Xinhai geming Jiangsu diqu shiliao*, 253, 294–96, 302–3, 305–6.

93. Ibid., 287, 298, 303–9, 320–28.

94. Ibid., 130–32, 177–81; Zhang Pengyuan, *Lixianpai yu Xinhai geming*, 260, 314.

95. *Jiading xian xuzhi*, 2:38b, juanmo, 1a–4a.

Chapter 7

1. Zhongguo shixuehui, *Xinhai geming*, 8:4–5, 8; Liu Xingnan, "Xinhai gesheng daibiao huiyi rizhi," 248–49, 252.

2. Zhonghua minguo kaiguo wushinian wenxian bianzuan weiyuanhui, *Zhonghua minguo kaiguo wushinian wenxian*, 104.

3. Zhang Jian, *Zhang Jian quanji*, 6:661–62; *Shibao*, January 19, 1912.

4. Zhongguo renmin yinhang Shanghai shi fenhang, *Shanghai qianzhuang shiliao*, 71; Shanghai shehui kexueyuan lishi yanjiusuo, *Xinhai geming zai Shanghai shiliao*, 429–31; *Xinwen bao*, March 28, 1912; SZZZ, 1:117, 119; *Shanghai zongshanghui baogaolu*, wendu 17–20. Under pressure of the Shanghai GCC, Yuan Shikai's regime repaid the loan with bonds in 1913.

5. Shanghai shehui kexueyuan lishi yanjiusuo, *Xinhai geming zai Shanghai shiliao*, 535–37, 617, 983; Gao and Yan, *Jindai Wuxi cansiye ziliao xuanji*, 36–37; *Xinwen bao*, February 11, 1912.

6. SZZZ, 1:126–33; Shanghai shehui kexueyuan lishi yanjiusuo, *Xinhai geming zai Shanghai shiliao*, 725–26. The Chinese title of the new general chamber, *Shanghai zongshanghui*, is very similar to that of the preexisting Shanghai GCC.

7. Ma and Zhu, *Chuantong yu jindai de er'chong bianzou*, 423–32; Ma and Zu, *Suzhou shanghui dang'an congbian*, 576, 595–610.

8. Zhang Jian, *Zhang Jian quanji*, 6:877; *Shibao*, January 19 and February 3, 1912; Xu and Qian, *Shanghai zongshanghui shi, 1902–1929*, 187; Zhou, *Xinhai geming ziliao huiji*, 5:305.

9. *Xinwen bao*, March 9, 1912.

10. Yu, *Shanghui yu Zhongguo zaoqi xiandaihua*, 296; Xu and Qian, *Shanghai zongshanghui shi, 1902–1929*, 165–66.

11. For the attitude toward Yuan among revolutionaries and the public opinion on the capital issue in early 1912, see Young, "Yuan Shih-k'ai's Rise to the Presidency," 420–23, 436–40.

12. *Minguo chunian quanguo gongshang huiyi baogaolu*, 23–33, 37–52.

13. TSDH, 1:291–99; *Shanghai zongshanghui baogaolu*, wendu 21–23, yi'an 3, 5, 15; Yu, *Shanghui yu Zhongguo zaoqi xiandaihua*, 108–9.

14. *Minguo chunian quanguo gongshang huiyi baogaolu*, 116–58, esp. 147–55; TSDH, 1:206–97; Zhu, *Zhuanxing shiqi de shehui yu guojia*, 477–82.

5. Tianjin shi dang'anguan, Tianjin shehui kexueyuan lishi yanjiusuo, and Tianjin shi ongshangye lianhehui, *Tianjin shanghui dang'an huibian, 1912–1928*, 4:4411–26; Chen and Wang, *Tianjin shi Lishi bowuguan cang Beiyang junfa shiliao*, 719–21.

16. Shanghai shi gongshangye lianhehui, *Shanghai zongshanghui yishilu*, 1:38; Yu, *Shanghui yu Zhongguo zaoqi xiandaihua*, 108–9.

17. Young, *The Presidency of Yuan Shih-k'ai*, 113–14, 129–37, 148–52.

18. Shanghai shi gongshangye lianhehui, *Shanghai zongshanghui yishilu*, 1:351–53, 364–66; 2:491–95, 508–9, 518–19; Zhu, *Zhuanxing shiqi de shehui yu guojia*, 462–82.

19. Yu, *Shanghui yu Zhongguo zaoqi xiandaihua*, 306–11.

20. Duara, *Culture, Power, and the State*, 43.

21. Close, "The Chinese Chamber-Power for Progress," 37, 40–41.

22. Fewsmith, *Party, State, and Local Elites in Republican China*, 130–65; Xu and Qian, *Shanghai Zongshanghui shi, 1902–1929*, 390–401; SZZZ, 2:534–656.

23. Yu, *Shanghui yu Zhongguo zaoqi xiandaihua*, 334, 366; Xu and Qian, *Shanghai zongshanghui shi, 1902–1929*, 400–401; Xiaobo Zhang, "Merchant Associational Activism in Early Twentieth-Century China," 685–86.

24. Tsin, *Nation, Governance, and Modernity in China*, 10, 18–19.

Conclusion

1. Miller, *The Moral Foundations of Social Institutions*, 12.

2. The increasing integration of the Chinese bourgeoisie within the institutional context of chambers of commerce is especially stressed by Yu's *Shanghui yu Zhongguo zaoqi xiandaihua*, 99–123.

3. On the power struggles among Lower Yangzi elites in the late Qing educational reforms and self-government movement, see Keenan, *Imperial China's Last Classical Academies*, 125–40; Thompson, *China's Local Councils in the Age of Constitutional Reform, 1898–1911*, 137–61.

4. Esherick, *Reform and Revolution in China*, 215, 257–58.

5. Rhoads, *China's Republican Revolution*, 276–77.

6. For a critique of Huang's concept of the third realm, see R. Bin Wong, "Great Expectations," 37–39.

7. For a critical review of previous scholarship on this subject, see Wakeman, "The Civil Society and Public Sphere Debate," 108–38.

8. Xiaoqun Xu, *Chinese Professionals and the Republican State*, 1, 15–16. Xu regards the mutual legitimization of the Republican governments and professional associations as an example of their interdependence, but these associations also used their social legitimacy to challenge state authorities, as previous chapters have shown.

9. Ma Min, "Cong gongshanglian dao shanghui," 74, 81.

10. Yu, Wang, Huang, and Li, *Minjian shanghui yu difang zhengfu*, 74–76, 183–84.

Character List

Anhui　安徽

banghang huiyou　帮行会友

banshi zongdong　办事总董

baoanhui　保安会

Baohuanghui　保皇会

Bei Runsheng　贝润生

benbu　本部

Cai Song　蔡松

Canshihui　参事会

Canyiyuan　参议院

changhui　常会

Changlu yanyunsi　长芦盐运司

Changshu　常熟

Changzhou (prefecture)　常州

Changzhou (county)　长洲

Chaozhou　潮州

Chaye huiguan　茶业会馆

Chen Gan (Shengjiao)　陈淦（笙郊）

Chen Guojun　陈国钧

Chen Kuilong　陈夔龙

Chen Qimei　陈其美

Chen Runfu　陈潤夫

Chen Ziqin　陈子琴

Cheng　呈

Cheng Dequan　程德全

chengguan gongjian　呈官公建

Chenghuangmiao　城隍庙

Chu Fucheng　褚辅成

chupinsuo　出品所

chupin xiehui　出品协会

Chuzhou　处州

Cixi　慈禧

dan　石

Danyang　丹阳

daotai　道台

Da-Qing yinhang　大清银行

daxueshi　大学士

Dianbao zongju　电报总局

diecheng　牒呈

Difang gongyi yanjiuhui　地方公益研究会

Difang zizhi yanjiuhui　地方自治研究会

difang zizhiju　地方自治局

Ding Jiahou　丁价候

Ding Zhongli　丁中立

Dinghai　定海

Dongnancheng difang lianhehui　东南城地方联合会

dongshi　董事

Dongtangshi　东唐市

Dongya bingfu　东亚病夫
Douye gongsuo-Cuixiutang
　豆业公所萃秀堂
duan'an　断案
Duanfang　端方
Duzhibu　度支部
Fan Gongxu　樊恭煦
Fang Huan　方还
faren shetuan　法人社团
Fenghua　奉化
Fengxian　奉贤
Fotang　佛堂
fu　府
Fujian　福建
fusheng　附生
Fuzhou　福州
Fuzongli　副总理
Gangyi　刚毅
Ganyu　赣榆
Gao Baoquan　高宝铨
Gao De　高德
Gao Shan　高山
Gaoyou　高邮
Ge Pengyun　戈朋云
geren huiyou　个人会友
Gezhi shuyuan　格致书院
gongche shangshu　公车上书
Gongchenqiao　拱宸桥
gonghang xiansheng　公行先生
gonghui　公会
Gongshangbu　工商部
gongsheng　贡生
Gongsifa　公司法
gongsuo　公所
gongtuan　公团
Gu Hongzao　顾鸿藻
Gu Songqing　顾松庆
Gu Xinyi (Lügui)　顾馨一（履桂）
Gu Zhao　顾钊
guandu shangban　官督商办
Guang-Zhao gongsuo　广肇公所
Guangdong　广东
Guangfuhui　光复会

Guangxi　广西
Guangxu　光绪
Guangzhou　广州
Guanqianjie shimin gongshe
　观前街市民公社
guanshang heban　官商合办
guanxi　关系
Gui Hanxiang　贵翰香
Guo Songtao　郭松焘
Guomindang　国民党
guominhui　国民会
guominjun　国民军
Haimen　海门
Haizhou　海州
Hang Zuliang (Xiaoxuan)
　杭祖良（筱轩）
Hangzhou　杭州
Hangzhou shangxue gonghui
　杭州商学公会
Hankou　汉口
Henan　河南
Hong Yulin　洪毓麟
Hu Shoukang　胡寿康
Hu Shouzang　胡寿臧
Hu Zaoqing (Huan)　胡藻青（焕）
Huai'an　淮安
Huashang gongyihui　华商公议会
Huashang ticaohui　华商体操会
Huating　华亭
huiban shangwu dachen　会办商务大臣
huiguan　会馆
huiyou　会友
huiyuan　会员
huizhang　会长
Huizhou　徽州
Hunan　湖南
Hunan shangwu fenhui　沪南商务分会
Hunan shangwu fensuo　沪南商务分所
Huxuehui　沪学会
Huzhou　湖州
Jiading　嘉定
Jiang Bingzhang　蒋炳章
Jiang Yixiu　江义修

Jiang-Zhe lianjun　江浙联军
Jiang-Zhe xiehui　江浙协会
Jiangdu　江都
Jiangnan shangwu gonghui
　　江南商务公会
Jiangnan shangwu zongju　江南商务总局
Jiangnan zhizaoju　江南制造局
Jiangning　江宁
Jiangsu　江苏
Jiangsu jiaoyu zonghui　江苏教育总会
Jiangsu tielu xiehui　江苏铁路协会
Jiangsu xuehui　江苏学会
Jiangsu xuewu zonghui　江苏学务总会
Jiangsu ziyiju　江苏谘议局
Jiangxi　江西
Jiangxi ciqi gongsi　江西瓷器公司
Jiangyan　姜堰
Jiangye gongsuo　酱业公所
Jiangyin　江阴
jiansheng　监生
jianyifa　简易法
Jiaxing　嘉兴
Jiazheng gailiang yanjiuhui
　　家政改良研究会
jijuren　寄居人
jimi toutongfa　机密投筒法
Jin Yuesheng　金月笙
Jing Yuanshan　经元善
Jingxi　荆溪
Jinkui　金匮
jinshi　进士
Jintan　金坛
ju　局
junji dachen　军机大臣
junzhengzhang　军政长
juren　举人
Kang Youwei　康有为
Kuaiji　会稽
Kun-Xin choubei zizhi gongsuo
　　昆新筹备自治公所
Kunshan　昆山
Lan Weiwen　蓝蔚雯
Li Hongxiang　李鸿祥

Li Hongzhang　李鸿章
Li Houyou　李厚佑
Li Qingzhao　李庆钊
Li Shuxun　李树勋
Li Tingbang　李廷榜
Li Weizhuang　李薇庄
Li Xieqing　李屑青
Li Yongshang　李咏裳
Li Zhengwu　李征五
Li Zhongjue (Pingshu)　李钟珏（平书）
Liang Cheng　梁诚
Liang Qichao　梁启超
Liangguang　两广
Liangjiang　两江
lianluo　联络
lijin　厘金
Lin Jingzhou　林景周
Linghu　菱湖
Lingnan huiguan　岭南会馆
lingxiu huiyou　领袖会友
lingxiu zongdong　领袖总董
Linshi canyiyuan　临时参议院
Lishenji　李慎记
lishu　隶属
Liu Guixin　刘桂馨
Liu Kunyi　刘坤一
Liu Shihang　刘士珩
Liu Xiejun　刘燮钧
Liyang　溧阳
Lu Runxiang　陆润庠
Lujiabang　菉葭浜
Lukou　禄口
Lumu　陆墓
Lunchuan zhaoshangju　轮船招商局
Luodian　罗店
Ma Jianzhong　马建忠
Ma Xiangbo　马相伯
Mao Zumo　毛祖模
Meili　梅里
miaojun　庙捐
Mimai zaliang gongsuo-Rengutang
　　米麦杂粮公所仁谷堂
mimaishui　米麦税

mingwang huiyuan　名望会员

mingyu huizhang　名誉会长

mingyu yiyuan　名誉议员

minzheng shiwusuo　民政事务所

Minzhengbu　民政部

minzhu dangpai　民主党派

Miye gongsuo-Jiagutang
　米业公所嘉谷堂

Nanbang huiye gongsuo
　南帮汇业公所

Nanjing　南京

Nanjing linshi zhengfu　南京临时政府

Nanshi shangtuan gonghui
　南市商团公会

Nanxiang　南翔

Nanxiang xuehui　南翔学会

Nanyang dachen　南洋大臣

Nanyang quanyehui　南洋劝业会

Nanyang'an　南洋岸

Neige　内阁

Neiyuan　内园

Ni Kaiding　倪开鼎

Ni Sijiu　倪思九

nianhui　年会

Ningbo　宁波

Nonggongshang bu　农工商部

nonghui　农会

nongtuan　农团

Pan Chiwen　潘赤文

Pan Tingcong　潘廷枞

Pan Zuqian　潘祖谦

Pang Yuanji　庞元济

Peng Fusun　彭福孙

Pingwang　平望

Qiangxuehui　强学会

Qianye zonggongsuo　钱业总公所

Qin Yunbing　秦运炳

Qing　清

Qingjiangpu　清江浦

Qingpu　青浦

Qixiang gongsuo　七襄公所

Quanguo nongwu lianhehui
　全国农务联合会

Quanguo shangtuan gonghui
　全国商团公会

quanxuesuo　劝学所

Quanzhou　泉州

renjuan　认捐

Rugao　如皋

Ruian　瑞安

Sanshan gongsuo　三山公所

Sha Yuanbing　沙元炳

Shaanxi　陕西

Shangbai　上栢

Shangban　商办

Shangbu　商部

Shangchuan huiguan　商船会馆

Shangfa zongze　商法总则

Shanghai beishi qianye huiguan
　上海北市钱业会馆

Shanghai cheng zizhi gongsuo
　上海城自治公所

Shanghai chengxiang neiwai
　zonggongcheng ju
　上海城厢内外总工程局

Shanghai renjitang　上海仁济堂

Shanghai shangtuan gonghui
　上海商团公会

Shanghai shangwu fenju　上海商务分局

Shanghai shangwuju　上海商务局

Shanghai shangye huiyi gongsuo
　上海商业会议公所

Shanghai xiezhen gongsuo
　上海协赈公所

Shanghai Yaxiya xiehui fenhui
　上海亚细亚协会分会

shanghui　商会

Shanghuifa　商会法

shanghui gongsuo　商会公所

Shangmin xiehui　商民协会

shangwu dachen　商务大臣

shangwu fenhui　商务分会

shangwu fenju　商务分局

shangwu fensuo　商务分所

Shangwu guanbao　商务官报

shangwuju　商务局

shangwu zonghui　商务总会

shangwu zongju　商务总局

Shangxue gonghui　商学公会

shangxuehui　商学会

shangye caipansuo　商业裁判所

shangye zonghui huiguan　商业总会会馆

shangye zonghui xieguan　商业总会协馆

Shangyu xuehui　商余协会

shanju zongdong　善局总董

shantang　善堂

Shanxi　山西

Shanyin　山阴

Shao Qintao　邵琴涛

Shao Xi　邵羲

Shaoxing　绍兴

Shen Manyun (Maozhao)　沈缦云　(懋昭)

Shen Shoulian　沈守廉

Shenbao　申报

Shendong　绅董

sheng　省

Sheng Pingzhi　盛萍旨

Sheng Xuanhuai　盛宣怀

Shengshi Weiyan　盛世危言

Shengze　盛泽

Shenshang　绅商

Shenshi　绅士

Shi Ying　施莹

Shi Zejing (Ziying)　施则敬　(子英)

Shibao　时报

shizhang　市长

Shuanglin　双林

Sichuan　四川

sijuan　丝捐

Siming gongsuo　四明公所

sinian dongshi　司年董事

sishi　司事

Sishu gailianghui　私塾改良会

Siye huiguan　丝业会馆

siyue dongshi　司月董事

Song Enquan　宋恩铨

Song Hanzhang　宋汉章

Song Jiaoren　宋教仁

Songjiang　松江

Su Benyan　苏本炎

Su-Zhe tielu dongshiju lianhehui　苏浙铁路董事局联合会

Sujing sichang　苏经丝厂

Sujun jiye gongsuo　苏郡机业公所

Sulun shachang　苏纶纱厂

Sun Duosen　孫多森

Sun Duoxin　孫多鑫

Sun Tiansheng　孙天生

Sun Yirang　孙诒让

Sunduan　孙端

Sushang tiyuhui　苏商体育会

Susheng difang zizhi diaocha yanjiuhui　苏省地方自治调查研究会

Susheng nonggongshangwu ju　苏省农工商务局

Susheng tielu gongsi　苏省铁路公司

Sushu shanghui lianhehui　苏属商会联合会

Suzhou　苏州

Suzhou jukuanhui　苏州拒款会

Suzhou nongwu zonghui　苏州农务总会

Suzhou xuewu gongsuo　苏州学务公所

Taicang　太仓

Taizhou (prefecture)　台州

Taizhou (county)　泰州

Tan Sitong　谭嗣同

Tang Shouqian　汤寿潜

tebie geren huiyou　特别个人会友

tebie huiyuan　特别会员

tehui　特会

Tianjin　天津

ticaohui　体操会

tidiao　提调

timian　体面

ting　厅

Tinglin　亭林

tixueshi　提学使

Tong-Chong-Hai huaye zonghui　通崇海花业总会

Tong-Chong-Hai-Tai shangwu zonghui　通崇海泰商务总会

tong guanshang zhiyou　通官商之邮

tongjuan　统捐

Tongmenghui   同盟会

Tongren fuyuantang   同仁辅元堂

tongshang gonghui   通商公会

Tongzhou   通州

Tongzhou nongwu fenhui
    通州农务分会

waiwei chengyuan   外围成员

Waiwubu   外务部

Wang Dajun   汪大钧

Wang Kangnian   汪康年

Wang Pengyun   王鹏运

Wang Qingmu   王清穆

Wang Tao   王韬

Wang Tongyu   王同愈

Wang Weiliang   王维亮

Wang Weitai   王维泰

Wang Xifan   王锡蕃

Wang Xirong (Xiangquan)
    王锡荣 （湘泉）

Wang Yudian   王禹甸

Wang Zhen   王震

wangluo   网络

weichi gongyi   维持公益

wen   文

Wenzhou   温州

Wu   吴

Wu Chuanji   吴传基

Wu Enyuan   吴恩元

Wu Qing   吴清

Wu Zhaoen (Zemin)   吴兆恩 （泽民）

wuchanhui   物产会

Wuhan   武汉

Wujiang   吴江

Wukang   武康

wusheng   武生

Wusong   吴淞

Wuxi   无锡

Xiamen   厦门

xian   县

Xiashi   硖石

Xibeicheng difang lianhehui
    西北城地方联合会

Xie Lunhui   谢纶辉

xiezan hui   协赞会

Xin Zhongguo bao   新中国报

Xincheng yinhang   信成银行

Xinghua   兴化

Xinyang   新阳

Xinzheng   新政

xiucai   秀才

Xu Baoshan   徐宝山

Xu Dinglin   许鼎霖

Xu Guangpu   徐光溥

Xu Run   徐润

xuanjuju   选举局

Xuebu   学部

xuehui   学会

xuewu gongsuo   学务公所

xuezheng   学政

Yan Xinhou   严信厚

Yan Yibin   严义彬

Yancheng   盐城

Yang Shiqi   杨士琦

Yang Xinzhi   杨信之

Yangzhou   扬州

Yangzi   扬子

Yanzhou   严州

Yao Wennan   姚文枏

Ye Huijun   叶惠钧

Yexie   叶榭

yi   移

yidong   议董

Yihui   议会

yinhuashui   印花税

Yiwu   义乌

Yixing   宜兴

yiyuan (deliberative members)   议员

yiyuan (parliament)   议院

yizhang   议长

Yongqin gongsuo   咏勤公所

You Xianjia   尤先甲

youcanyi   右参议

Youchuanbu   邮传部

Yu Dingyi   于定一

Yu Dingyuan   于鼎源

Yu Pinghan (Huaizhi)   郁屏翰 （怀智）

Yu Qiaqing   虞洽卿

Yuan Shikai   袁世凯

Yuan Shuxun   袁树勋

Yuanfengrun yinhao   源丰潤银号

Yuanhe   元和

Yubei lixian gonghui   预备立宪公会

Yun Yuding   恽毓鼎

Yun Zuqi   恽祖祁

Yunjin gongsuo   云锦公所

Yuyingtang   育婴堂

Yuyuan   豫园

Zaifeng   载沣

Zeng Zhu   曾铸

zha   札

Zhang Cha   张察

Zhang Guang'en (Youqi)   张广恩 （右企）

Zhang Jian   张謇

Zhang Lejun (Jianian)   张乐君 （嘉年）

Zhang Lüqian (Yuejie)   张履谦 （月阶）

Zhang Yugao   张遇高

Zhang Zhenxiang   张振庠

Zhang Zhidong   张之洞

Zhangyan   张堰

Zhangzhou   漳州

Zhaoqing   肇庆

Zhaowen   昭文

Zhe-Ning huiguan   浙宁会馆

Zhejiang   浙江

Zhejiang guomin jukuan gonghui
    浙江国民拒款公会

Zhejiang tielu gongsi   浙江铁路公司

Zhejiang ziyiju   浙江谘议局

Zhendetang   振德堂

Zheng Guanying   郑观应

Zheng Xianzi   郑贤滋

Zhenjiang   镇江

Zhenkang   镇康

Zhenwu zongshe   振武宗社

Zhenze   震泽

Zhifu (Yantai)   芝罘 （烟台）

zhihui   支会

zhiliting   直隶厅

zhilizhou   直隶州

Zhong Tianwei   钟天纬

Zhongguo guomin zonghui
    中国国民总会

Zhongguo huashang yinhang
    中国华商银行

Zhongguo tongshang yinhang
    中国通商银行

Zhonghua minguo   中华民国

Zhonghua quanguo shanghui lianhehui
    中华全国商会联合会

Zhonghua yinhang   中华银行

Zhongyiyuan   众议院

zhou   州

Zhou Jinbiao   周晋镳

Zhou Shiheng   周世恒

Zhou Shunian   周树年

Zhou Tingbi   周廷弼

Zhu Baosan   朱葆三

Zhu Dachun   祝大椿

Zhu Jinshou   朱金绶

Zhu Wulou   朱五楼

Zhuangyuan   状元

zhu-Hu diaochayuan   驻沪调查员

ziyiju   谘议局

Zizhengyuan   资政院

zizhihui   自治会

zongban   总办

zongdong   总董

zongli   总理

Zongli yamen   总理衙门

zongshiwu suo   总事务所

Zou Zongqi   邹宗琪

zuoban   坐办

Bibliography

Rare Sources

This section lists unpublished archival materials and other rare sources that are frequently cited by this book but have been rarely or never been used by previous studies. Their institutional holders are indicated by the following English titles:

Fudan University Library (Fudan daxue tushuguan)
Nantong Municipal Archives (Nantong shi dang'anguan)
Shanghai Academy of Social Sciences (Shanghai Shehui kexueyuan)
Shanghai History Museum (Shanghai shi lishi bowuguan)
Shanghai Municipal Archives (Shanghai shi dang'anguan)
Shanghai Union of Industry and Commerce (Shanghai shi gongshangye lianhehui)
Suzhou Municipal Archives (Suzhou shi dang'anguang)

Shanghai shangwu zonghui tongrenlu: Bingwunian (Register of the Shanghai General Chamber of Commerce, 1906). Shanghai, 1906. Fudan University Library.
Shanghai shangwu zonghui tongrenlu: Dingweinian (Register of the Shanghai General Chamber of Commerce, 1907). Shanghai, 1908. Fudan University Library.
Shanghai shangwu zonghui tongrenlu: Gengxunian (Register of the Shanghai General Chamber of Commerce, 1910). Shanghai, 1910. Fudan University Library.
Shanghai shangwu zonghui tongrenlu: Jiyounian (Register of the Shanghai General Chamber of Commerce, 1909). Shanghai, 1909. Fudan University Library.
Shanghai shangwu zonghui tongrenlu: Xinhainian (Register of the Shanghai General Chamber of Commerce, 1911). Shanghai, 1911. Fudan University Library.
Shanghai wanguo guanshang shishen zhiye zhuzhilu (Occupations and addresses of Chinese and foreign officials, merchants, and gentry in Shanghai). Shanghai: Gongyi shushe, 1908. Shanghai History Museum.
Shanghai [Western] General Chamber of Commerce. *Annual Report for 1868–69.* Shanghai, 1870. Shanghai Municipal Archives.

———. *Annual Report for 1869–70*. Shanghai, 1871. Shanghai Municipal Archives.

———. *Annual Report for 1876*. Shanghai, 1877. Shanghai Municipal Archives.

———. *Annual Report for 1880*. Shanghai, 1881. Shanghai Municipal Archives.

———. *Annual Report for 1890*. Shanghai, 1891. Shanghai Municipal Archives.

———. *Annual Report for 1891*. Shanghai, 1892. Shanghai Municipal Archives.

———. *Annual Report for 1892*. Shanghai, 1893. Shanghai Municipal Archives.

———. *Annual Report for 1896*. Shanghai, 1897. Shanghai Municipal Archives.

———. *Annual Report for 1897*. Shanghai, 1898. Shanghai Municipal Archives.

———. *Annual Report for 1900*. Shanghai, 1901. Shanghai Municipal Archives.

———. *Minutes of a General Meeting, December 31, 1869*. Shanghai, 1870. Shanghai Municipal Archives.

———. *Minutes of the Annual General Meeting, November 26, 1869*. Shanghai, 1870. Shanghai Municipal Archives.

———. *Minutes of the Annual General Meeting on March 31, 1898*. Shanghai, 1899. Shanghai Municipal Archives.

———. *Report of the Committee of the Shanghai General Chamber of Commerce for the Year Ended 31 December 1904 and Minutes of the Annual General Meeting of Members Held on 27 March 1905*. Shanghai, 1905. Shanghai Municipal Archives.

"Shouxian Sunshi jingying Fufeng mianfenchang ji youguan caituan suoshu qiye shiliaogao" (Draft history of the Sun lineage of Shou county, its Fufeng Flour Mill and other enterprises under its financial group). Shanghai Union of Industry and Commerce, archival no. (juanhao): 159.

"Sulu gongsi wubaigu yishang gudong mingdan" (The Jiangsu Railroad Company's register of holders of more than 500 shares of stock). Nantong Municipal Archives, Sectional no. (quanzonghao): B401, Index no. (muluhao): 111, vol. 24.

"Suzhou shanghui dang'an" (Archival materials concerning Suzhou chambers of commerce). Suzhou Municipal Archives, Sectional no. (quanzonghao): 2. 2, Index no. (muluhao): 1.

Zizhihui, ed. *Nanxiang jinshi diaochalu* (Surveys of current affairs in Nanxiang). n.p., n.d. Shanghai Academy of Social Sciences.

Other Sources

Arnold, Julean. *China: A Commercial and Industrial Handbook*. Washington, DC: Government Printing Office, 1926.

Associated Chambers of Commerce of the Pacific Coast. *A Visit to China*. San Francisco, 1911.

Bao Tianxiao. *Chuanyinglou huiyilu* (Reminiscences of the bracelet shadow chamber). Hong Kong: Dahua chubanshe, 1971.

Baoshan xian xuzhi (Continuation of Baoshan county gazetteer). N.p., 1921.

Bergère, Marie-Claire. *The Golden Age of the Chinese Bourgeoisie, 1911–1937*. Cambridge: Cambridge University Press, 1989.

———. "The Role of the Bourgeoisie." In Wright, ed., *China in Revolution*, 229–95.

Bian Xiaoxuan and Tang Wenquan, eds. *Minguo renwu beizhuanji* (Collection of grave inscriptions of personages of Republican China). Beijing: Tuanji chubanshe, 1995.

Brunnert, H. S., and V. V. Hagelstrom. *Present Day Political Organization of China*, trans. A. Beltchenko. Shanghai: Kelly and Walsh, 1912; repr., New York: Paragon Book Gallery, n.d.

Cai Song. *Shuanglin zhenzhi xinbu* (Supplement to the gazetteer of Shuanglin town). In *Zhongguo difangzhi jicheng: Xiangzhenzhi zhuanji* (Chinese gazetteer series: Special collection of township gazetteers), vol. 22, part 2. Nanjing: Jiangsu guji chubanshe, 1992.

Cameron, Meribeth E. *The Reform Movement in China, 1898–1912.* Stanford, CA: Stanford University Press, 1931.

Chan, Wellington K. K. *Merchants, Mandarins, and Modern Enterprise in Late Ch'ing China.* Cambridge, MA: East Asian Research Center, Harvard University, 1977.

Chang Chung-li. *The Chinese Gentry: Studies on Their Role in Nineteenth-Century Chinese Society.* Seattle: University of Washington Press, 1955.

———. *The Income of the Chinese Gentry.* Seattle: University of Washington Press, 1962.

Changzhoushi minjian and Gongshanglian wenshi ziliao ban'gongshi. "Wujin xian shanghui ji gongshangye fazhan shiluo" (A brief history of the development of chambers of commerce, industries, and commerce in Wujin county). *Changzhou difang shiliao xuanbian* (Selected materials concerning the local history of Changzhou) 14 (1987): 101–39.

Ch'en, Jerome. *State Economic Policies of the Ch'ing Government, 1840–1895.* New York: Garland Publishing, 1980.

Chen, Zhongping. "Beneath the Republican Revolution, Beyond Revolutionary Politics: Elite Associations and Social Transformation in Lower Yangzi Towns, 1903–1912." *Late Imperial China* 28, no. 1 (2007): 92–127.

———. "Business and Politics: Chinese Chambers of Commerce in the Lower Yangzi Region, 1902–1912." PhD diss., University of Hawaii, 1998.

———. "The Rise of Chinese Chambers of Commerce in Late Qing: Elite Opinion and Official Policy." In Yen-P'ing Hao and Hsiu-Mei Wei, eds., *Tradition and Metamorphosis in Modern Chinese History*, vol. 2, 1091–113. Taibei: Academia Sinica, 1998.

Chen Baoliang. *Zhongguo de she yu hui* (Chinese social organizations). Hangzhou: Zhejiang renmin chubanshe, 1996.

Chen Ruifang and Wang Huijuan, eds. *Tianjin shi Lishi bowuguan cang Beiyang junfa shiliao: Yuan Shikai juan* (The Tianjin Municipal Museum's historical materials concerning the Beiyang warlords: The volume regarding Yuan Shikai). Tianjin: Tianjin guji chubanshe, 1992.

Cheng Xinjin. "Jiushidai de Hangzhou shanghui" (Hangzhou chambers of commerce in old times). *Zhejiang wenshi ziliao xuanji* (Selected materials concerning the culture and history of Zhejiang) 9 (1964): 121–51.

Chi, Madeleine. "Shanghai-Hangchow-Ningpo Railway Loan: A Case Study of the Rights Recovery Movement." *Modern Asian Studies* 7, no. 1 (1973): 85–106.

China: Imperial Maritime Customs. *Decennial Reports, 1892–1901.* Shanghai, 1906.

Chu, Samuel C. *Reformer in Modern China: Chang Chien, 1853–1926.* New York: Columbia University Press, 1965.

Close, Upton. "The Chinese Chamber-Power for Progress." *Transpacific* 3, no. 1 (1920): 37–42.

Cochran, Sherman. *Encountering Chinese Networks: Western, Japanese, and Chinese Corporations in China, 1880–1937.* Berkeley: University of California Press, 2000.

Dillon, Nara, and Jean C. Oi, eds. *At the Crossroads of Empires: Middlemen, Social Networks, and State-Building in Republican Shanghai.* Stanford, CA: Stanford University Press, 2008.

———. "Middlemen, Social Networks, and State-Building in Republican Shanghai." In Dillon and Oi, eds., *At the Crossroads of Empires*, 3–21.

Ding Richu. "Shanghai Capitalists before the 1911 Revolution." *Chinese Studies in History* 18, no. 3–4 (1985): 33–82.

Dittmer, Lowell. "Chinese Informal Politics." *The China Journal* 34 (1995): 1–34.

Dollar, Robert. *Memoirs of Robert Dollar*. San Francisco: W. S. Van Cott, 1918.

Dongfang zazhi (The Eastern miscellany). Shanghai, 1904–1912.

Du, Yongtao. "Translocal Lineage and the Romance of Homeland Attachment: The Pans of Suzhou in Qing China." *Late Imperial China* 27, no. 1 (2006): 37–65.

Du Xuncheng and Zhou Yuangao. "Summary of Studies of the Bourgeoisie since 1949." *Chinese Studies in History* 16, no. 3–4 (1983): 104–37.

Duara, Prasenjit. *Culture, Power, and the State: Rural North China, 1900–1942*. Stanford, CA: Stanford University Press, 1988.

Eastman, Lloyd E. *The Abortive Revolution: China under Nationalist Rule, 1927–1937*. Cambridge, MA: Harvard University Press, 1974.

Eitel, E. J. *Europe in China*. London, 1895; repr., Taibei, 1968.

Elvin, Mark. "The Administration of Shanghai, 1905–1914." In Elvin and Skinner, eds., *The Chinese City between Two Worlds*, 239–62.

———. "The Gentry Democracy in Chinese Shanghai, 1905–1914." In Jack Gray, ed., *Modern China's Search for a Political Form*, 41–65. London: Oxford University Press, 1969.

Elvin, Mark, and G. William Skinner, eds. *The Chinese City between Two Worlds*. Stanford, CA: Stanford University Press, 1974.

Esherick, Joseph W. "1911: A Review." *Modern China* 2, no. 2 (1976): 141–84.

———. *Reform and Revolution in China: The 1911 Revolution in Hunan and Hubei*. Berkeley: University of California Press, 1976.

Esherick, Joseph W., and Mary Backus Rankin, eds. *Chinese Local Elites and Patterns of Dominance*. Berkeley: University of California Press, 1990.

———. "Introduction." In Esherick and Rankin, eds., *Chinese Local Elites and Patterns of Dominance*, 1–24.

Fairbank, John King. *Trade and Diplomacy on the China Coast: The Opening of the Treaty Ports, 1842–1854*. Cambridge, MA: Harvard University Press, 1953.

Fairbank, John King, and S. Y. Teng, "On the Types and Uses of Ch'ing Documents." In John K. Fairbank and Ssu-Yu Teng, eds., *Ch'ing Administration: Three Studies*, 36–106. Cambridge, MA: Harvard University Press, 1961.

Fan Jinmin. *Ming-Qing Jiangnan shangye de fazhan* (Commercial development in Jiangnan during the Ming-Qing period). Nanjing: Nanjing daxue chubanshe, 1998.

Fang Zhiqin, ed. *Kang-Liang yu Baohuanghui: Tan Liang zai Meiguo suocang ziliao huibian* (Kang Youwei, Liang Qichao, and the Chinese Empire Reform Association: A collection of materials preserved by Tan Liang in the United States). Tianjin: Tianjin guji chubanshe, 1997.

Fei Xiaotong. *From the Soil: The Foundation of Chinese Society*, trans. Gary G. Hamilton and Wang Zheng. Berkeley: University of California Press, 1992.

Feng Xiaocai. "Zhongguo shanghuishi yanjiu zhi huigu yu fansi" (A review and reflection on historical studies of Chinese chambers of commerce). *Lishi yanjiu* (Journal of historical research) 5 (2001): 148–67.

Feuerwerker, Albert. *China's Early Industrialization: Sheng Hsuan-Huai (1844–1916) and Mandarin Enterprise*. Cambridge, MA: Harvard University Press, 1958.

Fewsmith, Joseph. *Party, State, and Local Elites in Republican China: Merchant Organizations and Politics in Shanghai, 1890–1930*. Honolulu: University of Hawaii Press, 1985.

Field, Margaret. "The Chinese Boycott of 1905." *Papers on China* 2 (1957): 63–98.

Fincher, John H. *Chinese Democracy: The Self-Government Movement in Local, Provincial and National Politics, 1905–1914.* Canberra: Australian National University Press, 1981.

Fu Rucheng, ed. *Jindai Zhongguo tielushi ziliao* (Historical materials concerning the railroad history of modern China). Beijing: Zhonghua shuju, 1963.

Fujii Masao. "Shimmatsu Kō-Setsu ni okeru tetsuro mondai to burujoa seiryoku no ichi sokumen" (The late Qing railroad issue in Jiangsu and Zhejiang and one aspect of the bourgeois power). *Rekishigaku kenkyū* (Journal of historical studies) 5 (1955): 22–30.

Fuma Susumu. *Chūgoku zenkai zendoshi kenkyū* (A study of charitable societies and halls in China). Kyoto: Dōhōsha, 1997.

Gao Jingyue and Yan Xuexi, eds. *Jindai Wuxi cansiye ziliao xuanji* (Selected materials concerning the cocoon and silk industries in modern Wuxi). Nanjing: Jiangsu renmin chubanshe and Jiangsu guji chubanshe, 1987.

Garrett, Shirley S. "The Chambers of Commerce and the YMCA." In Elvin and Skinner, eds., *The Chinese City between Two Worlds,* 213–38.

Ge Shirui, ed. *Huangchao jingshiwen xubian* (Continuation of collection of Qing statecraft essays). Shanghai, 1888.

Geisert, Bradley K. *Radicalism and Its Demise: The Chinese Nationalist Party, Factionalism, and Local Elites in Jiangsu Province, 1924–1931.* Ann Arbor: University of Michigan Center for Chinese Studies, 2001.

Gesheng shanghui dahui jishi (Record of the general conference of chambers of commerce from various provinces). N.p., 1910.

Golas, Peter J. "Early Ch'ing Guilds." In Skinner, ed., *The City in Late Imperial China,* 555–80.

Gold, Thomas, Doug Guthrie, and David Wank. "An Introduction to the Study of Guanxi." In Gold, Guthrie, and Wank, eds., *Social Connections in China,* 3–20.

———, eds. *Social Connections in China: Institutions, Culture, and the Changing Nature of Guanxi.* Cambridge: Cambridge University Press, 2002.

Gongshang xuebao (Journal of industrial and commercial learning). Shanghai, 1898.

Goodman, Bryna. *Native Place, City, and Nation: Regional Networks and Identities in Shanghai, 1853–1937.* Berkeley: University of California Press, 1995.

Gordon, Stewart. "Social Networking in Pre-Modern Asian History." *IIAS* (International Institute for Asian Studies) *Newsletter* 48 (2008): 16.

Grove, Linda. *A Chinese Economic Revolution: Rural Entrepreneurship in the Twentieth Century.* Lanham, MD: Rowman & Littlefield, 2006.

Gu Zhentao. *Wumen biaoyin* (Historical highlights of Suzhou). Nanjing: Jiangsu guji chubanshe, 1986.

Gugong bowuyuan Ming-Qing dang'anbu, ed. *Qingmo choubei lixian dang'an shiliao* (Archival materials concerning preparations for constitutional government at the end of the Qing dynasty). Beijing: Zhonghua shuju, 1979.

Guo Songtao. *Lundun yu Bali riji* (Diary in London and Paris). Changsha: Yuelu shushe, 1984.

Guohui qingyuan daibiao di'erci cheng Duchayuan daizoushu huilu (Collection of pleas for a parliament submitted via the Censorate by delegates during the second petition). N.p., n.d.

Guojia dang'anju Ming-Qing dang'anguan, ed. *Wuxu bianfa dang'an shiliao* (Archival materials concerning the 1898 Reform). Beijing: Zhonghua shuju, 1958.

Habermas, Jürgen. *The Structural Transformation of the Public Sphere: An Inquiry into a Category of Bourgeois Society.* Cambridge, MA: MIT Press, 1989.

Haining Xiashi zhenzhi banzuan weiyuanhui, ed. *Haining Xiashi zhenzhi* (Gazetteer of Xiashi town in Haining). Hangzhou: Zhejiang renmin chubanshe, 1992.

Haining zhou zhigao (Draft gazetteer of Haining department). N.p., 1922.

Hamilton, Gary G., ed. *Asian Business Networks.* Berlin: Walter de Gruyter, 1996.

Hangzhou shangye zazhi (Journal of Hangzhou commerce). Hangzhou, 1909.

He Bingdi. *Zhongguo huiguan shilun* (A historical survey of Chinese *landsmannschaften*). Taibei: Xuesheng shuju, 1966.

He Zuo, ed. "Yijiu lingwu nian fan-Mei aiguo yundong" (The anti-American and patriotic movement of 1905). *Jindaishi ziliao* (Historical materials concerning modern China) 1 (1956): 1–90.

Hinde, Robert. A. *Towards Understanding Relationships.* London: Academic Press, 1979.

Huang, Philip C. C. "'Public Sphere'/'Civil Society' in China? The Third Realm between State and Society." *Modern China* 19, no. 2 (1993): 216–40.

Huashang lianhebao (Journal of united Chinese merchants). Shanghai, 1909–1910.

Huashang lianhehui bao (Journal of the Chinese merchant confederation). Shanghai, 1910.

Hubei shangwubao (Commercial journal of Hubei Province). Wuchang, 1899–1900.

Hunan Shangwu Fenhui baogao timingce (Reports and register of the South Shanghai Affiliated Chamber of Commerce). N.p., n.d.

Ichiko, Chūzō. "The Role of the Gentry: An Hypothesis." In Wright, ed., *China in Revolution,* 297–317.

Ikegami, Eiko. *Bonds of Civility: Aesthetic Networks and the Political Origins of Japanese Culture.* New York: Cambridge University Press, 2005.

Ji, Zhaojin. *A History of Modern Shanghai Banking: The Rise and Decline of China's Finance Capitalism.* Armonk, NY: M. E. Sharpe, 2003.

Jia Zhongfu. *Zhong-Mei shangren tuanti yu jindai guomin waijiao, 1905–1927* (Chinese and American merchant groups and modern people's diplomacy, 1905–1927). Beijing: Zhongguo shehui kexue chubanshe, 2008.

Jiading xian Nanxiang zhenzhi bianzuan weiyuanhui, ed. *Nanxiang zhenzhi* (Gazetteer of Nanxiang town). Shanghai: Shanghai renmin chubanshe, 1992.

Jiading xian xuzhi (Continuation of Jiading county gazetteer). N.p., 1930.

Jiang Shaozhen. "Xu Run" (Xu Run). In Li Xin and Sun Sibai, eds., *Minguo renwuzhuan* (Biographies of personages in Republican China). vol. 1, 266–69. Beijing: Zhonghua shuju, 1978.

Jiangdu xian xuzhi (Continuation of Jiangdu county gazetteer). N.p., 1930.

Jiangnan shangwu bao (Journal of Jiangnan commercial affairs). Jiangning, 1900–1901.

Jiangsu jiaoyu zonghui. "Jiangsu jiaoyu zonghui huiyuan xingming yilanbiao" (Membership list of the Jiangsu General Association for Education). In Jiangsu jiaoyu zonghui, ed., *Jiangsu sheng jiaoyu zonghui zhangcheng guize yilanbiao* (Regulations, bylaws, and tables of the Jiangsu General Association for Education), 1–35. Shanghai, 1909.

———. "Jiangsu quansheng jiaoyuhui yilanbiao" (Table of the educational associations in Jiangsu province). In Jiangsu jiaoyu zonghui, ed., *Jiangsu jiaoyu zonghui wendu sanbian* (Documents of the Jiangsu General Association for Education: Third collection), part 2, 91–112. Shanghai, 1908.

Jiangsu sheng bowuguan, ed. *Jiangsu sheng Ming-Qing yilai beike ziliao xuanji* (Selected materials from the stone inscriptions of Jiangsu Province since the Ming-Qing period). Beijing: Shenghuo dushu xinzhi sanlian shudian, 1959.

Jiangsu sheng shangyeting and Zhongguo di'er lishi dang'anguan, eds. *Zhonghua minguo shangye dang'an ziliao huibian* (A collection of archival materials concerning commerce in the Republic of China). Beijing: Zhongguo shangye chubanshe, 1991.

Jiangsu sheng Sushu difang zizhi choubanchu, ed. *Jiangsu zizhi gongbao leibian* (Classified collection of the Jiangsu Self-Government Gazette). In Shen Yunlong, ed., *Jindai Zhongguo shiliao conkan sanbian* (Third collection of historical materials concerning modern China). Taibei: Wenhai chubanshe, n.d.

Jiangsu sheng ziyiju lijin gaiban renjun wendu (Jiangsu Provincial Assembly's documents concerning the reform of *lijin* taxation with merchant tax-farming system). N.p., n.d.

Jiangsu xuewu zonghui wendu (Documents of the Jiangsu General Association for Educational Affairs). Shanghai: Shangwu yinshuguan, 1906.

Jiangsu ziyiju diyiniandu baogao (The first annual report of the Jiangsu Provincial Assembly). N.p., n.d.

Jiaxing xian shanghui diyiqi baogao (First report of the Jiaxing County's chamber of commerce). N.p., 1935.

Jing Yuanshan. *Jing Yuanshan ji* (Collected writings of Jing Yuanshan). Wuhan: Huazhong shifan daxue chubanshe, 1988.

Jingji xuehui, ed. *Zhejiang quansheng caizheng shuomingshu* (Explanatory booklet of fiscal administration in Zhejiang Province). N.p., n.d.

Jones, Susan Mann. "The Ningpo Pang and Financial Power at Shanghai." In Elvin and Skinner, eds., *The Chinese City between Two Worlds*, 73–96.

Judge, Joan. *Print and Politics: "Shibao" and the Culture of Reform in Late Qing China.* Stanford, CA: Stanford University Press, 1996.

Keenan, Barry C. *Imperial China's Last Classical Academies: Social Change in the Lower Yangzi, 1864–1911.* Berkeley: Institute of East Asian Studies, University of California, 1994.

Kipnis, Andrew B. *Producing Guanxi: Sentiment, Self, and Subculture in a North China Village.* Durham, NC: Duke University Press, 1997.

Knoke, David. "Networks of Elite Structure and Decision Making." In Stanley Wasserman and Joseph Galaskiewicz, eds., *Advances in Social Network Analysis: Research in the Social and Behavioral Sciences*, 274–94. London: Sage Publications, 1994.

Kohama Masako. *Kindai Shanhai no kōkyōsei to kokka* (The public and the state in modern Shanghai). Tokyo: Kembun shuppan, 2000.

Kojima Yoshio. "The Chinese National Association and the 1911 Revolution." In Etō Shinkichi and Harold Z. Schiffrin, eds., *The 1911 Revolution in China: Interpretive Essays*, 175–92. Tokyo: University of Tokyo Press, 1984.

Köll, Elisabeth. *From Cotton Mill to Business Empire: The Emergence of Regional Enterprises in Modern China.* Cambridge, MA: Harvard University Asia Center, 2003.

Kotenev, A. M. *Shanghai: Its Mixed Court and Council.* Shanghai, 1925.

Kuai Shixun. "Shanghai gonggong zujie Huaguwen hui de shizhong" (The beginning and end of the Chinese Consultative Committee in the International Settlement of Shanghai). *Shanghai tongzhiguan qikan* (Journal of the Shanghai Gazetteer Office) 1, no. 4 (1934): 919–30.

Kuhn, Philip. *Rebellion and Its Enemies in Late Imperial China: Militarization and Social Structure, 1796–1864.* Cambridge, MA: Harvard University Press, 1970.

Kurahashi Masanao. "Shinmatsu no shōkai to Chūgoku burujoajī" (The late Qing chambers of commerce and the Chinese bourgeoisie). *Rekishigaku kenkyū* (Journal of historical research), special issue (1976): 117–26.

Larson, Jane Leung. "The Chinese Empire Reform Association (Baohuanghui) and the 1905 Anti-American Boycott: The Power of a Voluntary Association." In Susie Lan Cassel, ed., *The Chinese in America: A History from Gold Mountain to the New Millennium*, 195–216. Walnut Creek, CA: AltaMira Press, 2002.

Lee, En-han. "The Chekiang Gentry-Merchants vs. the Peking Court Officials: China's Struggle for Recovery of the British Soochow-Hangchow-Ningpo Railway Concession, 1905–1911." *Zhongyang yanjiuyuan jindaishi yanjiusuo jikan* (Bulletin of the Institute of Modern History, Academia Sinica) 3, no.1 (1972): 223–68.

Leung Yuen Sang. "Regional Rivalry in Mid-Nineteenth Century Shanghai: Cantonese vs. Ningpo Men." *Ch'ing-shih wen-t'i* (Qing studies) 4 (1982): 29–50.

Li Peide, ed. *Jindai Zhongguo de shanghui wangluo ji shehui gongneng* (Networks of chambers of commerce and their social functions in modern China). Hong Kong: Xianggang daxue chubanshe, 2009.

Li Pingshu. *Li Pingshu qishi zixu* (Autobiography of Li Pingshu at the age of seventy). *Shanghai tan yu Shanghai ren congshu* (Collection of books on Shanghai and its personages). Shanghai: Shanghai guji chubanshe, 1989.

Liang Shuming. *Zhongguo wenhua yaoyi* (Essential meanings of Chinese culture). Chengdu: Luming shudian, 1949.

Liaotian yihe (A crane in the vast sky). Shanghai, 1910.

Lin Duanfu. "Ningbo guangfu qinliji" (My personal experience in the Ningbo revolution during 1911). In Zhongguo renmin zhengzhi xieshang huiyi quanguo weiyuanhui wenshi ziliao yanjiu weiyuanhui, ed., *Xinhai geming huiyilu*, vol. 4, 174–82.

Liu, Kwang-ching. "Chinese Merchant Guilds: An Historical Inquiry." *Pacific Historical Review* 57, no. 1 (1988): 1–23.

Liu Jinzao, ed. *Qingchao xu wenxian tongkao* (Continuation of the survey of the Qing political documents). Shanghai, 1932; repr., Taibei: Xinxing shuju, 1963.

Liu Kunyi. *Liu Kunyi yiji* (Posthumously collected works of Liu Kunyi). Beijing: Zhonghua shuju, 1959.

Liu Xingnan. "Xinhai gesheng daibiao huiyi rizhi" (Daily record of the meeting of provincial delegates in 1911). In Zhongguo renmin zhengzhi xieshang huiyi quanguo weiyuanhui wenshi ziliao yanjiu weiyuanhui, ed., *Xinhai geming huiyilu*, vol. 6, 241–60.

Lü Zuoxie. "Ming-Qing shiqi de *huiguan* bingfei gongshangye hanghui" (*Huiguan* in the Ming-Qing period were not artisan and merchant guilds). *Zhongguo shi yanjiu* (Journal of Chinese history) 2 (1982): 66–79.

———. "Ming-Qing shiqi Suzhou de huiguan he gongsuo" (Suzhou *huiguan* and *gongsuo* in the Ming-Qing period). *Zhongguo shehui jingjishi yanjiu* (Journal of Chinese socioeconomic history) 2 (1984): 10–24.

Ma Jianzhong. *Shikezhai jiyan* (Records of sayings in the Shike Studio). Beijing: Zhonghua shuju, 1960.

Ma Min. "Cong gongshanglian dao shanghui: Zhongguo shanghui de xiandai yanbian" (From unions of industry and commerce to chambers of commerce: The transformation of Chinese chambers of commerce in contemporary period). In Li Peide, ed., *Shanghui yu jindai Zhongguo zhengzhi bianqian* (Chambers of commerce and political change in modern China), 73–90. Hong Kong: Xianggang daxue chubanshe, 2009.

———. *Guanshang zhijian: Shehui jubianzhong de jindai shenshang* (Linkage men between officials and merchants: Gentry-merchants amid radical social changes in the modern period). Tianjin: Tianjin renmin chubanshe, 1995.

———. "Shangshi caipan yu shanghui: Lun wan-Qing Suzhou shangshi jiufen de tiao-chu" (Settlement of business cases and chambers of commerce: A study of the mediation in business disputes in late Qing Suzhou). *Lishi Yanjiu* (Journal of historical research) 1 (1996): 30–43.

Ma Min and Zhu Ying. *Chuantong yu jindai de er'chong bianzou: Wan-Qing Suzhou shanghui yanjiu* (Variations on traditionalism and modernity: A case study of Suzhou chambers of commerce in the late Qing period). Chengdu: Bashu shushe, 1993.

Ma Min and Zu Su. *Suzhou shanghui dang'an congbian, 1912–1919* (Collection of archival materials of the Suzhou General Chamber of Commerce, 1912–1919). Wuchang: Huazhong shifang daxue chubanshe, 2004.

MacGowan, D. J. "Chinese Guilds or Chambers of Commerce and Trades Unions." *Journal of the China Branch of the Royal Asiatic Society* 21, no. 3 (1886–1887): 133–92.

Miller, Seumas. *The Moral Foundations of Social Institutions: A Philosophical Study.* New York: Cambridge University Press, 2010.

Min Tu-ki. "The Late-Ch'ing Provincial Assembly." In Philip A. Kuhn and Timothy Brook, eds., *National Polity and Local Power: The Transformation of Late Imperial China*, 137–79. Cambridge, MA: Council on East Asian Studies, Harvard University, 1989.

Minguo chunian quanguo gongshang huiyi baogaolu (Report on the national conference of industry and commerce of 1912). Beijing, 1913; repr., Beijing: Quanguo tushuguan wenxian suowei fuzhi zhongxin, 2009.

Minli bao (The people's stand). Shanghai, 1911.

Mo Bei, ed. *Jiang-Zhe tielu fengchao* (The agitation over Jiangsu and Zhejiang railroads). Shanghai, 1907; repr., Taibei, 1968.

Morse, Hosea Ballou. *The Gilds of China.* London, 1909.

———. *The Trade and Administration of China.* New York: Russell & Russell, 1967.

Murphey, Rhoads. *Shanghai: Key to Modern China.* Cambridge, MA: Harvard University Press, 1953.

Nanhui xian xuzhi (Continuation of the gazetteer of Nanhui County). N.p., 1929.

Nantong difang zizhi shijiunian zhi chengji (The achievements of self-government in Nantong during the past nineteen years). N.p., 1914.

Nanyang shangbao (Commercial journal of southern China). Jiangning, 1910.

Nanyang shangwubao (Commercial journal of southern China). Jiangning, 1906–1909.

Nathan, Andrew J. "A Factionalism Model for CCP Politics." *China Quarterly* 53 (1973): 34–66.

———. *Peking Politics, 1918–1923: Factionalism and the Failure of Constitutionalism.* Berkeley: University of California Press, 1976.

Negishi Tadashi. *Chūgoku no girudo* (The guilds of China). Tokyo: Nippon hyōron shinsha, 1953.

———. *Shanhai no girudo* (The guilds of Shanghai). Tokyo: Nippon hyōronsha, 1951.

"Ni Zhongguo jianli shangye zonghui zhangcheng" (Draft regulations for the establishment of the general chamber of commerce in China). *Xiangxue bao* (Journal of Hunan learning) 26 (1898): 25a–27b; 27 (1898): 18a–21b; 28 (1898): 22a–25b.

Nonggongshang bu tongjibiao: Di'erci (Statistical tables prepared by the Ministry of Agriculture, Industry, and Commerce: The second collection). Beijing, 1909.

Nonggongshang bu tongjibiao: Diyici (Statistical tables prepared by the Ministry of Agriculture, Industry, and Commerce: The first collection). Beijing, 1908.

Nongshangbu zongwuting tongjike, ed. *Zhonghua minguo yuannian diyici nongshang tongjibiao* (First collection of statistical tables about agriculture and commerce in the Republic of China, 1912). Shanghai: Zhonghua shuju, 1914.

North China Herald. Shanghai, 1902–1905.

Peng Zeyi. "Daolun: Zhongguo gongshang hanghuishi yanjiu de jige wenti" (Introduction: A few issues in historical research on artisan and merchant guilds of China). In Peng, ed., *Zhongguo gongshang hanghui shiliaoji*, vol. 1, 1–32.

———, ed. *Zhongguo gongshang hanghui shiliaoji* (Collection of historical materials concerning the artisan and merchant guilds of China). Beijing: Zhonghua shuju, 1995.

Perlman, Daniel, and Anita L. Vangelisti. "Personal Relationships: An Introduction." In Anita L. Vangelisti and Daniel Perlman, eds., *The Cambridge Handbook of Personal Relationships*, 3–7. New York: Cambridge University Press, 2006.

Perry, Elizabeth J. *Shanghai on Strike: The Politics of Chinese Labor.* Stanford, CA: Stanford University Press, 1993.

Pugach, Noel H. "Keep an Idea Alive: The Establishment of a Sino-American Bank, 1910–1920." *Business History Review* 56, no. 2 (1982): 265–93.

Pusey, James Reeve. *China and Charles Darwin.* Cambridge, MA: Council on East Asian Studies, Harvard University, 1984.

Puyuanzhi (Gazetteer of Puyuan town). N.p., 1927.

Qi Longwei. "Lun Qingmo de tielu fengchao" (On the railroad agitations at the end of the Qing dynasty). *Lishi yanjiu* (Journal of historical research) 2 (1964): 33–60.

Qingpu xian xuzhi (Continuation of Qingpu county gazetteer). N.p., 1934.

Qiu Baichuan. "Wenzhou shanghui zhi chuangli yu yange" (The formation and evolution of the chamber of commerce in Wenzhou). *Wenzhou wenshi ziliao* (Materials on the culture and history of Wenzhou) 3 (1987): 156–64.

Quanyehui xunbao (Ten-day newsletter of the Nanyang Expo). Jiangning, 1910.

Quan-Zhe gongbao (The Zhejiang gazette). Hangzhou, 1911.

Rankin, Mary Backus. *Early Chinese Revolutionaries: Radical Intellectuals in Shanghai and Chekiang, 1902–1911.* Cambridge, MA: Harvard University Press, 1971.

———. *Elite Activism and Political Transformation in China: Zhejiang Province, 1865–1911.* Stanford, CA: Stanford University Press, 1986.

———. "Some Observations on a Chinese Public Sphere." *Modern China* 19, no. 2 (1993): 158–82.

Redding, S. Gordon. *The Spirit of Chinese Capitalism.* Berlin: Walter de Gruyter, 1990.

Reynolds, Douglas R. *China, 1898–1912: The Xinzheng Revolution and Japan.* Cambridge, MA: Council on East Asian Studies, Harvard University, 1993.

Rhoads, Edward J. M. *China's Republican Revolution: The Case of Kwangtung, 1895–1913.* Cambridge, MA: Harvard University Press, 1975.

Rowe, William T. *Hankow: Commerce and Society in a Chinese City, 1796–1889.* Stanford, CA: Stanford University Press, 1984.

———. *Hankow: Conflict and Community in a Chinese City, 1796–1895.* Stanford, CA: Stanford University Press, 1989.

———. "The Problem of 'Civil Society' in Late Imperial China." *Modern China* 19, no. 2 (1993): 139–57.

Sanxu Gaoyou zhouzhi (Third continuation of the gazetteer of Gaoyou department). N.p., 1922.

Schoppa, R. Keith. *Chinese Elites and Political Change: Zhejiang Province in the Early Twentieth Century.* Cambridge, MA: Harvard University Press, 1982.

Scott, John. *Social Network Analysis: A Handbook.* London: Sage, 1991.

Shangban Quan-Zhe tielu youxian gongsi Zhonghua minguo yuannianfen diqijie baogao (Seventh report of the merchant-owned Zhejiang Railroad Company, 1912). N.p., n.d.

Shangban Zhejiang quansheng tielu youxian gongsi gudonghui diyici yishilu (Minutes of the first shareholders' meeting of the merchant-owned Zhejiang Railroad Company). N.p., n.d.

Shanghai bowuguan tushu ziliaoshi, ed. *Shanghai beike ziliao xuanji* (Selected materials from Shanghai stone inscriptions). Shanghai: Shanghai renmin chubanshe, 1981.

Shanghai renjitang zhengxinlu (Veritable record of the Shanghai Hall for Benevolent Assistance). Shanghai, 1897.

Shanghai shehui kexueyuan lishi yanjiusuo, ed. *Xinhai geming zai Shanghai shiliao* (Historical materials concerning the 1911 Revolution in Shanghai). Shanghai: Shanghai renmin chubanshe, 1981.

Shanghai shi gongshangye lianhehui, ed. *Shanghai zongshanghui yishilu* (Minutes of the Shanghai General Chamber of Commerce). Shanghai: Shanghai guji chubanshe, 2001.

Shanghai shi gongshangye lianhehui and Fudan daxue lishixi, eds. *Shanghai zongshanghui zuzhishi ziliao huibian* (A collection of materials concerning the organization of the Shanghai General Chamber of Commerce). Shanghai: Shanghai guji chubanshe, 2004.

Shanghai Tongren Fuyuantang zhengxinlu (Veritable record of the Hall of Impartial Altruism and Support for the Fundamental in Shanghai). Shanghai, 1905.

Shanghai tongshe, ed. *Shanghai yanjiu ziliao xuji* (Shanghai research materials: Second collection). Shanghai, 1936.

Shanghai tushuguan, ed. *Wang Kangnian shiyou xinzha* (Letters from Wang Kangnian's teachers and friends). Shanghai: Shanghai guji chubanshe, 1986.

Shanghai xian xuzhi (Continuation of Shanghai County gazetteer). N.p., 1918.

Shanghai xianzhi (Gazetteer of Shanghai County). N.p., 1936.

"Shanghai xishang zonghui zhangcheng" (The rules of the Shanghai Western General Chamber of Commerce). *Shiwubao* (The Chinese progress) 23 (1899): 17a–25b.

Shanghai zongshanghui baogaolu (Reports of the Shanghai General Chamber of Commerce). Shanghai, 1913.

Shanghai zongshanghui luyin cuoshang gongxie youdai Huashang cheng'an (Shanghai General Chamber of Commerce's records of negotiations with the Mixed Court for preferential treatment of Chinese merchants). Shanghai, 1917.

Shangwu bao (Journal of commercial affairs). Beijing, 1903–1906.

Shangwu guanbao (Gazette of Commercial Administration). Beijing, 1906–1911.

Shangwu yinshuguan bianyisuo. *Nanyang quanyehui youji* (Travel notes on the Nanyang Expo). Shanghai: Shangwu yinshuguan, 1910.

Shangxue gonghui tongrenlu (Register of the Public Society for Commercial Studies). Shanghai, 1908.

Shen Yuwu. "Wei Ningbobang kailu de Yan Xinhou" (Yan Xinhou: Pioneer of Ningbo merchant group). *Zhejiang wenshi ziliao xuanji* (Collection of selected materials concerning Zhejiang history and culture) 39 (1989): 65–71.

Shenbao (Shanghai Daily). Shanghai, 1878, 1902–1912.

Sheng Xuanhuai. *Yuzhai cungao* (Extant manuscript of the Yu Studio). Wujin: 1939; repr., Taibei: Wenhai chubanshe, 1963.

Shenzhou ribao (China Daily). Shanghai, 1911.

Shibao (The Eastern Times). Shanghai, 1904–1912.

Shils, Edward. "The Virtue of Civil Society." *Government and Opposition* 26, no. 1 (1991): 3–20.

Shiyebu. *Da-Qing fagui daquan* (Complete collection of Qing laws and rules). Taibei: Hongye shuju, 1972.

Shuanglin zhenzhi (Gazetteer of Shuanglin town). Shanghai: Shangwu yinshuguan, 1917.

Skinner, G. William, ed. *The City in Late Imperial China*. Stanford, CA: Stanford University Press, 1977.

———. "Regional Urbanization in Nineteenth-Century China." In Skinner, ed., *The City in Late Imperial China*, 211–49.

Soda Saburo. "Shōkai no setsuritsu" (The establishment of chambers of commerce). *Rekishigaku kenkyū* (Journal of historical research) 422 (1975): 43–55.

Song Meiyun. *Jindai Tianjin shanghui* (The chambers of commerce around modern Tianjin). Tianjin: Tianjin shehui kexueyuan chubanshe, 2002.

Strand, David. *Rickshaw Beijing: City People and Politics in the 1920s*. Berkeley: University of California Press, 1989.

Su Shaobing, ed. *Shanzhong ji* (Mountain Bell Collection). Shanghai: Hongwen shuju, 1906.

Sun, E-tu Zen. "The Shanghai-Hangchow-Ningpo Railway Loan of 1908." *Far Eastern Quarterly* 10, no. 2 (1951): 136–50.

Sun Choucheng et al. "Yu Qiaqing shilue" (A biographical sketch of Yu Qiaqing). *Zhejiang wenshi ziliao xuanji* (Collection of selected materials concerning Zhejiang history and culture) 32 (1986): 104–28.

Suzhou lishi bowuguan and Jiangsu shifan xueyuan lishixi, eds. *Ming-Qing Suzhou gongshangye beikeji* (Collection of stone inscriptions concerning handicraft industry and commerce in Ming-Qing Suzhou). Nanjing: Jiangsu renmin chubanshe, 1981.

Suzhou shi dang'anguang. "Suzhou shimin gongshe dangan xuanji" (Selected archival materials regarding urban residents' associations in Suzhou). In Xinhai geming congkan bianjizu, ed., *Xinhai geming congkan* (Collection of materials on the 1911 Revolution), vol. 4, 53–197. Beijing: Zhonghua shuju, 1982.

Szonyi, Michael. *Practicing Kinship: Lineage and Descent in Late Imperial China*. Stanford, CA: Stanford University Press, 2002.

Tahara Tennan [Tahara Teijiro]. *Shinmatsu minsho Chūgoku kanshin jimmei roku* (Biographical dictionary of officials and gentry in the late Qing and early Republican periods). Beijing: Chūgoku kenkyūkai, 1918.

Tang Zhijun. *Wuxu shiqi de xuehui he baokan* (Study societies, newspapers, and journals during the 1898 Reform). Taibei: Taiwan shangwu yinshuguan, 1993.

Thelen, Kathleen, and Sven Steinmo. "Historical Institutionalism in Comparative Politics." In Sven Steinmo, Kathleen Thelen, and Frank Longstreth, eds., *Structuring Politics: Historical Institutionalism in Comparative Analysis*, 1–32. New York: Cambridge University Press, 1992.

Thompson, Roger R. *China's Local Councils in the Age of Constitutional Reform, 1898–1911*. Cambridge, MA: Council on East Asian Studies, Harvard University, 1995.

Tianjin shi dang'anguan, Tianjin shehui kexueyuan lishi yanjiusuo, and Tianjin shi gongshangye lianhehui, eds. *Tianjin shanghui dang'an huibian, 1903–1911* (Collection of archival materials of the Tianjin General Chamber of Commerce, 1903–1911). Tianjin: Tianjin renmin chubanshe, 1989.

———. *Tianjin shanghui dang'an huibian, 1912–1928* (Collection of archival materials of the Tianjin General Chamber of Commerce, 1912–1928). Tianjin: Tianjin renmin chubanshe, 1992.

Tōa dōbun shoin. *Shinkoku shōgyō kanshū to kinyū jijō* (Commercial customs and financial affairs in Qing China). Shanghai: Tōa dōbun shoin, 1904.

Tōa dōbunkai. *Shina keizai zensho* (Encyclopedia of Chinese economy). Tokyo: Tōa dōbunkai, 1907–1908.

———. *Shina shōbetsu zenshi* (Gazetteer of the provinces in China). Tokyo: Tōa dōbunkai, 1917–1920.

"Tong-Chong-Hai shangwu zonghui bing Tongzhou fenhui shiban zhangcheng" (Draft regulations of the Tongzhou-Chongming-Haimen General Chamber of Commerce and the Tongzhou Affiliated Chamber of Commerce). *Jiangnan baifanlu* (Records of a Jiangnan book vendor). N.p., n.d.

Tsai, Shih-shan Henry. *China and the Overseas Chinese in the United States, 1868–1911*. Fayetteville: University of Arkansas Press, 1983.

Tsin, Michael. *Nation, Governance, and Modernity in China: Canton, 1900–1927*. Stanford, CA: Stanford University Press, 1999.

Tsou, Tang. "Prolegomenon to the Study of Informal Groups in CCP Politics." *China Quarterly* 65 (1976): 98–114.

Wakeman, Frederic, Jr. "The Civil Society and Public Sphere Debate." *Modern China* 19, no. 2 (1993): 108–38.

Wang, Guanhua. *In Search of Justice: The 1905–1906 Chinese Anti-American Boycott*. Cambridge, MA: Harvard University Press, 2001.

Wang, Yeh-chien. *Land Taxation in Imperial China, 1750–1911*. Cambridge, MA: Harvard University Press, 1973.

Wang Er'min. "Zhongguo jindai zhi gongshang zhifulun yu shangmao tizhi zhi xihua" (The ideology of pursuing industrial and commercial wealth and the Westernization of commercial institutions in modern China). In Zhongguo jindai xiandai shilunji bianji weiyuanhui, ed., *Zhongguo jindai xiandai shilunji* (Collection of articles on modern and contemporary Chinese history). vol. 9, 71–150. Taibei: Taiwan shangwu yinshuguan, 1985.

Wang Er'min and Chen Shanwei, eds. *Qingmo yiding zhongwai shangyue jiaoshe: Sheng Xuanhuai wanglai handiangao* (The negotiation over Chinese-foreign trade treaties in the late Qing period: Letters and telegrams from and to Sheng Xuanhuai). Hong Kong: Zhongwen daxue chubanshe, 1993.

Wang Guoping and Tang Lixing, eds. *Ming-Qing yilai Suzhou shehuishi beikeji* (Collection of stone inscriptions concerning social history of Suzhou since the Ming-Qing period). Suzhou: Suzhou daxue chubanshe, 1998.

Wang Jingyu. *Zhongguo jindai gongyeshi ziliao, 1895–1914* (Materials concerning the history of modern Chinese industries, 1895–1914). Beijing: Kexue chubanshe, 1957.

Wang Junshi. "Huaiyin shanghui zuzhi jiankuang" (A brief introduction to the organization of Huaiyin chambers of commerce). *Huiyin wenshi ziliao* (Cultural and historical materials concerning Huaiyin) 1 (1983): 140–42.

Wang Laidi. "The 'Peaceful Independence' of the Constitutionalists and the 1911 Revolution." *Chinese Studies in History* 18, no. 3–4 (1985): 3–32.

Wang Shuhuai. *Zhongguo xiandaihua de quyu yanjiu: Jiangsu sheng, 1860–1916* (A regional study of Chinese modernization: Jiangsu Province, 1860–1916). Taibei: Zhongyang yanjiuyuan jindaishi suo, 1984.

Wang Suijin. "Zhenhai Xiaogang Lishi jiazu shilue" (Brief history of the Li lineage from Xiaogang of Zhenhai). *Zhejiang wenshi ziliao xuanji* (Collection of selected materials concerning Zhejiang history and culture) 39 (1989): 123–31.

Wasserman, Stanley, and Katherine Faust. *Social Network Analysis: Methods and Applications.* Cambridge: Cambridge University Press, 1994.

Wei Bozhen. "Xinhai Ningbo guangfu de huiyi" (Recollection of the Ningbo revolution in 1911). In Zhongguo renmin zhengzhi xieshang huiyi Zhejiang sheng weiyuanhui wenshi ziliao yanjiu weiyuanhui, ed., *Zhejiang Xinhai geming huiyilu* (Recollections of the 1911 Revolution in Zhejiang), 204–19. Hangzhou: Zhejiang renmin chubanshe, 1981.

Wellman, Barry. "Structural Analysis: From Method and Metaphor to Theory and Substance." In Barry Wellman and S. D. Berkowitz, eds., *Social Structures: A Network Approach*, 19–61. Cambridge: Cambridge University Press, 1988.

Wellman, Barry, Wenhong Chen, and Dong Weizhen. "Networking *Guanxi*." In Gold, Guthrie, and Wank, eds., *Social Connections in China*, 221–41.

Williams, S. Wells. *The Middle Kingdom.* New York: Charles Scribner's Sons, 1883.

Wong, Owen Hong-hin. *The First Chinese Minister to Great Britain.* Hong Kong: Chung Hwa Book Co., 1987.

Wong, R. Bin. "Great Expectations: The 'Public Sphere' and the Search for Modern Times in Chinese History." *Studies in Chinese History* 3 (1993): 7–49.

Wong Sin Kiong. *China's Anti-American Boycott in 1905: A Study of Urban Protest.* New York: Peter Lang, 2002.

Woqiu Zhongzi (Fei Xingjian). *Jindai mingren zhuan* (Biographies of eminent people of the modern period). Hong Kong: Zhongshan tushu gongsi, 1973.

Wright, Mary Clabaugh, ed. *China in Revolution: The First Phase, 1900–1913.* New Haven, CT: Yale University Press, 1968.

Wu Qin. "Guanyu You Xianjia shiliao yize" (A historical document about You Xianjia). *Suzhou shizhi ziliao xuanji* (Selected historical and gazetteer materials on Suzhou) 17 (1991): 146–50.

Wu Xinmu, "Xinhai geming shiqi de Xiashi shangtuan he gongbing tiedao dadui" (The Xiashi merchant militia and the Railroad Engineer Brigade during the 1911 Revolution). In Zhongguo renmin zhengzhi xieshang huiyi quanguo weiyuanhui wenshi ziliao yanjiu weiyuanhui, ed., *Xinhai geming huiyilu*, vol. 4, 170–73.

Wu Yixiong. "Guangzhou waiqiao zongshanghui yu Yapian zhanzheng qianxi de Zhong-Ying guanxi" (The general chamber of commerce of foreign sojourners in Canton and Sino-Anglo relations on the eve of the Opium War). *Jindaishi yanjiu* (Journal of modern history) 2 (2004): 91–116.

Wuxian zhi (Gazetteer of Wu County). N.p., 1933.

Xi Dichen. "Da'nao gongtang'an" (The Mixed Court uproar). *Shanghai Tongzhiguan qikan* (Journal of the Shanghai Gazetteer Office) 1, no. 2 (1933): 407–40.

Xia Dongyuan, ed. *Zheng Guanying ji* (The collection of Zheng Guanying). Shanghai: Shanghai renmin chubanshe, 1982.

"Xinhai Shanghai guangfu qianhou" (Shanghai around the 1911 Revolution). In Zhongguo renmin zhengzhi xieshang huiyi quanguo weiyuanhui wenshi ziliao yanjiu weiyuanhui, ed., *Xinhai geming huiyilu*, vol. 4, 1–19.

Xinwen bao (News Daily). Shanghai, 1902–1912.

Xu, Xiaoqun. *Chinese Professionals and the Republican State: The Rise of Professional Associations in Shanghai, 1912–1937.* Cambridge: Cambridge University Press, 2001.

Xu Daling. *Qingdai juanna zhidu* (The system of purchasing offices through contribution during the Qing period). Beijing: Yanjing daxue, 1950.

Xu Dingxin. "Shanghai gongshang tuanti de jindaihua" (The modernization of Shanghai craftsman and merchant groups). In Zhang Zhongli, ed., *Jindai shanghai chengshi yanjiu* (A study on modern Shanghai), 509–91. Shanghai: Shanghai renmin chubanshe, 1990.

Xu Dingxin and Qian Xiaoming. *Shanghai zongshanghui shi, 1902–1929* (A history of the Shanghai General Chamber of Commerce, 1902–1929). Shanghai: Shanghai shehui kexueyuan chubanshe, 1991.

Xu Qisong and Li Zongwu. "Zhengduo Hu-jun dudu xianchang mujiji" (Eyewitness account of the fight for the Shanghai military governorship). In *Ershi shiji Shanghai wenshi ziliao wenku* (Collection of cultural and historical materials regarding twentieth-century Shanghai), vol. 1, 29–31. Shanghai: Shanghai shudian chubanshe, 1999.

Xu Run. *Xu Yuzhai zixu nianpu* (Chronological autobiography of Xu Run). Shanghai, 1927.

Xu Zaiping and Xu Ruifang. *Qingmo sishinian Shenbao shiliao* (Historical materials concerning the *Shanghai Daily* in the last forty years of the Qing period). Beijing: Xinhua chubanshe, 1988.

Xuantong yuannianfen shangban Quan-Zhe tielu youxian gongsi shouzhi zhanglue (General account book of income and outlays of the Zhejiang Railroad Company in 1909). Shanghai: Shangwu yinshuguan, 1910.

Xuewu gongsuo, ed. *Xuantong yuannianfen Zhejiang jiaoyu tongjibiao* (Statistical table of educational data of Zhejiang Province in 1909). N.p, n.d.

Xuzuan Taizhou zhi (Continuation of Taizhou County gazetteer). N.p., 1924.

Yan, Yunxiang. *The Flow of Gifts: Reciprocity and Social Networks in a Chinese Village*. Stanford, CA: Stanford University Press, 1996.

Yang, Mayfair Mei-hui. *Gifts, Favors, and Banquets: The Art of Social Relationships in China*. Ithaca, NY: Cornell University Press, 1994.

Yang Fangyi. "Zhenjiang shanghui shimo" (A history of Zhenjiang chambers of commerce). In *Zhenjiang wenshi ziliao* (Cultural and historical materials concerning Zhenjiang) 4 (1982): 7–28.

Yang Liqiang and Shen Weibin. "Shanghai shangtuan yu Xinhai geming" (Shanghai merchant militias and the 1911 Revolution). In Yang Liqiang, *Qingmo minchu zichanjieji yu shehui biandong* (The bourgeois class and social change in the late Qing and early Republican periods), 106–37. Shanghai: Shanghai renmin chubanshe, 2003.

Yang Yi, ed. *Shanghai shi zizhizhi* (Self-government gazetteer of Shanghai city). Shanghai, 1915.

Yangzhou shifan xueyuan lishixi, ed. *Xinhai geming Jiangsu diqu shiliao* (Historical materials concerning the 1911 Revolution in Jiangsu). Nanjing: Jiangsu renmin chubanshe, 1961.

Ye Changchi. *Yuandulu rijichao* (Excerpts from a diary of the Yuandu studio). Shanghai, 1932.

Yeh, Wen-hsin. "Huang Yanpei and the Chinese Society of Vocational Education in Shanghai Networking." In Dillon and Oi, eds., *At the Crossroads of Empires*, 25–44.

Yi-Jing xuzhi (Continuation of Yixing and Jingxi Counties' gazetteer). N.p., 1912.

Ying Liya. *Tianjin shanghui zuzhi wangluo yanjiu* (A study of the organizational networks of chambers of commerce around Tianjin). Xiamen: Xiamen daxue chubanshe, 2006.

Yinxian tongzhi (A general gazetteer of Yin County). N.p., 1933.

Young, Ernest P. *The Presidency of Yuan Shih-k'ai: Liberalism and Dictatorship in Early Republican China*. Ann Arbor: University of Michigan Press, 1977.

———. "Yuan Shih-k'ai's Rise to the Presidency." In Wright, ed., *China in Revolution*, 419–42.

Yu Heping. *Shanghui yu Zhongguo zaoqi xiandaihua* (Chambers of commerce and the early modernization of China). Shanghai: Shanghai renmin chubanshe, 1993.

Yu Jianxing, Wang Shizong, Huang Honghua, and Li Jianqin. *Minjian shanghui yu difang zhengfu: Jiyu Zhejiang sheng Wenzhou shi de yanjiu* (Chambers of commerce and local governments: A study of the Wenzhou case in Zhejiang Province). Beijing: Jingji kexue chubanshe, 2006.

Yubei lixian gonghui bao (Journal of the Society for Constitutional Preparation). Shanghai, 1908–1909.

Yun Yuding. *Yun Yuding Chengzhai riji* (Yun Yudiang's diary in the Cheng studio), ed. Shi Xiaofeng. Hangzhou: Zhejiang guji chubanshe, 2004.

Zhang, Xiaobo. "Merchant Associational Activism in Early Twentieth-Century China: The Tianjin General Chamber of Commerce, 1904–1928." PhD diss., Columbia University, 1995.

Zhang Cunwu. *Guangxu sayinian Zhong-Mei gongyue fengchao* (The agitation over the Sino-American labor treaty in 1905). Taibei: Zhongyang yanjiuyuan jindaishi yanjiusuo, 1966.

Zhang Guogan. *Xinhai geming shiliao* (Historical materials concerning the 1911 Revolution). Shanghai: Longmen lianhe shudian, 1958.

Zhang Guohui. *Yangwu yundong yu Zhongguo jindai qiye* (The foreign affairs movement and modern Chinese enterprises). Beijing: Zhongguo shehui kexue chubanshe, 1979.

Zhang Hailin. *Suzhou zaoqi chengshi xiandaihua yanjiu* (A study of early modernization in Suzhou). Nanjing: Nanjing daxue chubanshe, 1999.

Zhang Huanzhong. *Shanghai zongshanghui yanjiu, 1902–1929* (A study of the Shanghai General Chamber of Commerce, 1902–1929). Taibei: Zhishufang chubanshe, 1996.

Zhang Jian. *Zhang Jian quanji* (Complete collection of Zhang Jian). Nanjing: Jiangsu guji chubanshe, 1994.

Zhang Kaiyuan. "The 1911 Revolution and the Jiang-Zhe Bourgeoisie." *Chinese Studies in History* 18, no. 3–4 (1985): 83–133.

Zhang Kaiyuan, Liu Wangling, and Ye Wanzhong, eds. *Suzhou shanghui dang'an congbian, 1905–1911* (Collection of archival materials of the Suzhou General Chamber of Commerce, 1905–1911). Wuchang: Huazhong shifang daxue chubanshe, 1991.

Zhang Kaiyuan, Zhu Ying, Zu Su, and Ye Wanzhong, eds. *Suzhou Shangtuan dang'an huibian, 1905–1911* (Collection of archival materials of Suzhou merchant militias). Chengdu: Bashu shushe, 2008.

Zhang Pengyuan. *Lixianpai yu Xinhai geming* (The constitutionalists and the 1911 Revolution). Taibei: Zhongyang yanjiuyuan jindaishi yanjiusuo, 1983.

Zhang Yufa. *Qingji de lixian tuanti* (Constitutionalist associations in the late Qing period). Taibei: Zhongyang yanjiuyuan jidaishi yanjiusuo, 1971.

———. "Wuxu shiqi de xuehui yundong" (Study societies in the era of the 1898 Reform). *Lishi yanjiu* (Journal of historical research) 5 (1998): 5–26.

Zhang Zhidong. *Zhang Wenxianggong quanji* (The complete works of Zhang Zhidong). Beijing, 1937; repr., Taibei: Wenhai chubanshe, 1963.

Zhao Jinyu. "Su-Hang-Yong tielu jiekuan he Jiang-Zhe renmin de jukuan yundong" (The Suzhou-Hangzhou-Ningbo Railroad loan and the anti-loan movement by the people of Jiangsu and Zhejiang). *Lishi yanjiu* (Journal of historical research) 9 (1959): 51–60.

Zhejiang guanbao (Zhejiang gazette). Hangzhou, 1909–1911.

Zhejiang Quanye Gongsuo diyijie chengji baogaoshu (First report on the achievements of the Industrial Promotion Office of Zhejiang Province). N.p., n.d.

Zhejiang ribao (Zhejiang Daily). Hangzhou, 1908–1911.

Zhejiang sheng Xinhai geming shi yanjiuhui and Zhejiang sheng tushuguan, eds. *Xinhai geming Zhejiang shiliao xuanji* (Selected materials concerning the 1911 Revolution in Zhejiang). Hangzhou: Zhejiang renmin chubanshe, 1981.

Zhejiang tongxianghui ganshi, ed. *Zhe-Gan tielu shijian* (The Zhejiang-Jiangxi railroad incident). Tokyo, 1905.

Zhejiang ziyiju di'erjie changnianhui yishilu (Minutes of the second annual session of the Zhejiang Provincial Assembly). N.p., n.d.

Zhelu daibiao lü-Jin shenshang feizhang baolü gongdu (Petitioins of representatives of the Zhejiang Railroad Company and Zhejiang gentry-merchants in Tianjin for the abrogation of the loan agreement and the protection of commercial laws). N.p., n.d.

Zhelu Dongshiju baogao (Report of the directorate of the Zhejiang Railroad Company). N.p., 1911.

Zheng Guanying. *Shengshi weiyan houbian* (Supplement to the warnings to a seemingly prosperous age). Shanghai, 1909; repr., Taibei: Datong shuju, 1969.

Zhengxie Zhejiang sheng Xiaoshan shi weiyuanhui wenshi gongzuo weiyuanhui, ed. *Tang Shouqian shiliao zhuanji* (Special collection of historical materials concerning Tan Shouqian). Xiaoshan, 1993.

Zhengzhi guanbao (Government administration gazette). Beijing, 1907–1911.

Zhenyang xianzhi (Zhenyang County gazetteer). N.p., 1918.

Zhong Tianwei. "Kuochong shangwu shitiao" (Ten suggestions for commercial development). In Ge, ed., *Huangchao jingshiwen xubian*, vol. 116, 4a–8a.

Zhong Xiangcai. "Zhong Tianwei sixiang lunyao" (A general discussion on Zhong Tianwei's thought). In *Shanghai yanjiu luncong* (Collection of articles in Shanghai studies), vol. 6, 261–69. Shanghai: Shanghai shehui kexueyuan chubanshe, 1991.

Zhongguo diyi lishi dang'anguan. "Qingmo gesheng sheli shanghui shiliao" (Historical materials regarding the formation of chambers of commerce in provinces during the late Qing period). *Lishi dang'an* (Journal of historical archives) 2 (1996): 48–60.

Zhongguo renmin yinhang Shanghai shi fenhang, ed. *Shanghai qianzhuang shiliao* (Historical materials concerning native banks in Shanghai). Shanghai: Shanghai renmin chubanshe, 1960.

Zhongguo renmin yinhang Shanghai shi fenhang jinrong yanjiushi, ed. *Zhongguo diyijia yinhang* (The first Chinese bank). Beijing: Zhongguo shehui kexue chubanshe, 1982.

Zhongguo renmin zhengzhi xieshang huiyi quanguo weiyuanhui wenshi ziliao yanjiu weiyuanhui, ed. *Xinhai geming huiyilu* (Collection of memoirs on the 1911 Revolution). Beijing: Zhonghua shuju, 1961–1963.

Zhongguo shixuehui, ed. *Wuxu bianfa* (The 1898 Reform). Shanghai: Shenzhou guoguangshe, 1953.

———. *Xinhai geming* (The 1911 Revolution). Shanghai: Shanghai renmin chubanshe, 1957.

Zhonghua minguo kaiguo wushinian wenxian bianzuan weiyuanhui, ed. *Zhonghua minguo kaiguo wushinian wenxian* (Documents on the fiftieth anniversary of the Republic of China). Part 2, *Gesheng guangfu* (Restoration of each province), vol. 3. Taibei: Zhengzhong shuju, 1975.

Zhongwai ribao (Chinese and Foreign Daily). Shanghai, 1906–1912.

Zhongyang yanjiuyuan jindaishi yanjiusuo, ed. *Haifang dang* (Archival records of coastal defense). Taibei: Zhongyang yanjiuyuan jindaishi yanjiusuo, 1957.

Zhou Kangxie, ed. *Xinhai geming ziliao huiji* (Collection of materials concerning the 1911 Revolution). Hong Kong: Dadong tushu gongsi, 1980.

Zhu Ying. "Xinhai geming qian de nonghui" (Agricultural associations prior to the 1911 Revolution). *Lishi yanjiu* (Journal of historical research) 5 (1991): 19–35.

————. *Xinhai geming shiqi xinshi shangren shetuan yanjiu* (A study of new-style merchant associations during the 1911 Revolution). Beijing: Zhongguo renmin daxue chubanshe, 1991.

————. *Zhuanxing shiqi de shehui yu guojia: Yi jindai shanghui wei zhuti de lishi toushi* (Society and state in a transitional period: A historical analysis centered on modern chambers of commerce). Wuhan: Huazhong shifan daxue chubanshe, 1997.

Index